CREATIVE LIVING

Basic Concepts in Home Economics

Third Edition

Consulting Authors

Personal & Family Relationships

Josephine A. Foster, Ph.D
Assistant Principal for Instruction
Alexander Central High School
Taylorsville, North Carolina

Consumer & Home Management

M. Janice Hogan, Ph.D
Head, Family Social Science Department
University of Minnesota

Foods & Nutrition

Bettie M. Herring, Ph.D
Director of Vocational and Adult Education
Fort Worth Independent School District

Clothing & Textiles

Audrey G. Gieseking-Williams, Ph.D
Chair, Department of Home Economics
California State University, Los Angeles

Co-developed by

Glencoe Publishing Company
Mission Hills, California
&
Visual Education Corporation
Princeton, New Jersey

Special Home Economics Editorial Consultants:
Ramona Myers-Rowan
Jeanette Weber

Visual Education Corporation
Editorial staff: Bob Waterhouse, Dale Anderson, Ann
Falivena, Hettie Jones, Wendy Warren Keebler, Candace
Botha Roman, Elaine Sedito, Renee Skelton, Elizabeth
Tener, Harry Wagner, Esther Luckett, Janet Stern,
Sue Sweet

Special Acknowledgments: Cindy Feldner, Adrienne Klein,
Dick Lidz, Sharon Lucas

Photographers
R. S. Beck 76, 92, 108; Jim Bradshaw 56, 184A; Joe Cole
87; Dudley's Photos 13, 69, 90, 126, 126C, 134, 141, 145,
154, 516; Tony Freeman 30, 85, 192, 258, 259, 479, 498;
P. Grant 267, 381; Richard Hutchings 9, 14, 15, 25, 31, 32,
35, 59, 98, 111, 165, 169, 171, 216, 265, 327, 360;
Marozi's Photos 107; Ronald L. Marty 137; Stephen
McBrady 12B, 20, 71, 88, 102, 128, 129, 143A, 158, 168,
186, 187, 188, 193, 286, 288, 292, 297, 306, 333, 379,
384, 455, 459, 480, 486, 489A, 492, 499, 501, 509, 511;
James L. Schaffer 94; Kay Shaw 67, 96, 132, 149, 185;
Barbara Baker Stephenson 41, 65, 77, 113, 147, 382;
Wide World Photos 91.

Illustrators
Dick Cole
Terra Muzick
Phyllis Rockne
Gretchen Shields
Sally Shimizu
Ed Tabor
Diana Thewlis

Send all inquiries to:
Glencoe Publishing Company
15319 Chatsworth Street, P.O. Box 9509
Mission Hills, California 91345-9509

ISBN 0-02-640910-0 (Student)
ISBN 0-02-641020-6 (Teacher's Annotated Edition)

7 8 9   92 91 90

Contents

(Continued)

Child Care and Child Development

(Continued)

Foods and Nutrition *258*

(Continued)

(Continued)

FEATURES

TEEN ISSUES

TABLES

FOCUS ON YOU

You probably spend a lot of time thinking about how other people see you. Maybe you have a hard time figuring out who you are and how you should act. You might be good at making people laugh. But one or two people think that you're a show-off.

Or maybe you're quiet. Your close friends know that you can express yourself very well, but you prefer not to say much. Other people think that you're too shy.

Maybe you don't seem to have many friends. You're lonely, but you don't know how to meet the kinds of people that you like.

What should you do? Should you stop being funny because some people don't like it? Should you join a club, as your parents suggest?

You may wonder about the changes that you're going through. You're growing, and you're taking on more responsibilities.

You enjoy your new responsibilities, but you also wonder about them. Suddenly you have more decisions to make than you used to. How should you use your allowance? What should you do to plan for your future? Should you go with the group this weekend?

One way to help yourself make these decisions is to discover what's important to you. You'll find that the most interesting subject you can study is you. What activities do you enjoy? What abilities and aims do you have? How do you get along with other people? Answering these questions is exciting. As you learn more about yourself each day, you'll gain in understanding and confidence.

In these chapters, you'll find some ideas on how to answer questions like these. You'll learn how to find out who you are, what you like, and how to act. And you'll find suggestions that will help you get a good start in the adventure that is to be your life.

1 You As an Individual

After reading this chapter, you will be able to:

☐ *compare your view of yourself with how others see you,*

☐ *explain how you can strengthen your self-concept.*

"He had dark, brooding eyes, and when he was with people he held himself apart from them, as if afraid to be drawn in by their friendliness."

"Her admirers knew her by what she did rather than by her appearance. She was average to look at, medium height, medium weight, medium brown hair, pleasant-looking but not striking. But her friends admired her for her actions, which were always kindnesses done without a hint of seeking any repayment."

"He had a special way of talking which put everyone at their ease right away."

To tell us about a person's character, an author uses **characteristics**, or *special features or traits of the person being described.* These features or traits may relate to how people look or to how they act. One way of looking at yourself is in terms of your characteristics, as others see you.

Views of Yourself

Looking at your physical, emotional, and mental characteristics will help you to form a picture of yourself. So will examining how you act and respond to people and situations.

Your Body

Think about all the things that people might notice about you. Some are physical characteristics—you are tall or short, straight-haired or curly-haired. Perhaps you are a fast runner, but you get out of breath easily. Your nose is upturned or your voice is husky. All of these features, and many others like them, affect the way people see

Look at any group of friends and you will notice a variety of individual differences in appearance, dress, and personality types.

you. Some of the features may please you. Others may make you feel self-conscious.

Your Emotions

Emotional characteristics also play a part in how others see you. Perhaps you have a tendency to be good tempered, or maybe you feel things deeply. Perhaps you find your emotions very changeable, as you swing from feeling happy one hour to feeling down the next. Even if they vary from moment to moment, your emotions and how you handle them influence how others see you.

Your Mind

Still other characteristics that affect how people see you relate to your mind—how you think and what you like. You like animals, perhaps, or you are interested in baseball statistics. You can express your thoughts well. You are good at social studies, but poor at math. You are good at suggesting solutions to your friends' problems. Whatever they are, your abilities, attitudes, and interests make you good company for other people. They also help you to express who you are and to enjoy yourself.

Your Actions

Your behavior with others also helps define your personality. Are you a good listener? Do you prefer spending time with a group of people or with only one special friend? Do you like sharing with others? Are you a leader of a group? These are social characteristics that people notice—they, too, add to the picture of who you are.

F E A T U R E

Wanted: A Positive You

PERSON WANTED. Female, named Judy. 15 years old, 5 feet 2 inches tall, 110 pounds, brown eyes, and short, curly brown hair. Must like cats, baseball, math, and the color red. Must be able to sing, change a tire, and bowl. Will give special attention to applicants with two little brothers and a best friend named Martha. B average in school helpful. Newspaper delivery or babysitting experience a plus.

Could you answer this ad? Probably not. The characteristics described belong to a unique individual. But you can write your own ad, one that lists all of your own spe-cial qualities. Make a list which includes the following:

- Appearance (height, weight, eye color, hair color and style)
- Favorite things (colors, sports, animals, celebrities, clothes, songs, school sub-jects, books)
- Special skills (writing, music, crafts, mechanics, cooking, sports, dancing, art, computers)
- Friends and family (names, ages, special qualities)
- School (classes, grades, favorite teachers)
- Jobs or chores (after-school or summer jobs, babysitting, food shopping)

The You That Others See

People see the world from different view-points. This means that each person will notice different characteristics in you.

To your parents, you are their child. They may notice acts like your kindness to a younger sister or your unwillingness to help unload groceries.

To your teachers, you are a student who is good in some subjects and not as good in others.

To your friends, you are ... well, to one friend, you are a person who listens and shares secrets. To another friend, you are a person who plays a good game of tennis.

To a stranger, you are an attractive per-son, someone to get to know better.

People sometimes judge you by things that aren't really typical of you. When Jan first met you, your hair was a mess and your clothes were wrinkled and dirty. You'd been working on your brother's car. Jan still calls you "Sloppy," even though you are usually well groomed.

Nobody's picture of you is complete. To fully appreciate yourself, you must realize that you are all of the people that others see, and more.

Your Personal View

You, too, have a view of yourself. You know things about yourself that nobody else can know—unless you tell them. The things that make you sad, the kinds of people you admire, your dreams for your future—these are also characteristics, parts of the picture of who you are.

Yet, even with all this inside knowledge, your own picture of yourself is probably incomplete. It may be even more incomplete than the picture that others have of you.

Other people may see things that you've never realized about yourself. George knows many people, but feels that he doesn't have anyone he can call a real friend. However, many people admire him because he is so friendly and comfortable with new acquaintances. He hasn't seen this positive part of his character.

Your Self-Concept

Your **Self-concept** is *the picture you have of yourself.* It includes your views about what you like and what you think you're

A strong, positive self-concept helps other people to feel comfortable and to enjoy being around you.

good at. You may see yourself as an athlete or a computer whiz, a good cook or a mechanic. Your self-concept also includes what you see as your weaknesses. Perhaps you are shy around others, or maybe you feel ashamed of having a messy room.

Your self-concept is very important to you in a number of ways. It not only affects the way you feel about yourself, but can also influence the way you act. Your self-concept can influence how others see you. For example, you may think of yourself as a cheerful person. If you greet everyone happily and in a friendly way, others also will think of you as cheerful.

When Your Self-Concept Began

You started forming your self-concept when you were very young. Perhaps your grandfather always commented on your warm smile or happy laugh. Maybe your mother praised you for running fast or for always helping out. Your sister may have teased you about your freckles. All of these comments helped build your self-concept.

You still have some of these characteristics. You're still the fastest runner on the block. You've outgrown other characteristics, however. Your freckles are all gone now, but you still remember your sister's teasing. As you change, your self-concept also changes. It adjusts to match the different way you see yourself.

Your self-concept is growing. And you are not alone—your friends are in the same situation. They, like you, have recently begun thinking about who they are. And, like you, they are also changing fast.

As teenagers, you will all have to adjust to the fact that some of your childhood characteristics may be changing. You'll also find that many new qualities are developing. There is still much to learn about yourself.

No one is ever finished developing his or her self-concept. Older people also experience changes and learn new things about themselves. But now is the time to lay the foundation for a positive self-concept.

Developing Your Self-Concept

Your self-concept is a key to becoming the person you want to be. With a strong self-concept, you'll know who you are and how you want to act. You'll be better able to focus on your good points, and you'll have the confidence to improve the things about yourself that you don't accept.

Needing a Strong Self-Concept

Jody has a problem that other teenagers describe. She feels totally different when she's with different people. With her par-

ents, she acts like a "good child." She does things that she feels her friends would laugh at her for. But with her friends, she's often led to do things that she knows her parents wouldn't accept.

Either way, she ends up feeling badly about herself. She finds herself doing what she feels people expect her to do. She doesn't have a clear idea of who she is and what she should expect of herself.

Jody lacks a strong self-concept. She depends on the views of others instead of relying on her own views. Because other people's views differ, she gets drawn into conflicting situations that make her feel uncomfortable.

Negative self-concepts can contribute to real problems. Some people can become so unsure of themselves that they are afraid to participate in group activities.

Others may try to act as if they are perfect, dismissing any criticism by saying, "He's just an idiot," or, "Who is she to tell me that?" But inside they still lack confidence, fearing that the opinions of others may be right.

TABLE 1 **Strengths and Weaknesses**

Something that bothers you about yourself may be what others like most about you. Look below at how these "weaknesses" can really be strengths.

Weakness	Strength
Friends are always telling you their problems.	Friends trust you and believe that you can help them.
You take longer to do homework than others do.	You read and study carefully, and finish all assignments.
Your parents always ask you to watch your little sister.	Your parents think that you are responsible.
You have too much to do.	You enjoy many different activities.
You always cry at sad movies.	You have deep feelings.

Strengthening Your Self-Concept

There are four major ways to strengthen your self-concept and keep it functioning well:

■ *Look for your good points.* The first step toward strengthening your self-concept is to recognize that you have many positive characteristics. Everybody has some. You are very important to other people. Perhaps you help a friend with problems, or always have a few pleasant words for a neighbor. Other people's positive feelings about you reflect your good points. Get to know those good points by thinking about what others have said to you or how they act with you.

■ *Don't sell yourself short.* Perhaps you have a hard time thinking of any good points. You have difficulty believing the positive things people say about you. If someone thinks well of you, you might secretly feel that you are "fooling" that person. He or she doesn't know how "worthless" you really are.

In thinking this way, you are only fooling yourself. People praise you because they feel you really deserve it. Think about what they say. Use their comments to discover your good points, and then develop those characteristics until everyone sees them.

■ *Be active with others.* Put your strengths to use in some activity, preferably helping others. If, like George earlier in this chapter, people have praised you for being friendly, you could join a group that welcomes new people to your community. You could make a point of seeking out lonely people at your school, or being available to help new students who enter your school.

■ *Learn from everything you do.* Be ready to feel good about yourself when you are successful—and be ready to accept other people's praise. Thank people for complimenting you and remember the quality they admired in you. If you make a mistake, don't withdraw, but try to learn from it.

A strong and positive self-concept can make you feel a lot more comfortable about yourself and a lot surer about how to act. And a strong self-concept can also influence how others see you. If you recognize and focus on your strengths, others will notice them, too.

Words to Remember

characteristic: a special feature or trait of a person being described

self-concept: the picture that you have of yourself

Questions

1. Is any person's picture of you complete? Is your own? Why or why not?
2. How can your self-concept influence how others see you?
3. How can you develop a positive self-concept?

Chapter 2 # Growing and Changing

After reading this chapter, you will be able to:

☐ *give examples of the physical, emotional, mental, and social changes you undergo in adolescence,*

☐ *explain how you can take good care of yourself, test and explore new ideas and activities, and learn from your mistakes.*

Jeff was so happy! "At last, my first job!" he said to himself. "Now I have money to do some of the things I want to do. Now I can be really independent!"

Six months later, Jeff was again thinking to himself, "Working isn't easy. It does get me money, but I don't want to bag groceries forever. I guess at this time of my life, I'd better start thinking about my future and get down to some studying, too."

Your teen years, *the time of growth from child to adult,* are called **adolescence.** This period is marked by new feelings and experiences as you become a new person.

It can be a troubling time, because you cannot see where all the changes will lead. It can be confusing, because what you feel one day is often quite different from what you felt the day before.

But all these changes and new feelings are signs that you're growing.

A Time of Change

Adolescence is the last important growth stage before adulthood itself. This stage affects your physical, mental, and social characteristics. The changes you undergo during adolescence will open up a whole new world of relationships and a whole new way of seeing things.

Physical Changes

Probably the first changes you notice in this period are physical. One classmate seems to grow six inches overnight. Some begin to develop adult figures. Others develop acne. Changes like acne are usually temporary—they go away as you age. Most of these physical changes will last, however. Your body is taking its adult form.

The materials that make up your body change. Leg bones get longer, making you taller. The proportion of fat and muscle in your body changes. And your body begins producing substances called **hormones.** These are *chemicals that cause you to grow and mature.*

The table lists other changes that occur. The result of all these changes is that you are becoming more adult.

Of course, how quickly these changes occur varies from person to person. One friend may grow slowly over a long time, while another has a great spurt of growth early and then doesn't grow again.

The ways adolescents react to these changes also vary. You might feel embarrassed about your voice cracking when you're excited, or awkward if you are the tallest in your class. Or you might feel proud that you are growing, happy with your new adult shape.

Emotional Changes

The hormones released in your body also produce emotional changes. You may feel your emotions more strongly than before. And you'll feel new emotions. For example, you may be annoyed at how your parents treat you, although it never bothered you before. You may be more sensitive to teasing—you used to laugh, but it hurts you now.

TABLE 1 **Changes in Adolescence**

☐ Girls' growth spurt begins between ages 10 and 13. (At ages 11 and 12, the average girl is taller than the average boy.)	☐ Your hair darkens.
	☐ Your voice lowers.
☐ Boys' growth spurt begins between ages 12 and 15. (In adulthood, the average man is taller than the average woman.)	☐ Your nose and chin become more sharply defined.
☐ You develop more muscles and curves.	☐ Your skin becomes oilier and you perspire more.
☐ Your legs and arms grow longer.	☐ Your lungs and stomach can hold more air and food.
☐ Your hands and feet grow bigger.	☐ You develop sexual maturity.

Thought-provoking games and activities in school and out of school promote critical thinking and reasoning skills. They also help you learn about people and about how you react in situations.

Because your body is trying to adjust to these changes, your emotions may go up and down like a roller coaster. One day you may feel lonely and want to be with friends. The next day, you may want to be by yourself.

Slowly, though, you'll learn to adjust to these emotions. And the emotional swings you may feel probably will stop as the levels of hormones in your body balance out.

Mental Changes

The mental changes you experience continue throughout your adult life. As you grow, you learn to reason and think more abstractly. You can understand concepts like justice and responsibility. You also dis-cover how ideas, emotions, and situations relate to one another.

You'll probably begin to question things by asking, for example "Why is that true?" or, "Why not do it this way?" Your new mental abilities will help you to see other ways of living or of reaching goals. You'll begin to test new ideas and learn to think for yourself. Unfortunately, this will some-times lead to tension with your family, teachers, or friends. But, even then, you'll learn from your experiences.

Social Changes

Your developing **self-awareness**, *the sense of who you are and what you're like,* helps you to learn how to act with others. And your ability to feel more deeply helps you to consider others' needs as well as your own. Because you see that they need help, you may offer to set the table when your mother is very busy, or show your little sister how to ride a bike.

Your skill in getting along with other people grows with experience. The more time you spend with people, the more you learn about them. Helping others and enjoying their company gives you more confidence.

Living with Change

You can take action to make sure that the changes you undergo lead in the direction you want. Use these years to advantage by giving yourself the best chance, by explor-ing new options, and by learning from mistakes.

FEATURE

Nature or Nurture or You?

Have you ever wondered why you are the way you are? Scientists have long debated the source of each person's characteristics and actions. Some trace the origin of all traits to your **heredity**, *the genes you inherit from your parents*. Nature, they say, is the source of what makes you uniquely you. Others claim that it's your **environment**, *the culture you have been reared in*. Nurture, or how you're reared, is their answer.

In truth, it seems to be a product of both. Your genes do determine certain features—the color of your eyes, whether your hair is curly or straight, and whether you have asthma. Some talents also may be inherited—musical ability, for instance.

Still, your environment plays an important role in shaping your life. As a result of better nutrition, human beings are generally taller now than they used to be. And many skilled musicians come from non-musical families.

Parents influence you through heredity and the way they rear you. But you are largely responsible for the final product that is you. Your parents can buy you a guitar and pay for lessons, but you must do the practicing to learn the skill. You also have the responsibility for keeping your body healthy and fit.

Accepting responsibility for yourself is part of growing up. Take advantage of or improve on what you have inherited. Make the most of your environment, or even make it better. By taking action, you can work at making yourself into the best possible you.

Giving Yourself the Best Chance

Taking good care of your health helps you to maintain your strength so that you can reach your full potential. Help yourself grow to be a strong and healthy adult in these ways:

- Eat a balanced diet.
- Get plenty of rest.
- Take time for regular exercise.
- Avoid all harmful substances that are known to have harmful effects, like tobacco, alcohol, and drugs.

You will find some ideas about exercise in the Teen Tips at the end of this unit. Unit 4 will explain how to eat a balanced diet.

Healthy eating habits and good nutrition supply teens with the energy they need for their rapidly growing bodies and their active lifestyles.

Exploring New Options

Your teen years are a time for testing and exploring. You try many new ways of acting and reacting. Babysitting, for instance, can teach you about the responsibilities and rewards of parenthood. Being with different kinds of people helps you to learn what characteristics you like or don't like in others.

You can also explore different ways of looking. You may want to change your haircut or your style of dress, searching for the fashion that reflects the real you. You may try different activities—painting, horseback riding, playing basketball, or being a hospital volunteer.

This exploring will teach you more about yourself. You'll add what you've learned to your growing self-concept, bringing that picture of yourself into sharper focus.

Learning from Mistakes

Some learning will come from mistakes. You may wear something inappropriate to a party and feel uncomfortable. You may be nervous and say something that sounds rude. Everyone makes mistakes like these. Developing the social skills you'll have as an adult takes practice.

You can help yourself to acquire the skills you want more quickly by learning from your mistakes—then you won't have to make the same ones again! Think about what happened and why. Were you dressed too casually for the party because you forgot to ask what to wear when you were invited? Next time you can ask and avoid the problem.

Learn from your mistakes, but don't dwell on them. If you think only about what you do wrong, you'll develop mostly negative ideas about yourself. Remember your strengths. If it's the only way you can remember them, write them down and read the list before leaving for school every day.

Use your teen years to develop a positive self-concept. Then you'll be ready to meet the challenges of adulthood.

Words to Remember

adolescence: the time of growth from child to adult

environment: the culture you're reared in

heredity: the genes you inherit from your parents

hormones: chemicals that cause you to grow and mature

self-awareness: the sense of who you are and what you're like

Questions

1. List some of the physical changes that happen in adolescence. What causes those changes?
2. What mental abilities do you have today that you didn't have two years ago?
3. What changes have you seen in your relationships with other people?
4. Give two specific examples of things you can do now to adjust to the changes you're experiencing.

Chapter **3** # What You Communicate about Yourself

Objectives

After reading this chapter, you will be able to:

☐ *explain how your body language, appearance, and manners affect how others see you,*

☐ *learn about yourself by considering others' views of you,*

☐ *improve your appearance and behavior to become the person you want to be.*

Has your best friend ever asked you, "What's wrong?" before you've said a word? How could your best friend know something was wrong? He or she could probably sense that something was different about you. Perhaps you were walking more slowly than usual. Perhaps you were looking at the ground. Or maybe it was just that you didn't say "Hi."

Communicating is *sending messages from one person to another.* But those messages aren't always sent by words. If you've ever seen a silent movie or a mime artist, you know that someone's facial expression can speak very clearly. The way you stand or sit, the clothes you wear, how you move, and how you speak all send messages about you to others.

25

Your Hidden Messages

When people first meet you, they receive many different messages. They put together all that they see and hear and create a picture of you. *The images people have of someone they've just met* are their **first impressions**. They use those impressions to decide whether they want to get to know that person better. After first meeting someone, have you ever said, "I don't like him; he's a showoff"?

Sometimes, first impressions can be wrong. Someone who seems unfriendly may simply be sad that day. Get to know people better before you decide what they're like. And keep in mind that many people make judgments based on first impressions. If someone just met you, what would he or she learn about you?

Your Body Language

The way you use your eyes tells something about who you are and how you feel. A girl who doesn't look at someone who speaks to her may be shy. By avoiding eye contact, she sends the message that others shouldn't approach her. Someone who looks directly at a new acquaintance appears friendlier.

Your posture and how you move also affect how others see you. A boy who slouches gives the impression that he doesn't think much of himself. A person who stands straight shows that she respects herself. Others will take that as a cue to respect her.

Your Appearance

How you look to others should be important to you, because it affects how they think of you. **Grooming** is *making yourself look neat, clean, and trim*. It includes things like regular bathing and shampooing, cleaning your teeth, and using deodorants or antiperspirants. Neatness and cleanliness communicate to others that you care about yourself. You show that you want to take the time and effort to look attractive.

The Teen Tips at the end of this unit give you some ideas on how to practice good grooming.

TABLE 1 **Clues to Who You Are**

What You Do or Say	What It Means
Wave your arms when you talk.	You're expressive.
Shake hands and smile at a new acquaintance.	You're friendly.
Look away when someone else talks.	You're not listening.
Fold your arms.	You're uncomfortable.
Interrupt someone who is speaking.	You're rude.
Tap your fingers on a table.	You're impatient.
Sit near someone.	You find that person interesting.

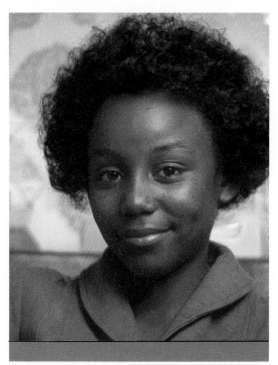

A neat, clean personal appearance creates a positive first impression and communicates to others that you care about yourself.

and friendly, strangers learn that you care about them as human beings. No one wants to get to know rude people.

How you react to things also can tell people about you. If you get angry very easily, others may see you as immature. If you can solve a problem calmly, they'll respect you.

Your voice can send messages—and sometimes those messages conflict with your words. Your little brother excitedly says, "Look at the picture I drew!" You answer, "That's terrific." But *how* you say those words tells the whole story.

If your voice shows enthusiasm, your brother will be pleased that you like the drawing. But if you speak in a flat tone of voice and don't look up from your magazine, your brother understands that you don't really care. And he may be hurt. Thinking before you act or talk can prevent problems like this one from happening.

Of course, with your family and friends, who you know well, you can be more casual. But looking your best is very important on special occasions, such as when you meet new people.

Another part of grooming is caring for your clothes. Keep them neat and clean. Wash them regularly, mend any rips or tears, and replace any buttons that are lost.

Your Actions and Your Speech

How you act is another way you communicate. Your **manners** are *the way you behave toward other people.* If you are polite

Learning About Your Messages

You can learn to read the messages that you send in two ways: by talking to others and by reading their messages to you.

Talking to Others

If you are concerned about how you appear to others, your family and friends can help. Ask someone that you trust how you appear. Does your voice sound harsh or friendly? Are you usually polite to others? A good friend can give honest answers that won't hurt you.

F E A T U R E

A Guide to Manners

Many people fear that good manners are complex rituals of behavior often painful to perform. They shudder at the thought of learning all that's written in the 1,000-page encyclopedias of manners.

But manners aren't hard to understand. They're really just common sense, depending on where you are and whom you're with. You may be more casual at home with friends than you are in public. But it's important to know good manners to be able to use them. To see how much you know, take this little test.

1. When you meet adults, you should:
   a. call them by their nicknames,
   b. call them by their first names,
   c. call them by their last names unless you're told otherwise.

2. When your parents call you to dinner, you should:
   a. tell them that you've already eaten,
   b. finish what you're doing before coming to the table,
   c. wash your hands and come to the table.

3. If a meal at your aunt's house includes a vegetable that you don't like, you should:
   a. ask not to be given any of the vegetable,
   b. not say anything, and then not eat what you're served,
   c. ask to be served only a little and eat that amount.

4. When you leave a party, you should:
   a. get your coat and go home,
   b. say good-bye and go home,
   c. thank your host or hostess and go home.

If you gave answer c for each question, you know more about manners than you think.

Reading Others' Messages to You

The other way to learn about the messages you send is to watch how others react to you. If someone who meets you seems to enjoy talking to you, you probably appear to be a friendly person. If someone backs away from you while you're talking, you may be speaking too loudly.

At home, when your mother lets you stay overnight at a friend's house, she is showing you that she trusts you. When your father gives you some extra dollars, he's telling you that he approves of you.

A Message to Yourself

You also send messages to yourself. If you are sad, you may walk with your head down. But it also happens that if you walk with your head down, you may begin to feel sad. On the other hand, smiling can make you feel better on a gloomy day. One way to change yourself, then, is simply to act positively—it may become a habit.

Of course, smiling all day isn't a replacement for talking to someone if a serious problem bothers you. But having a positive attitude can help a good deal.

Walk around during the day with a smile and a happy, positive attitude. Extend a friendly greeting to the people you see. Notice how it makes you and those around you feel good.

Controlling Your Messages

You have control over much of what you communicate. Often, you can choose what image you present to others. The key to making this choice wisely is knowing clearly what your feelings and ideas are. Then see if you're communicating them.

It isn't a good idea to change the way you dress or how you wear your hair just to please other people. Everyone has different likes and dislikes. Throughout your life, you will meet so many people that you couldn't possibly please them all!

Your goal isn't to become someone you aren't, but to show who you are. Take a close look at the image you present. Then you can see whether the messages you're sending are the ones you want to send.

Throughout, keep your image of yourself positive. It will help you to get over some of the smaller bumps of life and to face the bigger ones.

Words to Remember

communicating: sending messages from one person to another

first impression: the image people have of someone they've just met

grooming: making yourself look neat, clean, and trim

manners: the way you behave toward other people

Questions

1. Think of your first impression of someone you met recently. Once you got to know that person better, how did that first impression change?

2. Give one example each of how people stand, sit, walk, talk, or act that tells you something about them.

3. Describe how you think three people you know see you. Why does one person see you one way and another person see you differently?

4. Think of two messages you would like to send. How can you start sending them?

Chapter **4** # What's Important to You

Objectives

After reading this chapter, you will be able to:

☐ *identify some of your basic needs, wants, and principles,*

☐ *identify your goals,*

☐ *prepare for action by deciding which goals are most important to you.*

Every day you face problems, both large and small, that require you to make choices based on the things that are important to you. For example, suppose that you belong to the school band. This year the band has been invited to play at a special program in the state capital. All the members are excited about going, and they are working on weekends to raise the money to go. Everyone must take part in this fund raising, or there won't be enough money. You have been assigned to wash cars on weekends, and you have promised that you would definitely do the work.

But one month into the project, you have a problem. Your parents need you to stay home and watch your little brother and sister—on a day you have been assigned to wash cars. What can you do?

Needs, Wants, and Principles

One way of settling problems like this one is to sort out what's most important to you. You can do this a little more easily if you understand how your needs, your wants, and your principles differ.

What You Need

Everybody needs certain things to survive. You need food to eat and water to drink, clothes to wear, and a place to live. **Needs** are *things that are essential*—things that you can't get along without.

But meeting these physical needs alone wouldn't make life totally satisfying. You need other things, too. You need the love and companionship of people like your family and friends. You also need to feel that there are people you can turn to when you need help.

In addition, you need to do things that make you feel good about yourself. Making the soccer team or getting an A on a test makes you feel special. You also need some independence to make decisions and to try new things. New experiences help you learn and grow. These are necessary for your development.

What You Want

Wants are *things you desire to make life more enjoyable*. Some wants are also needs. Everyone has the need to eat, for example. But in the school cafeteria, you get a hamburger and your friend gets a salad. You both satisfy the *need* to eat differently because you both have different *wants*.

Some wants are things you set your mind on simply because they please you. You might want to take a trip to another city to visit a friend who has moved away. Or you might want to save enough money for a favorite album.

What You Believe In

Some of your actions are based not on your needs or wants, but on your principles. **Principles** are *your beliefs about what is right and what is wrong, and your guidelines for living with yourself and with others.*

Suppose that a friend has taken an exam the period before you and offers to give you the answers. What should you do?

Your principles are shaped by what you learn in school and in your religion. They are also shaped by the beliefs of those people you like and respect. They can be parents and friends, or they can be famous

The school cafeteria is a good example of a place in which you make individual choices daily.

people whom you admire, such as heroes from history or athletes of today. Likewise, television programs, politicians, and many other influences shape your principles.

Sometimes, you hear many different opinions about what is right, or wrong, or important. You may find it hard to know what to think. At those times, you may want to talk about these things to someone older, whom you respect.

Or you could think by yourself, away from others and their influences. List some principles that you know are important to you. How do they help you to make a decision? How are they helpful in guiding you?

Goals

The way you put your needs, wants, and principles into action is by setting goals. **Goals** are *the targets we set for ourselves to accomplish.*

Types of Goals

There are three types of goals. *Some goals meet basic needs*, such as getting food to eat, or clothing to wear, or having a place to live.

Other goals supply the things you want to make life more pleasant. Perhaps you decide to save up for a bicycle or a cassette player. Or maybe you start to learn to play tennis.

Some goals come from your principles. These are things that you do as much for others as for yourself. John spends two hours each Saturday helping an elderly neighbor, Mr. Jenkins, around his house. He could go out and play football with his friends. But John knows that Mr. Jenkins appreciates help.

Short-Term and Long-Term Goals

Goals also differ, depending on when they'll be reached. A **short-term goal** is *something that you can accomplish right away.* Short-term goals include such activities as going on a hike this weekend, losing five pounds, taking tennis lessons, or reading a new mystery novel. These are all things you can do in the near future.

A **long-term goal** is *something that you plan to accomplish farther in the future.* Your goal may be to do something in six months, or one year, or five years. Buying a used car when you get your driver's license is a long-term goal. So is saving for summer camp.

You can often use short-term goals as steps toward reaching a long-term goal. Suppose that you want to buy a computer. You can build toward that long-term goal in two ways. First, you can save money for the computer. Second, you can read magazines to learn which computer would be best for you to buy.

Principle goals often involve helping others, such as visiting a sick friend, helping the needy, recycling old clothes, and working with the elderly.

TABLE 1   **Short-Term Goals and Long-Term Goals**

You can achieve many long-term goals by building toward them slowly with short-term goals.

Long-term goal	Short-term goal
Buy a new radio.	Save $2 a week.
Use time more efficiently.	Plan your activities for a day.
Learn to play the piano.	Practice for 30 minutes each day.
Expand your wardrobe.	Make a new piece of clothing every month.
Improve your jump shot in basketball.	Shoot 50 jump shots a day.

Setting Priorities

Sometimes, you will be forced to choose between conflicting goals. Such a choice will be a lot easier if you spend some time examining your goals first.

Need, Want, or Principle?

In the example at the beginning of this chapter, your goals seem equally desirable. You want to help the band earn the money for the trip, and you also want to help your parents. To choose one of these goals, you need to look at each of them more closely.

The first step is to list the two goals on a piece of paper—writing things down makes them easier to compare. It also prevents you from forgetting anything.

Next to each goal, write whether it meets a need, a want, or a principle. Helping the band and taking care of your brother and sister are probably both principle goals.

Now note whether the goals are long term or short term. Both are short term, but one is more complex. Working with the band also helps meet the long-term goal of

going on the trip. So far, you seem to be stuck.

Fixed or Flexible?

Another thing to think about is whether the goal is fixed or flexible. **Fixed goals** *can only be met at a certain time.* Your parents' need for your help is fixed—it must be met that afternoon.

Flexible goals *can be reached at different times.* You can reorganize your closet any day you have the time.

Sometimes, a goal starts out being flexible but becomes fixed. If you want to study for a test coming up next week, it is a flexible goal for the first few days. But as the test gets closer, studying becomes a fixed goal—you can't put it off much longer!

Fixed and flexible do not mean important and unimportant. A television show you like is shown at a fixed time, but there may be a week when watching it is much less important than doing something else.

Working with the band seems to be a flexible goal. While the participation of each band member is important, the fund-

FEATURE

A Plan to Improve Yourself

If you want to change something about yourself, it helps to have a plan. That way, you'll be able to think carefully about what you want to be like and how to become that way. And with a plan you can check your progress.

Here's a simple plan in six steps.

1. *Find the problem.* First you have to know what you want to change. Be as specific as possible in stating the problem. You can only change if you have a concrete goal—like losing five pounds. It's much harder to follow a plan to simply "weigh less." For the sample plan, let's suppose that you want to overcome some of your shyness. That's your goal.

2. *Analyze your behavior.* Before deciding what to do to overcome your shyness, you need to see what you're doing now that keeps you being shy. Watch yourself for a week or so. Do you always sit alone in the cafeteria? Do you answer questions briefly to discourage more talking? Do you look away when others look at you? Good, now you're beginning to analyze your behavior.

3. *Make a plan.* Make a chart like the one below.

   For each day of the week, fill in the "Action planned" box with a short-term goal to help you overcome your shyness. Make each goal different. One day, you could stop to talk to a neighbor for five minutes. Another day, you could simply raise your hand in class to give an answer that you know is right.

4. *Follow the plan.* Each morning before you leave the house, review your goal for the day. Then, during the day, be sure to take the action you planned. Withhold something you want—say, your favorite television show—until you meet your goal. Each night before going to sleep, record in your chart the action you took.

5. *Reward yourself.* At the end of the week, see how you did each day. If you met your goal, treat yourself to something—a new record or an ice cream. Or you can doubly reward yourself by inviting one of your new acquaintances to a movie!

6. Repeat steps 3 through 5 for a few more weeks until you feel more confident.

	Sun.	Mon.	Tue.	Wed.	Thu.	Fri.	Sat.
Action Planned							
Action Taken							

raising activities will continue for a few months. You can work two days on another weekend to make up for the day you'll miss this time.

Choosing Goals

You seem to have solved your problem. You'll help your parents by taking care of your brother and sister. You can meet your obligation to the band at a later time—that goal was more flexible.

By examining your goals, you were able to set **priorities**. You could decide *which of the goals was most important to you*. That made choosing between the goals much easier.

A good way to order your goals is to write down five of the top goals in your life at this time. Write them in any order, and study them. Then, rewrite them in the order of importance to you.

Words to Remember

fixed goal: a goal that can only be met at a certain time

flexible goal: a goal that can be reached at many different times

goal: the targets we set for ourselves to accomplish

long-term goal: something that you plan to accomplish farther in the future

needs: things that are essential

principles: your beliefs about what is right and what is wrong, and your guidelines for living with yourself and with others

priority: the goal that is most important to you

short-term goal: something that you can accomplish right away

wants: things you desire to make life more enjoyable

Questions

1. Name five things that we need to survive.
2. What are some of the things that you want in life?
3. List three of your principles.
4. What are two of your short-term goals? What are two of your long-term goals? How do you intend to reach them?
5. Are fixed goals more important than flexible goals? Why or why not?

Chapter **5 Making Decisions for Now and for Your Future**

Objectives

After reading this chapter, you will be able to:

☐ *explain how the decisions you make affect you and others,*

☐ *make intelligent and successful decisions,*

☐ *begin to plan for your future.*

Chris and Jenny are partners in a neighborhood gardening service in the afternoons. One month after the girls start working together, Jenny is offered the chance to work as a volunteer in the local hospital. She would love to do it—Jenny thinks that she would like to study medicine and become a doctor. But if she volunteers at the hospital, Jenny will have to stop working with Chris. Since Chris can't handle the job alone, she would have to give up the gardening work.

Jenny's goals conflict, so she must set some priorities. Jenny likes working with Chris, and it's a way to earn money. But by volunteering at the hospital, she can get experience that may be valuable in the future. Then there's the problem of principles. Would it be right to leave Chris, knowing that she couldn't keep the gardening service going alone?

Decisions and You

Decisions, decisions, decisions—life is full of them. A **decision** is *the choice you make between different possibilities.* There are many different types of decisions, but every decision affects you and the others around you in some way. You are responsible for every decision you make, and you can learn something from every decision.

Types of Decisions

Decisions can be of major or minor importance. They can be easy or difficult to make. They can be made by you alone or by a group. Even *not* making a decision is a decision.

And decisions are a part of every area of your life. You make decisions about family matters, such as how to divide telephone time or household chores. You make decisions about friends, too—when you choose to spend more time with one friend rather than with another, for instance, or when you decide to go to a movie with one friend rather than bowling with another. You also make time and money decisions, planning your studying schedule or preparing a budget for yourself.

Other decisions that affect your daily life relate to food, clothing, and housing. Will you snack on chocolate or an apple? Will you buy jeans or a pair of corduroys? How can you organize your room to make it look nicer?

How Your Decisions Affect You

Decisions vary in the ways they affect you. The smaller, minor decisions you make every day determine the way you live right now. For example, you might decide to go to a movie tonight and study longer tomorrow night.

Larger, major decisions affect you today and in your future. For instance, Jenny's decision about working at the hospital will affect her future career choice.

How Your Decisions Affect Others

You aren't the only one affected by the decisions you make—Jenny's decision shows that. Other people almost always are involved, especially your family and friends. Your day-to-day decisions about

The decisions that you make affect other people around you, even when you cook.

things like chores and parties affect their lives and the ways they spend their time.

Sometimes your decisions affect their feelings, too—your brother will appreciate your help with the dishes, and he'll know that you care about him. That great birthday gift you gave your friend shows how much you think of her.

Your family and friends can also be hurt by things you say or do, so you must choose your words and actions carefully. This is also true for strangers you meet. Choosing to use good manners helps show people that you care about their feelings.

Your major decisions—those that are more important for your future—also influence other people. Personal decisions about friendship and dating are closely tied to the lives of others. These choices may lead to close relationships and commitments that will be just as important to the other people as they are to you.

Taking Responsibility for Your Decisions

You are responsible for your own behavior. Even though your decisions affect other people as well as you, you are the only one who can make them.

This doesn't mean that you should do whatever you feel like doing. You must recognize how your decisions will affect others. You can get helpful advice from parents, teachers, and community.

Being responsible for your decisions means thinking and planning carefully. Listen to others, look around you, and learn all you can about your choices and the possible results of each one.

Learning from Your Decisions

Some decisions benefit you in obvious ways. When you decide to take a home economics class, you choose to learn many useful skills. If Jenny takes the hospital job, she will learn something about medicine and caring for others. But making decisions is a skill in itself. As you make more and more decisions, you'll learn to find **alternatives**, or *ways of solving a problem*. And you'll develop your skill at choosing the best one.

Making Decisions

You've seen how the different types of decisions affect you and others. But how can you make these decisions? Some ways are outlined in the box. However, to make a decision thoughtfully, you need to use a more organized method.

Listen to others, and seek advice from family as well as friends when making major decisions.

FEATURE

Some Ways to Make Decisions

People don't always use an organized method to make decisions. Let's look at some other ways decisions are made.

- *Default.* You're at home studying when a friend drops by to talk. If you keep talking to your friend until it's too late to study, you've decided to talk rather than study by **default.** This means *backing into a decision by not deciding.*

- *Imitation.* You may make decisions by following the examples of others. Imitating others can lead to good decisions—a swimmer does well to follow the example of his coach. But in matters of style or ways of living, be careful not to adopt a fashion that doesn't suit your appearance, habits, or talents.

- *Habit.* We all do many things by habit—we wake up at the same time every day or take the same route to school. For simple matters, these habits provide shortcuts. Sometimes, though, habits get out of date. Be sure to change your habits if they don't provide you with shortcuts anymore.

- *Impulse.* You walk past a store window and see a new album by your favorite band. If you run into the store and buy it, you are deciding on **impulse.** You are *doing what you feel like doing.*

- *Coin toss.* Which movie will you see tonight? Some people make decisions like this by tossing a coin, leaving the answer to chance.

Each of these ways of deciding can be useful when the decision is minor. But when deciding more important and more complex matters, the six-step method discussed in this chapter will help you make more intelligent decisions.

The Decision-Making Method

Every successful decision follows the same basic, six-step method:
1. define your problem,
2. gather information and identify your choices,
3. review your wants, needs, principles, and goals,
4. examine the possible outcomes of each choice in terms of your wants, needs, principles, and goals,
5. make the choice and accept responsibility for it,
6. accept and evaluate your decision.

For small, quick decisions, you might follow these steps in seconds, without even being aware of them. More important decisions might take more time and effort. But the same basic steps apply to all decisions.

How the Method Works

Let's use the example of Jenny, whose problem is described at the beginning of this chapter.

First, Jenny must define her problem— she wants to work during her afternoons.

Next, Jenny indentifies her choices—she could start to volunteer at the hospital or continue working with Chris.

Jenny seems to be stuck. But in thinking about her problem some more, she comes up with another alternative. Why not find someone else who could work with Chris instead of her? Then she could learn about medicine, and Chris would be able to continue the gardening service. Jenny has made her choice—by giving more thought to her problem, she has found a way out.

After a few months, Jenny evaluates her decision and feels that she made the right choice. She is happy with her work at the hospital. And Chris and Tina—the friend Jenny suggested—are enjoying working together.

Decisions for Your Future

In the next few years, you will make many major decisions about your relationships, your health, your lifestyle, and your career. After high school, will you get a job or go to college? Where will you live? You will need to give time, thought, and energy to these decisions.

Gaining Knowledge

During these next years, you can prepare for the future. Start by learning about yourself. While you're in your teens, you can test different ways of thinking or acting. You can learn what you're like and what your abilities are.

You can also get help from this book. Here you'll read suggestions about what to consider when making many decisions.

Each unit of this book also has a chapter outlining many careers in a particular field. You can add to that information by doing research in the library, talking to your counselor, or speaking with people who work in the field.

With this information, you'll be able to make good decisions for your future.

Words to Remember

alternative: a way of solving a problem

decision: the choice you make between different possibilities

default: backing into a decision by not deciding

impulse: doing what you feel like doing at the moment

Questions

1. Give three examples of minor decisions that would affect you now.
2. Give three examples of major decisions that would affect you in the future.
3. What can you learn from your decisions?
4. What are the six basic steps in making a thoughtful decision?

When you focus on yourself, what do you see? You're happy with many things about yourself, but would like to improve others. Here are some ideas to help you make yourself the way you want to be.

1. What to do when they say you've done something wrong.

2. Getting fit and staying active.

3. Looking your best.

What to Do When They Say You've Done Something Wrong

Nobody likes to be criticized. But it's a big mistake either to dismiss criticism or to accept it without question. Finding that middle path—not getting upset, but calmly thinking about what the other person has said and deciding whether you agree with the comment—is difficult. Yet it isn't impossible. Here are some ways of handling your reactions.

1. If your English teacher scolds you for talking, *don't* take it personally. He isn't criticizing *you*, but something you did.

2. If your coach tries to tell you how to improve your jump shot, *do* listen—what she says may be helpful.

3. If your best friend complains that you revealed a secret, *don't* start defending yourself. Have an open mind and try to understand the point that he is making.

4. If your counselor says you don't try hard enough, *do* listen and ask questions to find out why he thinks so.

5. If your parent scolds you for not taking out the garbage, *don't* get emotional. Anger will only block your ability to learn and to get the job done.

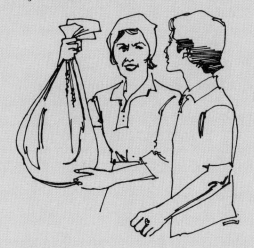

7. If a member of your club says that you aren't a good club president, *do* think about why he is criticizing you—is the comment true, or is he just jealous?

6. If your sister says that you didn't vacuum well, *don't* answer by listing her faults. Try to learn what you did that made her make the comment.

8. If everyone seems to be picking on you, *do* remember that you have good points, too. They are criticizing only one thing about you, not many.

Getting Fit and Staying Active

To get fit and stay that way, you need to follow a good program as much as a good diet.

Here are ten popular, healthy, and cheap activities you might choose from, as well as the kinds of benefits you can get from each. (Of course, there are many other kinds of exercise besides these, but they're a start.) And special facilities, like basketball and tennis courts and pools, are often free and open to the public.

These activities require no formal instruction, although everyone can benefit from lessons or coaching. To be sure of doing it right, you can borrow or buy a book or two when you start an activity. It's also a good idea to start slowly, working up gradually to more advanced skills or longer periods of exercise. Talk to your doctor before you begin an exercise program.

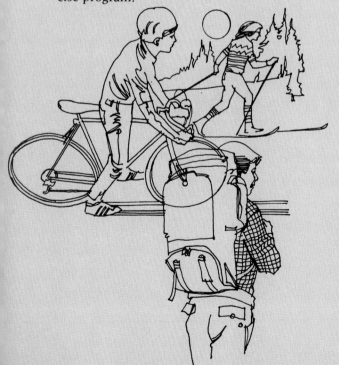

Basketball

Heart and lungs—good
Fat loss—good
Strength—no benefit
Flexibility—good

Bicycling

Heart and lungs—no benefit (at 5 mph);
good (at 8 mph)
Fat loss—no benefit (at 5 mph);
good (at 8 mph)
Strength—no benefit (at either speed)
Flexibility—good (at both speeds)

Calisthenics

Heart and lungs—good
Fat loss—very good
Strength—good
Flexibility—very good

Cross-country skiing

Heart and lungs—good (at 2.5 mph);
very good (at 4 mph)
Fat loss—good (at 2.5 mph);
very good (at 4 mph)
Strength—no benefit (at 2.5 mph);
good (at 4 mph)
Flexibility—good (at both speeds)

Hiking (at 3 mph)

Heart and lungs—very good
Fat loss—very good
Strength—good
Flexibility—good

Karate

Heart and lungs—good
Fat loss—very good
Strength—very good
Flexibility—very good

Racquet sports *(tennis and racquetball)*

Heart and lungs—good (tennis); very
                            good (racquetball)
Fat loss—good (tennis); very
             good (racquetball)
Strength—no benefit (either sport)
Flexibility—good (both sports)

Running

Heart and lungs—good (at 5 mph);
                            very good (at 7 mph)
Fat loss—very good (at both speeds)
Strength—no benefit (at either speed)
Flexibility—good (at both speeds)

Swimming

Heart and lungs—good (crawl, backstroke);
                            very good (breaststroke,
                                butterfly, sidestroke)
Fat loss—good (all strokes)
Strength—no benefit (all strokes)
Flexibility—good (all strokes)

Weight training

Heart and lungs—no benefit
Fat loss—good
Strength—good
Flexibility—good

Looking Your Best

Good grooming is easy to learn and to practice. If you are neat and clean, you show others that you have pride in yourself. They will enjoy being with you, and you will feel better about yourself. Here are some ways of keeping yourself well groomed.

Face

Wash your face thoroughly two or more times a day. Use mild soap and warm water. Rinse it carefully.

Acne can usually be controlled by eating a healthy diet, washing carefully, and using anti-acne creams. You should also avoid getting too much sun, using greasy creams, and squeezing pimples. If you have a severe case, see a dermatologist.

If you use makeup, apply it carefully. Too much may spoil the effect you're trying to create.

Mouth

To help prevent tooth decay, brush your teeth at least once a day or after every meal. (Avoiding sweets helps, too.)

Floss every day to remove food particles and other matter between your teeth and to promote healthy gums.

Visit the dentist—even if just for a checkup and cleaning—twice a year.

Hair

Shampooing at least twice a week will keep your hair healthy and attractive. Oily hair may need to be washed every day. Use shampoos to suit your type of hair and how often you wash it.

Keep your hair neat and well brushed or combed, and have it trimmed or shaped regularly.

Set your hair dryer at a medium temperature to avoid making your hair brittle.

Hands

Always wash your hands before preparing or eating food. Use a nail brush to scrub your fingernails and toenails clean.

Trim your nails with nail scissors or clippers. Use an emery board to smooth the ends. Use an orange stick to push back the cuticles, but do not cut them.

Body

Bathe or shower every day to remove dirt, control body odors, and keep your skin healthy and clear.

Deodorants and antiperspirants come in many forms and brands. Choose one you like, and use it every day.

Introduction Review

people around you. If you follow a thoughtful and organized method of decision making, you can make choices now that will bring you satisfaction in the future.

Unit Summary

Chapter 1.

As an individual, you see yourself in a certain way, which may be different from how others see you. Your self-concept—whether positive or negative—affects the way you feel and act, and the way other people relate to you. With a strong self-concept as a foundation, you can work on increasing your strengths.

Chapter 2.

Your adolescent years are a time of great physical, emotional, mental, and social changes. During this time, you should take care of yourself, explore the opportunities around you, and learn as much as you can from the mistakes you make.

Chapter 3.

You send messages about yourself to others not only verbally, but also through body language, appearance, and manners. You can strengthen or change these messages to communicate a positive view of yourself to other people.

Chapter 4.

Your needs, wants, and principles are the things that matter most to you. They determine your goals and let you decide which goals are most important when you're solving a problem.

Chapter 5.

You make decisions of many types—major and minor, complex and simple. These decisions will all affect you somehow, now or in the future. And they will also affect the other

Questions

1. Why is it important to have a positive self-concept?
2. What four major types of changes take place during adolescence?
3. Give two examples of messages communicated by body language.
4. Is it difficult to learn manners? Why or why not?
5. Explain the differences between needs and wants.
6. Where do your principles come from?
7. What are the basic steps in making a decision?
8. How can knowledge about yourself help you prepare for a career?

Writing Activities

1. Write a short description of yourself, listing all of the good qualities you can think of. Then, ask another person to make a list of the things he or she likes about you. How many of those items are on your own list? Would you say that your self-concept is mainly positive or negative?
2. Write a conversation between you and someone else who criticized you. If you are unhappy with the way you reacted, rewrite the dialogue to show what you wish you had said and done.
3. List ten activities that you enjoy. What does your list show you about yourself?

4. Take a career preference test. (See your guidance counselor or librarian for details.) How do the results compare with your own ideas about the jobs or careers you'd like to pursue? Which five occupations do the test results indicate you would be happiest with?

5. Review the decision-making method. Then think of a girl who has to make a decision about whether to take a certain job or not after school. Include:

- the kind of job,
- her school responsibilities,
- her home responsibilities,
- the advantages and disadvantages of the job,
- any conflicts that job, school, and home responsibilities might bring about.

Apply the decision-making method to your character's case. Write out the situation in story form.

Reading Activities

1. Read the section of a life science, health, or biology textbook that describes changes in hormones during adolescence. Write two or three paragraphs in your own words to explain what occurs.

2. In a book about body language, read a chapter that describes some examples of this way of sending messages. List ten of these examples, and carry the list with you for a day. Make a mark on the list each time you see something like one of the examples.

3. Reread the box in chapter 5. In our own words, describe each of the ways of making a decision.

4. Thumb through this text and find a photo which you like, and which shows a situation that might be solved through the decision-making method. Find a photo whose caption gives you some ideas about a solution. Report to the class on the situation and how the decision-making method could be used to resolve it.

5. In your social studies book or in any biography or history book that you know, find an incident in which a person had to make a very important decision affecting many people. Report to the class about the decision and its effects on people. How did the person follow the decision-making method?

Group Projects

1. Play "Body Language Charades" with a team of four or five people each. A player can stand, walk, sit, or gesture—but *not* speak—to communicate a certain emotion or attitude, and his or her team must try to guess the message. Record how long it takes for a correct guess. To determine what feelings players will act out, you might write things like "Anger," "Distrust," "Love," or "Confidence" on slips of paper for them to draw out of a box. You might even write on the slips something like "Humor—eyes only" or "Nervous—fingers only" to be more challenging.

2. Have students design a "Me" bulletin board that is regularly changed so that each member of the class is featured. Each display should include a photo or drawing of the person, some indications of special interests, perhaps some quotes, photos of family and friends, and memories of special events. Have the student whose turn it is to be featured be responsible for the board. The students should discuss each board—do they think that the person is well represented? Are all his or her special qualities included?

YOUR FAMILY AND YOUR FRIENDS

Have you ever thought what you would be like if you were born into a different family? Without your parents, brothers, and sisters, you wouldn't be the person that you are today.

Your family helps to shape your personality—you learn how to think and act mainly from your parents. Your family teaches you what's important in life. It provides you with food, clothing, and shelter. More importantly, your family gives you emotional support.

You can help the other members of your family in the same way. How can you help your parents around the house? Is there any way to settle that argument with your sister over who gets to use the telephone? In this unit, you'll learn how to answer these questions.

You have many other relationships, too. As soon as you were able to talk, you began to form friendships outside your family. You enjoyed running, playing, and trying out new games and toys. Your playmates were your friends.

When you started school, some of your classmates became friends. Perhaps you singled out one person as a "best friend," or you and your friends formed groups. Friends became even more important as you entered your teens. Now, instead of going everywhere with your parents, you often go out with your friends.

To keep your friendships strong, you have to make many decisions. What should you say to a friend who tells a secret of yours? What should you do if someone you like doesn't want to be your friend?

Later, you may form a special relationship with someone of the opposite sex. Is what you feel love?

In this unit, you'll also find answers to these questions. You'll learn how to be a good friend and how to make friends.

Chapter 6 Relationships and You

Objectives

After reading this chapter, you will be able to:

☐ *give examples of some of the relationships that are important to you,*

☐ *describe how successful relationships involve both giving and receiving,*

☐ *think about what you expect from your relationships.*

Because people need people, they have always lived and worked in groups. Within those groups, they form *special bonds with other people*. These bonds are called **relationships.**

The first relationships you formed were with your parents, brothers and sisters, grandparents, and other family members. As you grew older, you began to form relationships with people your age—you made friends.

Your relationships with your family and those with your friends are different, but good relationships have some things in common. They are based on both giving and receiving, and they help everyone involved in them to grow. If a relationship doesn't do these things, chances are that it won't last. You will not feel comfortable in the relationship, and it will end.

The Importance of Relationships

Building Your Self-Concept

Where do you get the picture you have of yourself, your self-concept? A large part comes from the way other people treat you.

If your friend tells you that she really likes your new hair style, you feel pleased. But if the same friend laughs at the sneakers that your mother bought you, you may feel ashamed. You feel intelligent when your teacher tells you that your book report was good, but not so smart when your father yells at you for leaving the front door unlocked. You feel grown-up when your mother praises you for doing the food shopping well, but childish when you make a silly mistake that everybody seems to notice.

In other words, the way you see yourself largely comes from the way other people see you.

But relationships do more than help you build your self-concept. Since Jane played that new album for you, you've been buying nothing but jazz records. If it weren't for her, you might never have enjoyed that kind of music. Relationships also can introduce you to new experiences.

Most important of all, relationships provide you with love and security. If you have love and security as a child, you'll be able to form close relationships with others later.

Relationships and Principles

Think about *your* relationships. Which ones are most important to you? What is it about them that you like? What do you get out of them?

You might like to spend time with your parents doing things such as shopping, going to the beach or the library, or visiting relatives. Someone else might prefer to be with friends at the Y, to work with a friend on a class project, or to practice with the soccer team.

Your friends and family help to shape your principles, and the things you consider important. And their attitudes toward relationships affect yours. If your family is friendly and outgoing, you probably are, too. If your friends enjoy helping others, you probably do, too.

Relationships and Goals

Most people, whether they realize it or not, have goals for their relationships. You might want to communicate better with your parents or to make more friends. Knowing what your goals are will help you improve the relationships you have, as well as help you make new ones.

Perhaps you're tired of being thought of as Mary's younger brother. You want to be appreciated for yourself. The best way is to get involved in different activities and interests. Develop our own abilities—be yourself. Don't run for class office, as Mary did. Use your energy to run on the track team.

Relationships and Decisions

As you grow older, your relationships will probably become more complicated. You learn more about what you want and expect from people, and they learn to expect more from you.

T E E N   I S S U E

Peer Pressure and You

Peer pressure is *the influence your friends and others of your age exert on you.* It can be good or bad, depending on how it affects you and how you handle it. Perhaps the members of your group are wearing their hair in a certain way, but your parents won't let you wear yours in that style. If you can shrug it off and not let it bother you, fine. But if not looking like the group really bothers you, you've got a problem.

Peer pressure can get you to try new experiences and become involved in worthwhile projects. For example:

- You join the group that's collecting canned food for poor families because Tom is in it.

- You go over and say hello to the new girl in class because you noticed that Sandy and Karen did.

- You start to laugh when Sharon teases Joe, but stop when you see that Phil and Maria don't join in.

Sometimes, however, peer pressure can make you do things you know are wrong, or keep you from doing things you'd really like to do. For example:

- You don't participate in class, even though you're prepared, because Sally doesn't.

- You'd really like to read the poem you wrote for English, but you're afraid that your friends will laugh at you.

- You don't call your parents to say you'll be late, because you're afraid that the group will tease you.

It's not easy handling peer pressure. All of us want to have friends, to be part of the group. But the fear of losing those friends, of being laughed at, or being alone, can sometimes make us do things we know are wrong.

To avoid this conflict, you have to make your own decisions. This will be easier if you have the courage to stand your ground and refuse to do things that are dangerous or wrong.

Sometimes, explaining your decision won't help and an excuse comes in handy. "I'm all out of change" can get you out of staying later than you should at the video arcade. "I'm tired; I'm going home," can solve a lot of problems. Whatever you say, be sure to act according to what *you* think is right.

In the past, you enjoyed sharing a room with your sister, but now you'd like privacy. Still, if your family's apartment is small, you'll have to compromise. Talk it over. Maybe she'd be willing to study in the living room while you're on the phone. You could do the same for her.

You have to make decisions about all your relationships. You notice that Steve acts differently when Robin and Pete are around. He makes wisecracks and insults you. Telling him how you feel can be difficult. But after you do it you'll feel better, and it may help your relationship.

The Variety of Relationships

Many Relationships at Once

Life becomes complex when you have to meet the expectations of more than one relationship. Teri wants your company all the time, but George wants you to spend time with him. Your parents urge you to study hard, but your friends are always asking you to go ice skating with them. How can you handle all these demands?

■ *First, be honest with yourself.* As you build your self-concept, you'll learn which activities are most important to you.

■ *Second, be honest with others.* Don't box yourself into a corner by agreeing to be two places at the same time. Someone will have to be disappointed, and you'll end up feeling bad.

  For example, you'd like to walk to school with Jon, but you told Mike that you'd meet him outside his house on the way to school. Explain this to Jon, and tell him that you'll see him on the way home. He'll respect you for keeping your word to Mike. And he'll know that he can count on you another time, when your appointment is with him.

Giving and Receiving

There are two actions in a relationship—giving and receiving—but there can be more than two people involved. The players on a basketball team all get directions from one coach, but there is more than one player!

Whether you are enjoying music among friends or walking along together, lasting relationships involve two actions—giving and receiving.

Giving. In every relationship, at least one person is getting something from another. Students learn from teachers. Friends receive companionship from other friends.

Sometimes, it seems that all the giving is on one side. Your job as a hospital volunteer takes time from your already busy schedule. You get up early Saturday—the one day you could sleep late—work all day, and don't even get paid. In addition, some of the patients are always complaining. It seems that you're giving, but getting nothing in return.

Receiving. But stop and think. You felt good when you got the man in Room 404 to cheer up, especially since he'd been sad all day. And the experience you're getting will come in handy in the future if you choose a health-care career. So you *are* getting something from this relationship—in fact, you're getting a lot.

Few relationships are all give in one direction and all receive in the other. People usually won't stay in a relationship for long unless they get something in return for the effort.

Expectations and Conflict

Living in a relationship is not always smooth and easy. At one time or another, you can expect to have *some problems in almost all of your relationships*. Often, these **conflicts** occur because you and the other

Maintaining an honest and open communication among family members and others can help you learn, grow, and solve conflicts. By listening to others' advice and understanding their expectations, you will be better able to deal with different relationships.

person expect different things. Your relationships might work better if you understand your **expectations**, or *what each of you wants from the relationship.*

Why Conflict Occurs

Often, the expectations of two people in a relationship differ. You and Mary are very good friends and enjoy each other's company. You go to the movies. But you like to do things with other people, too—for example, you'd like to ask Beth and Amy to come along. Mary likes it better when the two of you are alone.

How can you and Mary solve this conflict in your relationship? One good way is to talk about your expectations of each other. Once you understand what each of you wants, you can decide what to do. You may decide not to invite the others along when you do things with Mary, but to see Beth and Amy at other times.

No matter who your relationship is with—your mother, your brother, your best friend, or your teammate—talking with the other person usually will help to make things better. You learn what they are expecting from you, and you get a chance to tell them what you expect.

Where Expectations Come From

Some expectations depend on your **roles**, *the parts you play when you interact with others.* Children, for instance, expect their parents to provide food when they're hungry or a blanket when they're cold. Students expect their teachers to know what they're talking about in class, and the teachers expect their students to have done their homework.

Remember that you don't have just one role. You are your parents' child, your teachers' student, and your friends' friend. All of these people have different expectations for you.

Other kinds of expectations are formed by a person's way of looking at life. Since everyone is different, these expectations are different in every relationship. You agreed to take out the garbage every day. Now your parents expect you to do it. Your friend may perform a different chore for her family, or may be expected to practice piano lessons.

Words to Remember

conflict: a problem that arises in a relationship

expectation: what you want from a relationship

peer pressure: the influence your friends and others of your age exert on you

relationship: a special bond formed with another person

role: a part you play when you interact with others

Questions

1. Think of two ways that relationships help you build your self-concept.
2. How can you meet the expectations of many different relationships?
3. What are the two actions of a relationship?
4. Why do conflicts arise in relationships? How can these problems be solved?

Chapter 7 **Families: Sharing and Caring**

Objectives

After reading this chapter, you will be able to:

☐ *explain how families satisfy needs, provide wants, and promote growth for their members,*

☐ *talk about the conflict that teenagers feel between limits and independence,*

☐ *describe your family's own unique style, or way of doing things.*

Can you remember your first steps, or who held your hand? Perhaps not, but chances are that someone in your family was there to help you along. Back then, you learned how to talk and that it hurt to touch a hot stove.

Many of your ideas, opinions, and tastes also came from your family. Do you like card games? You probably learned to play them at home. Do you love spicy food? Your family probably cooks it that way.

In addition, as you grew, your family taught you to value what's important in life. You not only developed a feeling about who you are, but also about what your place is in the world. And even after you no longer needed a hand to hold, you felt secure, a part of something. You belonged.

The Family as Provider

Satisfying Needs

A newborn baby needs a lot of care, so it's easy to see how necessary a family is at the beginning of a child's life. But the family must satisfy the basic needs of *all* its members, old and young alike. This job of providing the things we all need—food, clothing, and shelter—is a difficult one, and one that never ends. There are many different ways to do it.

In some families, two adults work outside their home. In others, one person works outside the home and the other inside. In still others, a single parent works outside or inside the home. Whatever the arrangement, it usually involves working together.

In most families, the older the children become, the more the adults count on them to do their part. At first, they might just tie their own shoes and get to school alone. These may not seem like big responsibilities, but by doing these things themselves, children free adults for other jobs.

Gradually, however, most children become involved in the family's job of taking care of everyone. They learn to feed the dog and walk it, not just to pet it properly. A list of after-school chores may be left for them on the refrigerator. Older children sometimes clean, cook, or do the family wash. Often, they watch their younger sisters or brothers. Many older teenagers get part-time jobs to earn money.

This sharing of the work benefits not only the adults in the family, but also the children, who are learning by doing, becoming independent, and getting the experience that they will need as adults.

Providing Wants

If families only satisfied needs, home life would be a lot less interesting and valuable than it is. But the family does much more— it helps improve the lives of its members. And it provides much of what they want by entertaining them, giving them things, and showing them what it is to share.

Helping You Grow. Families help you to grow. Growing up isn't just a matter of getting taller. Your mind grows just as your body does—you have to grow emotionally and socially, too. None of this happens all at once. It's gradual, and much of it happens in your family.

Learning about Feelings. Your family teaches you about feelings, like love and affection. Home is also where you learn to express your feelings. At home, you can even let out your anger and hurt, because you know your family cares if you're unhappy.

Each family is a combination of individuals, who provide the support which helps the family grow.

This kind of emotional support gives you strength. Just knowing that your family cares means a lot. It means, for instance, that if you have too much work to do or if you're disappointed about losing the class election, you have someone to turn to. It also teaches you to give support to others when it's your turn.

Getting Along. Families teach people how to get along with one another. Even before you could talk, you were helped to enjoy playmates and share toys. You were shown how older family members got along with their friends. You were taken to stores, parks, or schools, and helped to find your way around. You were introduced to new games and sports, and shown how to take on. new responsibilities. By watching

As you grow older, you gain more responsibility. Things which you do now around your home will help you to develop skills for your future.

your family, you learned the right way to speak and act with people outside the family.

You as a Teenager

When you were a child, you were fairly sure of your role in your family. In general, though you did certain things for yourself, your parents looked after you. You looked up to them and did what they told you to do.

Things Are Changing

Now that you are an adolescent, things are changing. Sometimes, your family will look at you differently, partly because physical changes will make you look and act differently. And at times you'll see the members of your family from a new and different point of view. For one thing, your parents won't seem nearly as tall as they used to! You'll probably disagree with them more often. And you'll sometimes want to make your own decisions.

Such differences often cause conflict. Some people feel that this conflict is necessary, even useful. Others disagree. Most do agree, however, that adolescence can be an important growth period because of the changes that go on during it.

One thing is certain about the teen years—you won't feel the same way all the time. One day, you may feel that too much is expected of you, and wish that you could be as carefree as you were when you were a child. The next day, just when your family decides to treat you like a child again, you may want to be seen as an adult. These shifts in feelings are normal—everyone goes through them.

Independent Person?

You are learning to be independent, ready to go anywhere and everywhere without your family. But your parents may feel that you're not ready for so much responsibility. They may insist that you be home at a certain time each night, while you feel that you're too old for such rules.

One way to convince your parents that you *are* ready for more responsibility is to prove that you can be counted on. When you realize that you're going to be late, call home. Be where you're supposed to be on time, keep your word, and leave phone numbers where you can be reached when you're with friends. All these easy steps will convince your parents that you're ready for independence a lot faster than any kind of argument will.

FEATURE

Families, Families, Families

Apart from what a family *does*, how do you know one when you see one? To start, you might define a **family** as a group that provides major support and care for its members. But all such groups are not alike—there are a number of different family structures, such as the ones described below:

Henry and Alice Binder have been married five years. Though they have no children, they're still a family.

The Molinos live in the city. They have a particular family structure, too. Mr. and Mrs. Molino and their children Maria, Anna, and Juan are an example of a **nuclear family**—*parents and children sharing a household.*

There's Mr. Webster, who is divorced. He's the head of still another type of family. He lives with his son Jeff, his daughter Lisa, and his adopted son Arthur. Because *this group has only one parent,* the Websters are called a **single-parent family**.

Mr. Webster is one of 4 million single parents in the United States, and over 10 million children, or 20 percent of all American children, are in single-parent families. Most live with their mothers, but there are a growing number of single-parent families headed by men.

Some single-parent families are headed by divorced or separated parents, and some by widows or widowers—people whose husbands or wives have died. Sue Watson and her baby daughter Miranda form a third kind of single-parent family, one headed by a parent who's never been married.

The Lewises are a **blended family**, *one created by the marriage of two people who were married before and had children.* Their new family consists of Mr. and Mrs. Lewis, plus Jill, Mrs. Lewis's child from her previous marriage, and Charles and Kathy, the children from Mr. Lewis's first marriage.

But some parents are unwilling to let their children go, even though they know the children are responsible. In these situations, arguments often result. What's to be done?

First, calm down. It's useless trying to talk about conflict when you're in the middle of it. When you do talk, consider your parents' point of view. Think about your own demands before you take a hard line. If your desire for responsibility causes your family to worry, maybe you can find a compromise. Give and take is the clue.

Accepting Your Family

Have you ever wished that your family did things differently? Are you afraid that your parents will embarrass you in front of your friends? Are you tired of your younger sister tagging along, or of your older brother acting like he knows everything?

Perhaps you envy your friend. She's an only child who isn't bothered by brothers and sisters. And she seems to have a perfect relationship with her parents.

Did you ever stop to think that your friend might envy you? To her, your larger family looks like fun—there are more people to do things with. And she wishes that she could talk to her parents the way you can to yours.

Family Styles

You and your friend see these family styles as better or worse than each other, but they are simply different. The fact is that all families are different—in size, in the way work is shared, and in the way members interact. And no one style is right, making all the others wrong. Each family finds a system that works well for its members.

Why the differences? Each family is unique, because its members have special abilities and characteristics. It doesn't make sense for all those different people to try to follow the same pattern.

The culture and traditions you come from also make your family different. Your parents may do things the way their own parents did, because they feel more comfortable with these ways.

Does your family always celebrate birthdays with a cake? What holiday is most important to your family? All these practices are family traditions. You'll probably do things in similar ways when you have your own family.

Give-and Take

Whatever the system, each family is built on give and take. Everyone provides something for the others, especially emotional support. The Molino family—Mr. and Mrs. Molino and their children Maria, Anna, and Juan—are in many ways typical. Both parents work, and all the children go to school. Everyone pitches in so that things run smoothly—but that's not what's most important.

Even though they both work hard, Mr. and Mrs. Molino try to spend at least a few minutes with all of the children before they go to bed. They talk over the day's events. They offer encouragement or support if it's needed. When one of the children has a problem, the parents are ready to help.

Sharing the evening dinner, talking about the day's events, and offering support are the benefits of family life. What traditions and values have you learned from your family?

The members of this family have made sure that no matter how busy they are, there's time for give-and-take. They all give, but they also all receive. It's the support of each family member that keeps the family going.

Another type of family is the **extended family**. It can *include grandparents, uncles, aunts, and cousins, as well as parents and children.* The DeLauras are an extended family. There's Mr. and Mrs. DeLaura, their two children, Dean and Joan, Mrs. DeLaura's mother Audrey Swensen, and Arthur De-Laura, Mr. DeLaura's father, who lives with them six months a year.

Though all these people live in different kinds of groups, each lives within a family structure. How many families like these do you know?

Words to Remember

blended family: a new family, created by the marriage of two people who were married before and had children

extended family: a family that includes not only parents and children, but also grandparents, and possibly uncles, aunts, and cousins as well

family: a group that provides major support and care for its members

nuclear family: parents and children sharing a household

single-parent family: a family headed by only one parent

Questions

1. List three ways that the family satisfies the needs of its own members.
2. Give two examples of how the family helps to guide social growth.
3. Think of three contributions you can make to your family.
4. What is the best way to handle teen-family conflict?
5. How would you describe your own family's structure?

Chapter 8 Understanding Your Family

Objectives

After reading this chapter, you will be able to:

☐ *explain how children's characteristics are influenced by their differences, age, and birth order,*

☐ *describe some personal needs that parents have,*

☐ *give examples of how you can help other family members.*

"My mother treats me like a child." "My kid brother is always getting into my stuff." "My parents favor my older sister—she gets everything, and I get the leftovers."

How often have you heard complaints like these, or even said them yourself? Sometimes, conflict among family members seems to be an unavoidable part of family life. Often, however, conflict comes from misunderstanding—about the needs of each family member and about the role each member plays in family life.

A family is a group of different people:

■ Each person in the group is unique.

■ Each has his or her own problems and point of view.

Understanding these different points of view will lead to greater family harmony.

Children

Have you thought about how the differences in age affect the roles we play in our families? For instance, a 15-year-old will be given both more freedom and more responsibility than a child of 5. The number of years between children also affects their roles.

How Many Years Apart?

The age span between brothers and sisters affects how they get along. **Age span** is *the number of years between children.* When the age span is more than three years, children may not have many of the same interests. John, who is 16, wants to learn about car engines. His 9-year-old brother would rather play ball.

Closeness in age often leads to greater companionship. Twins are usually very close. **Siblings**—*another word for brothers and sisters*—who are one or two years apart may share interests, problems, and friends. But sometimes, two children who are close in age compete with each other. Even twins should be treated as two different people.

Oldest, Middle, Youngest, or Only

Whether you were born first, last, or in the middle affects both how you feel about yourself and how your family treats you.

Oldest. Oldest children are often given more freedom than the others because their parents depend on them. And because they are used to helping out, oldest children are often confident about their abilities.

Sometimes, however, they may feel that too much is expected of them or that their parents want them to act more grown-up than they are. Sometimes, they feel that the younger children are allowed to do more than they were at that age.

Still, teaching your younger sister or brother to do things—to multiply numbers or to jump rope—can be fun and can improve your own skills. And having a young child admire you can make you feel good about yourself.

Children often depend on their older brothers and sisters for comfort, for help in solving problems, and for teaching them new things.

Middle. Being in the middle has its good and bad points, too. Your parents are more experienced in caring for children. They probably feel more relaxed about bringing you up. You may find that you have more privileges than your older sibling had at your age, as well as less pressure to be perfect.

On the other hand, you may feel left out. You have neither the privileges of the older children nor the attention given to the younger ones.

Still, with both older and younger siblings around, you can be pretty sure of never being bored!

Youngest. Youngest children often join older siblings in doing new and exciting things. Their parents are more experienced, and youngest children often are given more privileges.

Of course, following an older sister or brother through childhood can be difficult. If the older child had some special talent or ability, the younger children may feel they have to equal it.

Still, being the ''baby'' of the family has a few good points.

Only. Only children are much like oldest children. They receive a great deal of the parents' attention and often are given responsibility. They do not have to share their things or get along with other siblings.

But being an only child can be lonely. And if all your parents' hopes rest on you, you can feel a lot of pressure to please them.

On the other hand, your close relationship with your parents provides you with company. And your friends can give you the companionship that other children get from brothers and sisters.

Special Children

Some children have special needs. **Special children** *develop physically or mentally at a different rate than the average child*. Some of them are very intelligent. They are called *gifted children*. Others have physical or mental handicaps that cause them to develop more slowly than other children. They are called *handicapped children*.

Either way, other family members must show special children much patience and love. Handicapped children can often learn the same tasks as their siblings. They just take longer. Gifted children need to have their minds challenged, but others must remember that they are still children. You can read more about special children in chapter 18 of this text.

Some children are not born into the families they live with. These children need extra support from other family members to make them feel at home. A child living with a parent who remarries is the new parent's *stepchild*. These children often have to adjust from living in a one-parent family to having two parents again.

Some children are **adopted**. This means that *an adult who is not the child's birth parent becomes the child's legal parent*. Some people choose to adopt children rather than have their own.

Adopted children are taken into a family permanently. Sometimes *children from troubled homes are taken into families for shorter periods*. They are called **foster children**. These children often do well because of the support and love that their new families provide. It doesn't matter how children enter a family. The important thing is that they be treated as part of the family.

All the children in a family are truly family members, because a family is a group of people who love, care for, and support one another.

Parents

Understanding your family means thinking about your parents' role, too. When you were younger, you may have thought that your parents knew everything and could do anything.

As you grew older, you realized that they are people, too. They have their own good points and bad points and their own joys and problems. When they became parents, they took on many responsibilities.

What Parents Give

Parents are completely responsible for their children's health, both mental and physical. They must provide the food, clothing, and shelter the children need, as well as the extras—television, tickets to a ball game, or any special education that they would like the children to have.

Parents' *love* helps you build a strong self-concept. Their *caring* makes you feel safe. Their *guidance* helps you decide what's right. Their *listening* proves how important you are to them. And their *sharing* teaches you to give.

Private Needs

When children are young, most parents have little time for anything but caring for them. But parents don't stop being separate people when they become parents. They still need time for themselves.

Your parents may enjoy window shopping or talking on the phone with a friend. Whatever their needs are, fitting them in during a busy day can be difficult. Sometimes, their needs may interfere with things you want to do. But you should realize that your parents want to be treated as people. Help them out when you can.

Single Parents

Single parents support their families, care for their children, and run their households, just as couples do. But they must do these things alone. These parents have to spend more time and effort to keep the home running.

Children in single-parent homes can help by sharing in the household work. As they take on more responsibilities, children often become more confident and capable. And their parent comes to rely on them for extra help. Working together can build a strong relationship between parent and children.

Stepparents

When single parents remarry, everyone in the family has to make adjustments. Household routines are changed. Rivalries start between stepsiblings. And the parents themselves must adjust to each other, just as newlyweds must. At the same time, the new couple must continue to meet the responsibilities all parents have.

Sometimes children are resentful or jealous of the new stepparent. They may feel that he or she is destroying the relationship the children had with the single parent. Or they may still wish they were living with the parent who is gone. But the confusion caused by remarriage usually doesn't last. In time, the new family members learn to trust and feel close to one another.

Giving Support

In many ways, a family is a team, just like any other team. For a baseball team to win, each player must do his or her part, and no player should try to be in the limelight all the time. For a family to work, each member must give the other members support.

The people in your family need two kinds of support—physical and emotional. Physi-

---

FEATURE

Older Family Members

Children often have close relationships with their grandparents. As you've grown older, you've probably realized that your grandparents know a lot of good stories. They can tell you firsthand about the Great Depression or World War II—or simply what your neighborhood used to look like when they were young and rearing a family.

People used to think of all grandparents as being too old to work and always ill. But that's not really true. Many people never retire, and many grandparents plan to retire but don't wish to do so yet. Many grandparents exercise every day—some even run in marathons. In fact, grandparents are as different from each other as grandchildren are.

Grandparents may live with you or away from you. They may live on your block or across the country. You may see them often or seldom.

Some grandparents do have health problems. They may need special care. Often, that care is more welcome when it comes from a family member they love.

Some grandparents may be lonely. Perhaps their husband or wife has died, and they miss him or her. You can help cheer them up by spending some time with them. Include your grandparents in your life. Invite them along on a shopping trip, or ask them to help with your homework. If poor health keeps them at home, a simple visit would make them feel better.

You can have fun with your grandparents—and learn about your past—by asking them to tell you the family history. The Teen Tips at the end of this unit explains how to collect their stories.

Ask one of your grandparents what he or she did as a teen for entertainment, what styles were popular, and what events were taking place.

cal support includes such things as doing your share of housework and helping your brother with his homework.

Emotional support begins with understanding your parents and your siblings. Try to respect your parents' need for time to themselves. Plan activities that won't interfere with theirs.

If you're an older child, try to understand your younger siblings' feelings. Include them in your activities sometimes.

If you're a younger child, you can make family life easier by understanding your older siblings' need for privacy. And remember that if they have more privileges, they have more responsibilities, too.

Whether you are the oldest, the middle, or the youngest, when you feel pleased with a brother or sister, say so. Your affection and admiration probably mean more to him or her than you realize.

Everyone who has a brother or sister feels jealous sometimes. It's important to remember that parents love all their children. In treating each child as a unique person, they may not treat them all alike.

Words to Remember

adopted child: a child who is permanently taken into a new family through a legal agreement

age span: the number of years between children

foster child: a child who is taken into a family temporarily

sibling: a brother or sister

special children: children who develop physically or mentally at a different rate than the average child

Questions

1. Think of two ways that age span affects a child's relationship with brothers and sisters.

2. Are you an oldest, middle, youngest, or only child? List three ways that it has affected your relationship with your parents.

3. What personal needs do parents have?

4. How can you give your family physical support? Emotional support?

Chapter 9 Sharing Problems

Objectives

After reading this chapter, you will be able to:

☐ *explain how good communication among family members can help solve problems,*

☐ *identify sources of help for solving family problems.*

The members of your family often seem like your closest friends. But do you also feel at times that they are your worst enemies? Is your sister always talking on the phone when you're expecting a call? Does your father always give you a curfew that's one hour earlier than your friends' curfews? If you can answer yes to questions like these, you have experienced a normal part of family life: problems.

You think that curfews and cleanup details, for example, limit your independence. Your parents think these things will help you become more responsible. The result? You and your parents argue without solving the problem.

It's important to realize that family members will always have arguments. But most arguments can be worked through if you learn two simple things: figure out what the problem is, and talk with one another.

What's The Problem?

From Outside the Family

Some problems are caused by events outside the family—things that you usually can't control. Suppose that your mother gets laid off from her job. It means that there's less money coming in, and you have to stop doing many of the things you enjoy.

Or perhaps the landlord is selling the house you rent, forcing your family to move. You worry about changing schools and leaving your friends. For problems like these, the whole family has to join together to help one another.

Many of the communication skills that you learn in the classroom can be used in other areas of your life.

From Inside the Family

There are also conflicts between family members. You always seem to end up doing the dishes. Stephanie is supposed to do them every other night, but she's on the track team and gets home late. Often, your mother asks you to clean up on Stephanie's night, too.

Personal problems can lead to conflicts within the family. Suppose you're feeling low because your swim coach is making things difficult for you these days. Then you forget to clean up after a snack, and your parents say something about it that makes you angry. But it's not you and your parents who have the problem; it's you and someone else.

The first thing to do when you have a problem, then, is to think about what the *real* problem is. Are you angry at your parents or at your coach?

Talking It Over

Once you've decided what the problem is, you can work toward solving it. And the best way to do that is to communicate. The art of **communication** involves verbal give and take. It's *an exchange of ideas, opinions, beliefs, and values* between two or more people.

Here are a few pointers for good communication:

- *Choose the proper time and place.* Wait for a relaxing moment in a quiet place to talk to your mother about the dinner dishes. Don't try to talk about it when she's late leaving for work one morning. One thing is certain: she won't be listening.

- *Keep to the point.* Think through what you want to say before you begin. Be direct. Your family won't get your point if you can't state it clearly. Offer a reasonable solution.

■ *Keep calm.* If you're upset or angry, you won't be able to get your point across. Slamming doors won't change people's minds.

■ *Listen.* Listening well is just as important as speaking well—and sometimes the part people find the most difficult. Don't think about your side of the argument when someone else is talking.

■ *Avoid criticism, sarcasm, and threats.* Saying "You're wrong!" or "That's ridiculous!" can end communication fast. Showing respect for another person's ideas will help earn respect for your own ideas.

Whatever else you do, remember one thing—work together to solve family problems. It's worth the time and effort in the long run.

As you form your own ideas and opinions, you may experience disagreements. By practicing good communication skills, conflicts can be easily solved.

Family Discussions

Some problems can be solved best by the whole family. Finding a solution that everyone accepts isn't always easy. But by communicating openly and honestly, respecting each person's opinion, listening, and allowing give and take, conflicts can often be resolved.

Brainstorming

One way of finding solutions is by **brainstorming**. This *''free-for-all'' approach to problem solving* is an excellent way to get ideas flowing and to promote discussion. All it takes to brainstorm is a pen, a piece of paper, and several open minds.

Your family decides to brainstorm your conflict with Stephanie over the dinner dishes. A certain period of time for thinking of ideas is set aside. The family members write down anything they think of—and don't start talking about why it's a good idea or a bad one. The goal at the beginning is simply to list ideas.

Here are just a few of the solutions that might come up:

■ Stephanie could do the dishes after track, even though it's late and she's tired.

■ Stephanie could clean up after all three meals on the weekend.

■ Stephanie could do the dishes every evening that she doesn't have track and do half the vacuuming on weekends.

■ Stephanie could be given a different chore entirely, one that track wouldn't interfere with. Perhaps you could do the dishes every night, but she could vacuum the whole house on weekends.

Learning how to listen well is the first rule of good communication. Try to hear what the person is telling you. Sometimes, compromise helps to find that solution which satisfies all parties.

Once these ideas have been listed, each family member gets a chance to defend the solution he or she thinks will work best.

Support your position in a mature way, or your family won't take your ideas seriously. Try to give good reasons for feeling the way you do. Listen to your family's objections without getting upset.

Compromising

An important part of handling problems in a mature way is being able to compromise. In a **compromise**, *each person gives up something in order to find a solution that satisfies everyone.*

As a result of your brainstorming session, you and your family decide that, from now on, you'll do the dishes every night, and Stephanie will vacuum the house on weekends. She won't have to rush home after track, and you'll have your weekends free. Usually, if each family member is willing to compromise, a workable solution can be found.

Help From Outside

Sometimes, when there's a really serious problem, even talking openly and honestly may not help. Not every family problem can be solved at home. When you've tried everything and you're no closer to solving a problem, it's time to reach out into the community.

Sally's Problem

Sally, for example, knows that her family needs help. Sally's home has become a battlefield. Her parents fight and argue constantly. They are insulting and cruel to one another. Sally has even thought about running away. She'd prefer to stay and work things out—but what can she do?

Community Counseling

There are many places Sally can go for help:

- *Teachers and guidance counselors.* The adults you see in school every day are a good source of help. They may come up with solutions to the problem or send you to a community agency that can offer help.
- *Religious leaders.* Many ministers, priests, rabbis, and mullahs know a great deal about counseling. They sometimes set up workshops to deal with family problems.
- *Youth leaders.* Adults who volunteer to work with young people are usually willing to help out in any way they can. If

T E E N   I S S U E

Teen Runaways and Suicides

Teenage Runaways. Every year between 1 and 2 million teenagers between the ages of 10 and 17 run away from home. These teens believe that life in the "real world" is better than the life they have at home.

Once on the road, however, most runaways find that their new lives are not what they expected. Without food, money, or a place to live, they can be taken advantage of by drug dealers and criminals. Because they are too young and have no skills, they are unable to get jobs. They have no money.

Why do teens leave home? Many run away from physical violence. Other reasons include emotional problems, pregnancy, family breakup by divorce or separation, strict house rules, permissive house rules—in other words, anything that seems too much to bear.

Runaways want help. Running away is a form of communication—a clear message that help is needed.

Teenage Suicides. Each year, more than 7,000 teenagers commit suicide. Suicide is now the second leading cause of death for 10- to 25-year-olds. Teenagers who commit suicide felt unable to handle the pressures in their lives—at home, at school, or with their friends.

For many teens, *trying* to commit suicide is a way of asking for help or of getting attention. Many teens who tried suicide later admitted that they hoped they would be found before it was too late. Fortunately, they were—others were not so lucky.

Anyone thinking about running away or committing suicide should get help. The people and groups listed in this chapter should be able to offer counseling.

you are a scout or belong to the YWCA or YMCA, the 4-H, the Future Homemakers of America, or other organizations like these, ask your leader for help and guidance.

■ *Social workers.* These people are trained to listen and help people overcome their problems.

■ *Community agencies and organizations.* Many agencies and organizations help families deal with specific problems. *Al-Anon*, for example, has helped millions of family members who live with alcoholics. To find these groups in your neighborhood, check the white and yellow pages of your local phone directory.

■ *Crisis centers.* Crisis centers have volunteers who are very willing to help people with problems. Some of the centers operate telephone "hot lines" for people who need help immediately.

Sally's Solution

Sally felt uncomfortable and embarrassed about telling her problem to a stranger. Sharing personal problems with someone you don't know well isn't easy to do. The person you go to, however, knows that you are discussing important feelings. He or she will make you feel as comfortable as possible.

Sally decided to talk to her minister. He suggested that Sally and her parents come to a workshop being held at the church. After he talked with the whole family, Sally's parents finally agreed to attend. Together, as a family, the members were taking an important first step toward working out their problems.

The journey between deciding what a family's problem is and solving it can be a long one. But it will be shorter and easier if all the family members work together.

Words to Remember

brainstorming: a "free-for-all" approach to problem solving that gets you to think of all possible solutions to a problem

communication: an exchange of opinions, ideas, beliefs, and values between two or more people

compromise: a way of solving a problem in which each person gives up something in order to find a solution that satisfies everyone

Questions

1. Not all family conflicts are caused by problems within the family. What other causes are there?
2. Give three ways to improve family communication.
3. How is brainstorming done?
4. Why is compromise a necessary part of solving family problems?
5. Find the names of three agencies and organizations in your community that offer help in solving family problems.

Chapter 10 Changes in the Family

Objectives

After reading this chapter, you will be able to:

☐ *identify some sudden changes in family life,*

☐ *give examples of some gradual changes in family life,*

☐ *explain how to adjust to changes in family life.*

Vicky is very excited. There's going to be a change in her life, and she's looking forward to it.

Since her mother started working six months ago, it's been Vicky's job to start dinner. Yesterday Vicky's mother said that she was really pleased with the maturity and responsibility Vicky had shown over the past few months. Because of that—and because Vicky's brother is moving away from home—her parents decided that Vicky wouldn't need to share a room with her sister anymore. She could have her own room!

Vicky is looking forward to the change in her life. But, not every change is so exciting. Some change is confusing—it forces you to adjust your routine and your way of thinking. You can't always avoid change, but you can learn to adapt to it and, of course, learn from it.

Sudden Changes

Some changes happen all of a sudden. Good or bad news may require that you adapt to a new situation rapidly.

Employment Changes

A happy change occurs when your parent is offered a new job. Usually he or she is pleased. Many times a new job means that the family will have more money. But anyone who takes on a new job has to do a lot of adjusting. Your parent might be more tired at the end of the day and less willing to listen to your problems. Other members of the family can help make the adjustment easier by giving each other support.

If a parent suddenly loses his or her job, the whole family is immediately upset. When Gary's father was laid off, everyone felt worried and confused. Gary's father was angry. Gary felt bad for his father, but he was also disappointed. He was hoping for a new sound system for his birthday. After the first shock, though, the family got together to discuss how they could manage while Gary's parents looked for jobs.

Moving Away

Your family may decide to move to another community. Maybe a parent's job requires it, or perhaps you're moving closer to the rest of the family. Moving is a big change. Family members must get used to a new home, new friends, and new schools.

Getting to know a new community can be exciting, but there is also some loss involved. When Sara's mother was transferred, Sara found that she loved living near the beach, but she missed her old friends very much. It took several months before she began to feel less lonely.

New Family Members

When a new person comes to live with a family, there is usually more work for everyone: more laundry to do, more cleaning up, and more food to be prepared. New people in a home mean less privacy for family members and more confusion. But they also may make life far more interesting and fun.

A new baby brother or sister can be a bundle of joy, but babies are a 24-hour job. They require constant care and watching. Still, as you learn to help care for the baby, your love for it will grow.

The addition of new family members can bring an added amount of responsibility, as well as a lot more fun and enjoyment from life.

If your divorced parent remarries and you move in with your new stepparent, you may feel confused and upset at first. You may resent the new parent telling you what to do. But with time, real closeness can develop with your stepparent.

Perhaps your grandparent moves in with you. Or a sibling may return from college or the armed forces to live at home again. These changes require adjustment, but the family can look forward to pleasures, too. You can go shopping with your older sister again. Or you can get help on your homework from your grandfather.

Departures from the Family

When people leave the family, those who remain usually feel a sense of loss. The new, smaller family must adjust to the absence of a person who has meant a lot to them.

Death. The most obvious kind of departure is the death of a family member. Deaths are **traumatic**. In other words, *they cause family members severe emotional shock that may take some time to heal.*

When Ray's Uncle Jerry died, Ray had trouble coping with his feelings. At first, Ray tried not to think about Uncle Jerry at all. Then he felt guilty, as if his arguments with Jerry were somehow to blame for Jerry's death. He felt angry, too, as if it were Jerry's fault that he had died.

Ray's feelings frightened him. He felt there was something wrong with himself. But all these emotions—together with loneliness and grief—are natural after a death. Allow yourself to grieve. Don't be ashamed to cry. People who ignore their feelings sometimes suffer from more serious problems later.

When someone dies, everyone in the family needs care and consolation, even very small children. Family members need to take turns putting their own sad feelings aside and comforting each other. Helping a parent or a sibling may help you feel better, too.

Divorce. If your parents are divorcing, you may fear that you'll lose touch with the parent who is moving away. You may wonder if you'll still be loved and protected.

You may feel guilty, as if you caused the divorce. Children have to realize that parents divorce because of problems between themselves. Children are not the cause of divorce. In fact, many parents who are having troubles stay together because of children.

You may feel resentful toward your parents for divorcing. This reaction is natural—the change is unpleasant, and you wish it wasn't necessary. But in time you will adapt to the new family. And you will probably lose your resentment. After a period of adjustment, however, there's a good chance you'll be happier than before.

Leaving Home. Other kinds of family departures are not as traumatic as death or divorce, but still may cause a feeling of loss. When grown children leave the home, the family changes. Vicky may have fought with her brother, and she'll certainly be happy to have his old room, but she'll probably miss him, too.

Gradual Changes

Other family changes happen a little at a time instead of all at once.

The Family Life Cycle

Important changes occur within the family as its members grow and mature. These changes are part of the **family life cycle**, *the eight stages of life that the average family goes through*. It begins with a couple's marriage, continues through birth and growth of their children, and ends with the older, retired couple whose children have left home.

The table shows this life cycle. Of course, there are many variations on this "average" family. Many children today are being reared by a single parent. A couple may marry and choose to have no children. Partners may divorce, remarry other people, and raise new families.

Individual Development

As the changes within the life cycle take place, individuals are developing, too. Change is most obvious in children—the toddler becomes the school-age child who

TABLE 1 Eight Stages in the Family Life Cycle

Stage*	What Happens
1. Beginning family	A couple marries, establishes a home, and builds a relationship. *(Couples with no children skip the next five steps.)*
2. Childbearing family	Lasts from the birth of the first child until the child is 2½ years old. Parents adjust to having children.
3. Family with preschoolers	Lasts until the oldest child begins school. Parents adjust to more demands on time and energy.
4. Family with school children	Lasts until the oldest child is 13. Parents promote the child's education.
5. Family with teenagers and young adults	Lasts until the oldest child is 20–22. Parents help the child become independent.
6. Launching center	Begins when the oldest child leaves home, ends when the last child leaves. Parents help children adjust and adapt to the new way of living.
7. Empty nest	Lasts until the couple retires. The couple renews the marriage relationship, prepares for retirement.
8. Aging family	Lasts until both partners die. The couple adjusts to retirement.

*Couples may divorce at any stage. A single parent may remarry at any stage.

turns into the teenager. But parents also mature and go through changes. They may change careers or develop new interests.

You, as a teenager, are going through a great many developmental changes, all of which will help you become a mature and independent person. On certain days, you love the security of the family. On other days you are irritated by your parents' rules. You long to be grown-up and free.

Reaching out and pulling back again is very much part of being an adolescent. Give yourself room for mistakes. Gradually, you will become more confident as you learn to

T E E N   I S S U E

Coping With Stress

Stress is *physical or emotional strain or tension that can be caused by changes in our lives.* Your heart begins to pound when your turn comes to speak in front of the class. You scream and yell when your father makes you stay home one night. Both examples are responses to stress.

Stress can be valuable. If you weren't worried about your grades, you might not bother to study. If personal problems didn't upset you, you wouldn't try to solve them.

If stress becomes too great, life isn't very enjoyable. It may make you anxious all the time. Too much stress can even lead to high blood pressure and other diseases. Fortunately, we can control our stress.

1. *Face your problems.* Don't ignore a difficulty, hoping that it will go away. It usually won't.

2. *Talk out problems with someone you trust.* A close friend or family member can help you brainstorm some solutions.

3. *Don't overreact.* Many people panic over situations that aren't really serious. If you find yourself getting upset, stop and ask yourself, "What is the worst that can happen?"

4. *Develop good health and nutrition habits.* Getting the proper amount of sleep, eating three good meals a day, and avoiding empty-calorie foods will help your body withstand stress that may come upon you.

5. *Exercise at least three times a week.* Physical activity is one of the best ways to relax.

6. *Take a mind trip.* Set a little time aside to be alone every day. Close your eyes and think of nothing at all, or imagine a beautiful, quiet scene in nature. This will help you relax.

7. *Stay away from quick-and-easy "solutions."* If your friend says, "Relax and have a cigarette," don't. It won't help your stress. In fact, smoking may increase stress. Other "cures" that don't work are overeating, alcohol, and drugs.

8. *Sharpen your sense of humor.* Don't take things so seriously—see the lighter side of life. If you've had a tense week, get together with friends and go to a funny movie, or to an amusement park, or to a baseball game.

make your own decisions, earn your own living, and choose the people you wish to be close to.

Adjusting To Change

Changes can be challenging, confusing, and painful all at once. But there are ways you can adjust to them.

1. *Plan ahead.* When you know that a change is unavoidable, prepare for it in advance, even if you wish it weren't going to happen. Often, difficult changes aren't as bad as you thought they'd be—because you prepared for them.

2. *Discover something positive about the change.* This is not always easy to do. For example, what can be positive about a death in the family? Finding out that grief and sadness eventually pass—and that you can be happy again—will make you stronger and more mature.

3. *Be supportive.* While you are going through changes in your life, members of your family probably are changing, too. It helps to talk out your feelings

Family members know one another, and this helps to solve problems within a family.

within your family. Just having someone listen can ease your pain and confusion.

If someone in your family is trying to adjust to a new situation, help out. When Joanne's father was struggling to manage a job and take college classes at night, Joanne started to get up early and make breakfast for him. It was her way of showing her father how much she cared for and admired him.

Words to Remember

family life cycle: the stages a family goes through from the time the parents marry until after the last child leaves home

stress: physical or emotional strain or tension that can be caused by changes in our lives

traumatic: changes that cause severe emotional shock that may take some time to heal

Questions

1. Give three examples of sudden changes that affect a family.

2. Think of two gradual changes that have occurred in your family.

3. Does every family follow the family life cycle?

4. What three things can you do to adjust to change?

Chapter 11 Being a Friend

Objectives

After reading this chapter, you will be able to:

□ *explain how being reliable, loyal, sympathetic, and caring will help you to be a good friend,*

□ *describe why keeping strong friendships requires you to control your emotions,*

□ *give examples of how friends can support you throughout your life.*

Think of all the friends you have. You have longtime friends you've known since kindergarten and other friends you met this year. Some friends you see every day; others you may see only twice a year. You feel closer to some friends than to others.

Some people have many friends and some have very few. This does not mean that it is better to have more friends than less. The important thing to remember is to have deep and rewarding friendships—whether they are with many or few people.

Friendships grow differently and at different paces. They may come easily or they may take work to develop. All friendships, however, have some of the same qualities. If you help these qualities to grow, you can develop friendships that will last all your life.

Qualities of Friendship

A strong friendship is built on five qualities.

- *Sharing.* Friendships are often based on common interests. You and a friend may both work on the school newspaper, or perhaps you like to go shopping together. You can learn from your friends. You might show a friend how to play volleyball. He might show you the newest dance. Going places with someone else can give you a sense of security. Walking into a party with a friend is easier than walking in by yourself. And often, experiences are more enjoyable if you share them. A funny movie is funnier if you can laugh at it with a friend.

- *Reliability.* Being **reliable** means *being a person others can count on.* Suppose you agree to meet your friends for a ball game. If you cancel or arrive late, you probably won't be too popular. Have you ever carried books for a friend whose arm was in a cast? Have you ever gotten homework assignments for a friend who was home with the flu? If so, you were being reliable.

- *Loyalty.* Being **loyal** is *being faithful to others, especially when they need it.* It can mean simply being there to listen when things get rough. Loyalty can also involve actions. Suppose a friend who means a lot to you is the target of gossip. It can take a lot of courage to speak up for that friend, but such loyalty would make him or her feel better.

- *Sympathy.* Just as friends can increase happiness, they can make sadness easier to bear. Everybody has unhappy times. Friends can encourage you if you are feeling bad about a failure at school. They can help you face family problems.

When you're feeling down, you don't always see your situation clearly. Friends can help you see yourself and your problems from another point of view. Suppose you're feeling bad because you didn't make the volleyball team. Knowing that you're a strong swimmer, your friend suggests that you go out for swimming. You were so disappointed, you hadn't thought of that.

- *Caring.* The basic quality of friendship—the one from which all the others seem to grow—is caring. People are real friends when they truly care about each other. **Caring** is *the emotional bond that one person feels for another.* A friend who cares remembers birthdays or helps a friend rehearse for the school play. Caring means valuing your friends' feelings as much as your own. And it means making the effort to be reliable, loyal, and honest.

A superfriend does spectacular things, like helping with homework, giving advice, and sharing interests. What type of friend are you?

F E A T U R E

What Should You Do?

When one of your friends is in a tough situation, you want to help. But what should you do? Here are two such situations that friends might face. In each case, which solution would a friend choose?

1. Your friend has missed two hockey practices. She'll be dropped from the team if she misses the one today. Unfortunately, your group of friends is planning to go shopping this afternoon. You know your friend wants very much to go along. You could:

   ■ tell her that she can't come with you. She might be hurt, but you know that hockey is important to her, too.

   ■ reschedule the shopping trip for another afternoon. This will be a bother, but then everyone will be able to go.

   ■ let your friend decide what to do. She's old enough to make up her own mind.

(Your friend probably can make up her own mind, but temptation can be strong. A good friend would most likely reschedule the trip.)

2. Your friend is usually a good student, but this term he's failing English, your best subject. You could:

   ■ write his next composition. As his friend, you don't want him to fail.

   ■ let your friend solve his own problem. He can probably raise his grade if he really studies.

   ■ offer to study with him for the next exam. You may be able to help him get a better understanding of the material.

(Writing your friend's composition might get him a better grade, but it would be dishonest. A good friend would most likely choose to study with him.)

The Give-and-Take of Friendship

Even in the best of friendships, things can go wrong. If you want your friendships to last, you need to learn how to handle the disagreements that sometimes develop.

All real friendships are worth preserving, even if they take work. A few guidelines for controlling your feelings, communicating honestly, and being tolerant will help.

When Problems Develop in Friendships

Mark and Eric have been friends for years. They used to eat lunch together every day at school. But now that Mark's on the tennis team, he eats with his teammates at least half the time. And one Saturday, when they had planned to go to a movie, Mark never showed up. Eric later learned that the team had held an extra practice. He wondered why Mark hadn't told him.

Talking to a close friend—sharing your experiences, your hopes for the future, and the way you view things now—helps you and your friend to grow and mature.

Like Mark and Eric, Carrie and Pat have been friends for a long time. But lately, Carrie's been wondering if the friendship will continue. Carrie can go practically anywhere, but Pat's parents only let her go to certain places.

Carrie looks forward to going to new places, but her loyalty to Pat makes her feel guilty about leaving her behind. At the same time, her desire for new experiences makes her resent that feeling.

When problems like this develop in a friendship, the results can be painful. It hurts to find that a friend you counted on has been disloyal or thoughtless. But disagreements don't have to end friendships.

Controlling Your Feelings

When you have a disagreement with a friend, the thing you should *not* do is speak in anger. You will only be tempted to say something that will hurt the other person. You may even say something you don't really mean—something that will drive you and your friend further apart. Eric was so angry with Mark that he was ready to end the friendship on the spot.

Give yourself time to cool off. This doesn't mean that you shouldn't express your anger. You might talk about the problem with your parents, or with another friend. But don't try to work the problem out with your friend until you are calm enough to control your feelings.

Honest Communication

Once you are calm, try to talk to your friend about the problem. Mark probably wasn't even aware of how his actions were affecting Eric. If Eric had talked to Mark the first time he felt hurt, the problem might never have grown so serious.

If it's difficult for you to talk about your angry feelings, letting your friend know that is often a good way to get started. If you say something like, "This is hard for me to say . . . ," it may actually become easier. And it will show your friend that you care.

Tolerance

Tolerance is *the ability to accept people as they are*. It is sometimes difficult to accept that our friends don't behave exactly as we want them to. But to keep their friendship, we have to make allowances for their particular traits.

Tolerance is also needed when there are problems in a friendship. If Carrie can accept the limits to Pat's freedom, their friendship will probably continue. They might not spend all their free time together, but they can still go to some places.

Building for the Future

Your present friendships have value beyond the companionship they provide you now. Your friends are teaching you the art of being a friend. They are also helping you learn what qualities you value in a friend. Some of the friendships you have now may last into your adult years. But even if they don't, learning to be a good friend now will help you form other friendships later.

Words to Remember

caring: the emotional bond that one person feels for another

loyalty: being faithful to others, especially when they need it

reliability: being someone others can count on

tolerance: the ability to accept people as they are

Questions

1. How have your ideas about friendship changed as you've grown older?
2. What qualities do you look for in a friend?
3. What do you think your friends look for in you?
4. If you and a friend have a disagreement, how can you keep your emotions from making the problem worse?
5. Give two examples of things you can learn from having friends.

Chapter **12** # Stereotypes and Prejudice

Objectives

After reading this chapter, you will be able to:

☐ *explain how stereotypes hurt individuals,*

☐ *describe how prejudices can lead to false thinking,*

☐ *give examples of how you can learn to avoid prejudice in yourself and others.*

You're so tired of doing the family wash, you could scream! Twice a week it's the same thing. And besides, you've got a test to study for tonight. As usual, your brother's in his room listening to records—he never has homework. You've complained to your mother until you're blue in the face, but it doesn't do a bit of good. "Laundry is women's work," she says, and that's that.

You've always wanted to dance. You're good, and you know it. You win the dance contests at every school dance, and you've even been on "Dancin' on the Air" on television. That's fun, but you want real dance lessons. Yet when you raise the subject, your father hits the ceiling. "That's for sissies," he states, and that's that.

Looking at Others

Why are these parents being so unreasonable? You know that in the past certain jobs were reserved for women and others for men, but you thought those days were gone. Unfortunately, all too often **tradition**, or *the ways things were done in the past*, still shapes our views. We think in terms of stereotypes.

What Is a Stereotype?

A **stereotype** is *a fixed mental picture of what someone or something is like.* This picture may be completely wrong, but, once it's fixed in a person's mind, it can be very difficult to change. A mother's belief that boys shouldn't do laundry is a stereotype. So is a father's view that only girls should take dance lessons.

People may be stereotyped according to their physical characteristics, such as age, race, or sex. Have you ever heard the stereotypes that all old people are cranky or that all boys are stronger than girls?

Sometimes, people are stereotyped by where they come from. All New Englanders, for example, are supposed to be unfriendly. And some stereotypes are based on what people do: all athletes are dumb; all doctors are rich.

Whatever the cause, stereotypes make us like or dislike people before we even know them. Stereotypes cause harm in two ways:

- Stereotypes limit your chances of discovering and experiencing things. They put people into different groups without allowing you to find out if they really belong there. You may believe that someone who needs a wheelchair is sad all the time. That incorrect belief can stop you from getting to know a classmate.

- Stereotypes restrict your chances. If employers think that teenagers are untrustworthy, you'll have trouble getting a job, and for no reason.

Stereotypes are learned in many different ways. They are not confined to any one racial, ethnic, or cultural group. In all situations, they can limit an individual's growth.

F E A T U R E

Male or Female?

When we say that men act one way and women another, we help create stereotypes about the sexes. Do you hold stereotypes about men and women? Here is a list of 10 character traits. Write the number 1 to 10 on a piece of paper and mark each M or F, for masculine or feminine.

1. Helps others
2. Is aggressive
3. Is home-oriented
4. Is independent
5 Is quiet
6. Is active
7. Is emotional
8. Never cries
9. Is unable to make decisions
10. Makes decisions easily

When given this list, most people agree that men have the even-numbered traits and women the odd-numbered ones. But those general statements aren't really true of all men or all women.

You can help to end this stereotyping:

- Develop your own skills and interests. Don't limit yourself by believing stereotypes.

- Before you say "Girls shouldn't do that," or "Boys don't act that way," stop yourself. What you say can influence your brothers and sisters. Try to help them to be more flexible in how they think and act. If you encourage them, they are likely to think for and be themselves.

Where Do Stereotypes Come From?

We are all exposed to stereotypes from many sources. Tradition is one source. The opinions you hear from family and friends are another source. Often, these views were handed down to them from others.

Still another source of stereotypes is the **mass media**—*television, magazines, movies, and newspapers.* Because time and space are valuable to the media, they use a shorthand way—the stereotype—to present people. In this way, the media help to form stereotypes without even meaning to. That is why we have to be careful when forming opinions based on what the media presents.

Looking at Others Without Seeing Them

Stereotyped thinking can lead to **prejudice**. This is an *opinion or feeling that is not based on fact.* Prejudice can be in favor of people or against people. Either way, it means that you are not treating someone fairly.

Prejudice Hurts

In Favor of People. You may develop a prejudice about someone you admire and wish to be like. If you are blind to a movie star's faults, for example, you are not being fair to him or her. You have made up your mind that the movie star is perfect, but no one is.

When that person does something less than ideal, you are hurt and disappointed. Yet you never gave the person a chance. It wasn't the movie star's faults that caused the problem, but your prejudice.

Against People. A gas station owner refuses to even interview you for a job. He has the prejudiced view that women can't fix cars.

When there is prejudice against an entire group of people, the whole of society is hurt. If talented people are refused jobs or training because of their age, race, color, religion, or sex, everybody suffers. Society loses the work of people it needs. We, as individuals, lose the chance to meet people who might make our lives richer. And the ones who are the target of the prejudice obviously lose.

A balanced view of life is formed by using many different media sources and by talking with people of different backgrounds.

Prejudice Leads to Prejudice

Prejudice can lead you to make mistakes. It can also lead to more prejudices.

Linda has the idea that all cities are dirty and dangerous. When her parents took her on a weekend trip to a nearby city, she saw some litter on the first day and decided she was right. She refused to leave the hotel all weekend.

Back home, Linda told all her friends about how dirty the city was, even though she only saw it briefly. Now they think as she does. But their ideas are just prejudices based on no firm facts. She did not go out and see for herself how the city looked.

Dealing With Prejudice

Prejudiced and stereotyped thinking is lazy thinking. Avoiding prejudice means first getting into the habit of thinking for yourself.

Prejudice in Yourself

To deal with prejudice in yourself, ask questions. Learn to rely more on what you see than on what you are told. Make judgments based on *your own* experiences.

There may be groups of people about whom you've been told negative things. Try to meet some people in that group. Hold off making up your mind about them until you have a chance to know them personally.

Do they sound the way you thought they would? Do they have the ideas you thought they had? Are they as different from you as you thought they were? Get to know people as themselves, not as members of some group.

Prejudice in Others

Dealing with the prejudice of others is more difficult. They're not basing their opinions on facts, and it's hard to make them see how unfair they are. Always remember, though, that prejudice tells more about the person who is prejudiced than about the one who is the target of the prejudice.

For a long time, prejudice made people think that black baseball players could not compete in the major leagues. Now that idea has been shown to be not only untrue, but ridiculous. The truth first shows prejudiced thinking to be false, then plain silly.

The best way to meet prejudice is to continue to develop your own self. Concentrate on being *you* and on sharpening *your* talents. Remember that, whoever you are, you are *not* just part of a group someone else wants to put you in. You are *you*.

At one time, black baseball players like Jackie Robinson were not allowed to play on a national league. Such prejudicial thinking does not give each person a fair opportunity.

Words to Remember

mass media: television, magazines, movies, and newspapers

prejudice: an opinion or feeling that is not based on fact

stereotype: a fixed mental picture of what someone or something is like

tradition: the ways things were done in the past

Questions

1. What is a stereotype?
2. What is prejudice? How is prejudice harmful to (a) the holder of the prejudice, (b) those who are the target of the prejudice, and (c) society as a whole?
3. How can you best guard against prejudiced thinking in yourself?
4. How can you deal with prejudice in others?

Chapter 13 Making New Friends

After reading this chapter, you will be able to:

☐ *describe various ways of making friends,*

☐ *explain how fairness and patience can help a friendship develop,*

☐ *discuss how to handle friendships you do and do not want to pursue.*

No matter how many friends you have, it's nice to make new ones. Perhaps you move to a new town and a new school where everyone is a stranger. Or you want to take up a new activity—helping build sets for the school play, for example—and find that your friends are not interested in helping you.

That's when it helps to have a variety of friends to do different things with. It's great having Ricky next door. You two can always shoot baskets when there's nothing else to do. But you don't feel comfortable telling him your more personal thoughts. For that you need a really close friend to confide in.

Making new friends can be difficult, but everyone can do it. It just takes some effort to begin.

Making the Effort

Making friends is a skill. Like most skills, it improves with practice. If you want to meet people and make friends, you must be willing to take some action.

Meeting People

To make friends, you must first go where there are people. You won't make friends staying home alone.

■ *Join a club or group.* Talking with someone who likes the same things you do is much easier than talking with someone who has totally different interests. Remember to be yourself. Don't join the photo club to make friends if you hate taking pictures. You'll feel uncomfortable, and it will soon become clear that you're faking your interest. Since there are groups for every type of interest, you should be able to find one that suits you.

■ *Start a conversation with someone in one of your classes.* You'll have at least one thing to talk about—the work in that class.

■ *Join someone in some activity.* You could study for your next math test with someone in the class. Perhaps everyone in your grade is selling magazines to raise money. You could go around with someone new in your neighborhood.

FEATURE

The Quest For A Friend

Ellie went to school determined to make friends this year—no more shyness. As she was about to enter the school, another girl came up. Would you *(1) enter the school,* or *(2) say, "Hi, my name is Ellie—what's yours?"* (Go to the paragraph with the number you chose.)

1. Ellie felt awful as soon as she got through the door. So much for the new me, she thought. That girl probably thinks I'm a real snob. What a year this will be, she thought.

2. Jessica smiled and said her name. She said that she was new in town, and had Ms. King as homeroom teacher. "So do I," said Ellie. Would you *(2a) wait for Jessica to say something,* or *(2b) ask where she moved from.* (Go to the paragraph with the number you chose.)

2a. They walked on in silence until Jessica asked directions to her homeroom. Ellie showed the way, and the two of them stood in the hall, waiting. Finally, Jessica said, "Well, I guess I'd better get going." As she turned away, Ellie mumbled, "Maybe we'll see each other again."

2b. Jessica described where she used to live. She liked it better here, she said—"The people are friendlier." Ellie asked what street Jessica lived on. Since her house was only a block away from Ellie's , they agreed to walk home together. Ellie smiled. What a year this will be, she thought!

Relaxing with Others

Many people are nervous when talking to new people. After all, meeting strangers means facing the unknown. And it's human nature to feel a bit uncomfortable about the unknown.

Most of our fears about dealing with new people come from doubts about ourselves. We imagine that other people are judging us—finding us too tall or too short, too this or too that. But don't forget that they may be feeling the same way. Try to accept yourself as you are, and concentrate on putting the other person at ease. You'll both feel more comfortable.

Try to act self-confident, even if you don't feel that way. When you enter a room full of strangers, such as a new classroom or the cafeteria, walk tall and straight, look directly at other people, and smile.

If you see someone you'd like to speak to, say something. Don't wait for the other person to start a conversation. One of the Teen Tips at the end of this unit gives ideas on what to say to someone new.

Giving Others A Chance

Just meeting someone new doesn't mean that you will make friends with that person. Friendships are based on mutual liking and give and take. They take time

Frequently shared experiences, such as eating lunch together, joining a school club, or enjoying recreational activities in common brings people together and leads to new friendships. What activities bring you together with new friends?

and effort to develop. And there are things that can keep a new friendship from growing.

Snap Judgments

Sometimes when you meet someone new, the two of you hit it off right away. At other times, you feel sorry that you made no effort to start a conversation. But don't be too quick to dislike someone. If you judge people on first impressions, you may misjudge them.

The person who doesn't smile and look friendly when you say hello may be shy or nervous about meeting you.

The person who talks a mile a minute also may be nervous. He may be worried that the conversation will come to a dead end if there's a silence.

Avoid thinking in stereotypes. If your sister won't date a football player because she thinks that brawn doesn't go with brains, she's not judging that person fairly. She's treating him as a stereotype instead of as an individual.

Taking Advantage of Others

John started the school year with a plan to raise his math grade. He'd made friends with Ralph, who always got an A in math, and studied with him for every test. But by October, Ralph wasn't returning John's phone calls. He was always busy the night before a test. Ralph had quickly figured out that he was being used.

For a friendship to work, two people must be truly interested in each other. Give as well as take; nobody likes to feel used all the time. Spend some time and energy getting to know people you really like and relate to. Then you'll develop friendships that last.

Handling Friendships

Meeting new people and getting to know them may or may not lead to new friendships. Not all hoped-for friendships work out. Learning how to handle these situations is an important part of the skill of making friends.

Keeping Your Distance

If you've decided not to pursue a new friendship, try to keep your distance without hurting the other person's feelings. You can do this by being polite, fair, and honest.

Be pleasant when your acquaintance calls, but keep the call short. Explain that other interests and activities are keeping you busy. And don't accept invitations and favors.

Sometimes, you may have to tell someone that you don't think you have enough in common for a friendship to develop. If you do this in a positive way—by complimenting the interests and traits of the other person—you're less likely to hurt his or her feelings.

Keeping Your Self-Confidence

What should you do when a new acquaintance seems cool toward you?

■ First, don't assume that there's no future for a friendship. Find out if your impression is based on fact. Explain that you had hoped to get together more often, and ask if there's a reason why you haven't. Perhaps your acquaintance has just been too busy to call.

Talking on the phone is an easy way to keep in touch with friends that have moved away, and with new acquaintances.

■ Your acquaintance may have decided not to pursue the friendship. Although it's easy to feel hurt, stop and think. When friendships don't work out, it's rarely the "fault" of either person. Busy schedules, different interests, or similar problems are usually the cause. You would be wrong to blame yourself or your acquaintance.

Helping New Friendships Develop

Friendships don't develop on their own—they require effort to grow. After your first conversation with someone, one of you will have to make a second move. If you don't hear from new acquaintances, don't assume they aren't interested in you. They may be waiting for you to call, or they may simply be busy. Make the move yourself. Follow up with a telephone call or an invitation to do something together.

Each time you meet or talk to your friends, you are likely to find new interests in common. You share your experiences and problems and, just as important, you listen to your friends' experiences and problems. These things become the cement that holds friendships together and makes them last.

Questions

1. Can you think of times when you wanted to make new friends? When?
2. What groups or clubs could you join that would match your interests and introduce you to new people?
3. How would you open a conversation with a new person in your class? With a new neighbor?
4. How can you keep your distance from an acquaintance without hurting his or her feelings?
5. How can you help a new friendship develop?

14 Dating and Love

After reading this chapter, you will be able to:

☐ *explain how dating is a special way to explore relationships,*

☐ *describe how having a crush teaches you to love,*

☐ *explain how a successful relationship is built on expressing emotions honestly and thoughtfully.*

At some point during your teens, you will probably notice a change in the way you feel about the opposite sex. You no longer think of each other as dull, the way you did when you were little. And you're not as mysterious to each other as you used to be.

Almost everybody goes through these changes, but not at the same time. Some young people begin dating in their early teens. Others don't start until they are in college or working.

These are some of the things to think about now regarding dating and love. In this chapter, we will talk about dating in groups and as a couple. We will also talk about love and crushes—what they are and what is different about them. We will also talk about handling emotions and feelings when relating to the opposite sex.

Going Out in a Group

Sometimes dating starts with a group of friends who have fun together. Boys and girls might meet for bowling, skating, parties, or movies. It's easier to talk in a group—people are less self-conscious with their friends around.

But maybe you're not part of a group. Perhaps you're a more private person with only one or two close friends, and you feel lost in a crowd. Don't worry—group activities are not the only way to start dating. You will have many chances to meet possible dates if you are friendly and willing to take the time to get to know someone.

Dating as a Couple

A date can take many forms. It can be as simple as going to the local fair, a basketball game, the dance at school, or biking to the beach for a swim. The idea is to have fun and to get to know the other person.

What to Do

When you start dating someone, try to choose an activity that will be natural and comfortable for both of you. If you both like animals, a visit to the zoo would be perfect. Go skating or hiking if you're both fairly athletic.

Perhaps the most popular thing to do on a first date is to see a movie, because you can relax while you're watching the film, without worrying about making conversation. The movie will give you something to talk about later. And what you both say about it can tell you a lot about each other.

Group activities, such as washing cars, playing team sports, and going places together, give you the opportunity to practice your social skills.

Relaxing

What if you go to a movie and spill popcorn all over your date? Or you laugh at the movie, but she doesn't?

If you do something awkward, you're probably not relaxed or being your real self. The more dates you have, the more comfortable you'll feel and the more successful they'll be.

Don't be upset if a date doesn't turn out the way you had hoped. You and your date may just not have been right for each other. Or perhaps something happened that you couldn't help, like rain at a picnic or a traffic jam that made you late for a movie.

If you relax, act yourself, and take time to get to know the other person, you can almost guarantee a successful date.

F E A T U R E

How to Have a Successful Date

- Choose an activity you'll both enjoy doing.
- Set the date up well ahead of time.
- Tell your parents where you'll be and who you'll be with.
- Arrive on time, or call if you're late.
- Be ready on time. Don't keep your date waiting.

- Don't cancel because you heard about something better to do.
- Don't take over the whole conversation.
- Ask questions to keep the conversation going.
- Relax and enjoy yourself.
- If you had fun, tell your date—he or she would like to know.

Is It Love?

Tanya's relationship with Fred was making her think about love. She had never before felt this way about anyone—at least not about anyone she really knew. There was that television actor she thought about last year, but now that seemed silly. With Fred, she felt more serious. She really cared about him, and he made her feel special. Was this love?

Crushes

Last year, Tanya had a **crush** on that actor. This *intense, but usually passing, love-like feeling* may be for a movie or television star, a musician, an athlete, or even an out-of-reach classmate.

The main thing about a crush is that, deep down, you don't really expect the other person to return your feelings. This makes it a safe way to prepare for the real love you're going to experience later. Through a crush, you learn to feel and express affection.

Although the other person may not know about them, your feelings for him or her are real. You enjoy imagining being with the person. This daydreaming gives you some idea of how you want to love and be loved.

Love

If crushes are practice, then love is the real thing. Now, daydreams aren't enough. You want to be together all the time. Your family can forget the phone—it's always busy. Your parents may keep telling you that you're too young, that you'll outgrow it. The teasing from your brother makes you angry.

Your love may last a long time or a short time. But chances are it *will* end. Both of you are still growing. And as people grow, their feelings change.

Breaking Up

Breaking up can be painful. You might feel hurt. If you want to break up and the other person doesn't, you might feel guilty. But you *can* make breaking up easier on you and the other person:

- In deciding whether to break up, face the truth. If you're enjoying the other person less now than in the past, try to fix the problem. But if one or both of you can't, it may be best to separate.

- In talking with the other person, be honest and gentle.

- Don't blame the other person or say harsh things.

- Give yourself time to recover from the hurt and disappointment. You'll soon find that you can have fun again.

- Remember that you and the other person can remain friends. The hobbies, classes or interests you share—which brought you together in the first place—can still be enjoyed.

Breaking up doesn't mean that your love was a waste. The experience of loving and being loved is part of you now. You've even learned from breaking up that you can bear the pain, and that it passes. Now, you're a slightly different person—a person who knows more about love.

Expressing Emotions

Fred and Tanya have just had their first fight, though they can't even remember what started it. But Fred remembers the awful way Tanya yelled at him, and she remembers how he walked out and slammed the door.

Now Fred thinks that walking away wasn't the best way to handle the problem. He never seems to express himself well with Tanya.

She is questioning her reactions, too.

Relationships change throughout a person's life. Many times it is possible to remain close to someone even after you have broken up. It is always best to part as friends.

Why does she have such a bad temper when it comes to Fred?

Strong Feelings

Along with happiness and excitement, love creates other strong emotions that aren't as easy to deal with.

Jealousy and possessiveness are part of most relationships. *You may feel hurt and resentful when your boyfriend or girlfriend spends time with someone else.* You may also get these feelings when he or she does something that doesn't include you.

You may feel anger, too. Sometimes the closer and deeper a relationship becomes, the more easily the partners get angry at each other.

These emotions are normal parts of all relationships—everyone has them. But that doesn't mean they should be ignored. If they build up, they can threaten the relationship.

Expressing with Care

To keep strong feelings from hurting your relationship, you have to communicate. You'll be amazed at how much good a simple talk can do. Fred and Tanya might have avoided their fight if they'd talked about what was bothering them.

Many people have trouble expressing their strong emotions—both the negative ones like anger and jealousy, and the positive ones like love. Maybe they're afraid of hurting someone or of being hurt themselves.

When you do express your emotions, then, think about how what you say will affect the other person. Be honest and calm, and you may be surprised at the results. You'll be less tense and worried, and you and your friend can relax and enjoy each other again. Being open to each other is always the best way to keep communication open between people.

Words to Remember

crush: an intense, but usually passing, love-like feeling

jealousy: feeling hurt and resentful when a boyfriend or girlfriend spends time with someone else

Questions

1. Why are group activities an easy way to start dating?
2. Is going to a movie a good idea for a first date? Why?
3. How can a crush be a good experience?
4. Think of two negative emotions that can hurt a love relationship.

Chapter 15 Looking at Your Future

After reading this chapter, you will be able to:

☐ describe how you and your friends may change over the years,

☐ list the basic skills for building a strong love relationship,

☐ give examples of the ways you might relate to your family in the future.

Your teen years are a time of preparation. In getting ready to be an adult, you learn how to be a friend and how to be a member of a family. The success of your future relationships might depend on what you learn now.

Of course, no one knows what your future relationships will be like. Everyone takes a different path. You may stay in your town and remain friends with the people you know now. You may go to college in a new city, form deep friendships, and decide to stay there. Or perhaps you'll go away for a period—in the armed services, for example—and then return to your home town to work at another job.

Whatever you do, wherever you go, there will always be people with whom you can form deep, satisfying relationships that will last.

F E A T U R E

You, the Fortune Teller

Flying cars. Wristwatch computers. Housecleaning robots. Space colonies. These are some of the exciting inventions we might see in the future. See if *you* can guess the future. On a piece of paper, write the answers to these questions about the future thirty years from now.

1. What will the single most important invention or discovery be?
2. How long will people live?
3. Will people live in colonies in outer space? What will they be like?
4. What kind of work will robots and computers do for people?
5. What will people's homes be like?

Next, write down how you think each answer will affect your relationships with friends and family.

Now answer these questions:

1. After high school, will you go right to work or get more schooling?
2. Will you live in your current hometown or somewhere else? If somewhere else, how far away?
3. Will you get married some day?
4. Do you want to have children some day?
5. What kind of work will you do? Will it be in an office, or a store, or a factory? Will you work for someone else or run your own business?

Finally, describe how *these* choices will affect your relationships with friends and family.

Friendships

As you get older, you and your friends may grow apart. Sometimes, a friend moves away and it's harder to keep the closeness over a long distance. Sometimes, you grow apart because of a change in interests.

But changes in your life don't mean that you *must* lose your current friends. You can have conversations about your new experiences when you meet.

New Friends at Work

People spend so much time at the factory or office that they often begin to make friends of the people they meet there. Of course, being friendly at work doesn't mean joking around all day. But it does make the workday more enjoyable.

The people you work with will have different opinions and personalities. But you will have to get along with all of them, not just the ones you like. If you hold a grudge, refuse to do your share, or avoid someone, everyone's work will suffer.

You'll also have to learn to follow suggestions and to accept criticism of your work. This can be difficult. Remember that your boss is discussing your *work*, not judging your character. It's natural to make mistakes. Your boss simply wants to help you learn from those mistakes.

New Friends at College

Perhaps you'll go to college away from home and live in a dormitory with a roommate. Living with another person is similar to living with your family, but it can be much more difficult. Both you and your roommate need to adjust to living with someone who has different habits. And you have to learn to share responsibilities.

Getting along will be easier if you speak honestly, listen patiently, and are considerate. A sense of humor and flexibility help, too.

Finding other friends at college—especially at a big school—may seem impossible. But, actually, it's like making friends in school now. You can meet people in classes, at the cafeteria, in special clubs, or on teams.

In seeking these friendships, remember to be yourself. You've built a self-concept and identified your interests. Now act on what you've learned.

You have adjustments to make once you leave home, including adjusting to different lifestyles.

Love

A big change that may be ahead of you is the development of one friendship into a loving relationship. Love is based on the give-and-take of two people who follow the four C's: *caring, commitment, communication,* and *compromise.*

The Four C's

■ The most satisfying part of a love relationship may be the *caring.* Knowing that someone else cares makes you feel good—more secure and worthy. If you remember how much better you feel knowing that the other person cares, you'll be sure to show how much you care, too. Help her when she's feeling low, or listen when he has a problem.

■ A strong relationship also depends on both people having a **commitment**. *Each partner must want to make the relationship work*—and work it is. Love relationships don't just happen—they require teamwork.

■ Commitment requires *communication.* Talking honestly can help solve the problems that arise. Certainly, keeping things to yourself won't get you past them. But just talking isn't enough; you must listen, too.

■ To settle differences, both partners must be willing to *compromise.* They must be willing to give a little so that the other will get something. The result is a stronger relationship.

Marriage

Deciding to marry someone is a major decision. It means being willing to practice the four C's every day. And it usually requires a lot of adjustment by each person. The first year or so, in particular, can be rough. But if both partners work hard, they can get over the rough spots. The joy that may result can make it all worthwhile to you.

Of course, not everyone chooses to marry. You may prefer to dedicate your life to a career. Single people can still have satisfying relationships with other people— old friends, new friends, and family.

Family

Your family relationships also will change in the future. You may start to care for younger siblings, or perhaps help take care of your grandparents. The thing that's most likely to happen, however, is that you'll move out of your home.

Independence and Moving Out

In many other countries, children—even grown ones—live with their parents until they're married, and sometimes even after. In our society, though, young adults often

Caring, commitment, communication, and compromise are especially important to practice when you marry. The everyday give and take in relationships should help to deepen love.

leave their homes and become **independent**. They *live on their own or with room-mates, and begin setting up their own household.*

It can be an exciting time. You fix up your own home. You sleep when you want and eat what you want. But this freedom carries its responsibilities. To pay the rent, you need a job. And you'll have to manage your money to meet your other expenses.

Still, as you meet the new challenges, you gain more confidence in yourself. You prepare yourself to take on even more. And it's always comforting to know that your family is still there to lend a helping hand.

New Family and Old

When you marry, you don't just get a spouse—each of you also gets a new family. Your spouse's family may be very different from what you're used to. And your family may be strange to your spouse. In fact, accepting one another may be difficult for everyone at first.

Remember that your spouse draws strength and love from his or her family, just as you do from yours. A good relationship with your new family is important to you and to your marriage.

Future Decisions

Whether with family or friends, your future relationships will involve many decisions. Will you go to work, to college, or to the army? Will you live at home, or move out with a friend? The skills you're learning now can help you make these decisions. You can prepare today to choose how you want to live tomorrow.

Words to Remember

commitment: wanting to make a love relationship work

independent living: living on your own and setting up your own household

Questions

1. In the future, how can you stay in touch with your current friends?
2. How can you help yourself make friends when you get a job or go away to school?
3. What are the four C's of a love relationship? How can you begin to develop each one?
4. How will your relationship with your family change in the future?

Chapter **16 Careers That Help with Relationships**

Objectives

After reading this chapter, you will be able to:

☐ *identify the skills required in the careers that help people form better relationships,*

☐ *give examples of jobs that involve working with families,*

☐ *give examples of jobs that involve working with individuals.*

Your elderly neighbor doesn't want to live alone, so his family hires a companion for him.

You join a youth group at the local community center, where a young adult plans all the activities.

A family down the street begins meeting weekly with a family therapist to help end the conflict it's experiencing.

Your mother hurt her leg and must wear braces. A physical therapist comes to the house to massage her legs and help her to walk in the braces.

These are only a few of the ways that people call on certain workers to help them with their relationships.

Characteristics Useful in Helping with Relationships

Levels of Jobs

Jobs dealing with relationships can be divided according to how much training they must have.

Some can be hired for **entry-level** jobs, *those for which little or no experience is needed.*

The next level of jobs are those for which some training is needed. That training could be education in a junior college or technical school, work in an apprenticeship program, or on-the-job training.

The third group of jobs requires at least a degree from a four-year college. Some jobs call for higher degrees as well.

Of course, a person can move from one job to another. Someone hired at the entry level could learn enough on the job—or by taking classes after work—to move into the second level, and then on to the third one.

Most of these jobs have some things in common. They aim at helping a **client**, *the person who is given advice and information.* And they require similar skills, both mental and emotional.

Mental Characteristics

- *Are you interested in people?* Most of your working hours would be spent with other people, and the experience is often very tiring. A drug abuse counselor spends many hours with people who may be suffering. You must be prepared to put a lot of energy into helping a client. Still, the rewards are often greater than the drain on your energy and time. When a client's problem is solved, you feel better, too.

- *Do you want to have a deep knowledge of people?* You need to understand people's fears and hopes, how they learn, and why they act as they do. Some of this knowledge comes from studying, but much is learned on the job.

- *Are you a good listener?* You need to learn about the particular client who wants help. You must be able to let the client tell his or her own story, while you keep an open mind.

- Can you allow the client to choose the solution to his or her problems? You must be careful to let the client choose what to do. If you force a client to take a certain action, it's very likely to fail.

School counselors help students identify mental characteristics to determine if they would be happy in a career that involves helping people.

- *Are you trustworthy?* A client may reveal deep and important secrets, and needs to feel confident that you will respect his or her privacy and not tell those secrets to others.

Emotional Characteristics

- *Do you have* **empathy?** You must have the ability to understand what the client is experiencing. You may feel that your client's problems are minor, but to the client they are major. You will not be able to offer much help if you don't see the problem as the client does.

- *Can you be* **objective?** To help a client, you must be *able to listen without becoming emotionally involved.* Balancing empathy and objectivity can be difficult.

- *Are you calm?* By being calm, you can put a client who is very upset at ease. Often, this helps the client see the solution that might solve the problem.

Jobs Working With Families

In many helping careers, the worker works with the family as a whole. (Other jobs aimed at helping the family are discussed in chapter 23.)

Entry-Level Jobs

One job that helps the family meet the needs of its members is the *companion.* A companion helps a person who is elderly, disabled, or recovering from illness. He or she might keep house, prepare meals, and even entertain the client.

Companions can work full-time or part-time. They can live in the house of the person they care for. In that case, room and board might be provided, along with a wage. Experience working in a hospital can be helpful for this job.

Government agencies hire *social worker aides.* **Aides** are *workers who assist higher-level workers with their jobs.* Some ask questions of clients to see if they can be part of income or job programs. Others give information or explain programs to clients who ask questions.

Social worker aides can work part-time or full-time. Typing skills can be valuable for this job.

Jobs That Require Training

More and more families are headed by a single parent who works, or by two parents who both work. These parents need someone to care for their children while they work.

As a result, the number of *day-care workers* is growing. These workers help preschool children grow emotionally, socially and mentally. They often get their training on the job, although some employers require a degree from a two-year college.

Among other duties, *police officers* handle family problems in emergencies. It is very important for them to act calmly, since these situations are sometimes dangerous.

To become a police officer, you first must pass a test. Then you will be trained in a police academy. The number of police jobs is expected to grow in the future, so there will be many openings for new workers.

F E A T U R E

Finding Out About Yourself

Finding the right career isn't always easy. One way to narrow them down and focus on just a few careers is to identify your skills and interests. Then you simply match these with the careers which match them.

Skills

Skills are *the things you can do well.* You can start to identify them by making a self-inventory chart.

1. *List any part-time or summer jobs you've had.* Include work you've done to help your parents around the house or to help them with their own jobs, and work you've done for school, church, or community groups in your neighborhood.
2. *List your education.* Write down what courses you've taken. Note which ones you've done well in, and any special honors or awards you have won in the past.
3. *Now go over both lists.* Ask yourself: Was I good at this job or course? Did I enjoy or dislike it? What exactly did I like or dislike about it? By looking at all your answers together, you may see that the things you're good at form a pattern. Perhaps you like shop courses and also enjoy fixing things around the house. It's easy to see how these skills might connect.

Now look at the list of ten characteristics below. Rate your level of skill for each: Are you average, above average, or below average?

1. *Analysis.* Are you able to look at a problem and figure out a solution to that problem?
2. *Artistry.* Are you talented in art or music?
3. *Athletics.* Are you talented in sports?
4. *Creativity.* Can you think of new ways of getting jobs done?
5. *Language.* Are you good at expressing yourself?
6. *Leadership.* Do people often look to you for guidance?
7. *Manual ability.* Are you good at working with your hands?
8. *Mathematics.* Are you good at arithmetic and science?
9. *Planning.* Are you able to organize the way you do a task and follow that plan?
10. *Understanding.* Are you able to listen to other people and offer them help when they need it?

Interests

Now try to identify your **interests,** *the things that you enjoy doing.* One way of discovering them is to list your hobbies. How you spend your free time—reading, running, building models, or sewing—hints at what you like.

Once you know what you're good at and what you like to do, finding a career should become easier.

Jobs That Require an Advanced Degree

Family therapists help families that are having conflicts. These highly trained people work with the whole family, rather than with one or two individuals. They can work for clinics and hospitals, or in private practices. Family therapists must have a college degree and usually a master's degree as well.

Social workers also help families solve their problems. They work in many different community groups—schools, hospitals, and government agencies. They can provide counseling and advice, help clients get government help, and hold classes to give information. Most social workers have a master's degree.

Jobs Working with Individuals

In many helping jobs, the worker works with one person, rather than with the entire family.

Entry-Level Jobs

Across the country, many groups have formed "hot lines"—telephone numbers that people can call for emergency help. Some hot lines help people who are thinking about committing suicide. Others assist people with drug problems.

The *hot-line workers* who answer the phones offer very important care to people who badly need it. These workers need to be calm and understanding. Most hot-line programs train their workers, but college courses in counseling will help.

Medical assistants work with doctors and nurses in providing health care. They might handle office records, do lab work, or do simple physical tests on patients. Most work in doctors' offices, though some are employed by hospitals. Usually, they are trained on the job, but some junior colleges offer courses for medical assistants.

Jobs That Require Training

Physical therapist assistants help people who are in pain due to illness or injury. They use equipment, exercise, and massage to help patients overcome their pain and physical problems. They might also instruct patients in using wheelchairs or braces. Training is given in two-year colleges.

Whether as a paid employee or as a volunteer, the hot-line worker helps people identify and solve their problems.

Many communities have built centers for young people to gather for recreation. Running the programs at these centers are *youth group workers*. They plan activities, teach, and help young people solve their problems. College study of psychology and on-the-job experience are both helpful.

Jobs That Require an Advanced Degree

Many people turn to a member of the **clergy** for help when they need it. Priest, minister, rabbi, or mullah, these *religious workers* can be important sources of comfort and advice. Training varies from one religious group to another, but it usually involves a college degree and study at a religious school.

Psychologists are people who have studied how the mind works. They offer counseling to clients who have difficulty solving their problems. Psychologists have a college degree and usually an advanced degree. They also get extra training by talking with patients and helping them resolve difficulties. These professionals can work in a hospital or have their own practice.

Words to Remember

aides: workers who assist higher-level workers with their jobs

clergy: religious workers

client: the person who is given advice and information

empathy: a helper's ability to understand what the client is experiencing

entry-level job: a job in which little or no experience is needed

interests: the things you enjoy doing

objective: being able to listen without becoming emotionally involved

skills: the things you can do well

Questions

1. What mental characteristics do helping careers require?
2. What emotional characteristics do helping careers require?
3. Name three jobs aimed at helping families—one at each job level.
4. Name three jobs aimed at helping individuals rather than whole families—one at each job level.

You've seen how many different kinds of relationships you have and how important they are to you. Right now, you have relationships with many people—parents, siblings, grandparents, other relatives, friends, acquaintances, and teachers. Later, you may have relationships with a spouse, in-laws, children, bosses, employees, and others. Building all these relationships and keeping them strong is a challenge. The tips in this section may help.

1. Showing your responsibility.

2. Tracing your roots.

3. The ABCs of good communication.

4. What do you say?

5. What to do?

Showing Your Responsibility

It's important to you to show your responsibility these days—to show that you deserve those privileges you've been asking for. Below are some ways you can do that. By taking these actions, you can help your parents see that you are ready to take on more responsibilities.

As a son or daughter, you can help around the house by cleaning up, fixing a dinner, or keeping your room neat.

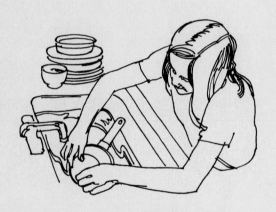

As a grandchild, you can write a thank-you note for the gift your grandparents gave you, or call them up occasionally.

As a brother or sister, you can help your younger siblings with their homework, and comfort them when they hurt themselves.

As a niece or nephew, you can thank your aunt or uncle when they prepare the family holiday meal.

As a cousin, you can teach your younger cousins how to make a craft item for their room.

As a lab partner, you can do your share of the clean up after the experiment.

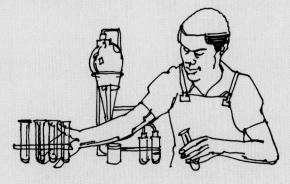

As a student, you can turn your homework in on time, and don't be tardy for classes.

As a best friend, you can send that birthday card to get there on time.

As a teammate, you can put the equipment away after practice.

As a neighbor, you can take care of your neighbors' pets when they are on vacation.

Tracing Your Roots

Have you ever wondered where your family came from? How many brothers and sisters your grandfather had? Why everybody always talks about "crazy Uncle Harry"?

Maybe you asked your mother once, but forgot her answer. One way you can remember your family's history is to make a family tree.

Starting Out

The first things you need are a pen and paper. Then, like any researcher, you need a resource. Scholars use libraries. You'll use a relative—but pick one with a good memory!

You might start with your parents. Ask them to tell you all they can remember about their brothers and sisters, parents, aunts and uncles, and grandparents.

What should you ask?

■ First, find out each person's name and birthday. You can also ask where the person was born—you may be able to trace your family's history to other countries.

■ For relatives who are dead, ask when they died. Find out which ones got married and to whom, and how many children they had, if any.

■ Once you've gotten all the information you can from your parents, turn to an older relative—a grandparent, great-aunt, or anyone else who might remember further back. See what you can learn from them.

Your Family History

Now put all your information together to make a family tree. You can follow the design shown on the next page.

Or you can use a simpler format, such as this one:

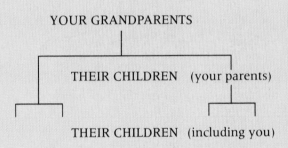

YOUR GRANDPARENTS

THEIR CHILDREN   (your parents)

THEIR CHILDREN   (including you)

Making a family tree is simple, especially if you keep a separate chart for each parent's family.

Family trees can be fun to make, but you can learn even more about your family by asking a few more questions. While you're talking to your relatives, ask them to tell you at least one story about each person they name—what work he or she did, hobbies, a funny incident that happened, a dangerous accident.

Write the story down, and you'll be able to remember that long-lost cousin more easily.

If you have a cassette or tape player, you can record your relatives telling these stories. Then, in later years, you'll be able to hear their voices and enjoy their great storytelling styles all over again.

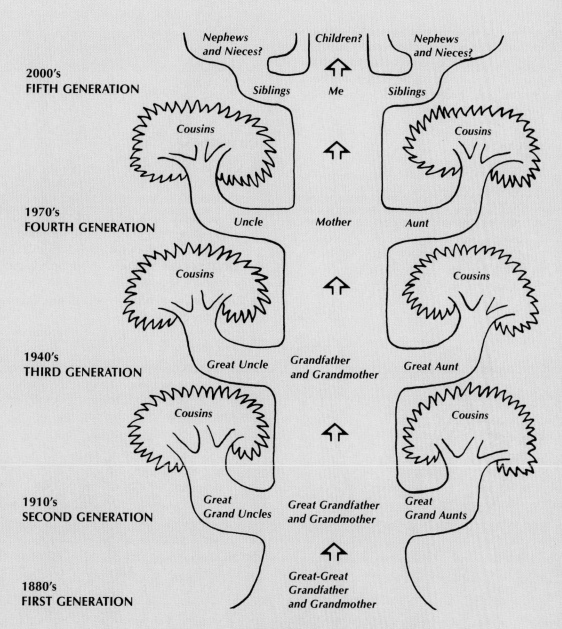

2000's
FIFTH GENERATION

1970's
FOURTH GENERATION

1940's
THIRD GENERATION

1910's
SECOND GENERATION

1880's
FIRST GENERATION

Nephews and Nieces?   *Children?*   *Nephews and Nieces?*

Siblings   *Me*   *Siblings*

Cousins   *Cousins*

Uncle   *Mother*   *Aunt*

Cousins   *Cousins*

Great Uncle   *Grandfather and Grandmother*   *Great Aunt*

Cousins   *Cousins*

Great Grand Uncles   *Great Grandfather and Grandmother*   *Great Grand Aunts*

Great-Great Grandfather and Grandmother

MOTHER'S FAMILY AND MYSELF

The ABCs of Good Communication

Good relationships require good communication. And good communication doesn't just happen. It's a skill—a skill that you learn, practice, and improve. Here are some hints that can spell better communication skills for you.

Face to Face

- Look directly at the speaker.
- Ask questions to show your interest—and to learn more.
- Introduce people to one another following custom. Introduce a younger person to an older person ("Mother, this is my friend, Phil"). Introduce a female to a male ("Grandpa, this is my coach, Ms. Scott").

On the Phone

- Answer the phone by saying your name ("Sue Jones speaking" or "the Ramirez residence").
- Use good phone manners. Don't talk too long—others may need to use the phone, too. And ask if the other person has time to talk. He or she may be in the middle of dinner when you call.
- Take complete messages when the call is for someone else. Write down the caller's name, telephone number, the date and time he or she called, and the best time to call back.
- Be safe on the phone. Don't tell strangers any important information, such as where parents work, when they're expected home, or how many children there are.

Running a Meeting

- Begin the meeting on time.
- Introduce any new members of the group to others.
- Make an agenda, or a list of topics to discuss at the meeting, and stick to it during the meeting.
- Be sure to give all members of the group a chance to speak about a topic.
- End the meeting on time.

Listening Effectively

- Ask questions such as who, when, what, where, and why to learn more about what the speaker is saying.
- Don't think about what you want to say, but really listen to the other person.
- If you don't have time to listen, tell the other person politely.

What Do You Say?

You're at a party. Your best friend brings over a new neighbor and introduces you. You think the person is interesting, and you'd like to start a conversation—but how?

Or maybe you're at a family reunion and you're sitting next to an aunt that you hardly know. What can you say to her? Here are a few hints for getting past those awkward pauses that happen when you're not sure what to say to that person you're interested in.

At a family reunion

Ask your aunt about her job, or what hobbies she has, or any travel she's done recently.

On a date

Ask your date what he or she thought of a recent movie or a well-known music group.

A stranger at a party

If the person is new in town, ask where he or she came from, why the family moved, and how they like it in the new place.

At the meeting of a new club

If you're new to the club, ask what topics they've talked about in the past. If someone else is new, ask why he or she decided to come to the meeting.

At a team practice or a music group rehearsal

This is easy—ask the other person what he or she likes about the sport or the music.

At a campground

Ask someone you meet where they come from. If you've been to the campground before, tell them what you know about it. If you haven't, ask if he or she has and ask for tips on what to do.

When your grandfather visits

Ask what he used to do for a living, if he's retired, or ask him to talk about his childhood or historical events he's lived through. You can even ask what your parents were like when they were your age!

When your cousin from the coast comes to stay for a week

Ask what she does for fun, or what her school is like.

What to Do?

It's Saturday, and you and your friend want something to do, but can't think of anything. There are hundreds of possibilities for you to choose from—you just have to think of them. Here are a few suggestions to get your ideas going.

Sports

Swim in the community pool
Play basketball
Roller skate or ice skate
Sled
Ride bikes

In the park

Picnic
Feed the birds
Play on the swings
Watch the people

At home

Write a puppet play
Create a new video game
Create the characters and plots for a television
    series about your school
Write a fan letter to your favorite singer

Crafts

Bake a loaf of bread
Work on a sewing project
Build a storage unit

On the town

Window shop
Take a factory tour to see how a product is
   made
See a matinee movie
See a city from an observation site at the top
   of its highest building

The cultural scene

Go to an art museum
Visit an aquarium
Explore in a science museum
Visit the zoo

Unit One Review

Chapter 6.

You have many kinds of relationships, and they are very important to you. They help satisfy your basic needs and help build your self-concept. To keep your relationships satisfying, you need to make many decisions.

Chapters 7 and 8.

Your family meets many of your basic needs and helps you learn how to have strong relationships. Each member of your family has different needs and responsibilities, but all can work together to provide the help that's needed from time to time. Your family also has its own unique way of doing things.

Chapters 9 and 10.

All families experience some problems and go through many changes. But these situations can be less troubling if you and other members of your family work together. By communicating and giving each other support, you can get through the tough times.

Chapters 11 and 12.

You have relationships with friends, too— many different kinds of friends. You keep those friendships strong by sharing and caring, and by being reliable, loyal, sympathetic, and honest. You can become friends with more people by looking at people as individuals, and not as stereotypes. Putting people into categories lessens them, and robs you of a chance to make some interesting friends.

Chapters 13 and 14.

You can make new friends by trying out new activities. But you need to give new relationships time to develop. And you need to deal with other people honestly. The same is true of your future dating relationships. By relaxing on a date and taking time to learn about the other person, you can learn how to have strong relationships in the future.

Chapter 15.

Your future can take many different directions. But whichever path you follow, you will probably have relationships that are important to you. You can prepare today to make those relationships strong and rewarding.

Chapter 16.

If people are very important to you, you might choose a career that helps people. While there are many different careers to pick from, most require these characteristics: an interest in people, an understanding of people, the ability to listen, empathy, objectivity, and calmness.

Questions

1. With whom were some of your earliest relationships formed?

2. What needs do families satisfy?

3. Describe four different family structures you might come across.

4. What advantages might the oldest child in a family have? The youngest child? The middle child? An only child? What disadvantages would each of these children have?

5. Give an example of the conflicts that might occur in a relationship:

   a. with a friend of the same sex,

   b. with a friend of the opposite sex,

   c. with a parent,

   d. with a sibling.

6. What is brainstorming? How can people use it to help solve problems?

7. Give three examples of changes your family might experience.

8. Suggest three ways of reducing the stress caused by change.

9. What five qualities are characteristic of good friends?

10. What harmful effects does stereotyping have?

11. Name two ways you can meet new friends.

12. What can you learn from a crush?

13. Describe two careers in which you would be helping people with their relationships. Pick one that requires quite a bit of education and training and one that requires very little.

Reading Activities

1. Read a letter in a newspaper advice column that describes a teenager who has a problem with family or friends—but don't read the answer. First, write your own answer, then read the one in the newspaper. How do they differ? Who do you think had the better solution?

2. Look through teen magazines to find advice on overcoming self-doubts and making friends. Explain which two hints you think are the most important.

3. Reread the list of characteristics in the box in chapter 16. Which ones do you think you have? Which ones don't you have?

Writing Activities

1. Write a paragraph describing an important decision you had to make about a relationship recently. What does your decision show about what you value in relationships?

2. Write a "Bill of Rights for Children." Write a "Bill of Rights for Parents." How are the two lists different?

3. Ask one of your grandparents or parents what his or her childhood was like. Write a paragraph pointing out the differences between that childhood and yours.

4. Write a paragraph describing what you think the ideal friend would be like.

5. Write a dramatic skit about an unfair stereotype.

Math Activities

1. Make a time line to illustrate the changes in your family. Include moves, new jobs, the arrival and departure of children, and any other major changes from the time your parents married. Figure out how much time passed between changes.

2. Ask five people outside your class to look at the ten characteristics listed in the box in chapter 12. Which do they think are largely true of males and which of females? How many people answer "either sex" for each characteristic?

Group Activities

1. Form a neighborhood information committee to write and hand out community information to families moving into your community.

2. Collect lines from different popular songs about love. Post them in the classroom. After everyone has studied the lyrics, poll your classmates to see which ones they think best express their ideas about love.

3. Find quotations that describe or comment on love, friendship, and loyalty. The class can be divided into three groups, and each group can be assigned one of the above topics. Each group can then make a poster display of the quotations it found.

CHILD CARE AND CHILD DEVELOPMENT

What must someone who cares for children know about them? What must he or she be able to do? Here's a quick quiz for you to take. The answers follow the quiz.

Questions

1. Who needs more care—younger or older children?
2. What is a better toy for a two-year-old—building blocks or a construction set?
3. How can you entertain a bored five-year-old while you're both waiting for the bus to go home?
4. What should you do if a child receives a small cut?
5. What emergency phone numbers should a babysitter have?
6. In childproofing a room for a one-year-old, what would you do about electrical outlets?

Answers

1. Infants need more attention when they're awake, but be sure not to ignore older children.
2. Building blocks are better. A two-year-old is not able to handle something as complex as a construction set.
3. Tell a story or make up a counting game based on the passing cars.
4. Wash the wound in warm water and bandage it.
5. A caregiver should have the phone numbers of the parents, the police, the fire department, the doctor, an ambulance, and the poison control center.
6. Cover them with special plastic caps.

How did you do on this quiz? After reading this unit, you'll learn enough to be able to answer all of these questions.

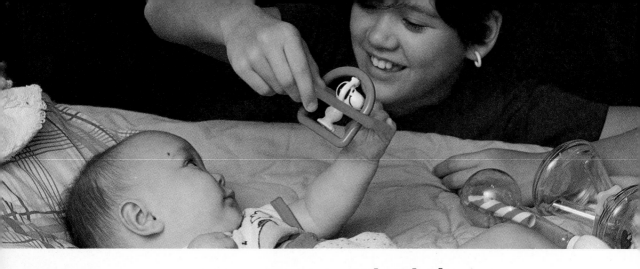

Chapter 17 Children and You

Objectives

After reading this chapter, you will be able to:

☐ *explain why parenting requires making decisions,*

☐ *identify the needs of children that are met by parenting,*

☐ *give examples of the things that a caregiver must know about children.*

Monica was feeling good—happy about the ten dollars she'd earned babysitting, and pleased with how well her day had gone. She was proud of the way she had handled the Vega children. Coaxing Linda to take a nap had been tricky, and she could tell that both children really liked the games she'd planned.

Mrs. Vega complimented Monica on her work. She even recommended Monica to a neighbor who needed a mother's helper two afternoons a week.

Monica thinks of herself as a babysitter, but she can also be called a caregiver. A **caregiver** is *someone who takes care of children*. Because Monica works only occasionally, she is called a *part-time caregiver*. The people who take the main responsibility for rearing children, usually the parents, are called *main caregivers*.

Rewards of Caregiving

Many young people like working as part-time caregivers. Their skills with children and the trust that adults place in them boost their self-esteem.

By caregiving, they also fulfill their own needs and wants. The ten dollars that Monica earned will go toward a skirt that she wants to buy. If she takes the mother's helper job, she might also put the money away toward nursing school. And, like everyone, Monica needs affection, so the children's clear fondness for her is another plus.

Monica's goals for her child-care job are *short-term goals*. She wants to do a good job with the children, to please her employer, and to earn money.

If she has children of her own some day, she'll find that her child-care goals are somewhat different. She'll still want to do a good job, but for different reasons. Her goals then will be *long-term goals*: to rear happy, healthy children who will grow into responsible, well-adjusted adults.

If you are either a part-time or full-time caregiver, you find yourself making many decisions. The decision-making skills that you learned in chapter 5 can help you. Monica has faced many decisions:

■ What shall I do to stop Linda's crying?

■ How can I fix lunch and give her a bottle at the same time?

■ What things are fun for a two-year-old?

Monica has the skills to make decisions in emergencies, too. She knows what to do if a fire starts or if a child is injured.

If Monica were the children's main caregiver, her decisions would affect their future. A parent's daily decisions about nutrition and interactions with others will have results throughout the child's whole life.

Knowing how to feed, comfort, and guide a child are responsibilities of the caregiver. Have you had any experience doing these things?

What Is Parenting?

Parenting means taking care of children in all the ways that children require. It means *meeting children's physical, emotional, mental, and social needs.* Parenting is not the same as *parenthood.* Many people can parent, including parents and babysitters. In some families, parenting is shared by the parents, grandparents, older brothers and sisters, and a day-care center.

F E A T U R E

Parenting in Other Cultures

In this country, children are reared in a variety of ways. In some families, both parents work and both care for the children. In others, one parent works and one cares for the children. And in some, the parents hire a person to watch their children. But caring for children is always seen as the parents' responsibility. They can choose whatever pattern and style of parenting they wish.

Other cultures see child care differently. In the Soviet Union, parents are seen as deputies of the government. Although they have the main responsibility for caring for children, the government has the final authority. Children are reared to value the group—they are meant to contribute to society. Fathers usually do very little to help with child care.

Other societies also rear children to put more value on society than on parents' wishes and needs. This is true in mainland China. It is also true, to some extent, in the kibbutzim, or communes, of Israel.

Some societies provide extra help to parents who are raising children. Both New Zealand and Sweden offer medical and dental care, as well as education for parenthood. Sweden even makes a yearly payment to all mothers with children under sixteen.

Many cultures help parents, but not through the government. In many Asian and African groups, relatives help mothers care for their children. In some societies, mothers do other work and leave child care to the grandmothers or other women.

Physical Needs

Food. Nutritious meals and snacks help children grow and develop. A variety of foods provides a balanced diet and different tastes.

Infants begin by drinking either milk from their mother or formula. During the first year, they begin eating strained foods and, later, food cut in small pieces. As they get older, children can eat the same meals as adults.

Rich, spicy, or fried foods can upset a child's digestion, so they should be avoided. Foods like nuts and popcorn are bad for a child, too. They might get stuck in his or her throat.

Clothing. Children need to be dressed properly. They shouldn't be too warm or too cold. Infants need fresh diapers—often! Other good clothes for infants include T-shirts, nightgowns, and sleepers.

Once children are able to dress and undress themselves, they need clothes that they can put on and take off easily. And whatever their age, children need clothing that's appropriate for the weather.

Rest. Children need more sleep than adults. They need naps during the day and

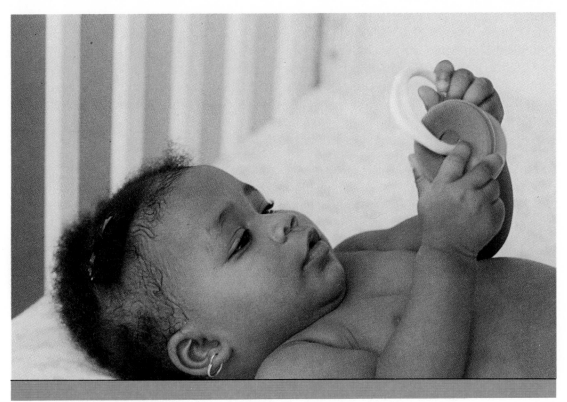

Children should be provided with a safe, comfortable, and stimulating environment that arouses curiosity and encourages safe exploration of surroundings.

many hours of sleep at night. Following the same routine each day and night helps them get to sleep.

Newborns can sleep in cradles or carriers. Once they are larger, they should sleep in cribs. Since they can hurt themselves by hitting the crib sides, the crib should have padded bumpers. Washable sheets and a waterproof pad covering the mattress are also useful.

Safe Environment. Children are not aware of the dangers of stairs, electric outlets, or poisons. They must be protected from accidents that their exploring can cause. Chapter 20 explains how to make the home safe for children.

Care. Children need to be bathed and washed when they're infants. Once they are older, they should be taught to clean themselves and brush their teeth. Young children also need toilet training, so they can learn to go to the bathroom themselves.

Mental Needs

Children are constantly learning because the whole world is new to them. To help them learn, they need stimulation—

chances to see, hear, touch, taste, and smell. Infants learn by exploring with their senses. Older children build on this base as they experience even more. Chapter 19 offers some ideas on how caregivers can help children learn.

Social Needs

Children need love and a sense of security. They need affection. They need someone to comfort them when they are hurt or upset. They need to know that people care.

As they grow older, children must learn to get along with others. First they learn how to relate to family members, then how to relate to friends.

Guidance

Finally, children need **guidance**, *to be told what behavior is acceptable and what is not.* Young children do not yet know right from wrong. If given complete freedom, they may be confused about what to do. They can even be frightened.

Caregivers help children by setting limits—telling them that they can go here, but not there, or that they can do this, but not that. Of course, a child may *test* that limit and purposely do the wrong thing. He or she isn't trying to be bad, but only wants to make sure that the caregiver meant what was said.

Setting these limits is the responsibility of the main caregiver. Part-time caregivers simply remind children what the limits are—and stick to them. Of course, it's the responsibility of the part-time caregivers to find out from the main caregiver what the limits are.

Skills for Parenting

Parenting is demanding work. It requires knowledge, skills, and personal qualities like understanding, patience, love, and respect. Some of these things can be learned in classes and by reading. Others are learned through experience.

Many people can share the parenting role, including grandparents, older brothers and sisters, babysitters, and even you.

Knowledge

Effective parenting requires knowing about children. One-year-olds can't do what two-year-olds can do, and two-year-olds aren't as advanced as five-year-olds. A caregiver—parent or babysitter—must understand the stages of development that children reach at various ages. Then, he or she can develop activities suitable for them.

Skills

The caregiver also needs certain skills. He or she must be able to:
- meet the child's physical needs
- meet the child's mental needs
- meet the child's social needs
- give the child guidance
- act wisely and quickly in an emergency

Personal Qualities

Increased knowledge will help you gain more understanding, patience, love, and respect for children. For example, under- standing a two-year-old's desire for independence—and his frustration at not being able to put on his own jacket—will make you more sympathetic.

Patience is valuable, too. Children are bound to try your patience at times, but losing your temper does neither of you any good. You'll be more likely to stay calm if you keep in mind the facts of child development. Katie is not trying to be bad when she throws all nine toys out of her playpen; she's just testing gravity in her own way.

And as for love and respect, these are qualities you learn from others around you. You even learn from the children, who show you their love and respect.

Learning

The chapters in this unit will start you on the way to getting the knowledge and to learning the skills of parenting. But as in all things, practice—working and playing with children—is one of the best ways to learn. And the experience of playing with children and watching them learn and grow is fun!

Words to Remember

caregiver: someone who takes care of children

guidance: telling children what behavior is acceptable and what is not

parenting: meeting children's physical, emotional, mental, and social needs

Questions

1. How is parenting different from parenthood?
2. What physical needs do children have?
3. What mental needs do children have? How can each be met?
4. What social needs do children have? How can caregivers meet those needs?
5. List three things that a caregiver needs to be able to parent effectively.

Chapter **18** Ages and Stages

Objectives

After reading this chapter, you will be able to:

☐ *explain how development occurs in stages,*

☐ *describe what tasks children master in developing physically, mentally, and socially,*

☐ *explain how children with special needs can learn to develop to their full ability.*

A nine-month-old crawls; and in some three more months she walks. A two-year-old speaks a few words. By three-and-a-half, he is talking in sentences. These examples show the **developmental tasks** that children learn—*the abilities that they acquire as they grow.*

After much study, researchers have seen that children master these tasks in the same order. Crawling usually comes before walking, and speaking a few words comes before talking in sentences. Children build on what they've learned the day before. A few words become sentences. Finger painting turns into drawing.

Developmental tasks are to be encouraged in children. If children are not helped to do some of these tasks, such as talking, they will not communicate well.

Stages of Development

Researchers list four stages that children go through:

- infant (birth to one year)
- toddler (one to three years)
- preschooler (three to five years)
- school-age (five to ten years)

These **stages** mark *periods when the child is able to perform new tasks*. The table shows what some of those tasks are for the first three stages. Of course, the ages given are just averages. One child may begin to walk at nine months, and another may start to walk at fourteen months.

Remember, too, that the stages are not rigid categories. An "infant" does not suddenly become a "toddler" the day after his first birthday. The change is very gradual. Still, you can refer to this table as you read the chapters in this unit to learn what things a young child has probably learned.

Infant

Physical Development

Although she is only a few days old, Gloria is already quite a complex individual. She has strong **reflexes**, or *automatic, involuntary responses*. If you stroke her cheek, she turns her head toward your hand and sucks. If you stand her up so that the soles of her feet touch the bed as you support her, her knees will bend as though she is walking.

Gloria cries to signal unhappiness. She can see, taste, hear, and smell. Gloria can also touch. As she gets older she will learn about shapes and textures by putting objects in her mouth.

Gloria's next year will be one of tremendous change and growth. Her weight will triple. She will learn to use her hands by grasping a rattle and reaching out for objects. Bringing objects to her mouth will help her learn *hand-eye coordination*.

Gloria will develop **gross-motor skills**. These skills show her *control over large muscles, such as those in the legs*. As her muscle control grows, she will roll over, sit up, crawl, and finally stand.

Mental Development

As a one-month-old baby, Gloria is alert for only short periods during her waking hours, but she is beginning to take notice of the world. She will follow a toy with her eyes when it is moved in front of her face.

As her vision develops, Gloria will become more aware of the mobile over her head. And she'll recognize familiar faces. With a rattle, she begins to learn about *cause and effect*—if she shakes the rattle, it makes a sound.

At first, Gloria's only way of communicating is by crying. But around her third month, she will begin to use sound to communicate pleasure. She'll gurgle and coo at familiar people and toys.

Social Development

Gloria will probably smile for the first time when she's three to five months old. She will coo when talked to at three months. At six to eight months, she may

TABLE 1 Stages, Ages, and Tasks

Stage (approximate age)	Physical Tasks	Mental Tasks	Social Tasks
Infant (birth to 1 year)	Lifts head (1–2 months) Grasps rattle (3 months) Rolls over (3–5 months) Puts objects in mouth (4–5 months) Sits (5–9 months) Crawls (5–9 months) Transfers objects from hand to hand (5–9 months) Begins teething (6 months) Eats finger foods (9 months) Stands (9–12 months)	Cries to communicate (birth) Follows object with eyes (1 month) Babbles (3 months) Forms sense of self (6 months) Explores by touch and taste (7 months)	Develops trust of caregivers (1–6 months) Smiles (3–5 months) Recognizes own name (4–12 months) Is afraid of strangers (6–8 months)
Toddler (1–3 years)	Walks (12–15 months) Climbs out of crib (12–15 months) Picks up small objects (12–15 months) Runs (15–18 months) Climbs stairs (15–22 months) Eats with spoon (15–22 months) Can undress self (18–30 months) Begins toilet training (1½–3 years)	Imitates words (12 months) Follows simple instructions (12 months) Points to objects when named (12–18 months) Makes single–word sentences (12–18 months) Makes 2-word sentences (18–24 months)	Learns meaning of "no" (12–15 months) Waves "bye-bye" (18–24 months) Has temper tantrums (2–2½ years) Can play in groups (2–3 years)
Preschooler (3–5 years)	Runs, jumps, hops, skips (3 years) Rides a tricycle (3 years) Feeds and dresses self (3 years) Climbs jungle gym (4 years) Makes drawings and clay models (4 years) Walks straight line (5 years) Skips rope (5 years) Pours liquids (5 years) Uses knife and fork (5 years)	Attention span lengthens (throughout) Identifies objects in pictures (3 years) Speaks 5- to 6-word sentences (3½ years) Learns counting and colors (4–5 years) Repeats rhymes, songs (4 years)	Develops sense of self (throughout) Begins using simple manners and grooming (3½ years) Begins cooperative group play (4 years) Learns fair play (5 years)

Reading aloud can help a child learn to talk. The child listens to the sounds and begins language development by imitating the sounds.

become afraid of new people. This is probably because she is learning to tell familiar faces from unfamiliar ones.

An infant begins to develop a sense of herself. Gloria begins to understand that she is separate from her parents. And between eight and twelve months of age, she will learn that people or toys exist even after they're gone from the room. This concept is called *object permanence.*

Toddler

Physical Development

Manuel's first steps were a thrill for him and his family. Once Manuel felt steady, he wanted to walk everywhere, including up every flight of stairs. After he became more sure of himself—by one-and-a-half to two years old—he often wanted to run everywhere—fast! His gross-motor skills are improving.

Manuel will also gain more *control over smaller muscles, such as those in his hands.* With these **fine-motor skills**, he can feed and dress himself. His family encourages these efforts. Some of his triumphs, such as climbing out of his crib and highchair, may not be as welcomed by his parents.

Mental Development

There is also much mental growth during the toddler years. Manuel will go from speaking single words to short phrases and finally to whole sentences. He will build on his knowledge of cause and effect by noticing that if he drops something, it falls.

Manuel will begin to learn about space—what's on top and on bottom, what is larger or smaller. Toddlers often experiment with putting toys together. He will learn what jobs objects are meant for. Spoons are for eating and a shirt is for wearing.

Social Development

Toddlers tend to play alongside each other, rather than together. This is called **parallel play**. They are not ready to play with each

FEATURE

Caring for the Unborn

A pregnant woman is responsible for two people at once—herself and her unborn child. Good care before birth is more likely to produce a healthy baby and safeguard the health of the mother.

Things To Do

There are several things a pregnant woman should do:

- She should go to a doctor or clinic if she thinks she is pregnant and have a test taken to be sure. The doctor will tell her how often she must return during the rest of her pregnancy.

- She should eat a balanced diet. Doctors now recommend that pregnant women gain about 24 to 30 pounds. That means adding about 300 calories a day to an average well-balanced diet. Usually the doctor will provide a special diet that the expectant mother can follow.

- She should get an adequate amount of exercise.

- She should talk over the facts of pregnancy and delivery with her doctor or the health workers at her clinic. She can also read books and pamphlets on the subject.

- She should keep a positive attitude and try to relax—pregnancy is a normal, healthy process.

Things To Avoid

There are also certain things a pregnant woman should avoid:

- *Tobacco.* Smoking may cause serious problems for a baby.

- *Alcohol.* This drug can damage a baby's mental and physical development.

- *Caffeine.* Present in coffee, tea, and many soda drinks, caffeine can harm babies, too.

- *Any medicines.* She should not take drugs, even nonprescription medicines, without first checking with her doctor.

- *German measles* (rubella) or *venereal disease.* These diseases are extremely dangerous to an unborn baby.

---

other until preschool or later.

Around the age of two years, children get caught in a struggle between their dependency on others and their desire for independence. This usually shows up in fits of frustration. Often, Manuel wants to do everything for himself and realizes that he can't. At the same time, he resents his parents' efforts to help. When he isn't able to feed himself, climb into his highchair, or put together a puzzle, he may have a temper tantrum.

Little by little, Manuel is beginning to acquire the ideas that will form his self-concept: the knowledge that he is unique, that he has his own feelings, that others have certain feelings about him.

Many of Manuel's early attitudes about himself will come from the people who care for him. Caregivers must help children to feel good about themselves, and must promote their self-esteem.

The Preschooler and the School-Age Child

Physical Development

After three and until the teens, the changes that occur in children's bodies are not as dramatic as those that took place in infancy. During the preschool years and middle childhood, children simply continue to get bigger and stronger and to have more control over their bodies and emotions.

Children at these stages eat the same food as adults. By the time they start school, they can handle such personal care as bathing and dressing. They also learn to be sensitive to their own feelings of wellness and illness.

Mental Development

The exploring and testing that began during infancy continue as a child grows. This is a time for exploring, asking questions, and thinking about things.

Preschoolers begin counting and learning colors. These skills show preschoolers' ability to think *abstractly*. Preschoolers become able to write their names and form complete sentences.

School-age children build on these skills to master more complex tasks. They learn arithmetic and reading. They refine their fine-motor skills to be able to draw and color.

Children in these stages are able to sit still with one activity for a longer time than toddlers can. These are also the years of imagination, when children may brag or have scary dreams.

Social Development

During the preschool years, a child begins to explore what it means to enjoy the company of others. Around age four or five, a child is likely to single out another child as a best friend.

In day care, nursery school, and kindergarten, children learn social behavior—how to get along in a group, how to share, how to play together.

Children in these stages also learn how to argue and how to compete. Winning contests becomes very important to them.

Sometimes, older children will feel caught between wanting to grow up and wanting to stay the same. An older child may suddenly want to sit on a lap or take a favorite stuffed animal to bed.

Children With Special Needs

Some children need special attention. They *may be mentally or physically handicapped*, or *have certain learning difficulties*. Or they may *be unusually bright*. All these children are called **children with special needs**.

Physical Development

It's important to remember that children with physical problems are children *first*. They have the same basic needs as other children—to be loved and to be stimulated. Like any child, Paul, who uses a wheelchair, needs to develop self-confidence.

Children with physical problems do best when they are given the chance to help themselves as soon as possible. Help them learn to wash and dress themselves. Give them chores that they are capable of doing. By accomplishing these tasks, special children will feel better about themselves.

Mental Development

The Mentally Handicapped Child. Mentally handicapped children must also be given every chance to develop as far as they can. They may be slower in completing a developmental task, but eventually they are able to do such things. Encouraging the children—and rewarding them for what they do learn—can lead to further learning. Whenever possible, emphasize what the children *can* do.

The Gifted Child. Children who are unusually intelligent need special attention, too. Dina is intellectually gifted. Her parents try to do everything possible to stimulate and interest her.

At school, Dina could be given extra projects. Or she could go to a special class as part of her school day. There she can do challenging work, but she can still take part in regular school activities.

Dina's parents are careful to treat her and their other children equally. She is given jobs equal to those of her brothers and sisters. Her parents are proud of her, but they also let her know they love her not because she is so intelligent, but because she is their child.

Words to Remember

developmental task: an ability mastered at a given stage, such as crawling in the first year or walking in the second

fine-motor skills: the control over smaller muscles, such as in the hands

gross-motor skills: the control over large muscles, such as those in the legs

parallel play: playing alongside each other, rather than together

reflex: an automatic, involuntary response

stage: a period when a child is able to perform new tasks

Questions

1. What are the four stages of childhood?
2. State one way that infants develop (a) physically, (b) mentally, and (c) socially.
3. State one way that toddlers develop (a) physically, (b) mentally, and (c) socially.
4. State one way that preschoolers develop (a) physically, (b) mentally, and (c) socially.
5. State one way that school-age children develop (a) physically, (b) mentally, and (c) emotionally.
6. What is the main thing to remember about children with special needs?

19 The Importance of Play

Objectives

After reading this chapter, you will be able to:

☐ *explain how children learn through play,*

☐ *give examples of activities that can help children develop physically, mentally, and socially,*

☐ *choose play activities suitable to a child's age and stage of development.*

Playing comes so naturally to children that you may never have given it much thought. If you sometimes take care of a younger brother or sister or your neighbors' children, you might just be grateful for children's games.

But there is more going on with child's play than just amusement for the children and a break for you. Playing teaches children about their environment. It also influences how they grow.

People have always known that adult play serves many purposes, including relaxation, learning, and social communication. But, only recently have we come to realize the great importance of play in children's learning about the things around them.

Play and Development

Just as children change as they grow, their play also changes. Play is an important part of every one of the stages of child development. But a child's play changes as he or she develops. An infant develops his fine-motor skills by grasping toys and bringing them to his mouth. A preschooler improves her fine-motor ability by making drawings.

When you know about the stages of development, you can provide children with play that matches their skills. Remember, though, that children develop at different rates and have different interests. One child can be ready for one kind of play before another of the same age. Adapt your play suggestions to their actual skills to get the best results.

The Play of Infants

Infants play by exploring their world through their senses. Here are some suggestions on how to play with infants:

- Provide objects to touch, suck, hear, and watch.
- Make sure that objects have no sharp edges or small parts, because at about three months infants begin putting objects in their mouths.
- Change toys occasionally, since infants' attention spans are short.
- Once they can sit up (at about five months), prop infants up in a comfortable and safe chair with two or three toys. Then they can see what is going on.
- Play catch with a soft ball.
- Talk to an infant to help her develop her babbling into language.

FEATURE

Matching the Toy to the Child

Infant
Mobiles, rattles, squeak toys, soft animals, crib-gym exercisers, plastic measuring cups, balls. All toys should be too large to swallow.

Toddler
Push-pull toys, books with rhymes and pictures to identify, stacking toys, simple songs and games such as "Ring around the Rosy," simple riding toys, small wagons, easy puzzles.

Preschooler
Low gym, wading pool and sandbox, tricycle, dolls, toy cars and trucks, wagons, materials for pretending such as child-size play furniture and kitchen, hobby horse, modeling dough, finger paints, crayons, building blocks, round-edge scissors and paper, paste and paper, play sets such as a farm or village.

School-age child
Board games, fashion dolls, doll houses, typewriter, racing cars, building sets, crafts, sports equipment, bicycle, books, computer games.

The Play of Toddlers

Here are some hints for playing with toddlers:

- Allow room for walking and running.
- Set aside time for active play so they can use energy and lose restlessness.
- Be prepared to change games when the child seems bored or frustrated.
- Help the child develop language by talking to him. Describe what you are doing or what you see on a walk.
- Don't be disturbed if the child seems aggressive when playing with other children. Be patient and correct the behavior in a gentle way.

The Play of Preschoolers

Preschoolers are proud of themselves and their abilities. Their muscles are developing rapidly. Their favorite words are "Watch me!" as they run, jump, and climb.

But children at this age tire quickly. Some still take a daily nap, and all need a change of pace from an hour of active play. That is the time for gluing a collage or looking at a book.

Because the preschooler can imagine and think well, and because his abilities are increasing quickly, he can learn much. He needs many more experiences from which to learn:

- Take him on a walk through the neighborhood or to the local store. Talk about whatever you see along the way.
- Encourage questions and safe exploration.

Can you remember dressing up in your mom's or dad's old clothing and playing

Young children develop fine motor skills by drawing and gross motor skills by exercising. They have fun dressing up in old clothes and pretending to be someone else.

house? Or maybe you had clothes or props for playing cowboys or pirates? Preschoolers also become interested in **role-playing,** which is *pretending to be someone else.* Providing children with old clothes and props will amuse them for a long time.

Passive Activities

Passive activities are *those that you watch or listen to, but do not join in.* Watching a baseball game is passive, as is watching television or reading a book.

Although passive activities don't get children into the action, they still affect them. Children learn how to do things by imitating people they watch. And their ideas and attitudes are affected by what they see and hear.

Watching Television

When you babysit for a child, it's tempting to make the television your helper. You might think of letting the child watch television so that you can do homework.

Keep in mind that television programs can have a great impact on children. They may contain violence or scary situations that children do not understand.

Get into the habit of sitting and watching television with children. Be ready to discuss what is going on and explain situations that may confuse them. Turn off the set or to another channel if the program is not suitable for children to watch. The table gives

TABLE 1 **Television Tips**

Watching television can be fun, and children can learn much from some programs. But don't rely on it to keep children occupied. Here are some do's and don'ts.

What to Do	What Not to Do
Check with the child's parents about what programs he or she can watch.	Let the child watch anything.
Stick to those shows and turn off the television when they are over.	Watch the shows that *you* want to see, but that the child isn't interested in.
Watch the program with the child.	Put the child in front of the television and leave the room.
Do other activities as well as watching television.	Tell the child to watch television when you can't think of anything else to do.
Talk about what you've seen.	Don't bother to comment on the show or answer questions.
Reassure the child if the program is violent or scary, and turn it off.	Let the children see shows that are not appropriate for them.
If there's more than one child, allow each to choose a program to watch.	Let the children fight over which show to watch.

you some other ideas about how to use television.

Watching television can be a good change of pace for children. But, like anything, too much can be harmful. Children shouldn't see television as the thing to do when they can't think of anything else. Challenge yourself to find interesting activities for children instead of relying on television.

Reading Books

Reading can be a time of quiet fun and exploration for young children. Try to get them to join in as much as possible. If they're old enough to read simple books, let them read to you or to younger children. Help them with words they don't know and give praise for the parts they do well. But don't be too quick to help. Children may just need a little more time to figure out a word.

Here are some tips on reading:

- Read simple stories in books that have pictures.
- Ask questions about the pictures or the story to involve the child.
- Read shorter stories to very young children. You can read them longer stories as they grow.
- Act out the stories when you're done.

Watching Real Things

Children are fascinated by watching people do things. You can use that as part of playing and learning. If you're looking for a change of pace, let the children help you make brownies or watch the neighbor work in his garden. You might just sit on the front porch or stoop together and watch people go by.

When you are reading a story, involve children. Stop and ask them questions about the characters, the setting, and the pictures. Finally, let them finish the story in their own way.

Playing in Groups

If you're taking care of more than one child, it's sometimes difficult to make sure that everyone is fully included in the activities you plan. But it is important that no child feels that he or she is being left out. To prevent this, plan activities in which everyone has to work together toward a common goal, such as putting together a puzzle or collecting rocks.

Each child has different abilities. It's easy for children to feel like failures if they are playing something in which they are not as good as the others around them. If you see that happening to one child, suggest a dif-ferent game, or help them master the game they are not good at by giving them practice.

Competitive Sports

If the children are playing competitive sports, be sure that some aren't left out from the start. A horrible feeling for a child is to be chosen last for teams all the time. Avoid the problem by finding an inventive way to choose teams. You might put all the children who like chocolate ice cream on one side, and all those who prefer strawberry on the other.

Finally, in any team game, try to play down the importance of winning. Make it clear that the main goal is to have fun.

Words to Learn

passive activities: activities that are watched or listened to, but not taken part in

role-playing: pretending to be someone else

Questions

1. Why is play important for children?
2. What kind of play is best for infants?
3. What kind of play is best for toddlers?
4. What kind of play is best for preschoolers?
5. What are passive activities? Do they have any effect on children?
6. Why should children go back and forth between active and passive activities?
7. What should you do if a child is being left out of games?

Chapter **20 Care and Safety**

Objectives

After reading this chapter, you will be able to:

☐ *care for children by meeting their needs,*

☐ *set limits and make rules for children.*

Children need an adult or teenager to care for them. They may be too young to feed or dress themselves. They need someone to protect them from danger. They may need someone to comfort them when they're upset. They rely on others to set limits for them.

Parents and other caregivers care for children by meeting these needs. They help guide children's behavior by setting limits and sticking to them.

All the children's needs must be met. This means meeting the child's physical, mental, and social needs. A caregiver not only feeds a child. He plays with the child and sees to it that the child feels comfortable and loved. A caregiver is always looking for opportunities to help the child learn. Through such activities children grow and become self-reliant.

147

Caring for Children

When you care for children, they look to you for all the things that their parents provide—from a glass of juice to a bedtime story. You must meet their physical, mental, and social needs.

Physical Needs

Caregivers meet children's physical needs in these ways:

- feeding them,
- dressing them appropriately,
- bathing them,
- getting them to bed on time,
- keeping them away from possible danger.

Feeding. If you are going to make a simple meal for the children, find out from their parents what foods are to be served. Make the children feel comfortable by following their usual mealtime routine. Have them eat in the same place and at the same time as they usually do. Feed them nutritious meals and snacks.

Bedtime. It also helps to follow the children's usual routine at bedtime. If sleepy children insist that it's not bedtime yet, a story or a word game will often help them change their minds. Once children are asleep, check on them often to be sure that they are asleep and safe.

Safety. Keeping children safe is important. Children will usually try anything, often more than once. Babies put things in their mouths; toddlers climb stairs; preschoolers may be fascinated by water; older children run, hide, and disappear. As much as possible, caregivers should **childproof**, or *make the area safe for children*.

Since babies constantly put things in their mouths, you should never give them small toys that they might swallow accidentally. Crawling babies and toddlers need space, but use gates to restrict them to places they can explore safely.

Older children can be hurt badly in the kitchen. Keep breakable glasses and dishes and hot pots away from them. Closets that contain dangerous substances should be locked securely.

Childproofing is usually done by parents, but a babysitter who knows what to look for can help make sure that a child is safe.

The Teen Tips section at the end of this unit suggests other ways to make children's environments safe and to make children comfortable.

Mental Needs

Caregivers can help children learn about the world and develop their mental skills in these ways:

- playing games that are appropriate to a child's skill,
- changing to a new game when a child tires of what he or she is doing,
- talking to the child to help him or her learn and develop language.

You can review some of the play ideas in this unit to help you meet children's mental needs.

Social Needs

Children look to caregivers for emotional support and guidance. Be ready to praise a drawing or a project that a child has done. Encourage a child who is tired or frustrated with a game or toy.

You can help children socially in other ways:

- giving them love and paying attention to them; this helps them feel loved and secure,
- responding quickly when they are hurt or upset,
- teaching children to get along with others—by sharing toys, for instance,
- helping children learn to communicate.

Young children may cry when their parents leave. Be understanding. Often, you can quiet them by interesting them in a toy or a song. They usually get over their unhappiness quickly.

Children who wake up frightened need to be reassured that they are safe. Never make fun of their fears. Comfort them by talking or singing to them, or by holding or rocking them.

If a child you are caring for does something wrong, there may be many reasons. Understanding the reason can help you deal with the situation. If the child is simply tired, try reading a story quietly or playing a record.

Sometimes, children may misbehave to test you. An important part of caring for children is knowing how to set and maintain limits.

Children need someone to comfort them and to reassure them with love and affection. Caregivers should not take the feelings of children lightly.

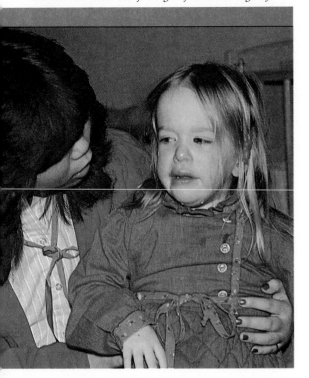

Rules and Limits

Children need to have limits placed on what they can do and where they can go. Setting these limits is the parents' responsibility, but other caregivers must uphold them. It's always important to ask parents what limits they have set.

Setting Limits

Some limits are set to protect the children's safety. You should refuse to take them in, or near, dangerous areas that cannot be childproofed.

If the children are going to be outdoors near water, make sure that you review their parents' rules for water play. If they are going to use bicycles or other wheel toys, point out how far the children can travel. Such boundaries prevent accidents.

Limits also apply to behavior, such as what time to go to bed or how two children should play together. Insisting on the regular bedtime is important. Stopping fights can help children learn how to get along with each other.

Testing the Limits

Sometimes, you'll get an argument from a child, even if a rule is strictly enforced by the parents. The child may tell you that she's allowed to cross the street or climb high trees.

Children like to try out forbidden activities when someone new is in charge of them. But they need to know that the limits hold true at all times. Be firm about what is permitted.

One way to handle this problem is to focus on what children may do, rather than on what they may not do. "You can run all the way to . . ." is a more positive way of suggesting limits than starting every sentence with *Don't.*

Of course, sometimes you can't enforce a limit by gentle reasoning. When a child chases a ball into the street, you don't have time to reason with him. You must take immediate and complete control. Either call out a sharp command or grab him, or do both.

Providing Distractions

A good way to prevent arguments over limits is to provide distractions. Children who are busy with safe, interesting play are far less likely to become restless and get into trouble. You can **distract** children, or *lead them away from something they shouldn't do by interesting them in another activity.*

Planning interesting activities is important. If it's raining and you're stuck indoors, try an art project. Finger painting, which preschoolers enjoy, can be set up with a minimum of effort and supplies.

While you're in the kitchen preparing lunch, arrange an area in sight but out of your way. There the children can keep

TABLE 1 **How to Set Limits**

Children will feel more secure if they know what their limits are. And they will be happier if they're told what they *can* do—not what they can't.

What to Say	What Not to Say
"Let's read a story."	"Stop running around!"
"You can play here in the living room."	"Get out of the kitchen!"
"You can phone George to say hello."	"Don't go out!"
"You can play on the swings."	"Stay off the jungle gym!"
"Let's play with the toy truck."	"Put down your brother's toys!"
"Pet the dog gently."	"Don't hit the dog!"
"You can stay up until 8:00."	"You have to go to bed soon."

T E E N   I S S U E

What You Should Know About Child Abuse

Child abuse occurs in all levels of society—among rich people and poor, among all races and minorities. Seventy-four percent of the victims are under five years old.

Parents who are unemployed, have marital problems, or are rearing children alone are more likely to abuse their children. Many have more worries than other parents. They may take out their frustrations or hurt on their children.

The pattern of child abuse is often passed on in families. Many parents who abuse their children were abused when they were small.

Child abuse can be defined as *harm, injury, or sexual molestation of a child, usually by a parent or guardian.* There are various forms of abuse.

- *Neglect* occurs when the parent fails to give the child basic love and care. A parent may not feed or clothe the child properly. He or she may not provide medical attention when the child is sick, or may leave the child unattended for long periods of time.

- *Assault* is physically harming a child.

- *Sexual molestation* takes place when an adult persuades or forces a child to have sexual contact with him or her. Most of the victims of molestation are girls. Eighty percent of the time, the abuser is a man the victim knows well, usually her father or a close family member.

- *Emotional abuse* occurs when a child is constantly yelled at, is tortured by teasing and ridicule, or is continually made to feel bad about himself.

If you suspect abuse of a child you know, seek guidance from your parents or another adult you can confide in. After you have talked it over, and if there really does seem to be a problem, the adult can call a local or national group that deals with child abuse.

---

busy, perhaps imitating your actions by using plastic bowls and spoons.

Races or ball games that you supervise can help children improve their coordination. Games also prevent the arguments and fights that result from boredom.

The Dangers of Anger

You may become frustrated and angry when children disobey or argue. At these times, it is very important to control your anger. Shouting, hitting, or calling children names will not help anyone. In fact, such behavior can make a bad situation worse.

Angry behavior from you sets a bad example for the child. Showing anger also tends to build up anger and resentment in the child. He or she will become less cooperative in the future. And the parents of the child will object if the child is not treated with respect.

Children have lots of energy and little fear of situations. The caregiver directs their energy into fun and safe activities, and does not endanger the children's physical health.

After David had pushed over his sister's building blocks three or four times, Annie, the babysitter, was furious. She really wanted to shake David. Instead, she took a deep breath and counted to ten. Then she led David off to the side.

"David, I get angry when I see you knocking down those blocks," she said, "especially when I've asked you not to. You're going to have to sit in the corner now until you learn to play with your sister without upsetting her."

Annie told David she was angry with him without acting out her feelings. When you're angry, there's often enough annoyance in your voice to make your point to the child without shouting or spanking. Communicating to the child in this way teaches that, with self-control, a person can express anger in acceptable ways that do not hurt others.

Words to Remember

child abuse: harm, injury, or sexual molestation of a child, usually by a parent or guardian

childproof: to make an area safe for children

distract: to lead children away from something they shouldn't do by interesting them in another activity

Questions

1. Think of two ways to meet children's physical needs.

2. List two ways to meet children's mental needs.

3. List two ways to meet children's social needs.

4. Why is it important to childproof an area or home?

5. What is a good way to state limits to children?

6. What are the dangers of showing anger to children?

Chapter **21 Babysitting: Earning and Learning**

HELP WANTED
Someone to care for and protect the most precious things in my world. Low pay, but great experience. Write Box 609.

A parent probably wouldn't phrase an ad for a babysitter in quite this way. But it describes the job you're being hired for each time you care for other people's children.

As a sitter, you take on the parents' responsibilities for the children's safety, welfare, and happiness while their parents are away. If a child whom you're watching is sick or hurt or unhappy, it's up to you to take the right action.

You might say that babysitting is a teen profession that takes knowledge and sympathy to care for another human being.

153

Being An Employee

Babysitting gives you valuable experience in caring for children, making decisions, and dealing with new people and new situations. It can help you decide if you'd like a career working with children. Sitting can also be fun. You may develop close relationships with the children you care for regularly.

You'll also earn money. Babysitting is a business. And you'll be most successful at it if you understand what the job requires, and if you're organized and businesslike.

When parents hire you to babysit for their children, you become their employee. Like any employee, you'll do a better job when you understand the responsibilities of your job.

Get the Information You Need

The Schedule. Before the parents leave, make sure of the following points:

- What is the schedule for mealtime and bedtime?
- Do the children take any medicines?
- What foods are they allowed to have for meals and snacks?
- Do they have any allergies or fears?
- What are the rules for watching television?

The House. Find out about the house, too.

- Where are the children's rooms and bathrooms?
- Where are the light switches?
- How do you work the appliances you will need to use?

- Where are flashlights and first-aid supplies kept?
- Where are the fire escapes?

Limits and Rules. You should also find out how the parents want you to guide their children. You need to know, for example, if it's acceptable to take away privileges when the child misbehaves.

Sometimes, it helps to go over rules with the parents while the children are there. Then the children know that you are aware of the limits.

Phone Numbers. You should also get some important phone numbers:

- the number where you can reach the parents

The skills that you learn as a babysitter (arriving on time, following directions, and assuming responsibility) can be transferred to other jobs.

- the fire department
- the police department
- the local poison control center
- the nearest hospital emergency room
- the child's doctor
- the local ambulance service
- a nearby family member or friend

The babysitter's checklist in the table shows you how to organize all these numbers.

Act Responsibly

Your employers may tell you to make yourself at home. But that doesn't mean that you can behave exactly as you would in your own home. Here are some do's and don'ts:

- Check with the parents about snacks and about using the phone, the television, and the stereo.
- If you do use the phone, keep the call short. You wouldn't want to tie up the line, because the parents might be trying to reach you.
- Don't entertain friends on the job. Your job is to watch the children, and friends would be a distraction.
- While the parents are out, you're responsible for their house. You should leave it at least as neat as you found it. If you prepare a meal or a snack for the children, you should clean up the dishes. Help them put away any toys or games they've gotten out to play with you.
- Take a few precautions. Don't give information over the phone. Don't say that you're a babysitter, or tell the caller where the parents are or when they'll be

back. If the caller insists, give the phone number of where the parents can be reached.

- Do not open the door to strangers. If someone shows up at the door asking to use the phone for an emergency call, offer to make the call yourself. Jot the number down for safekeeping.

Dealing with Problems

Sometimes accidents happen. Children tumble off swings and cut themselves or break bones. They pull heavy objects onto themselves. They get burned or bruised or scratched.

If an accident occurs, you must be ready and able to deal with it at once. One general rule to remember is to *stay calm.* You may feel upset, but getting excited will only make things worse.

The phone numbers that you got from the parents should be kept near the phone. Then, if an accident occurs, you can easily find the number to call.

First Aid

As the term suggests, **first aid** is *what can be done right away to help the victim of an accident.* It's important to know what you should or should *not* do. Incorrect handling or improper emergency treatment can cause further injury. The box describes some of the simple actions that you can take.

If you want to know more about first aid, you can take a class offered in your community.

FEATURE

First Aid

For anything beyond the simplest first aid, call an adult for help. For a child who is unconscious, has difficulty breathing, is badly burned, has broken a bone, or is bleeding severely, call the ambulance immediately.

Of course, you can treat minor problems yourself. But if you have a question about a cut, call the child's parents, a neighbor, or your own parents.

The following information will help you with problems that may arise:

- *Bites (animal or human):* Wash the wound with water, then clean it with soap and water. Cover the wound with gauze. Call the doctor.

- *Bites (insect):* For minor bites, wash and apply an antiseptic or calamine lotion. For bee, hornet, or wasp stings, remove the stinger with a tweezers, and apply either a paste of baking soda and water or vinegar. **Caution:** Some people are highly allergic to stings. If the child is short of breath or faint or has stomach pain, call the doctor immediately.

- *Burns (minor):* Immediately run cold water on the burn for about five minutes.

- *Choking:* Use the Heimlich maneuver. Stand behind the child with both your arms around him. Clasp your hands together, then place one fist into the area just over the child's navel. Press up rapidly several times until the object pops out. If the object doesn't come out, seek help immediately.

- *Earache:* Pain can be relieved by covering the ear with a warm towel or heating pad set on low. Call the doctor.

- *Electric shock:* Don't touch the child until his or her contact with electricity is broken, or you will be shocked. Turn off the electricity if you can. If you can't, pull or push the child away from the source of the shock with a stick, cloth, or rope—never with anything metal. If the child is not breathing, apply artificial respiration if you know how. Call the ambulance immediately.

- *Nosebleed:* Keep the child seated and tilt the head back slightly. Grasp the lower end of the nose and press in gently for a few minutes. If the pressure doesn't stop the bleeding, place a small strip of gauze in the bleeding nostril. Call the doctor if bleeding continues.

- *Poison:* Call the poison control center. Be sure to say just what the substance is: different poisons require different **antidotes,** or *remedies to counteract the effects of poisons.* Keep the container and take it with you if you go to the doctor or hospital.

- *Scrapes and bruises:* Clean scrapes with soap and water and apply antiseptic and gauze. For bruises, apply a clean washcloth wrung out in cold water.

- *Small cuts:* Apply pressure to stop the bleeding. Wash the area and apply a mild antiseptic and a bandage.

Fire

In case of fire, don't take the time to call the fire department or try to put out the blaze yourself. Be sure that you know where *all* the children are. Get them and then walk, don't run, to the nearest exit. Once you are all safely out, call the fire department from a neighbor's house.

If smoke becomes a problem, cover your faces with damp cloths and stay close to the floor. Feel each door before you open it to see if the next room is on fire.

Other Emergencies

Caring for children also means taking responsibility for them—as well as for yourself—during emergencies such as severe weather or break-ins. Each situation will be different, but follow these general rules:

- Don't panic.
- Use the telephone to call for help if you're not in immediate danger.
- If the emergency is threatening weather, listen to radio or television bulletins.

Remember that emergencies require quick thinking and common-sense decisions. Above all, *stay calm.*

Running a Babysitting Business

If you want your babysitting jobs to multiply, you'll have to be businesslike in your

TABLE 1 **A Babysitter's Emergency Card**

Parents' names _____

Phone number where parents can be reached _____

Fire department _____

Police department _____

Poison control center _____

Child's doctor _____

Ambulance _____

Hospital emergency room _____

Nearby relative or friend _____

    name _____

    number _____

dealings with your employers. Your rates, hours, and responsibilities should be clear to both you and your employers before you start work. And both parties should stick to the agreement.

Make Appointments and Keep Them

One of the biggest mistakes you can make as a babysitter is to forget a sitting appointment. Almost as bad in many parents' eyes is a last-minute cancellation.

To prevent these mistakes, keep an appointment calendar next to the telephone at home. Write everything in it—the club meeting, your brother's birthday party, and all your babysitting jobs. When someone calls to offer you a job, you'll be able to tell at a glance whether you're free on that day.

If you have to cancel, let your employers know as early as possible. They'll appreciate it if you try to find someone who can take your place.

Agree on Rates and Hours

When parents call, clearly state what you will charge for your babysitting services. You won't seem very businesslike if you tell

---

Before parents leave, get important information from them. Write down important phone numbers, and be sure to have parents tell you where they can be reached in emergencies.

your employers to pay you what they think is fair. And it's possible that you'll end up being underpaid.

Find out what other sitters in your area charge, and set about the same rate. Consider charging extra for difficult jobs—large families, infants, or late hours.

You should also establish the length of the job. Find out what time to arrive and what time the parents expect to return home. Make arrangements for transportation. Will the parents be picking you up? How will you get home? By being clear about these details from the start, you'll prevent confusion later on.

Do Work, Not Favors

As a babysitter, your job is to care for the children, not to clean the house or do the laundry. Some chores, like cleaning up the child's dishes after a snack, should be done. But if your employers begin to expect extra favors, like taking out the garbage or cleaning the living room, explain politely that your rate doesn't include housework. Also point out that the extra work takes you away from the children.

You have a right to expect certain things from your employers. They should provide you with the information and instructions you need to do your job. If they find themselves out later than planned, they should call to let you know. If they don't, tell them in a friendly way that you'd appreciate a call next time.

A Job Well Done

By being clear about things like rates, hours, and responsibilities, good sitters help themselves and their employers. And by acting responsibly and giving children their undivided attention, they live up to the trust their employers have placed in them.

Parents are always looking for good sitters, and word travels fast. Be a good babysitter, and you'll probably have more jobs than you can handle.

Words to Remember

antidotes: remedies to counteract the effects of poisons
first aid: what can be done right away to help the victim of an accident

Questions

1. List at least five telephone numbers you should have when babysitting.
2. Give examples of three pieces of information you need from parents before babysitting for their children.
3. What should you do when you're babysitting and a stranger calls?
4. What are the general rules for handling emergencies when you're babysitting?
5. What should you do in case of fire when you're babysitting?
6. What three topics should you discuss with parents to show that you're a businesslike babysitter?

Chapter 22 Ready for Parenthood?

Objectives

After reading this chapter, you will be able to:

☐ *list the challenges of parenthood,*

☐ *describe the financial and emotional costs of parenthood,*

☐ *give examples of the rewards of parenthood.*

"You know what the real difference is between babysitting and being a parent?" Donna asked as she changed the baby.

"What?" her friend Gilda wanted to know. She and Donna had been friends in high school, but now Donna was married and a mother.

"The real difference," Donna said, "is that there's no one returning home at eleven o'clock at night to take care of the child again. *You're* the one who's in charge. It's scary and exciting at the same time."

"I know," Gilda said. "I think about what fun it would be to be married and have a baby. But then I get a little frightened, too."

Donna put the baby in her playpen. "It's different when you're the one responsible. Little Jan depends on Mario and me. It makes you think."

The Challenge of Parenthood

Donna and Mario had fallen in love. They knew they were young for marriage, but they wanted to get married anyway.

Their parents asked them to wait. Donna's parents thought she ought to go to college so she could teach. Mario's mother wanted him to go to community college and study accounting.

But the young people overcame their parents' objections. Donna and Mario got married right after they graduated from high school.

Dreams and Reality

Two months later, Donna was pregnant. Neither of them had planned it that way or thought much about having a baby. Donna decided to give up her job, and she postponed plans for school. Mario withdrew his application to college and got a job driving a delivery truck.

Even with these changes in plans, however, they were both excited. They were in love with each other, and they looked forward to having a child. It was exciting to think about another human being, one they would care for and share their happiness with. They wanted to help this new person grow and learn. They were a little nervous, but they had each other and a lot of hope.

The Baby

Once Jan arrived, Donna's and Mario's lives changed completely. They still had their love, of course, and some fun, too. But they had a lot more besides. It was hard for them to believe that anything as small as an infant could require so much work.

There was washing and diapering and feeding around the clock—the list of needs seemed to go on and on. Donna and Mario found they had to rearrange their lives around Jan's needs.

But they were lucky, too. They cared for each other and for their baby. They were able to get help and advice from their parents. And they were smart enough to use that advice to help them over the rough spots.

A lot of time and energy is devoted to being a parent. Changing diapers is only one of the many tasks that parents and other caregivers need to do.

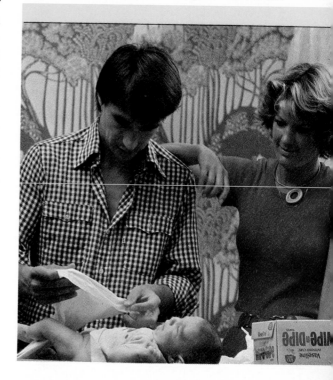

F E A T U R E

Scenes From a Marriage

Everybody seems to love the soaps on television. However, most of them give a pretty unreal view of the world. Here is a more down-to-earth picture of the lives of young parents.

Scene 1. It's Saturday, but the alarm rings at 7:00 A.M. Mario has taken a weekend job driving a truck for a small moving company. Donna's been up since 6:00, anyway, for Jan's 6:00 A.M. feeding. Because Jan was cranky this morning, it took Donna a full hour to get her fed and back to bed. Donna and Mario have a quick breakfast before he goes off to his job.

"Better try to get some sleep now," Mario says. "You were up for the 3:00 A.M. feeding, too."

"Too much to do," Donna says.

"Got to get Jan to the doctor for her three-month checkup and go buy a stroller."

Scene 2. Late afternoon. Mario is in the kitchen preparing dinner.

"Guess what, honey," Donna says when she comes in with Jan. "The doctor said that Jan has grown another inch and gained another 1½ pounds."

"That's my big girl!" Mario says as he picks the baby up.

"She was so funny in the waiting room this morning," Donna tells him. "She and two other babies were babbling and cooing to each other."

"She'll be a real talker," says Mario. "Did you find a stroller?"

"Yes—on sale, too," Donna answers. "We went shopping after I bought it, and I think Jan likes it. She was able to watch things as we walked."

The Cost of Parenthood

One way to measure the cost of anything is to figure out what you have to give up in order to get it. When you think of the costs of being a parent, think first of the things you have to give up.

Obvious Costs

First, you don't have as much time. The child needs attention and care. There's no time clock that you can punch at five o'clock.

Second, caring for the infant takes a lot of energy. Parents of young infants often find that they are too tired to do other things.

Third, children may be small, but they are not cheap. There are doctor bills and clothes to buy. Baby food and disposable diapers can get expensive, too. And while two may live in a snug apartment happily, three may need more space—and that means a higher rent.

For this reason, it is important to have **financial stability**. Parents need *the ability to meet all their expected everyday living costs.* Couples who cannot manage the extra costs should think twice about having a family until they can.

Less Obvious Costs

Parenthood has emotional costs as well. For instance, young parents may feel jealous of their child. They may feel that the child takes too much of their partner's time, leaving them out. This puts extra pressure on their relationship.

Also, loving an infant seems like a one-way street. The baby can't tell you how much it loves you. But a smile or a hug helps keep you going.

To meet these emotional demands, parents need something even more important than money—they need **emotional maturity**. They must *be secure enough in their own self-image to be able to meet the emotional demands and responsibilities they face.*

This maturity includes being able to give love without expecting it back right away. It also means being grown up enough so that they don't think of their own needs all the time.

Costs in Personal Development

Because being a parent is a twenty-four hour job, there may be little time left over for outside activities. Donna and Mario want to continue their education, but they have decided to wait.

Young adults are just beginning to get to know themselves and what they want out of life. Yet, all the exploring that needs to be done to develop a sense of self gets sidetracked when a baby comes.

Fortunately, babies grow to be toddlers, then preschoolers. Once children are older, parents can spend more time on their own interests. And parents and children can always enjoy doing things together.

The Rewards of Parenthood

There is more to parenthood than the costs—ask your own parents. Some moments make up for everything. Listen to the way parents speak of their children. Watch the light in their eyes when they say, "Do you know what my little David did yesterday?"

Children are long-term investments. The bond formed by love and shared experience, by two lives helping each other develop, is emotionally very rewarding.

In an effort to meet their baby's physical and mental needs, parents find that they have less time for themselves.

Children make you start thinking differently. Before you become a parent, you need to think only about yourself and, if you're married, about your partner. When you become a parent, you think about the future. What kind of world will it be when your child is grown? Is that what you want? What can you do to change it?

Helping children learn brings special satisfaction. Parents thrill to see their children master new skills. From the infant who begins to walk to the student graduating from high school, children give joy to their parents.

Parents enjoy watching a child grow, and they find it fascinating to observe a person develop. And seeing a child develop his or her self-concept leads parents to think about themselves, too. In fact, parents learn from children.

Becoming a parent may be the most rewarding step to take in life. It involves a lot and asks much of you. But if you're ready for parenthood, your life can be wonderfully rich.

Fathers share in primary responsibilities, such as changing diapers, feeding and entertaining, and showing love and affection.

Words to Remember

financial stability: the ability to meet all your expected everyday living costs

emotional maturity: being secure enough in your own self-image to be able to meet the emotional demands and responsibilities you face

Questions

1. Is being in love with someone enough reason to start a family? Why or why not?
2. What is the major difference between being a parent and being responsible for a child now and then?
3. Think of two costs of parenthood and two rewards of parenthood.
4. List three things you feel you need before you're ready for parenthood.

Chapter 23 Careers Helping Children

Objectives

After reading this chapter, you will be able to:

☐ *identify the traits that are useful for people who work with children,*

☐ *describe some jobs that involve working directly with children,*

☐ *describe some jobs that involve working for children.*

They cry, they spit up, they run around, they fight, and they constantly demand attention. Working with children can be exhausting. But when they smile at you or at something they've learned, the work seems worthwhile. People who enjoy children often find jobs that involve working with children. There are many possible jobs and they all call for such characteristics as an interest in children, creativity, sensitivity, and a sense of humor.

One job comes immediately to mind—a parent. The mother and father of a child have full-time responsibility for the child's health, safety, learning, and happiness. But many other people also work with and for children. Some even care for children while the parents work.

Characteristics Useful for Working with Children

Before exploring actual jobs and careers that involve working with children, let's find out what traits such careers call for. Some of the characteristics are mental and some are emotional.

Mental Characteristics

Child-care workers need to have certain mental abilities and interests to be able to work well with children:

- Are you interested in children and how they learn and grow?
- Are you adaptable? Child-care workers need to switch activities when children aren't enjoying something.
- Are you willing to learn about children?
- Can you treat each child as an individual, with his or her own unique qualities?
- Do you have **creativity**—*the ability to use your imagination to do things in new ways?* This characteristic can help you think of new and interesting activities for children.
- Do you respect children as people? You must show children that you take their play as seriously as they do.

Emotional Characteristics

It is important for child-care workers to have certain emotional traits.

- Are you enthusiastic and willing to join with children in their play? Playing with them shows them that you think they're important.

- Are you patient, tolerant, and calm? These qualities can help you play long, repetitive games and settle arguments.
- Can you put yourself in the children's place? If so, you'll be able to calm their fears.
- Do you have a sense of humor? Having one can help you make a toddler laugh at a fall, instead of crying.

If you have these qualities, you may be interested in some of the careers described below. Although this is just a sampling of the many jobs available, it should give you a basic idea of the variety of work you can do.

Jobs Working Directly with Children

Many people work directly with children. Some provide health care; others help children learn. Some perform the many tasks that are called *parenting*. Still others help children play. Let's look at some of these jobs more closely.

Entry-Level Jobs

A *mother's helper* cares for the children of a working parent or parents. This work is usually done in the child's home. (A day-care worker, which you read about in chapter 16, does similar work in a day-care center.)

A mother's helper sometimes lives with the family and cares for the child in the evenings as well. In that case, he or she is often paid room and board as well as a salary. Babysitting experience and home

F E A T U R E

Learning About Careers

An important step in searching for a career is to learn about various careers. First, however, decide what you want in a career.

Making a Career Decision

Do you want to work indoors or outdoors? In an office, a store, a factory, or a home? Alone or with others? Leading others or being supervised? Part-time or full-time? Days or nights? Do you want to earn a lot of money, or will you accept less if other conditions are to your liking? Do you want to travel or stay close to home?

Answering these questions prepares you to analyze which careers match what you want. The basic things to learn about a career are what kind of work it involves, what the working conditions are like, what training is required, and what the future of the career is.

Finding Out About Careers

Reading and Inquiring. How can you learn these facts about careers? Some jobs are described in this book. To learn about others—and to get even more information on the ones discussed here—you can turn to counselors, teachers, and school and public librarians.

You can also write to a **trade or professional association.** This is a *group of workers that educates the public about the work they perform.* Such groups can give you expert, up-to-date information about careers. A librarian can help you find the names and addresses of these groups.

Interviewing. Another way to learn about a career is to talk to someone in that job. People who enjoy their work love to talk about it. And you'll appreciate the chance to find out exactly what you want to know. If you do talk to someone about his or her career, follow these steps:

- Make an appointment when it's convenient for the worker.

- Show up on time.

- Write down your questions beforehand, so you can ask them in an organized way and not waste the person's time.

- Ask if you could take a tour if one is allowed.

- Ask for a brochure or flyer which describes the job.

- Say thank you, and—better yet—send a thank-you note. The thoughtfulness you show will be appreciated.

economics courses are helpful for this job.

A *camp counselor* works with children in a very satisfying way. Many children spend part or all of their summers in camps. There they learn new skills, such as swimming and making crafts, and enjoy the outdoors. These skills are often taught by high school and college students. Such students also work in day camps that care for children after school.

Jobs That Require Extra Training

A *teacher's aide* helps a teacher either with paperwork or with actual instruction in the classroom. The training needed for this job varies from one school system to another. Many two-year colleges offer a course of study leading to a degree for teacher's aides. With extra course work, the aide can eventually become a teacher.

A *team coach* works with children who enjoy athletics. Many coaches are hired by school systems, but some work for the community parks department. Coaches have a very important role. They instruct children not only in the basic skills of a particular sport, but also in good sportsmanship. Many young adults look up to their coaches.

Jobs That Require a Degree

How heavy is the earth? How many breeds of dog are there? These are the kinds of questions asked of a *children's librarian.* Whether they work in a school or a public library, librarians help children find information and good books. Someone hired to be a librarian needs to have a college degree, and often a master's degree as well.

The doctors who care for children are called *pediatricians.* (**Pediatrics** means *the study of children's health.*) Like all doctors, they've gotten extensive training in both college and medical school, as well as in an internship at a hospital. They may have their own practice or work in a hospital. The work can be demanding, but most pediatricians find happiness in helping children.

Coaches are needed for schools and for recreational departments of towns and cities. If you like sports, the outdoors, and working with people, a coaching job may be for you.

Teachers feel a great deal of satisfaction, too. Whatever their students' ages, teachers find many rewards in helping children learn new concepts and skills. Many teachers spend long hours at home planning lessons and grading papers. Some even plan lessons and gather material during their vacations.

Jobs Working for Children

Many people work in jobs that are related to children, but they don't work directly with children. These people may create products for children or work behind the scenes in a school. Whatever they do, they need to have the same characteristics as people who work with children.

Entry-Level Jobs

Cafeteria workers prepare food and serve it to children in the school. These workers should enjoy cooking and being with children. Patience and friendliness are a big help, too. Many mothers find this a convenient job, because it allows them to work when their children are at school and to be home after school is out.

Store clerks work in stores that sell clothes, books, toys, or sports equipment for children. It's important for store clerks to know about children's interests and abilities. A parent may ask the clerk to compare one toy with another, or to describe the safety features of various car seats. A clerk who can give an informative answer is very helpful.

Teaching is a wonderful opportunity to help young people learn and grow. Teaching new concepts and skills can be very rewarding.

Clerks can work either part time or full time, days or nights. Many also work on weekends. A high school diploma and math ability often help them in getting the job.

Jobs That Require Extra Training

Children's book writers write books for children. They may write picture books for toddlers or novels for teenagers. There is no single way of becoming a writer, though most writers have college degrees. The most important requirements are the desire to write and the creativity to capture children's interests.

A *toy designer* may seem an ideal job for someone who is creative and likes children. Designers often build a model of a new toy and test it by giving the toy to children and watching them play!

There is no school for toy design, but college courses in child psychology and behavior, as well as in art, help to prepare people for this career. Some toy designers work at home and sell their ideas to businesses. Others work for toy companies.

Jobs That Require a Degree

School administrators run one or more public schools. While they do not work with children every day, like teachers, their decisions affect what children learn and how. A *principal* heads up only one school. He or she makes sure that the school teaches what the community wants to have taught. A *school superintendent* controls many schools. This official works with the school board to decide what will be taught in every grade of the school system.

Both jobs require advanced college degrees in teaching and/or school administration. Teaching experience also helps.

A *school dietitian* plans and directs the purchase and preparation of the food in the school cafeteria. His or her aim is to provide food that meets a budget, appeals to children, and satisfies their nutritional needs. A strong knowledge of nutrition is essential, and dietitians usually have a college degree in foods or food service. Most also have a master's degree in food service. Management training is also a helpful background to have in this profession.

Words to Remember

creativity: the ability to use your imagination to do things in new ways

pediatrics: the study of children's health

trade or professional association: a group of workers that educates the public about the work they perform

Questions

1. List three mental characteristics that are important for working with children.
2. List three emotional characteristics that are important for working with children.
3. Think of three jobs that involve working with children, one at each job level.
4. Think of three jobs that involve working for children, one at each job level.

Here's a handy set of hints for anyone who babysits or watches a younger brother or sister. Much of what you need to know about caring for children is right here.

1. How to feed babies and toddlers.

2. How to diaper a baby.

3. How to bathe a child.

4. Child safety.

5. Making your own toys.

6. Quiet things to do.

How to Feed Babies and Toddlers

Babies

The baby is crying, and you're sure it's hunger. In the refrigerator is a bottle ready to use—but now what? Here are some hints on how to feed a bottle to a baby.

Warm the milk by running the bottle under warm tap water for one or two minutes. Or set the bottle in a bowl of warm tap water so that you can hold the baby while you're heating the milk.

Check the temperature of the milk by shaking the bottle upside down so that a few drops fall on your wrist.

Pick up the baby by putting one hand behind her head and neck and the other on her bottom.

Cuddle the baby, supporting her with your arm and holding her close. After a while, hold the baby with your other arm.

Make sure that the neck of the bottle is full of liquid so that the baby takes in less air.

Midway through feeding the baby, you need to burp her to let out the air that may have entered her stomach.

This is the most common way to burp a baby, and it's comfortable for both her and you. Pat the baby firmly but gently on the back until she burps. This may take several minutes. Cover your shoulder with a towel in case some milk comes up.

You can also burp the baby by sitting her up on your lap. Hold her steady with one hand and pat her gently on the back with the other.

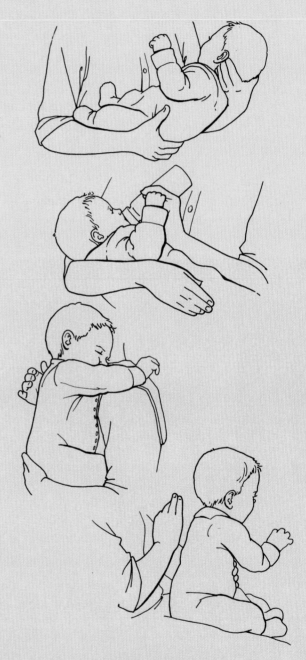

Toddlers

Before the meal, make sure that the high chair is in a safe location, out of reach of the stove and other dangers. If possible, strap the child into the chair. Keep the child company during the meal.

Heat the food, but don't make it too hot. What is warm to you might be hot to a toddler.

Toddlers enjoy feeding themselves. Cut meat, vegetables, fruit, or cheese into tiny pieces. Put bite-sized pieces of food on a plastic plate, or right on the tray of the high chair if the food won't cause a mess.

Food like applesauce, of course, calls for spoons. Give the toddler a low bowl and a small spoon. Allowing him to practice eating with a spoon is more important than keeping his face clean.

Toddlers can drink from a cup. Serve liquids in a two-handled plastic cup or a training cup that has a cover.

Encourage the toddler to feed himself by smiling and praising his efforts. Make up stories about the food. If food spills, don't yell—accidents are bound to happen.

Don't force a child to eat something if he refuses. When the parents return, tell them what the child ate. When the meal is finished, clean the toddler's hands and face. Then clean up everything else—high chair, plate, floor, walls, and you!

How to Diaper a Baby

Diapering may not be the most fun you'll ever have when caring for a baby, but it really isn't that bad. Parents may use either disposable or cloth diapers. A well-prepared babysitter should be able to handle each kind. But before putting the clean diaper on, you have to take the old one off!

Cleaning the baby

Take off the old diaper, putting it in the garbage or diaper pail. Clean the baby using warm water or diaper towels. Be sure to wipe from front to back. Add powder or baby oil if the parents use it.

Putting on the diaper

Now you're ready to put the diaper on the baby. Lift the baby's legs by holding both ankles with one hand. Slide the diaper underneath.

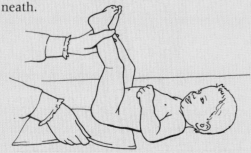

If you're using a disposable diaper, simply fasten it using the tapes on the diaper.

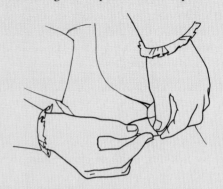

If you're using a cloth diaper, you must fasten it with pins. Always put your finger inside the diaper to protect the baby when you pin the diaper.

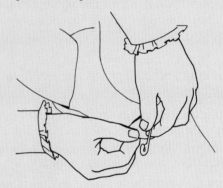

Diapering tips

■ Use a clean, flat surface, like a changing table, crib, or a pad or towel on the floor.
■ Don't leave the baby alone on a table—he may turn over and fall off.
■ If the baby has a diaper rash, apply ointment or powder.
■ Play with the baby while diapering.

How to Bathe a Child

Parents may ask you to bathe the child you're sitting for. Bath time can be fun for both of you if you allow the child to play and enjoy herself. But the object of a bath is to clean the child.

Bathing an infant

Fill with water a small tub or a sink lined with a towel. The water should come up to the baby's navel when she is put in the bath. Test the temperature of the water by using your elbow—it should be warm and not hot.

Hold the infant securely in the tub. Keep her away from the fixtures in the sink. And be sure to keep her head out of the water.

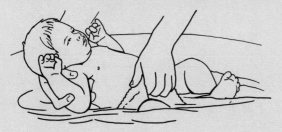

With a face towel, wash her head and face first. Use a very mild baby soap. Then rinse them and dry her head. After washing and rinsing the rest of her body, remove her from the water and wrap her in a towel to dry.

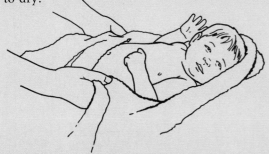

Bathing a Toddler

Toddlers can sit up in the bathroom tub. Add a small amount of warm water and some plastic toys and watch them play. Don't leave the bathroom!

To wash a toddler's hair, use a baby shampoo and rinse by pouring water on his head away from his face.

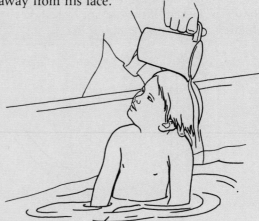

Once you've washed and rinsed the toddler, take him out of the tub and dry him off. The toddler may be able to help dress himself, but you can assist him with the rest.

Child Safety

To learn about their world, children explore. Sometimes these explorations aren't safe, but since they haven't learned yet, the children don't know it. Caregivers are responsible for making sure that children are safe at all times.

When changing diapers, never leave an infant alone on a table. She may turn over and fall off.

When bathing an infant, never leave her alone in the water. She may fall in and drown.

Toddlers love to *climb furniture*. Take them off tables that aren't sturdy. Also take them off if they're reaching too far and might lose their balance.

Toddlers love to look into *kitchen cabinets*. If they contain dangerous material, cabinets should be locked. If they're not locked, keep children away from them.

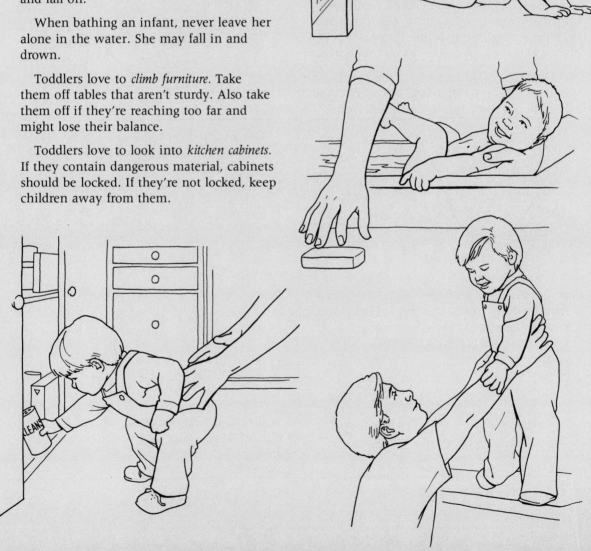

Parents should install *gates* at the top and bottom of stairs until children can climb stairs safely. If there are no gates, keep the children away from the stairs.

Some playthings can be dangerous. Infants should play with large, *soft toys*— nothing that has small, breakable, or sharp parts.

Keep *plastic bags* away from a child—he could suffocate.

Don't let children play with *electric outlets or wires*. Distract them with another toy, or simply take them to another spot.

In a car, a child should *always* ride in a *child car seat,* no matter how short the trip. The safest spot for a child is in the middle of the back seat.

Toddlers like to *run outside*. Always watch them to prevent their running into the street.

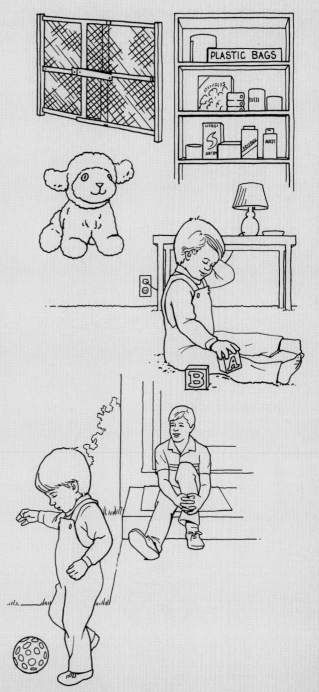

Making Your Own Toys

You can have some fun—and provide quiet play—for pre-schoolers and older children by turning some common objects into toys. If you bring some supplies along when you're babysitting, you can pull them out when the children get restless. They'll be delighted with the new toys.

Making masks

Small shopping bags, crayons, scissors, construction paper, and glue.

Play dough

Combine 1 cup flour, 1 cup water, ½ cup salt, 1 tablespoon oil, ½ teaspoon cream of tartar, and food coloring. Cook on the stove until thick. Store in a plastic bag.

Making hats and crowns

Construction paper, glue, scissors, sequins, buttons, and braid.

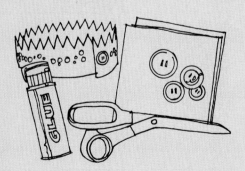

Wooden dolls

Painted scraps of wood—blocks, dowels, or circles.

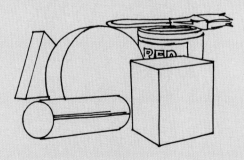

Homemade building blocks

Popsicle sticks and cardboard, notched to hold the sticks.

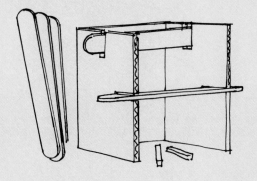

Finger paints

Mix equal parts of powdered tempera paint and water. Store in containers.

Flash cards

3″ × 5″ cards with numbers, letters, colors, or objects on them.

Science center

Magnet and large paper clips, magnifying glass and small objects.

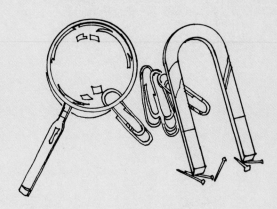

Quiet Things to Do

One way to maintain peace and quiet when you're babysitting is to get the children interested in quiet activities. Here are a few things you can try.

Read a story aloud.

Make up stories.

Identify shapes.

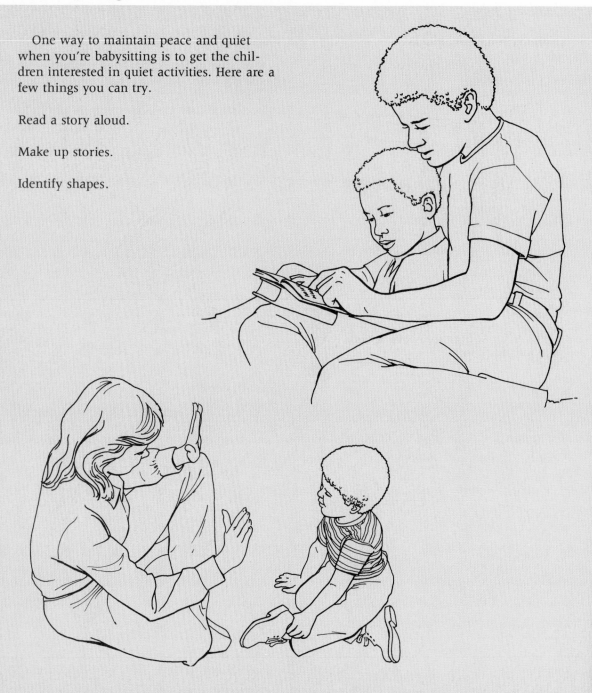

Identify animals in pictures (This activity may become less quiet if children decide to make animal noises!)

Draw.

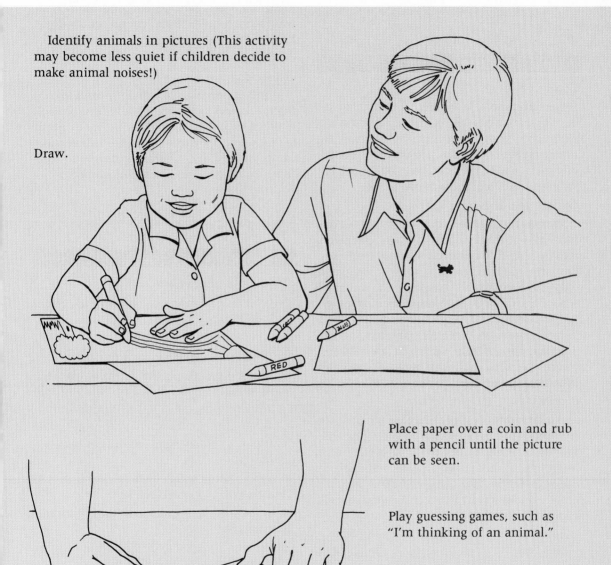

Place paper over a coin and rub with a pencil until the picture can be seen.

Play guessing games, such as "I'm thinking of an animal."

Unit Two Review

Unit Summary

Chapter 17.

Caregivers may be parents, other relatives, or babysitters, but they can all do a better job when they know the basics of child care. By understanding children's physical, mental, and social needs, they can meet children's basic needs and help them learn.

Chapters 18 and 19.

By learning about the stages of development that children pass through, caregivers will be able to recognize an infant's reflexes, have the patience to cope with a two-year-old's tantrums, and comfort an unhappy school-age child. A good caregiver also knows the importance of play. Choosing toys and games appropriate to a child's abilities and understanding can help the child grow. Caregivers also need to switch between activities because children need variety.

Chapter 20.

An important part of child care is caring for children. This means meeting their physical, mental, and social needs. A caregiver must learn how to childproof a home and keep an eye open for possible dangers. Caring for children includes setting limits and rules that will lessen the chance of injury.

Chapter 21.

Working as a babysitter gives teenagers a chance to earn money and to learn more about children. In this job, you can put to use all that you have learned about child care and development. If you are businesslike with your employers, you can help yourself get more work.

Chapter 22.

Becoming a parent is a big step, one that changes a person's life completely and permanently. Although parenthood is very rewarding, it requires time, energy, and money. People should be sure that they're ready for parenthood before taking on the responsibility.

Chapter 23.

If you enjoy children, you may want to consider a career working either directly with children or for children. There are many possible jobs, and they call for such characteristics as an interest in children, creativity, sensitivity, calmness, and a sense of humor.

Review Questions

1. What is a caregiver?
2. What kinds of needs do children have?
3. What should you do when you get angry with a child's behavior?
4. Describe two reflexes of an infant.
5. Why do you think the two-year-old stage is sometimes known as "the terrible twos?"
6. What kind of children have special needs?
7. What do infants do when they pick up objects?
8. What should you keep in mind when children want to watch television?
9. What are three quiet activities that children might enjoy?
10. When is it useful to distract children? Describe how you might do it.
11. What emergency phone numbers should you have near the phone?
12. What are the general rules for action in an emergency? Give an example and how you might handle it.

13. How does a babysitter meet a child's physical needs?

14. How can you show your employers that you're businesslike about babysitting?

15. How does a couple's life together change once a baby arrives?

16. What are some of the financial costs of being a parent?

17. Why is it important for a parent to be emotionally mature?

18. What are the rewards of parenthood?

19. List four personal characteristics that are important for someone planning a career with children.

20. Which medical careers involve work with children? Which recreational careers?

Reading Activities

1. Read the help-wanted ads from a Sunday newspaper. Clip out those ads that require working with children. Using those ads as models, write an ad of your own for a job in child care. Put all the ads together on a poster to share with the class.

2. Reread the quiz that opened this unit. Choose one of the questions and write a paragraph explaining why the answer to it is true.

Writing Activities

1. Put together a recipe booklet of easy-to-make healthful snacks for children. Divide the booklet into snacks for toddlers, preschool children, and school children. For instance, a hamburger would be good for some preschool and most schoolchildren, but not for a toddler.

2. Write a "Babysitter's checklist," with questions to ask parents and advice to remember. Check with parents for additional suggestions not included in this unit. Duplicate the checklist for your classmates.

3. Imagine that you are a parent. Write one or two paragraphs instructing the teenager who will babysit for your child.

Math Activities

1. Figure out the financial costs for a baby's first two months of life. Find out the typical hospital and doctor fees for the mother and infant. (For this example, assume that medical insurance pays 75 percent of these fees.) Add to this amount the cost of clothing, formula, and baby equipment, such as diapers, a crib, and a car seat. If possible, ask the parents of a newborn to help you in this activity.

2. In the library, find the average height and weight for a newborn, a one-year-old, a three-year-old, a five-year-old, and a ten-year-old. How much do height and weight increase from one age to the next?

Group Projects

1. Work with another person or a small group to prepare a debate on the following subject: "Children should not be allowed to watch television."

2. With two other students, make a time line showing the physical, mental, and social changes that take place in a child between the ages of one and three. Each student should be responsible for recording one type of development.

MANAGING AND BUYING

Managing—that's what business executives do, right? That's true, but executives aren't the only ones who manage. You're often in situations that require management. Remember the time your parents wanted you to clean your room and you had the history paper due? What about the time your friends wanted another player for basketball, but you had a dentist's appointment? Then there was the time you didn't have enough money for that sweater you liked.

In each of these cases, you had to solve the problem by compromising with someone else. Or you solved it by managing your time, your energy, or your money. Managing is simply finding the best ways to use your resources to meet your goals. You make management decisions every day. Will you walk or get a ride to school? Which class will you study for first?

As you grow older, more of your management decisions will involve money. You will earn more and have more opportunities to get the things you need and want. It becomes important to use your money carefully. By doing so, you can meet more of your goals. You are also a consumer. You probably make more of your own purchases now than when you were younger. You may buy clothes, as well as school lunches, albums, movie tickets, and school supplies. You need management skills to help you make decisions about what to buy. These are just a few of the many decisions that you'll make as a manager and as a consumer. In the chapters in this unit, you'll find information that will help you make those decisions. As a result, you should be better able to manage your life.

Chapter 24 Management and You

Margo woke in the morning with a start. Today was the first day of her summer job as a camp counselor at a day camp on the outskirts of the city.

Already she was late! It was nearly 8:15 and she was supposed to be at camp at 9:00 A.M. sharp. With a sinking feeling, Margo phoned the camp office to tell them that she'd be half an hour late.

When she arrived at the camp, the children were lined up. A counselor was at the head of each line, except Margo's. The counselor next to Margo's line was taking care of both her own and Margo's line of children.

"Hey, Margo," the counselor in the next row whispered, "if you can't manage to get yourself out of bed in the morning, how are you going to manage these little ones?" Margo could only nod grimly and think to herself, "She's right."

Benefits of Management

Managing means *planning to make the best use of your time, money, and abilities.* When Margo did a poor job of managing her time, she disappointed herself and irritated the other counselors. She had wanted to do the right thing, but she just hadn't been organized enough to accomplish what she wanted.

We all make some mistakes in managing. Sometimes we even forget to manage. You may forget the tryouts for the school play, or spend your money on records so that there's nothing left for lunch. Or you may go out for soccer to be with your friends, even though you don't really like the game. Learning to be a good manager results in making fewer mistakes like the ones above.

In a store, you select a style, size and color of clothing based on your principles, needs and wants. These may differ among family and peers.

Improving Your Self-Concept

By learning to manage successfully, you can improve your self-concept. You'll feel better about yourself because you'll be able to do more. You'll be more relaxed because you'll accomplish the goals you set for yourself. Others will feel better about you, too—because you're reliable, they'll be able to count on you.

Using Your Resources Well

Good management has another benefit. It will help you get the most out of your **resources**. These are your time, your possessions, your money, and your talents—*all the things you use to help you meet your goals.*

The other people in your family and the community are also resources. By using your resources well, you won't be caught with three new records and no lunch money. You'll have extra time to finish that special project.

Influences on Management

How would you spend one million dollars? Years ago, there was a television series devoted to that question. Each week's program showed a different person who had been given a million dollars by a mysterious stranger. How each character used the money, and how it affected his or her life, depended mostly on that person's principles, needs, and wants.

Principles are *your beliefs about what is right and wrong and your guidelines for living* *with yourself and others*. A woman who thought that free time and friendship were important might retire from her job after receiving one million dollars. She would use the money for plane tickets to visit friends in other parts of the country.

Someone else might spend the money on needed medical care. Yet another person might want to buy a large house or a private plane.

All decisions are influenced by principles, needs, and wants. Suppose that you're thinking about dropping study hall to take an art course. Would you rather stay with your friends in study hall, or are you more interested in taking a class where you'll meet new people? Do you need the study time to finish your homework, or is the art practice more important to you?

Meeting Your Goals

In making a choice, you probably have to make a **trade-off**—you have to *give up something in exchange for something that you want more*. You can have the art practice, but lose the chance to be with your friends. Or you can stay in study hall, but pass up the opportunity for art lessons. But you don't have the time to do both.

To choose between study hall and art class, you need to know what your goals are. Sit down with a piece of paper and a pencil. What do you want to accomplish today? This week? The things you wish to accomplish in the near future are your short-term goals.

Perhaps your short-term goals include improving your drawing—that's why you want to take art class. You may also want to lose ten pounds, read a new novel, and save money for art supplies.

You also have long-term goals. These are the things you wish to accomplish in the more distant future. They may include winning the art contest next term or making the basketball team next year.

Because your goal of improving your art skills is important, you decide to take the art lessons. You know that this work will help you meet your long-term goal of winning the art contest.

Making Decisions

Management skills can help you make decisions. Margo faced a difficult decision soon after coming to camp. She was still

The conflicting goals and priorities of individuals in a group may lead to problems. Compromise may be the only solution.

FEATURE

Setting Goals for a Group

"I think we should start by buying floor mats," said Dave.

"We need a practice bar around the wall, and mirrors, too," said Lisa.

"We have to be realistic," said Ellen. "The school fund drive last year raised $300. We might be able to raise more money this year, but we might not."

"But we *have* to have the practice bar," Lisa protested.

"Wait a minute, Lisa, the mats are a must," Dave repeated.

And so the year's first meeting of the Athletic Club began. Students interested in judo, ballet, gymnastics, and exercise were meeting to discuss the upcoming fund drive.

Ellen, the president of the club, got to the heart of the group's problem. "We need equipment. But no one seems to be able to agree on which equipment to buy. I'd like all of you to write down what pieces of equipment you think we'll need, and give your suggestions to me."

Ellen temporarily got around a problem of the group—loud arguments—by asking people to write down suggestions.

When Ellen read the equipment suggestions aloud, the arguments started again.

"Wait a minute," said Ellen, "we can't make a decision until we know two things: which piece of equipment will get used the most, and how much it will cost."

She had just identified two short-term goals for the group—to do some research into group needs and to look into equipment costs. The long-term goal was to get the equipment that most of the group could use and enjoy.

"Everybody write down the one piece of equipment you'd use the most. Then find out how much it costs." Ellen was getting the others involved in a constructive way. "We'll meet again in two days to discuss the suggestions and go over what we've found out."

---

having trouble being on time. Should she quit? She had $35 in savings that could tide her over until she found another job.

Margo decided to make a short list of her choices:

1. Use the money for spending and look for another job.
2. Keep the job and spend the money on a clock radio to wake her up.

Then Margo got out the list of goals that she had made last spring. The list read:

1. Get a camp job.
2. Pass a lifesaving course.

The camp job was one that Margo had wanted for a long time. She wanted to be outdoors and work with children. In addition, the camp job offered lifesaving instruction after the morning session. With a lifesaving certificate, she could get a better-paying job as a camp lifeguard next summer.

Once she reviewed her goals, Margo decided to keep the job. If she bought a clock radio for no more than $25, she would still have some money left over for other activities during the summer. What other options might she have?

Considering Others

Sometimes you have to consider not only your own goals, but also those of others around you. This happens in your three roles as family member, friend, and member of a community.

- *As a Family Member.* What if your family depends on you to make dinner? What if you are supposed to clean your room—or the living room—before a guest comes over? How you manage those tasks will affect whether your family is happy and its guests feel comfortable.

- *As a Friend.* Your friend may rely on you to pick up homework for him when he's out sick one day. Perhaps the group relies on you to make posters for the dance. Or maybe the band needs you to practice. You need to come through for these people and not let them down.

- *As a Community Member.* How you use public property affects others. You may not care if the library book you have is overdue, but what if someone else needs it for a school paper? How would you feel if you couldn't get a book that you needed?

Managing requires you to think about more than just yourself. Sometimes you make decisions as part of a group. Then you have to try to fit your goals in with the goals of the others in the group.

Words to Remember

managing: planning to make the best use of time, money, abilities, and other resources

resources: the things you use to help you meet your goals

trade-off: giving up something in exchange for something else that you want more

Questions

1. What is managing? How can it help you feel better about yourself?
2. Name three principles that are important to you. Do you share these principles with your friends? If not, how are your friends' principles different?
3. What are trade-offs?
4. What steps are helpful when you are making a difficult decision?
5. Why is it important to be able to compromise when trying to achieve goals with others?

Chapter 25 Your Resources

Objectives

After reading this chapter, you will be able to:

☐ *identify and describe the many resources available to you,*

☐ *identify and describe human resources and use them to increase other resources,*

☐ *list outside resources and describe their importance to you,*

☐ *explain how to substitute and trade resources.*

Megan never seemed to have enough money to do all the things she wanted to do. Yesterday didn't work out at all. She did go shopping for a new sweater, but she spent too much money for it.

The result was that she didn't have enough money to go to the movies that evening with Kathy. Instead, she called up Eunice and they both went to the neighborhood video arcade. Megan spent the rest of her money and forgot to keep enough for bus fare home. She had to borrow it from Eunice.

To Megan, Carl was a mystery. He always seemed to be involved in some project or other. Yesterday, she'd seen him taking pictures of the school with a professional-looking camera. Last week he'd run in the Charity Marathon. She'd heard that he had a guitar, too.

"Where does he get the money?"

Your Own Resources

Carl laughed when Megan asked him about his "wealth." "You're wearing jogging shoes, too," he said. Megan's face reddened. "But what about the camera?" she asked.

"It's my older sister's," explained Carl. "She and her husband bought a nice one so they could photograph their kids. In fact, that's part of the deal. My sister lent me the camera this week because I said I'd watch the kids all day on Saturday."

"And the guitar?" asked Megan.

"I'm renting it from the music store where I take lessons. If I decide to buy the guitar, the rental fees will go toward the sales price. Right now, I just want to rent until I'm sure that the guitar is the instrument I'll stay with."

So, Carl's "wealth" was not just money. In fact he spent very little money. What Megan had noticed were Carl's resources—his sister's camera and a rented guitar. A resource, you may remember, is anything you use to meet your goals. In fact, Carl had resources more important than the camera and guitar. His imagination and knowledge helped him get the camera and the guitar in the first place.

Like Megan, you've probably wished for more—more money, possessions, time, or even skills and imagination. But there's no need to wish. Let's find out what resources you have and how to use them to your best advantage.

Possessions

The toaster in your kitchen is a resource, because you use it to get something done. The toaster, like many other possessions, helps you meet your goals. Some possessions, like toasters and books, can be used over and over again. Others, like ball-point pens, need to be replaced often.

Some possessions are **material**, *things that you use to make other things.* Food is a resource for cooking; paint and wallpaper are resources for decorating a room.

Other possessions are **tools**. They *help you use other resources more efficiently.* A bicy-

---

You can save time and money by using tools. The tools increase productivity and help you use other resources more efficiently. What tools are most valuable to you at home?

cle speeds travel and conserves time. Some tools, such as a sewing machine or lawnmower, help you increase your other resources. By sewing, you can have more clothes. By using your lawnmower to mow other people's lawns, you can increase the amount of money you have.

Money

Money is a special resource because it is commonly accepted for the goods and services we buy. The family toaster would not be accepted by a pizza maker in exchange for a pizza. The restaurant owner would rather have money, which he or she can use to buy supplies. Money, unlike a toaster, is a flexible resource because it can be traded for almost anything.

Human Resources

We also have **human resources**. These are *personal qualities that each of us possess*.

Knowledge is a human resource that is closely related to information. When you learn some information, it becomes knowledge that you carry around with you. And, unlike some of the other resources, knowledge cannot be used up. When you cook a hamburger, for example, you don't use up your knowledge of how to cook one. The next time you want a hamburger, you'll still know how to cook it!

In fact, you'll probably cook it better. With practice, you can improve your **skills**, another human resource. Skills are worth developing. They enable you to reach goals quickly and efficiently.

Imagination picks up where knowledge and skills leave off. If you need to do some-

Research a future career, listen to others, and ask questions to gain useful information that will help you achieve your goals.

thing but don't know how, you can use your imagination to think of a way to do it. Imagination helps you to use your skills to accomplish what you want.

Energy is one of the most valuable human resources. It is the power that allows you to get things done. Mental and physical energy are always needed to reach a goal. Using objects, money, knowledge, or imagination can mean using less energy. But if you don't have enough of the other resources, determination and physical energy can often help you reach your goal.

Time

Time is a resource with limits. Each day has only 24 hours. And we cannot *save* time—we can only use it wisely. Carl needs time—an entire Saturday—to stay with his sister's children. But that weekend Carl also has to do a big homework assignment, jog five miles on Sunday, and practice his guitar.

Carl's weekend schedule seems very full. But he has thought of ways to manage it. Carl has decided to bike wherever he has to go during the weekend. Biking is faster than walking and will provide a substitute for the five-mile jog he planned for Sunday. While still keeping in shape, Carl will be able to save a few hours. How else could Carl have managed his time?

Outside Resources

You can use many outside resources, too. Your *family* gives you emotional support. It helps you meet your basic needs. Other family members have skills and knowledge that you can draw on.

Friends are also valuable resources. They might have skills that you don't have—and sometimes you can trade your skills for theirs. You might help a friend with homework in return for her sewing a button back on your shirt. You can rely on friends to go places with you and to listen when you need to talk.

Many people at *school* also serve as resources. Teachers, coaches, and counselors all help you increase your knowledge and improve your skills. At school, you get the chance to explore different interests—art, foreign languages, child care, and computers. And schools have facilities like libraries and gymnasiums that you can use.

Businesses are other outside resources. Banks, clothing stores, movie theaters, and restaurants all provide you with goods and services.

Your *community* has many resources you can visit to learn things and have fun. These resources, like museums and zoos, enrich your life.

An important outside resource is *information*. You can find this resource in many places—family, friends, school, business, and community. And as you learn things, you also become a resource for information.

When a group works together to achieve a goal, all members pool their skills. The more resources each member shares with others, the more successful the group will be.

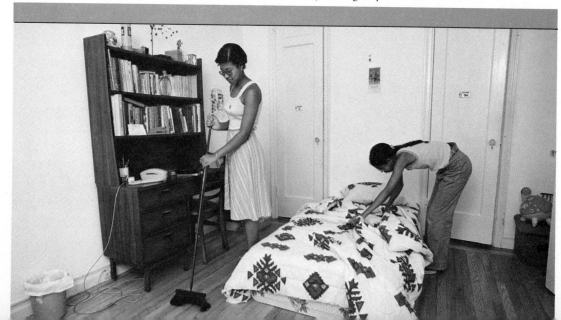

F E A T U R E

Increasing Your Resources

You can increase your resources in many ways.

■ *More possessions.* You can care for the things you own to make them last longer. You may be able to make or trade some things. And you can use your money wisely.

■ *More money.* By careful planning and budgeting, you can get the most out of your money. And you can work part-time to earn more.

■ *More time.* If you plan how to use your time, you'll be able to use it more wisely. That way you'll be able to get more done.

■ *More energy.* Getting proper rest, eating nutritious foods, exercising, and avoiding harmful substances are the four steps to having more energy.

■ *More knowledge.* By reading, talking to people, and asking questions, you can build up your knowledge.

■ *More skills.* Practicing is the best way to master skills. Reading and getting advice from skilled people also help.

■ *More imagination.* You can even add to this resource. Give yourself time to think out problems and find creative ways to solve them. Use brainstorming to develop new ideas. Imagine new stories, or think of what it would be like to be someone else or live somewhere else. Adding to this resource should be fun.

Adding to Resources

The number of resources you have can change. Resources such as time get used up, but many others can be increased in any number of ways:

■ Your energy, for instance, can actually grow if you follow four guidelines: get plenty of rest, eat nutritious food, exercise, and avoid harmful substances.

■ Money grows by being invested in banking institutions.

■ Knowledge and skills increase as you learn things.

■ Your store of possessions grows each time you buy something.

Exchanging Resources

Money is only one resource that can be traded for something else. You can also exchange other resources directly with another person. That's what Carl and his sister did—they exchanged the use of her possessions for the use of his skill and time. This kind of *direct exchange of one resource for another* is called **barter**.

Many people make indirect exchanges. They use their human resources to work for an employer in return for money. With the money they've earned, they buy the possessions they want. The right to use community resources is usually based on taxes paid by local citizens.

Substituting Resources

You can also *use one resource in place of another*. By **substituting** resources, you can spend the resources that you have more of and conserve those that you have in short supply. For instance, if you'd like curtains for your room, you can make a choice from a number of options. You can:

- buy them ready-made (using money but little time, energy, or skill).
- buy material and sew them yourself (using less money, but more of your time, energy, and skill).
- find a used set of curtains and shorten them to fit your windows (using little money and skill, but more time and energy).

We substitute resources every day. It is important to make thoughtful and worthwhile substitutions so we can reach many goals. Our resources are too valuable to waste.

Choosing Resources

You can use different resources to accomplish the same goal.

Suppose that washing the family car is Joe's job. Joe can use his own time and energy to do the job. Or, if he is busy or feeling lazy, he can spend money to have it done at the local car wash.

However, suppose Joe is lazy, but doesn't have money to spend at the car wash. Then he might use his imagination and skill to persuade his little brother that washing the car is fun. He could strike a bargain with him to do the job for less money than what the car wash would charge. Joe could then save energy, time, and money—and still get the job done!

If you use resources wisely, you will reach more of your goals. When you use your time and energy to wash a car, you reserve your money for things your energy can't produce—a ticket for a concert, for example.

Words to Remember

barter: the direct exchange of one resource for another

human resources: personal qualities that each of us possesses

material: a possession that you use to make other things

substituting: using one resource in place of another

tool: a possession that helps you use your other resources more efficiently

Questions

1. What is a resource? Identify four types of resources.
2. What human resources do we all possess?
3. How can your school be a resource? What about your community?
4. List some of the ways your family increases your own pool of resources. Then list three ways you increase your family's resource pool.
5. What are two ways of adding to your resources? What kinds of resources would you use to do it?

Chapter 26 Managing Your Time

Objectives

After reading this chapter, you will be able to:

☐ *identify the four benefits of good time management,*

☐ *make a schedule that you can use to meet your goals,*

☐ *list and explain some techniques for carrying out a schedule.*

"Can you make the meeting tonight?" a member of your club asks you.

"Sure," you say. "I don't see any problem. I'll be there."

You say this because you have planned your day fairly well. You expect to go home right after school. You'll have a snack and do the house chores you're supposed to take care of. Then you'll play basketball with your friends, do your homework, eat your dinner, and still get to the meeting on time.

You think your day is going to go smoothly, but what if something comes up that you hadn't planned on? Managing your time helps you handle all your normal problems and tasks. It also makes it easier to meet the unexpected things that can arise during any day's activity at home, in school, or with your friends.

197

Making Time Work for You

There are only 24 hours in a day. Time is one resource you can't expand. But even though you can't change the quantity of time you have, you can change the way you use it.

Managing your time well will allow you to do several things.

- You'll be better able to achieve your goals.

- You'll be able to get more done by fitting in more activities that are important to you, or just by taking a moment to relax.

- You'll be less likely to leave important tasks undone.

- You'll be able to do all that's expected of you—at the time when it's expected. Others will be able to rely on you, and they'll appreciate that.

- You'll gain extra time to do the things you enjoy, or just to relax.

When you offer your assistance to friends, be sure that you arrive prepared and on time. This will gain you a reputation of being reliable.

Looking at the Big Picture

Before you can start managing time, you need to know what you're managing *for*. You need to examine your actions. In short, you must start out by setting your goals.

Setting Your Goals

Some goals will be short term—you may want to write a thank-you note, do homework, or go out with friends. Others will be long-term goals, such as making the basketball team or raising your math grade.

Once you've identified your goals, you can decide which are most important to you. Those are the ones to set aside time for. You may want to practice basketball every day to improve your shot. If your goal is to have more friends, you'll want to set aside time for meeting people and doing things together.

Time Management

The advantage of looking at the big picture is that you can change your plans if your goals change or if something unforeseen comes up. Looking at all your goals together also helps you group tasks. If you want to buy a new sweater and get a birthday card, you can save time by scheduling one shopping trip.

This kind of planning also helps you break large tasks up into smaller units. Instead of studying for the big test two hours the night before, you can spend 20 minutes each night. One of the Teen Tips at the end of this unit shows you how to divide your tasks in this way.

You can plan these tasks by using the two tools of time management: a calendar and a schedule:

- A *calendar* is a monthly or yearly record of what you want to accomplish. It shows you the total picture of your goals.
- A *schedule* is your daily or weekly plan for achieving those goals. Let's find out how to make and use a schedule wisely and well.

Making a Schedule

How do you control your time and make it work for you? One excellent way is with a simple device—a "To-Do" list. Each day, list what you must do and want to do on that day. Divide the tasks into three groups, A, B, and C:

- The A items on your list are your "must-do" items. These tasks are the ones with **deadlines**—*dates by which tasks must be completed.*
- The B items are important, but they don't have to be done that day.
- The C items are those you would like to get done, but can be put aside with little loss.

You must be honest with yourself in dividing your tasks into these categories. And you must concentrate on *getting the A items done.*

Some things don't need to be scheduled. You don't have to write down: "Have fun. (A)," or "See movie with Charley. (B)." In fact, you may not have to draw up a schedule every day. You have a sense of what you need and want to do, and you can fit it all in.

Tuesday - To Do

A. Turn in math assignment
~~Pick up lettuce for dinner~~

B. Clean Room
~~Fix bike lock~~
Put dirty clothes in laundry

C. Watch 8:00 P.M. TV movie
Read 2 chapters of <u>Lincoln</u>
for next week

Make a "To Do" list every day. This will eliminate wasteful time and prevent you from forgetting important tasks.

But when you seem to have many tasks to accomplish, or when someone else is counting on you, a schedule can help you. Here's what to do.

Setting Up a List

Start your day by making your "To-Do" list for that day. Each day will have its own new list, different from the day before. Your list may even change once or twice during the day.

The list itself doesn't have to be complex. You can just jot it down on a piece of notepaper. Keep the list with you all day. And remember to *cross out each task as you complete it*—you'll feel better when you see that you're getting things done.

By following these simple steps, you will manage your time better. But what happens when something new comes up?

Let's look at the scene that opened this chapter and list the activities A, B, C:

- Walk and feed the dog. (A)
- Do homework. (A)
- Attend club meeting. (A)
- Practice basketball. (B)
- Do house chores. (B)
- Watch new television comedy. (C)

When you get home from school, you're ready to start on your tasks, but you're faced with a small crisis. Your mother has left you a note saying that she's gone to pick up your grandmother and will be back with her around 9:00 P.M. You'll have to heat up the stew for your dinner. And you must get the extra room ready for Grandma. You have a **contingency**, *an unforeseen event.*

Using Your List to Help Plan Your Time

You need to change your list to reflect the new situation. Your A list must now include getting the room ready and fixing dinner. To fit those tasks in, you have to make some other changes. Your revised list might look like this:

- Fix Grandma's room. (A)
- Walk and feed the dog. (A)
- Do homework. (A)
- Prepare and eat dinner. (A)
- Attend club meeting. (B)
- Practice basketball. (B)
- Do house chores. (C)
- Watch new television comedy. (C)

You think you can fix up the room and walk and feed the dog by 4:00 P.M. Then you can still meet your friends for an hour's practice. You had wanted to play for two hours, but you must cut it short to meet your other responsibilities.

You can get home from basketball by a little after 5:00. You can heat the stew, eat it, and clean up by 6:00. That will give you an hour for homework until the club meeting at 7:00. You will get back around

Some tasks are like sporting events—they go into overtime. Be sure to allow ample time in your schedule for activities that may take longer than you plan.

8:30 from the meeting, which will give you more time for homework before going to bed.

Your new list means putting off house chores for another day. It may have to get an A rating on tomorrow's list. You also put aside the television show for another week. It wasn't that important.

Carrying Out a Schedule

The "To-Do" list is only a device to help you plan your time. It doesn't have to be perfect—an imperfect plan is better than no plan at all. When you get into the habit of making the list every day, and crossing out the items as you achieve them, you will become more skilled in using the list.

T E E N   I S S U E

The Time Bandits— Most Wanted List

Often you don't feel robbed of time; it just seems to slip away. A number of habits waste time for you and leave you short on time when you need it the most.

- *Wrong information.* Not paying attention and forgetting are costly time bandits. You come to class prepared to discuss chapter 10. Then you realize that the homework was to read *chapter 11.* Not paying attention or writing down the assignment cost you precious time.

- *No set priorities.* It's easy to spend time on a minor task while letting a major one go by. There's nothing wrong with checking out the new video game at the pizza parlor. But be sure to get your chores done, too. When you spend the time you need for a "must-do" task on a "may-do" basis, *you* come up short.

- *Procrastination.* This is another word for *putting things off.* It's very easy to **procrastinate** on a job you dislike. There are lots of excuses—"I'll have time to do it tomorrow," or, "I'm too

tired now." You probably recognize all of them. But these excuses don't get the job done, so spare yourself the effort of making excuses.

- *The telephone.* You call Dan to tell him that tomorrow's practice has been canceled, and 45 minutes later you're still on the phone. If you really didn't have anything else to do, that's no problem. But you had promised to wash the car. Next time, combine business with pleasure. Invite Dan over to keep you company while you wash the car. Or agree to call him back when you've finished washing the car.

- *Repeating yourself.* There are few things more frustrating than doing things twice—walking back to school because you forgot your jacket the first time, having to put in a zipper twice because you were in too much of a rush before. No one has to tell you that you've made a mistake in planning. You have plenty of time to tell yourself—while you do the job for the second time.

Hints For Good Time Management

Follow these tips to use time effectively:

- *Group activities together to save time.* Suppose you have two A errands during the school day—getting a form from your counselor and turning in an assignment. Since both stops are in the same part of the building, do both errands on the same trip.

- *Alternate chores with more enjoyable tasks.* Having something pleasant to look forward to will help you finish a chore more quickly.

- *Do unpleasant tasks first.* They're easier if you get them out of the way.

- *Don't overload.* If you try to do too much, you may do something wrong. Then you'll have to spend time to fix it.

- *Allow enough time to do things.* You can bet that a problem will occur if your schedule is too tight. If you planned on spending only one hour to write a paper that actually takes two hours, your whole day's schedule will be off.

- *Look out for time wasters.* See the box for some common problems to avoid.

- *Be prepared.* Even the best time plan can fail if you don't organize each task. Before you begin a task, think it through and decide what you will need to accomplish it. If you're cleaning your room, bring both the vacuum cleaner and the dust cloth. If you have to go back to the broom closet twice, you're wasting time.

- *Learn from your mistakes.* If you find it hard to get all your A items done, don't be discouraged. Step back and think. Try to find out what went wrong. Are you putting too many items on your A list? Are you allowing too little time for each item, so that you can't possibly get them all done? Learn to limit your commitments and to leave a little extra time in the schedule—just in case.

Once you learn to plan your time, you'll find that you have more of it. Once you finish the essentials, take a minute to relax, or turn to an item on your C list that you thought you might not get to. Reward yourself for your good work.

Words to Remember

contingency: an unforeseen event

deadline: the date by which a task must be completed

procrastination: the tendency to put things off, to delay

Questions

1. What are four benefits of time management?
2. What's the difference between a calendar and a schedule?
3. How can you make a schedule?
4. Give three hints for carrying out your schedule.

Chapter **27 Managing Your Money**

Objectives

After reading this chapter, you will be able to:

☐ *describe different ways of buying things,*

☐ *explain the importance of money management,*

☐ *make a budget that you can use to meet your goals,*

☐ *explain how to carry out a budget.*

"Mention money and the whole world goes silent." (*German Proverb*)

"A heavy purse makes a light heart." (*Irish proverb*)

"When money is not a servant it is a master." (*Italian proverb*)

"Money makes money." (*Chinese proverb*)

"When money speaks, the truth is silent." (*Russian proverb*)

These wise sayings show us that money can bring happiness and sorrow, so use it wisely.

Money is not the most important thing in life, but you need it to get many of the things you want. You may need money for bus fare, record albums, and college tuition. You may also need money for unplanned expenses, such as a birthday present for a friend. That's why it's important not only to make money, but also to use it wisely.

Types of Money

What is money? You're probably thinking of the coins or paper bills you carry around in your pocket. They are money, but so are checks, credit cards, and some other things as well.

Money, in whatever form, is just *something that has an agreed-upon trading value.* The value of the money becomes real only when you spend it—that is, trade it for other things.

You can spend money for two kinds of things. You can spend it for goods like jeans or hot dogs, or for services like bicycle repairs or haircuts.

- *Cash.* This is the kind of money that you're probably most familiar with. The coins in your pocket and bills in your wallet are made by the government and given a certain value. You can exchange them at a store or with another person for something of equal value.

- *Checks.* If you don't want to carry around lots of cash, you can put your money into a checking account. Then, when you purchase something, you can write a check instead of handing over the cash. That piece of paper is a promise that the money you owe is in your bank account. And it gives the store the right to collect that money.

- *Credit Cards.* **Credit** is *permission to borrow money.* Borrowing is what you are doing when you use a credit card. Businesses usually issue credit cards to people over 18 who show that they will pay their bills. When using a credit card, you borrow from the business. That company then bills you for the money you borrowed, which you must pay back, usually on a monthly basis. You may also need to pay an extra charge to the business that allowed you to borrow.

The Goals of Money Management

Although you can buy some of the things that you want, it's almost impossible to have money for them all. But you are more likely to have money for the most important things by learning to use your money wisely.

Money for the Things You Need

It's essential to have money to meet your needs. You might have to put aside money for bus fare to and from school, as well as for food and clothing. Good money management can be the key to providing for your basic needs.

Cash, checks and credit cards are convenient and flexible methods of exchange for goods and services.

F E A T U R E

Electronic Money

It's now possible to *bank and pay bills automatically with the use of computers.* The method is called **electronic funds transfer** (EFT). EFT cards can be used to move your money from one place to another with just the push of a button. Here are some EFT services.

■ *Automatic teller machines.* You can skip the long lines at the bank by using these machines. The bank gives you a plastic EFT card and a secret identification number. You put your card into a machine and punch in your secret number on a keyboard. You can then make deposits or withdrawals, pay bills, or move money from one account to another.

■ *Point of sale terminals.* These machines are located in stores. Instead of paying cash or using a check, you put your EFT card into one of the machines. It instantly transfers the money from your account to the account of the store.

■ *Preauthorized payments.* This system allows for the transfer of money to or from your account. An employer may deposit a paycheck directly into a worker's bank account each week. Or the money for a monthly gas bill can be automatically taken out of a consumer's account and put in the gas company's account.

■ *Telephone transfers.* You can call some banks on the phone and have them transfer money from one account to another. You can also have them take money out of your account to pay your bills for you. EFT systems can be very convenient.

But, there are some important things to keep in mind when using EFTs.

■ Never keep your secret identification number in the same place as your EFT card or write your number on the card.

■ Never tell anyone your number or let anyone see the number as you punch it in.

If you think there has been a theft of your money or a bank error, call the bank as soon as you spot the problem. Give your name, account number, and the date, and then describe the situation.

Money for the Things You Want

Being able to buy some of the things you want makes life more pleasurable. New clothes, records, snacks, movies, and trips are some of the things enjoyed by teens.

However, most people never have enough money to buy everything they want. Some people must spend almost all of their money on needs. They must wait until they have better-paying jobs before they can begin to buy things they want.

Money for Unplanned Expenses

It's also important to manage your money so that there is some left in case of an unexpected expense. Suppose someone invites you to a party and you need to buy a present to take with you. Or perhaps your stereo needle breaks and must be replaced. By putting some of your money aside, just in case, you'll have extra to take care of things like that broken stereo needle.

Making a Budget

One of the best ways to manage your money is to make a budget. A **budget** is *a plan for spending your money*. A budget doesn't somehow get you more money. But it will help you decide how to use the money you have.

When making a budget, it's important to keep in mind what your goals are. Short-term goals might include paying club dues or getting a new album. Long-term goals could be saving for summer camp or for a car, once you have a driver's license.

Before you start a budget, make a list of your needs and wants. Set some priorities. Which of the wants are most important?

Set aside money for these goals before allowing money for extras. If you want to have more clothes, use your money for that before spending it on movies.

Your Income

Before you start to plan the use of your money, you have to figure out how much money you have available to spend. *The money you take in and have available to spend* is called your **income**. Income can be salary from a job, money earned from a business like babysitting or mowing lawns, gift money from relatives, or an allowance.

To figure out your income, decide on a period of time—maybe a week or a month. Then add together all the money you expect to receive over that period of time. The total is the amount you have to spend in your budget.

Savings

Once you figure out how much money you have to spend, you can start deciding

Following a budget is not easy, especially when something that you want attracts your attention. If this happens, review your budget and reorganize your wants.

TABLE 1   Susan's Budget

Weekly Income		Weekly Expenses	
Allowance for chores	$10.00	Savings	
Babysitting (twice a week)	10.00	Emergencies	$ 2.00
		For stereo	3.00
		Fixed expenses	
		Nutrition snacks	4.50
		Flexible expenses	
		Entertainment	6.00
		Clothes	3.00
		School supplies	1.50
Total	$20.00	Total	$20.00

what to do with it. If you can, save something each time you receive money—then you'll have money for expensive items and for emergencies.

Some people figure out everything they need or want to spend money on first. Then they plan to save any money left over. The problem with that method is that there often isn't anything left over.

The best way to solve this problem is to save first. Put aside a little each week or month—even if it's just a dollar or two.

Saving can help you buy the really big, costly things you want. By saving a little at a time, you'll eventually have enough for that stereo you want.

Expenses

Your **expenses** are *the things that you spend your money on.* Once you've set aside your savings, look at your expenses. There are two types.

- **Fixed expenses.** These are *the important set expenses that you need to pay—costs that you are committed to.* You might have a piano lesson each week that you have to put aside money for. Or you might need money to buy lunch each day at school.

- **Flexible expenses.** These are *expenses that don't stay the same, which you can make new decisions about in each budget.* You go bowling some weeks but not others. You don't buy clothes every week.

Sometimes it can be hard to estimate your expenses. If you have a lot of trouble estimating expenses, keep track of every amount you actually spend for two or three weeks. Write everything down. Then, take an average. For instance, if you spent $3.94 for school supplies for three weeks, you spent an average of $1.31 each week. You might decide to put aside $1.50 each week for school supplies. Do this math for each item you want to budget.

Using Your Budget

Making a budget is a waste of time unless you use it. But to use it well, you have to keep track of all you take in and all you spend. Then see how well it's working. Sometimes you might make changes.

Keeping Records

During the first few weeks that you use your budget, write down all the money that you take in and everything you spend. No amount is too small to note. Write down even the cost of candy or bubble gum.

Remaining Flexible

If you aren't coming close to your budget, it's not right for you yet. Are you getting caught short of lunch money at the end of the week? Do you always find yourself with entertainment money left over? You might want to adjust your budget to allow less for entertainment and more for lunch.

Perhaps your income will change. You may earn money from a paper route, or maybe your allowance will go up. Your aunt might give you a gift of $10.00 on your birthday. You can adjust your budget to include changes in income as well as changes in expenses.

Learning from the Budget

Making and using your budget is a learning experience. You haven't failed if it doesn't work out exactly right the first time. Change things and try again until you are getting what you want from your money.

Words to Remember

budget: a plan for spending your money

credit: the extension of permission to borrow money

expenses: the things that you spend your money on

fixed expenses: important set expenses that you need to pay—costs that you are committed to

flexible expenses: expenses that don't stay the same, which you can make new decisions about in each budget

income: the money you take in and have available to spend

money: something that has an agreed-upon trading value

Questions

1. What are the different forms of money?
2. What are the three goals of money management?
3. What is a budget? How do both income and expenses relate to a budget?
4. What is the purpose of saving?
5. What are fixed expenses? What are flexible expenses? Is one more important than the other?
6. Why is it a good idea to change a budget?

Chapter **28** Saving and Borrowing

Objectives

After reading this chapter, you will be able to:

☐ *explain what interest is,*

☐ *describe a variety of savings plans,*

☐ *explain how credit cards, bank loans, and layaway plans operate.*

"A penny saved is a penny earned." (*English proverb*)

"Though you live near a forest do not waste firewood." (*Chinese proverb*)

"Through saving comes having." (*Scottish proverb*)

"Borrow sparingly, save abundantly." (*Arab proverb*)

You want to get the most for your money so you can increase your buying power. As you already know, budgeting your money can help make that possible. Part of your budget can be savings. Saving increases your buying power because it allows you to gather larger amounts of money to buy more expensive things.

Once in a while, however, people find that even saving isn't quite enough. They might need a large sum of money right away. At such times, people might consider borrowing money.

Any Interest in Money?

You earn money by working. You can also earn money by making your money work for you. If you put money in certain bank accounts, the bank will add money to your account. The money that you earn in this way is called *interest*.

Banks don't pay you interest because they are generous. **Interest** is *a fee paid for the use of money*. The bank uses your money to make investments or loans. The people who borrow money pay a fee—interest—to the bank. In turn, the bank pays some of that money as interest to you.

How does the bank know how much interest to pay you? That's determined by two factors:

- The first is your **principal**, which is *the amount of money you have in your bank account.*
- The second factor is the **interest rate**, or *the percentage of the principal that will be paid as interest.*

Suppose that you have $50 in your savings account, and there is an interest rate of 5 percent per year. At the end of the year, your $50 will have earned an extra 5 percent of that $50, or $2.50. The bank adds that to your savings account, giving you a total of $52.50.

Once the interest is added on, it becomes part of your principal. Since your principal is now $52.50, you will earn even more interest dollars the next year.

Ways of Saving

There are many ways to save money. Each one has advantages and disadvantages. It's a good idea to take a look at a few of these ways to see what each has to offer.

Keeping Your Money at Home

You can keep your money at home in a locked box, a safe, or even a piggy bank. It

---

Wise consumers compare and evaluate the benefits and risks involved in various savings plans. Then they choose the plan that will best serve their needs and goals.

TABLE 1 Comparing Compound Interest

A $100 deposit with 5% interest.

	Compounded Annually	Compounded Semiannually	Compounded Quarterly
Deposit	$100	$100	$100
Interest	5	5.06	5.62
Total after 1 year	$105	$105.06	$105.62

will always be right there when you want to use it. But you might be tempted to reach into your savings every time you get an urge to buy something.

Another problem with saving at home is that your money doesn't earn interest. There is also the question of safety. Money in the bank is insured. If the bank is robbed or goes out of business, you still get your money back. If your house is robbed, chances are that your money is lost forever.

Savings Accounts

A **savings account** is *an account that holds your savings.* You can open these accounts at a bank, savings and loan association, or credit union.

When you open an account, you usually get a small book called a *passbook.* It shows how much money is in your account. You can withdraw the money whenever you want, and the money is insured. But savings accounts differ, so shop around before settling on one.

The most important thing to find out about these accounts is how much interest your money will earn. Of course, the higher the interest rate, the more you will earn.

But you also want to find out how often your interest is **compounded.** That means *figuring the interest due and adding it to your principal.*

Interest may be compounded daily, quarterly (every three months), or yearly. Daily compounding will pay you the most interest.

You should also find out if you have to leave a certain amount of money in your account to get interest. And ask whether you lose interest if you withdraw money often.

Savings Bonds

Savings bonds are *certificates that represent money that you lend to the government.* The bonds pay you interest as long as you own them. They are insured, and you can cash them in any time you want. They are sold in smaller amounts than other kinds of bonds.

Savings bonds do not pay as much interest as some other ways of saving. Since you earn more money the longer you keep the bond, buy bonds only if you know that you will not need to use the money right away. You do not make as much interest if you cash the bond in early.

The government issues U.S. savings bonds. It takes a few years before the bonds reach full maturity, so it is best to buy bonds if you know that you will not need to use the money soon.

Savings Clubs

The most common kind of savings club is a Christmas Club. People pay a certain amount of money to a bank Christmas Club, usually every week during a year. The money adds up until, before Christmas, the people cash in the account and use the money to buy presents.

The advantage of a savings club is that it forces you to save. Then you have a large amount of money when you finally need it.

A disadvantage of savings clubs is that the money may not earn any interest, or at least not as much as that of other savings accounts. And you may have to leave the money in the club for an entire year to earn any interest at all.

Compare the club rules with those of a normal savings account to see which type of saving is better for you.

Other Ways to Save Money

There are other ways that you can save money. Some are more complicated than the ones mentioned above. You need more money and an understanding of how banking and money systems work to use them.

Stocks. Companies need money to operate. They get it by selling shares of *stock*. When you buy stock, you buy a share in the business.

Owners of stock gain when the company makes money. They may be paid part of its profits. They also benefit if the value of the stock goes up and they sell it for a higher price than they paid for it.

Since no one knows for sure how successful a company will be, buying stocks is something of a gamble. If stock prices fall, people can lose money. They must wait for the stock to rise again before they sell it. That's why it's a good idea to buy stocks carefully, using extra money that you do not need to meet the daily expenses that you have.

Bonds. Some businesses sell *bonds*. The people who buy them are lending the company money. In return, they are paid interest. Usually, investors must have a lot of money to buy a bond—a thousand dollars or more.

Mutual Funds. Mutual funds are a method of saving and investing for people who don't want to buy stocks and bonds on their own. Mutual fund companies pool the money of many people to buy stocks, bonds, and other investments. Then they divide any money that the investments earn. People can invest smaller amounts of money by joining mutual funds than by buying bonds on their own.

F E A T U R E

Credit Rights

Getting credit and keeping your credit records straight can sometimes present problems. Certain laws can help you if problems arise.

- Under the *Equal Credit Opportunity Act,* you cannot be discriminated against when applying for credit because of your race, color, sex, religion, marital status, or age (provided you are 18 years old, or, in some states, 21). You must be notified of the approval or disapproval of credit within 30 days. If you are turned down, you must be told in writing why you were denied credit.

- The *Truth-in-Lending Act* requires lenders to give you full information when you shop for credit. Stores must tell you both the cash purchase price and the total purchase price of an item after the finance charge is added. Lenders must state the annual percentage rate (APR) so that you can compare different borrowing plans.

- Stores or banks decide whether to give credit based on records kept by credit agencies. The *Fair Credit Reporting Act* gives you the right to see your credit records. If you find mistakes, you have the right to have them corrected. If a company refuses to give you credit because of information they have received from a credit agency, you have the right to see the credit report, or a summary of it, and to comment on it.

- The *Fair Credit Billing Act* protects you from billing problems. If you feel that a mistake has been made on your bill after a credit purchase, you must notify the creditor in writing within 60 days. Give your name, address, account number, the item, and amount in question, and explain why you think there is a mistake. The creditor must answer your letter within 30 days and must clear up the problem within 90 days. Until the problem is solved, you do not have to pay the amount in question.

Borrowing Money

Financial institutions lend money because they believe the borrower will repay it. An older person who pays bills promptly and has money in the bank probably has a good credit record. But young people just starting out may have trouble getting loans until they prove themselves trustworthy to a bank.

Getting Credit

Companies that offer credit look for certain qualities in the people they lend to. They want borrowers to be of a certain age, usually at least 18 years old. They want them to have some steady source of income, such as a job. They also want the borrower to have shown that he or she was responsible about paying off past debts.

When you're ready to borrow money, or to request a credit card in your name, there are some things you can do to get a company to offer you credit. First, you can get a parent to co-sign the loan. The parent must agree to be responsible for payments if you can't meet them.

You can also establish a credit record. You might start out by getting a checking account to show that you can pay bills and handle money. Then you might get a credit card from a store. By using it wisely, you can build a good credit record.

Another method of establishing a credit record is to get a small loan from a bank. Put the borrowed money into a savings account in another bank. Withdraw it to make payments on the loan each month, making sure that you pay on time. By repaying the loan, you establish a good credit record.

Shopping for Credit

The best source of credit is one with the lowest annual finance charge. The **finance charge** is *the money that you pay to the lender for allowing you credit*. It includes interest, service charges, and other fees.

For example, if you borrow $100 you might pay $18 in interest. In addition, there might be a service charge of $1. That would make the total finance charge $19 for the year.

A good way to compare finance charges is by using the **annual percentage rate** (APR). It is *the percentage cost of credit on a yearly basis*. The APR in the example above is 19 percent; you would pay $19 in one year for a $100 loan. The lower the APR, the better. Banks, stores, car dealers, and other lenders must tell you how much their fi-

nance charges and APR rates are. Be sure to get these figures in writing and choose the lowest APR.

Layaway

The coat you want is on sale for $50, but you only have $25 saved. You can buy the coat at the sale price by using the store's layaway plan. But instead of charging the coat, and wearing it while you pay off the debt, you have the store set the coat aside for you.

You first make a **down payment**, which is *your first, partial payment on something you*

Before signing a credit contract, be sure that you fully understand it. Read the fine print regarding interest rates, service charges, and other fees.

buy. The store agrees to hold the coat for you. Then you pay the rest of the money at specific times, perhaps ten dollars every two weeks. Of course, there is a limit to how much time you have to pay for the coat. And there's usually a fee added that increases the cost of the coat.

Making the Most of Savings and Credit

You can use savings and credit wisely to expand your resources. Money in a savings account grows and gives you more to spend. Using credit usually costs money, but it increases your buying power.

Be careful of buying on credit. With the freedom to purchase comes the obligation to pay for the product, plus its extra costs. It may be best to wait until you can pay cash for a purchase. You can put the money in an interest-bearing account until you have enough. You won't have to pay finance charges, and you'll earn interest, too.

When you think about savings and borrowing, remember to start simply. Open a savings account. Build your credit record carefully. Once you feel comfortable, you can move to more complex financial arrangements when you need them.

Words to Remember

annual percentage rate (APR): the percentage cost of credit on a yearly basis

compound: to figure interest due and add it to the principal

down payment: a first, partial payment on something you buy

finance charge: the money that you pay to the lender for allowing you to use credit

interest: a fee paid for the use of money

interest rate: the percentage of the principal that will be paid as interest

principal: the amount of money you have in a bank account

savings account: an account that holds your savings

savings bond: certificate that represents money that you lend to the government

Questions

1. What is interest? What is principal? How are they related?
2. List three ways of saving money. What are the advantages and disadvantages of each?
3. What kinds of things do companies look for when deciding whether to loan you money?
4. Why is it important to establish a good credit record for yourself? How can you begin?
5. How can you use the annual percentage rate to help you shop for credit?
6. Explain how layaway works.

Chapter

29 You in the Marketplace

Objectives

After reading this chapter, you will be able to:

- □ *separate the information in advertisements from selling techniques,*

- □ *find reliable sources of consumer information,*

- □ *identify the store that's best for a particular purchase,*

- □ *explain why retailers have sales,*

- □ *shop at sales wisely.*

When Angela needed to buy new running shoes, she decided to buy them at a sporting goods store. She had seen in a newspaper ad that her favorite brand was on sale. She didn't want to go back to the store where she'd gotten her last pair. Paying for them had taken forever, and the shoes hadn't lasted.

Angela went to the new shop. She shopped carefully and found just the right pair of shoes. They were on sale and a real bargain. Angela was able to pay for them quickly and leave. After the purchase, Angela felt good about herself and her new shoes.

In deciding where to shop, Angela was casting her vote as a **consumer**, *a user of goods and services.* Just as people express their choices with ballots in elections, you express your choice with dollars every time you buy something.

The Pros and Cons of Advertising

The decisions that consumers make about where and when to spend their money give them power in the marketplace. Without consumer dollars, products go off the market and stores close. You and your dollars are important to the people who make and sell things. How do they get your attention and your dollars? They try to offer attractive products, and they advertise.

Advertisements are everywhere—on television and radio, in newspapers, on buses, and on roadside signs. All the sellers are eager to tell you that you need their products.

The Purpose of Advertising

Can you think of how you came to know a particular product that you wanted? Did your friends have it? Or did you learn about it through advertising? Whatever the product—radio, bicycle, blue jeans—advertising probably played a large part in your desire to buy one.

Advertising has its benefits. For one thing, it lets you know what's available. For example, it tells you when a new movie comes out. Advertising can actually lower the cost of some products by making it possible to sell more products to more people. Ads also provide consumers with useful information.

Forewarned Is Forearmed

Will a new pair of designer jeans really make you more popular, as the ad suggests?

Probably not, but the "popularity ploy" is just one of the ways that advertisers use to persuade you to buy what you may not really need.

Another common technique is the **testimonial**, in which *a public figure is shown to use a product to promote sales.*

Some ads use a misleading comparison such as, "Use Bounce Shampoo for livelier hair." What exactly is livelier hair?

There's also the "gift that counts" ad: "Only *Mystique* can tell her how much you love her." Why not tell her yourself?

All these techniques are **emotional appeals**. They are *aimed at persuading you that buying a particular product will make you feel better about yourself.* Often ads have little or nothing to do with the nature of the product or its value to you. Does a soft drink taste better because of the catchy commercials?

Be on the lookout. Don't be easily convinced that products are good because the advertising says so. Find out for yourself.

Other Sources of Information

If your friend José owns a stereo and if you're thinking of buying the same model, you'd naturally ask him some questions about it. Questioning friends and relatives is an easy way to get information about a product.

For more information, you can turn to consumer magazines. The two main ones are *Consumer Reports* and *Consumers' Research.* They test many different products and services and sometimes rate them. Their tests are thorough, and they can compare more brands than friends and relatives can. You may find it helpful to turn to these sources. At your local library you can find the *Consumer Index*, which lists what products and services have been reviewed in these consumer magazines.

You can also get information from consumer magazines such as *Changing Times*, *Consumer Digest*, and *Money*.

Knowing Your Stores

Different kinds of stores serve different purposes. Consumers can save themselves time and money by shopping first at the most appropriate store.

- The **convenience store** offers *quick service from early morning until late at night, usually seven days a week*. This store generally sells a limited selection of items at high prices. You pay for the convenience of being able to buy something at 10:30 P.M.

- A **specialty store** *sells only a certain type of merchandise*, such as records or jeans. At a specialty shop, you may find a better selection of the item you're looking for.

- The **department store** offers consumers the convenience of *a wide variety of items, often in several different price ranges, all for sale under one roof*. Department stores hire many salespeople and issue their own credit cards. They offer many services, such as delivery, gift wrapping, alterations, bridal registry, and fashion and interior decorating.

- The **discount store** usually *carries nationally advertised brands at reduced prices*, as well as merchandise with the store's own private label. These stores offer the least service, but they are also the least expensive.

- In the **factory outlet**, *the manufacturer of a product sells merchandise directly to consumers*. Sometimes the goods are imperfect, or they may be styles that are no longer made. Prices are low because there is no separate store owner who must mark up the prices to make a profit.

Good bargains can be found in almost any store, if you have the time and patience to shop wisely.

Mail Order

Shopping by mail may be another way you want to shop. The mail-order company sends you a catalog. You mark what you want on a form and return it with a check or money order. In addition to the cost of each item, you pay a fee for postage and handling. Delivery takes a few weeks.

Many mail-order firms specialize. Some deal in outdoor equipment and clothing, some in old-fashioned items that may be hard to find elsewhere. Other mail-order firms sell foods. There are even a few that deal only in supplies for left-handed people!

Because you don't get to examine mail-order merchandise before you actually purchase it, you should take your time when ordering. Read carefully all the catalog information about size, weight, fabric, or warranty.

For your own protection, there are also a few other points to remember when dealing with mail-order firms.

Never pay cash. Pay only by check, credit card, or money order. Keep a record of your purchase, including the catalog ad and a copy of your order form with the company's name and address.

Know your rights. There are laws covering purchases by mail (but not by phone):

- Merchandise ordered must be shipped within 30 days of receipt of your payment. If it isn't, and the company doesn't explain why, you can cancel the order and the company must issue a refund.

- Damaged or spoiled articles can be returned in the original wrapper for no additional postage. Mark the package "refused."

- If you find a product to be unsatisfactory, contact the company about replacing it, repairing it, or refunding your money. If you don't get any results, contact the Postal Inspection Service.

Other ways to shop include buying from *mail-order companies* (see the box), and *door-to-door* as well as *telephone salespersons.*

In addition, there are *consumer co-op organizations* that buy in bulk, pay wholesale prices, and then pass on the savings to their members. *Thrift shops* offer used merchandise at low prices. And finally, of course, you can buy used goods from another consumer at a *yard* or *garage sale* or a *flea market.*

Understanding Sales

Stores use sales for two purposes—to attract new and regular customers, and to clear out merchandise that may be selling poorly or slowly. Retailers also hope that while you're there you'll be attracted to regular-price items and buy them, as well as the sale merchandise that is offered to the interested buyers.

When shopping for sales, be sure that you are buying something that you want. A sale is not a bargain if you buy an item that you don't need.

When Stores Hold Sales

You'll often see sales at certain times of the year. Fall clothes, for example, go on sale in January. Sometimes sales become traditions, such as Columbus Day coat sales. Stores that are closing sometimes sell their remaining stock in one final going-out-of-business sale. Sales are also held in response to competition from other stores.

Points to Remember at Sales

Is the Product Worthwhile? Check the label of anything you buy. If it says "as is," there's a flaw somewhere on the product. "Seconds" or "irregular" merchandise will also have flaws. These may still be worthwhile purchases if the flaws are minor. If the label says "final sale," the product is not returnable.

TABLE 1 Good Times to Buy

Month	Items to Buy
January	coats, cosmetics, shoes, stationery
February	musical instruments, stormwear, Washington's birthday sale items
March	winter clearance items
April	fabric, paint
May	bicycle tires, jewelry, summer sportswear
June	camping and camera gear, clothing, typewriters
July	sports gear, summer clothes, swimwear
August	back-to-school specials, summer clearance items
September	auto accessories, fall clothes
October	Columbus Day specials, fall and winter clothes
November	Christmas gifts, jewelry, radios and stereos, televisions
December	after-Christmas specials on toys, cards, wrapping, gifts

Is the Product Dated? Be aware that what's on sale may be out of fashion or out of season. In the case of food, sale items may have only a limited shelf life left (that is, the time during which they may be legally sold).

Can You Control Your Buying Urges? Once you are in a store that's having a sale, the temptation to pick up other goods is great. This is **impulse buying**, or *buying something you hadn't intended to*. Avoid the urge to buy something just because it's there and looks attractive. Chances are you'll regret the purchase by the time you get home.

Detecting Suspicious Sales

Here are the terms used in ads for sales.

■ The *list price*, included on products by the manufacturer, is seldom the retailer's ac-tual selling price. "Twenty percent off list" may not be a bargain if the store never sold the product at list price.

■ *Below manufacturer's cost* suggests that both the manufacturer and the retailer will lose money on the sale, which isn't likely. Check the merchandise—is it out of date? Are parts for it unavailable?

■ *Comparable to $49.95 value* is just the opinion of the advertiser. The merchandise may be worth only the $29.95 you pay for it.

■ *Special purchase* items may not be of the store's usual quality.

■ *Regularly $9.95, now $5.95* tells you the item is on sale if the store used to charge $9.95, and will raise the price to $9.95 again. But sometimes the lower price becomes permanent—and that's no sale.

Words to Remember

consumer: a user of goods and services

convenience store: a store that is open long hours and offers quick service at high prices

department store: a store offering a wide variety of items in several different price ranges under one roof

discount store: a store that sells nationally adver-tised brands at reduced prices

emotional appeal: the suggestion that an adver-tised product will make you feel better about yourself

factory outlet: a store in which a manufacturer sells extra merchandise directly to consumers

impulse buying: buying something without having intended to

specialty store: a store that sells only a certain type of merchandise

testimonial: an ad in which a public figure is shown to use a product to promote sales

Questions

1. What is a consumer? Why do consumers have power?

2. How does advertising benefit the con-sumer? How might it be misleading?

3. In addition to ads, how can you find out about a product?

4. Name three types of stores.

5. What should you remember when buying merchandise on sale?

30 Shopping
for Price
and Quality

Objectives

After reading this chapter, you will be able to:

- *explain the connection between price and quality,*

- *identify the characteristics you want in goods and services,*

- *comparison shop before buying,*

- *evaluate the hidden costs that may accompany your purchase.*

Apples, braces, coats, dog food, earrings, jogging suits, ketchup, lipstick—can you go on with this alphabetical list of goods and services?

Even if you go all the way to zippers, your list will be only a small sample of goods and services available. You can choose from a tremendous variety of **goods**, or *merchandise that can be bought.* You also have many choices of **services**, or *the work performed by one person for another.*

How, then, do you choose? How do you get the most for your money? What are the qualities to look for? What should you avoid? The following guidelines can help you make the wisest decisions about price and quality when you are shopping for goods and services.

Price and Quality

If money were no object, you could always buy the highest-quality item available. But most of the time, price, as well as quality, influences your purchasing decisions. Often, you will have to make a trade-off, or a compromise. You must give up one thing to get another. The usual trade-off is between what you can afford and what you'd really like if money was unlimited. You can make the best trade-offs by planning before you shop. Start out by setting a minimum level of quality and a maximum price.

Standards

What is quality anyway? What's called quality varies from product to product. In general, though, quality can be said to depend on five important factors.

- *Performance.* How well does the product work? Is the video game fun? Is the cereal nutritious as well as delicious?
- *Durability.* How strong, sturdy, or well made is the product? Will the sweater shrink after washing? Will the schoolbag hold your books, or will it fall apart in a few weeks?
- *Convenience.* Is the product easy to open, close, use, and store? Do you have to fight those boots to get them on? Does the shampoo bottle tend to pour more than it should?
- *Maintenance.* How much care will a product require during its lifetime? Will the watch need expensive repairs if you get it wet? Does the portable television come with a warranty? And are there

service centers nearby in case repairs are needed?
- *Safety.* Are there any potential hazards involved in using the product? Is the handle of the typewriter case strong enough? Does that hair dryer come with the Underwriter's Laboratory (UL) seal of safety?

Price

There are several things to consider when you're deciding how much you're willing to pay. A higher price doesn't always mean better quality. And paying a low price at a discount store may not be a bargain if you have to travel far.

Emergencies may cause you to pay more. If your glasses break, and only an expensive repair shop is open, the price may be less important than getting your glasses fixed in a hurry. Your need for, and intended use of,

Be careful to check labels and to read the warranty on a product. In many cases, you will be glad that you did.

a product is as important a consideration as its price.

You'll usually get more for your money when you plan ahead. If that $3 wallet is a perfect gift for your sister, buy it now if you can afford it. Six months from now, when her birthday arrives, you might pay $10 for a last-minute gift that neither of you is pleased with.

Suitability

Having some idea of what you need before you shop makes all the difference when you're in the store looking at rows and rows of products. Take a few minutes to think about your purchase.

Suppose you've saved money to buy a watch. What features are most important to you? Do you want a stopwatch? Do you want one with a calendar? Or are you more interested in a better-looking watch with neither of those features?

Once you've decided what you require, find out which product in your price range comes closest to fulfilling your needs.

Comparison Shopping

If you're about to make an expensive purchase—a portable cassette player, for instance—you probably won't want to buy the first one you see. More than likely you'll want to look at several models and *compare the features and prices of each before you buy.* Such **comparison shopping** is a good habit even if the product is a relatively small item, like a box of cereal.

In chapter 29, you found out where to go for consumer information about products. You must also know what information to get from these sources. Your comparisons should include the important points mentioned below.

Price and Performance

You may think that a difference of a dime on a food purchase isn't that much. But what are the reasons for the 10-cent difference? Read the labels of two similar products carefully. Is the nutritional value the same? Is there as much in one package

When you shop, be careful to look for quality and durability in clothing, as well as a good fit and an appealing price.

as in the other? Should you buy the larger or smaller size?

Using **unit prices**, or *the prices of items by ounce or by count*, will help you find the best value.

Suppose that 15 ounces of your favorite shampoo costs $3.69, and 12 ounces of a new brand is $3.39. You wonder if the new brand is cheaper. Reading the unit prices of the two shampoos shows that your brand costs less. The other is priced at $4.52 per pint, but yours is only $3.94 per pint.

The only way to find out if something expensive is really worth the extra money is to compare performance.

Start by looking up cassette players in the *Consumer Index.* Read all you can find about different brands and models. A more expensive brand may not be better. It might not have the features you want, or it may have features you don't need. It might have gotten a very low rating from a consumer magazine.

Next, go to the store and ask for a demonstration. You may prefer the sound of one model over another, or like the location of the dials better.

Contents and Durability

If the item is packaged, ask to see a sample so that you can get a "hands-on" idea of what you're buying. If you're considering a pair of boots, try them on, of course, but also look them over carefully to see how well they're made. Check a bicycle to see if it feels sturdy.

Labels help you compare the contents of products like food and clothing. You'll read more about these labels in units 4 and 5 of this book.

Unit price labels help you to find out which product costs less. What other factors should you consider when buying a product?

Convenience and Maintenance

If you're buying something that you'll need to assemble yourself, be sure that the instructions are included in the package. Ask at the store if someone will be available to answer questions should you have trouble.

Look for care instructions on clothing labels, and consider the cost of such care before you make your purchase. Most wool clothing, for instance, requires dry cleaning. Appliance packages should come with service manuals. These booklets describe how to use and care for a machine properly.

Safety

A **warranty** (or guarantee) is *a written statement from the manufacturer or retailer, promising to repair or replace a defective product, or to*

F E A T U R E

Tips Against Sales Traps

Sometimes it's hard to resist. The salesperson has you cornered. The watch seems like a bargain, though the strap does look a bit flimsy. "Only $19.95!" he says. You're reaching for your wallet, but something tells you . . .

Don't. Don't give in to sales pressure when you have doubts about a purchase. Buy what you want, not what the salesperson wants you to buy.

Pressure from salespeople is only one way that skillful merchandising can part you from your money. You can save money by being aware of such techniques. Follow these suggestions:

■ *Know what you want.* Avoid impulse buying—make a list and stick to it.

■ *If you're not sure whether to buy a particular item, wait.* A store may be willing to hold an item aside for you for several hours. This allows you time to check a few other stores.

■ *Get the facts.* Ask questions. Dismiss any information that you recognize as an emotional appeal. Buying the "official running shorts of marathon winners" will not improve your running. It will only take more money.

■ *Avoid bait and switch advertising, which is illegal.* If you go to a store to see an advertised product, and you're told that item is out of stock but are shown something more expensive, watch out.

■ *Beware of stores that have continuous sales.* If "sale" signs are unchanged after a few weeks, it's likely that there was no real sale in the first place. Be especially careful about "going out of business" signs that are up for months.

■ *Don't be taken in by "free offer" ads.* Free means *free.* If you have to buy something else to get the free offer, be sure you know the details. Is the cost of the item you must purchase higher than usual?

■ *Use "cents-off" coupons carefully.* Even with the discount, the product may cost more than the brand you usually use. Even if it's a bargain, is it something you really need?

■ *Wherever you are, in every shopping situation, use your common sense.* Stay alert. Be critical. Put your consumer power to work for *you.*

refund your money. A warranty should include the following information:

■ The name and address of the company.

■ An exact statement of what is covered. Does the company agree to pay for parts and labor, or only parts?

■ The length of time of the coverage.

■ The procedure to be followed in case of a defect. For example, who will pay shipping costs to send the product back?

■ Whom the owner must contact to get the warranty fulfilled.

■ The length of time the company has to take action on a problem.

- Any requirements that the purchaser must meet, such as sending in a registration card.

Remember to keep your warranties in a safe place in case you need them.

Avoiding Hidden Costs

Some costs are hidden because they are not part of the price of something, but they still must be paid. A few common ones are listed below.

- *Travel.* When comparison shopping, don't forget to include the cost of transportation. Consider the time, energy, and money required to have your hair cut across town. It might cost less to go to a more expensive salon around the corner.
- *Stores.* The cost of something at a store that gives poor service can skyrocket if you have trouble with an exchange or refund.

- *Repairs.* Before buying a product, check the warranty for coverage. There may be a copy attached to the floor model. If not, ask to see one. Stores are required by law to show you warranties. Ask about the costs of repairs not covered by the warranty. If they seem high, compare them to repair costs for other models of the same products.

- *Accessories.* "Battery not included" can mean another expense before the product you've bought is actually going to work. Some accessories, such as shoulder straps for schoolbags and stuff sacks for sleeping bags, are conveniences you might need as much as the item itself.

- *Exchanges.* If something goes wrong with a product you purchased, take it back to the store with the receipt. Usually, stores have policies and time limits for refunds and exchanges. For your own protection, find out about these at the time of purchase.

Words to Remember

comparison shopping: comparing features and prices of different brands of the same item before you buy

goods: merchandise that can be bought

services: the work performed by one person for another

unit prices: the prices of items by ounce or by count

warranty: a written statement from a manufacturer or retailer, promising to repair or replace a defective product, or to refund your money

Questions

1. What factors might you want to consider when buying a bicycle?
2. What are two considerations that may outweigh price?
3. How do you use unit prices?
4. Give three pieces of information that a warranty should include.
5. Name three hidden costs.

Chapter **31** Voicing Your Opinion

After reading this chapter, you will be able to:

☐ *make an effective consumer complaint to the right person,*

☐ *take other steps if your complaint is not satisfied,*

☐ *explain why you should tell businesses whether you are satisfied or dissatisfied with them.*

Jeff had saved twenty-five dollars for a new pair of pants. He wanted a special pair that he could wear to parties and other places during the summer.

Jeff is a careful shopper so he went to several stores to find the right pair of pants. Finally he found a pair that was well-made and just the right color—navy blue.

Jeff enjoyed wearing the pants, but after the third time he wore them, the navy blue color of the pants turned to a blotchy blue and green. The sun had faded the pants in just a few wearings. Jeff was really mad, but he didn't know what to do.

Sometimes you aren't happy with a purchase you made. Perhaps a product is missing parts. Or maybe a service was not done correctly. At such times, it's important to know how to use another consumer skill: *voicing your opinion.* This step gives you a second chance to become satisfied.

Your Consumer Rights

Making a complaint is not just a skill; it's a right. In 1962, the late President John Kennedy introduced the "Consumer Bill of Rights." It includes:

■ *The right to safety.* Consumers are protected from the selling of dangerous products.

■ *The right to be informed.* Consumers are protected from misleading advertising. They can ask for all the facts needed to make good choices.

■ *The right to choose.* Consumers are given the chance to make their own choices.

■ *The right to be heard.* Consumers can speak out when they aren't satisfied. They have a voice in the making of consumer laws.

During the 1970s, former President Richard Nixon added another right: *the right to redress.* This means that consumers who have a wrong done to them have the right to get that wrong corrected.

Former President Gerald Ford also added a right—*the right to consumer education.*

When Is it Fair to Complain?

Every consumer expects manufacturers and sellers to be fair. They expect to be offered goods and services at fair prices. Consumers must also be fair by voicing their opinions only when the complaint is a real one.

For example, Donna bought a wool-blend sweater. The care label on the sweater said, "Hand wash, using a cold-water wash product." Donna washed the sweater by hand in cold water, but it shrank. Donna has a real complaint against the sweater manufacturer.

Generally, a complaint is fair if you purchased a product that was damaged, or if it was not sold at the advertised price. You would also have a right to complain if a service you paid for was not done correctly.

Complaining in Person

If you do have a fair complaint, act soon. Delaying may make it harder to solve the problem. First, find your sales receipt and warranty. Always save these; they can help you state your case.

Then follow these five steps:

1. *Check to see if the problem is covered by the warranty.* If so, follow the directions listed on it and go to step 5. If not, take the next three steps.

2. *Write down exactly what's wrong with the product.* Use these notes to guide you when you explain the problem.

3. *Go to the store where you made your purchase.* Ask a salesperson to help you or to direct you to someone who can, such as the department store manager or store owner.

4. *Explain your problem clearly and briefly.* Be polite, firm, and willing to compromise. Remember that the store worker will probably want to settle the problem. A satisfied customer means future sales.

5. *Propose a solution to the store worker.* You may want the product to be repaired, to receive a replacement, or to get your money back.

Writing a Letter of Complaint

The problem may not be solved by visiting the store. If not, it's time to write a letter. Send it to the company that makes or sells the product or supplies the service. Address the letter to a particular person, such as the vice-president, rather than "To Whom It May Concern." This makes it more likely that your letter will be read.

If the company is local, check your phone book for the name and address. For a national company, go to the library. You can find the company's address in a business reference book or a consumer complaint guide.

A complaint letter should have the following information:

- Your name and address.
- The date you are writing the letter.
- The name, job title, and address of the person you're writing to.
- The product or service name, style, and model number.

Find the right address before you send in your complaint letter. Calling a company to find who to send the letter to is also a good idea.

- The name and address of the store where you made your purchase, and the date you bought it.
- What sales receipts, bills, or warranties you are including with your letter (always send copies of these papers, not the originals).
- A simple and brief explanation of why you are unhappy with the product or service, and how you would like to see the problem solved.

Taking Further Action

In most cases, visiting the store or writing a letter will settle the problem. But sometimes these actions are just not enough. In those cases, the consumer can get help from other sources.

Consumer Agencies

Business Consumer Agencies. The public relations department of a large company can help you. Another group is the Better Business Bureau (BBB), which is formed by businesses. If you wish to complain, for example, about the sales policy of a store in your area, you can contact the BBB. It may present your complaint to the store and help find a solution. There are 150 branches of the BBB helping consumers.

Consumer Action Panels (CAPs). These groups are formed by industries—automakers, for instance—to handle consumer complaints. If a consumer is not satisfied after complaining directly to the manufacturer, the CAP will try to find a solution.

F E A T U R E

How Would You React?

You are the head of a record company. One day, you receive the following three complaint letters. How would you react to each one?

---

775 West 82 Street
New York, New York 10024
March 15, 1987

Company Head
Top Quality Records
32 Platter Drive
Columbus, Ohio 43224

Dear Company Head:

Your company made <u>Reaching for the Stars</u>, but my copy is warped.

I want my money back.

Yours truly,

Barbara Palatino

Barbara Palatino

---

741 Planter Way
Dallas, Texas 75218
March 15, 1987

Ms. Joan Snelling
President
Top Quality Records
32 Platter Drive
Columbus, Ohio 43224

Dear Ms. Snelling:

Last week I bought the album, <u>Reaching for the Stars</u>, made by your company. Unfortunately, my copy is warped.

I took the album back to the store, Sound Effects, but the manager said that he had no more copies and suggested I write to you. I'm enclosing a copy of the sales slip.

I would like a new copy of the album, please. Also, please tell me what to do with the warped copy.

Thank you for your help.

Sincerely,

Wanda Ramirez

Wanda Ramirez

---

13 Weston Court
St. Louis, Missouri 63116
March 15, 1987

President
Top Quality Records
32 Platter Drive
Columbus, Ohio 43224

Dear President:

I bought the album, <u>Reaching for the Stars</u>. It is warped and will not play properly.

Please send me a new copy of the album or a refund. I would like your help in this.

Thank you very much for your time and attention.

Sincerely,

Alan Yamashita

Alan Yamashita

TABLE 1   Federal Consumer Agencies

Agency	Responsibilities
Consumer Product Safety Commission	Sets safety standards for household products
Department of Agriculture	Grades and inspects foods
Federal Communications Commission	Sets standards for radio and television advertising and broadcasting
Federal Trade Commission	Prevents misleading advertising and selling practices; regulates competition among businesses
Food and Drug Administration	Regulates food, drug, and cosmetic quality; inspects food and drug production plants
Interstate Commerce Commission	Regulates rates and sets standards for bus and train travel
Office of Consumer Affairs	Educates consumers
Postal Service	Regulates mail practices; protects consumers from being cheated through the mail
Securities and Exchange Commission	Regulates the sale of stocks and bonds

Government Consumer Agencies. Each level of the United States government has agencies that protect consumers. Local and state agencies enforce laws. They also make health and safety rules to protect consumers.

Consumer agencies in the national government have three major jobs that they are responsible for:

1. They make safety rules to protect consumers.

2. They make sure that manufacturers do not offer unsafe products.

3. They keep manufacturers and sellers from doing things that will mislead consumers.

The table above lists nine federal agencies that help consumers in various ways. They touch all aspects of our lives.

Joining with Other Consumers

Your community is another source of help. Why? All manufacturers and sellers know that when shoppers join together, they can give a company, store, or product a bad name. This can hurt sales. Of course, you should take action only when you have a fair complaint.

You can also make a complaint public by contacting people in the mass media. Newspapers and radio and television stations often have workers who help consumers.

Legal Assistance

If a complaint is still not settled, you can get legal help to solve the problem.

Hiring a lawyer to handle the complaint is one way, but it can be costly. Consumers usually choose this method only for serious problems.

Legal aid and legal services provide free legal help to consumers who can't pay lawyers' fees.

Most consumers with less serious complaints use the **small claims court**. In this court, *consumers and businesses present their complaints informally, and a judge decides the case.* Because you can present your own case, there are no legal fees. The small claims court fee is only $2 to $15. It is often paid back if you win your case. The court cases are short and simple to follow.

The Positive Power of Consumers

Suppose that you purchase a hair dryer. The first time you plug it in and turn on the switch, smoke pours out of the dryer's vent. That day, you write a letter to the maker of the hair dryer and describe what happened.

Your letter does something very impor-tant. It gives the manufacturer the chance to hear your complaint. The company may not even know the problem exists. A poorly made product could damage the company's name. This could mean fewer dryers sold. The business would rather know about the problem and fix it.

Putting in a Good Word

Consumers are often quick to complain. But they rarely take the time to tell a business when it's doing something right.

The next time you are happy with a purchase, think about writing a complimentary letter. Putting in a good word will encourage a business to continue making high-quality goods and services. It will also encourage the business to care about consumers.

Voicing your opinion takes time. It also takes extra effort. But it's worth it. By voicing your opinion, you can make a difference. With your complaints and your compliments, you help businesses learn about the needs and wants of consumers.

Word to Remember

small claims court: court in which consumers and businesses present their complaints informally, and a judge decides the case

Questions

1. What are the six consumer rights?
2. What are the five steps for complaining in person?
3. Why is it important to send a letter of complaint to a particular person at a company?
4. What type of legal action is usually best for less serious consumer complaints?
5. How can your complaint be helpful to a business or organization?

Chapter **32 Being a Responsible Consumer**

Objectives

After reading this chapter, you will be able to:

□ *identify dishonest consumer actions and explain why they harm consumers as well as businesses,*

□ *judge when a consumer complaint is unfair,*

□ *list ways that consumers can act responsibly for their own benefit and the benefit of others.*

Marlene answered the phone. It was her girlfriend, Anita.

"Marlene," Anita said. "Remember the yellow dress I wore to the party last night? Well, I just exchanged it. I told the store it didn't fit me well. Now I'm going to wear the new dress to the game tonight."

"Anita, that's not right," said Marlene.

"Why isn't it right?" asked Anita. "I didn't soil the dress or tear it!"

Consumers have the power to make their voices heard. They act to protect their rights. But along with their rights, consumers have some responsibilities. They should remember to be honest, fair, considerate, and responsible.

Being Honest

Consumers expect merchants to be honest with them. If a can of food is spoiled, they expect it to be taken off the shelves. If they ask the difference between one guitar and another, they expect an honest answer. Consumers, in turn, should be honest with sellers.

Honest or Dishonest?

Honest consumers pay the price that is marked on an item. Some consumers put saving money ahead of honesty. They may switch price tags, putting a lower price on the item they plan to buy. This practice is unfair to other consumers, who paid the correct price. In fact, this cheating makes prices higher. And it isn't fair to the store.

If a store cashier gives a customer too much change, an honest consumer returns it. It would be unfair for the store to charge too much for a purchase; keeping extra change is just as unfair. And it could be costly for the cashier, too. Some stores make cashiers pay for missing money out of their own pockets.

No Shoplifting

Have you ever entered a store where you were asked to leave your shopping bag at the cashier's counter? The owners wanted to be sure that you wouldn't hide anything in your bag. They were afraid of **shoplifting**, or *stealing goods from stores.*

Such stealing costs $26 billion each year. That figure covers the cost of the goods stolen, the cost of security systems aimed at preventing shoplifting, and the cost of tak-

Count your change when you receive it after a purchase. This prevents misunderstandings for both you and the sales clerk.

ing shoplifters to court. This money can be replaced in only one way—by raising prices. Experts say that shoplifting adds 2 percent to the prices in stores.

To try to stop shoplifting, stores are taking extra steps. They are putting special tags on clothes. These tags sound an alarm if the clothing is taken out the door. They are removed by the cashier if the garment is purchased.

Some stores hire security guards and use cameras. And many stores are no longer letting shoplifters go. If the shoplifter is young, store owners may hold the person until his or her parents come to the store. Shoplifting can be listed on a police record, which might cause problems when the person tries to get a job.

T E E N   I S S U E

The Costs of On-the-Job Crime

Good relationships between businesses and their customers are built on trust. Businesses also expect to establish the same kind of a trusting relationship with their employees. But many businesses have learned that employees are guilty of *on-the-job dishonesty* known as **worker theft.** Experts say that worker theft costs businesses about $40 billion a year.

What do you know about employee theft? Find out by taking the quiz below.

1. Taking an extra 20 minutes for lunch every day is an example of worker theft. (True or false.)
2. Businesses can afford the losses from worker theft; their insurance covers it. (True or false.)
3. Consumers are not affected by worker theft; only businesses suffer a loss. (True or false.)
4. Worker theft is a fact of life; nothing can be done to combat it. (True or false.)

Answers

1. True. By arriving late or going home early, a worker cheats an employer of some of the time and work that is being paid for.
2. False. Insurance rates for stores and businesses with high inventory losses have skyrocketed. Companies must find other ways to recover their losses.
3. False. Consumers, too, are victims of worker theft. Stores and businesses that lose too much to worker theft must increase their prices.
4. False. By being honest, fair, considerate, and responsible, workers can help cut the high costs of worker theft.

Being Fair

Consumers expect stores to sell their goods at fair prices and to give them good service. They expect sellers to answer complaints fairly. But consumers should also be fair toward sellers.

Many stores have a **return policy**. *A customer can return an item in exchange for another item, or perhaps for a cash refund.* Fair consumers use this policy when they need to—perhaps to return something that doesn't fit. Unfair consumers try to take advantage of this policy. They buy a sweater, wear it once or twice, and then return it. In the long run, this behavior hurts them. Handling too many returns and giving refunds force a store to raise its prices.

Some stores protect themselves by stating on signs that no item will be taken back if it is missing its *price tag*. These tags are fixed to the items in such a way that they cannot be put back if they are removed.

Being Considerate

A considerate consumer remembers that the store is someone else's property. Littering is unpleasant and makes a mess that employees must clean up. Consumers can help keep stores clean and neat by not littering.

Worse than litter is **vandalism**. This is when *someone mars or destroys someone else's property*, such as spraying paint on a store window or breaking products. Just like shoplifting, vandalism forces store owners to raise prices.

Considerate consumers also think of others. Have you ever brought home something new, only to find that one piece was missing? The piece could have been lost when a thoughtless shopper opened the box in the store. Don't open boxes. The person who buys the product wants it to be new, not dirty and incomplete. If you need to see the product, ask the store clerk to show you a floor sample.

You can help other consumers in another way, too. Simply putting things back where you found them can make it easier for the next shopper to find an item.

Being Responsible

Consumer responsibility goes beyond how you act in stores. It also includes how you use the products you buy, and how you use both your own resources and the resources of the whole nation.

The shop owner has the responsibility to sell undamaged products. The consumer has the responsibility never to return to the owner products that he or she has damaged.

Using Products Safely

Many products, like lawn mowers and floor cleaners, can be very dangerous if they are used improperly. A responsible consumer is aware of the possible dangers and uses products carefully.

Acting responsibly includes driving safely and not mixing drinking with driving. It also includes using knives properly when preparing food in the kitchen, and following manufacturers' instructions when using small appliances. Consumers should unplug them after use.

Consumers should stay informed about safety problems. Television and radio news reports and newspaper articles tell the public about products that are found to be unsafe. Sometimes a batch of food is bad. Several years ago, somebody added poison to bottles of medicine. As a result of this problem, many such medicines now have tamper-resistant lids.

By staying alert and informed, consumers can protect themselves. They can also protect each other. If you hear of a product with a safety problem, you should tell your friends and neighbors.

Using Resources Wisely

As a consumer, you use natural resources such as water, energy, and air. The choices you make about them can help the nation use those resources more efficiently.

■ People who choose energy-saving appliances, for instance, are helping to reduce the amount of coal, oil, or gas used daily.

■ Certain shower heads use less water than others. They reduce the amount of water needed in households.

■ Using paper products carefully and avoiding those with wasteful paper packaging will mean cutting down fewer trees.

■ Recycling aluminum cans and paper means fewer resources will be used up to produce new products.

All the above steps can also mean lower prices for everybody.

Acting responsibly, then, benefits everyone. Being honest, fair, and considerate makes relations between consumers and sellers better. It can also help keep prices lower—and that makes all consumers happy!

Words to Remember

return policy: a store's rules for allowing a customer to return an item in exchange for another item, or perhaps for cash

shoplifting: stealing goods from stores

vandalism: marring or destroying someone else's property

worker theft: on-the-job dishonesty

Questions

1. List three ways by which consumers can be dishonest.
2. What are the costs of shoplifting to the person who shoplifts and to all consumers?
3. In what ways can consumers be fair? In what ways can they be considerate?
4. What two things are involved in being responsible?

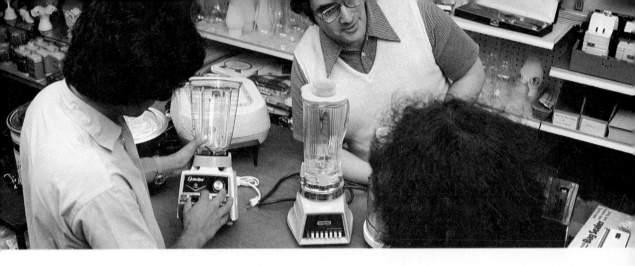

Chapter 33 Management and Consumer-Related Careers

Objectives

After reading this chapter, you will be able to:

☐ *identify areas in the job market in which you can use the skills learned in this unit,*

☐ *describe particular jobs in these areas.*

You manage your resources so that you can achieve as many goals as possible. Businesses and other groups do the same thing. They hire workers who plan for the future and organize ways to get work done. Studying home economics can help prepare you for these careers.

Managing and consumer careers are many and varied. They range from store clerks to fish hatchery workers. They include bookkeepers, financial advisers, and environmental scientists. Lawyers and comparison shoppers are also people who help us manage our resources.

Characteristics Useful in Managing and Consumer Careers

Managing and consumer careers call for many similar characteristics.

Mental Characteristics

■ *Are you good at math?* Managers and consumer workers often need math skills. Whether the worker is a bank teller counting out bills or a financial adviser suggesting ways to pay for college, they must be able to make calculations without mistakes.

■ *Can you make decisions and solve problems?* Good managers also recognize when they need more information before making a decision. They know how to find the information they need.

■ *Can you set goals for yourself and then plan how to meet them?* Planning is an important skill for managing. Organizing is, too. Can you order your schoolwork and your chores so that you get both done? You may have this important quality for a management job.

■ *Have you ever explained to a younger brother or sister how to play a game?* Then you know how important it is to give clear directions and be a good listener. Managers must be able to talk with others about how to work.

■ *Are you good at making and keeping a schedule?* Managers also need to review their own work to see if their plans are being carried out. This often means keeping a schedule.

Social Characteristics

■ *Have you ever led a group of classmates in a school project?* If so, you are learning an important skill. Managers hire and give directions to workers. They must be able to judge others' abilities and know how to work efficiently with others.

■ *Have you ever walked out of a store because of a rude salesperson?* Then you know the importance of getting along with people. Employees may work poorly if they feel that their boss is unfair or doesn't trust them.

■ *Are you good at talking with others?* One way managers and consumer workers develop these important skills is by being good at communication. Managers need to know when their workers are having problems with a task. They also need to know how to explain the solution.

If you have these abilities and characteristics, you may want to think about some of these careers.

A good manager often meets with employees to discuss schedules and to solve problems.

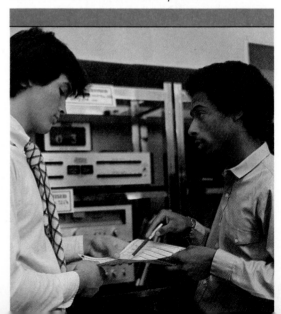

FEATURE

Writing a Résumé

Once you have identified a career that you are interested in, you are ready to write a résumé. A **résumé** is a paper *that states what career you are looking for and summarizes your background.* It shows an employer how you qualify.

The goal of the résumé is to interest the employer in you. It should show that you have the experience and skills that he or she needs. To make a good impression, you should prepare your résumé neatly. Follow these tips:

- Type it, if possible.

- Keep it no longer than one page. It should be short but informative.

- Begin it with your name, address, and phone number, so that the employer can contact you.

You should start your résumé by listing your career goal. You can keep this general (as in the sample), and send a cover letter with the résumé to apply for a particular job.

The main parts of your résumé are the next two sections—education and work experience. These sections show how your background qualifies you for the job you've chosen.

Some résumés, like the sample, include **references,** *the names of people who can tell an employer more about you.* Others say "References available upon request." If you choose to put that on your résumé, be sure to have the names of people handy when you have an interview. You should always ask someone in advance if he or she is willing to be a reference.

Andrea Thomas
650 West Twelfth Street
Coppstown, FL 33511
813-555-1212

JOB OBJECTIVE: Work in the food service industry

EDUCATION:
1982-1986   Coppstown High School
Took five home economics courses (including food service) with additional courses in business. Organized the glee club international food fair in junior and senior years.

WORK EXPERIENCE:
1985-1986   Kitchen worker, Sparky's Seafood, Coppstown, FL.
Part-time work cleaning, filleting, and cooking fish and shellfish.

1984-1985   Food server, Sparky's Seafood, Coppstown, FL.
Part-time work taking and filling orders and cleaning tables.

REFERENCES: Ms. Arlene Callison   Mr. Spartacus Argys
Home economics teacher   Owner, Sparky's Seafood
Coppstown High School

Management Careers

With the skills you have, you can work in many different types of management and consumer-related jobs. Because these jobs call for similar skills, you can even start in one area and change to another. You may start out working in a bank or department store. Years later you may use your skills to sell computers to businesses or plan how to use natural resources. You'll still be using similar skills, though.

Entry-Level Jobs

Many businesses keep all their supplies or products in large rooms or warehouses. They hire *stock clerks* to work in these areas and to locate items when they are needed in the store, office, or factory. These workers may be part time. The experience they gain in being part of a business will be very valu-able in their future jobs, even if they do other work.

Managers are often helped by *administrative assistants*. These workers prepare reports, schedule meetings, and communicate with other workers. They must be well organized. Many use computers and word processors to do their work.

A wide variety of workers is involved in managing resources. *Fish hatchery workers* and *farm workers,* for instance, are outdoors much of the time. Depending on where they live, these people may be seasonal workers—very active in some months, but less so in others.

Jobs That Require Extra Training

If you really like working with numbers, you may want to become a *bookkeeper.* These workers keep financial records so that managers know how much money is

---

Entry level and part-time jobs can give you insight to different business opportunities. Most people start "from the bottom" and work themselves into middle level jobs soon.

being spent and in what way. Bookkeepers are trained in two-year college programs.

People who want to be their own bosses become **entrepreneurs**. *They open a new business to provide a product or service that they think people will want to buy.* Being an entrepreneur is exciting. It offers independence and the chance to set your own goals. But it also presents many responsibilities and pressures. Entrepreneurs usually use their own savings to get the business going. If the new business does not do well, they can lose everything.

Many people start a business based on something they learned about in school, like hairstyling. Others learn by working for someone else first. Someone who works in a bookstore, for example, may eventually open his or her own store. Many business owners take courses in business management and financial planning to increase their chances of success. Many government and business groups give advice to new business owners.

Jobs That Require Advanced Degrees

Many people and groups turn for money information to *financial advisers.* These experts in managing money help clients set financial goals. Then they write a savings or investment plan to meet those goals. This career is expected to become very important in the future.

Most businesses have a *personnel manager* to help plan the company's employee needs. These managers make rules about hiring and firing and how workers should act on the job. They handle the health and life insurance policies provided by the company for the workers. They often have a college degree in business.

Environmental scientists plan how people use natural resources. They study an area to see what resources it contains. They also try to predict how long these resources will last. Or they may study how people and industry affect the way plants grow and animals live in an area. These scientists have at least four years of college.

Consumer-Related Careers

Many people work with and for consumers. They provide goods and services, or they help consumers get the most for their money.

Entry-Level Jobs

A person interested in working in a bank often starts out as a *bank teller.* A teller handles deposits and withdrawals for bank customers. Tellers must be very careful in their work to avoid making mistakes.

Comparison shoppers work for large stores. They travel to competing stores to check the prices and quality of similar products. Then they report to their managers. The store uses these reports to plan its own pricing and advertising.

Market survey interviewers ask people what they like. They take surveys at public places such as shopping malls to find out how people will respond to a new advertising campaign or a new product. They should be friendly, and willing to work in public.

Jobs That Require Extra Training

Many magazines and newspapers print articles about new products or how to manage resources. The *consumer writers* who write these articles know about these topics from research and from their own experience. They must be able to write clearly so that their readers understand what they say.

Credit managers work in banks or stores. They read the loan applications made by consumers and businesses. They must decide whether the person or business will be able to pay back the money borrowed. Most credit workers have a college background.

Jobs That Require Advanced Degrees

Many *lawyers* work on behalf of consumers. They study laws and court decisions about product safety and consumer rights. They may practice alone or work as part of a consumer group. Some write books or articles giving consumers valuable advice. These professionals go to college and then get an advanced degree.

Home economists have college degrees. They do a great range of work. Some teach in public schools, of course—but that's only the beginning! Nearly every county in the United States employs a home economist to answer consumer questions and to develop family living programs. They also organize 4-H clubs.

Many businesses such as banks and electric and gas companies hire home economists. These people advise families on how to manage their resources. They also write pamphlets, explaining how to use and care for appliances. Stores and manufacturers also hire home economists. They work with the public, explaining new products or new uses for old products.

Training in home economics, then, opens up many career possibilities. If you like managing and you like working with people, it may be for you.

Words to Remember

entrepreneur: someone who opens a new business to provide a product or service that he or she thinks people will want to buy

references: the names of people who can tell an employer more about you

résumé: a paper that states what career you are looking for and summarizes your background

Questions

1. Give two mental characteristics needed for management and consumer-related jobs.
2. Give two social characteristics needed for management and consumer-related jobs.
3. Name three jobs in management, one at each job level.
4. Name three consumer-related jobs, one at each job level.

"Okay," you say. "So it's great to save time and money, and be the perfect shopper. But that's easier said than done." You're right. But when you're armed with the right information, you'll have a much better chance to be a wise shopper and manager. Here is some information that will help.

1. Be an entrepreneur.

2. Tips on time.

3. Checking it out.

4. Borrowing basics.

5. Looking at labels.

Be an Entrepreneur

Many teens are identifying their skills and finding out that they can use them to make money. By running their own businesses, they also gain valuable experience.

Becoming an entrepreneur is a three-step process.

1. Identify your skill or interest.
2. Determine who would be willing to pay for your skill, and advertise yourself to those people.
3. Do a good job so that your customers will recommend you.

Here are some businesses that teens run. What could *you* do?

If your skill is working with children, you could babysit.

If you have good math or reading skills, you could tutor younger children.

If you enjoy working outside or with plants, you could mow lawns or do gardening.

If you are good at working with wood, you could make planters or wooden toys to sell at craft shows or flea markets.

If you are handy with a computer, you could write programs.

If you can play a musical instrument, you could join a band and play at parties.

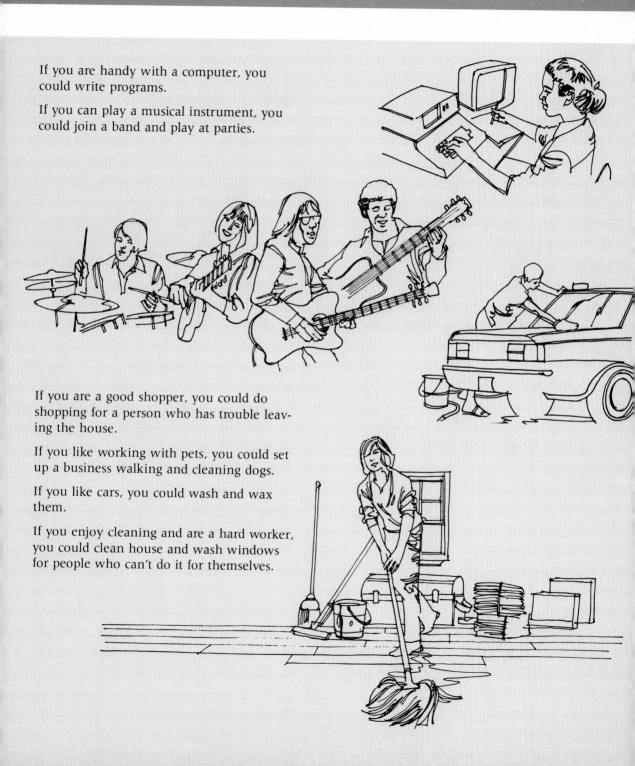

If you are a good shopper, you could do shopping for a person who has trouble leaving the house.

If you like working with pets, you could set up a business walking and cleaning dogs.

If you like cars, you could wash and wax them.

If you enjoy cleaning and are a hard worker, you could clean house and wash windows for people who can't do it for themselves.

Tips on Time

You have to turn in a book report in two weeks. "That's plenty of time!" you think. And it is. But if you're like most people, you don't *use* all that time. You shove the assignment to the back of your mind for one week. Then you spend two days thinking of it occasionally, but not starting on it. The next three days you spend worrying about the assignment—but you still don't read!

Finally, the night before the report is due, you skim the book, call your friend to ask more about the assignment, and frantically write your report.

There's an easier way. If you pace yourself, you can use a little time every day and get the job done with less worry. You'll probably even do a better job.

A Book Report Assignment

Day 13:   Get an overview of the book by reading the introduction, the jacket copy, and any information about the author. Scan the table of contents. Review the questions that your teacher wants you to answer.

Day 12:   Read one-quarter of the book—3 chapters of a 12-chapter book, for instance—and write a summary paragraph of each chapter.

Day 11:   Read the next quarter of the book and summarize it.

Day 10:   Read the next quarter of the book and summarize it.

Day 9:   Finish the book and summarize the last chapters.

Day 8:   Use the notes you've gathered over the last four days to write a one-page summary and review of the book.

Day 7:   Identify the main characters and theme of the book.

Day 6:   Answer the questions about the book that your teacher assigned.

Day 5: Read the rough draft of your report to a member of your family. Let them help you check for errors in spelling or grammar.

Day 4: Use your best handwriting to copy the report over.

Day 3: Read the new copy. Correct any errors you find.

Day 2: Get a good night's sleep—you're finished with a day to spare! This extra day gives you a cushion in case something happens on one of the other days to prevent you from getting the work done.

Day 1: Hand in your finished report.

You can use this method to accomplish any major task. Simply break up big projects into little segments that are easy to manage. Then you won't have to panic to get your work done.

Checking It Out

What does a properly written check look like? Here's an example, along with some pointers. Remember one thing: always write out a check in ink, not pencil, so it cannot be changed.

Randy Wu
1217 Kensington
Barclay, CA 91311

$\frac{1-11}{111}$

[1] *124*

[2] *December 1,* 19*86*

Pay to the
Order of [3] *Super Sound* _____ [4] $*17.92*

[5] *Seventeen and $\frac{92}{100}$* _____ Dollars

FIRST BANK

FOR [6] *records* _____   [7] *Randy Wu*

001–721–11100–092–3246–11

1. Fill in the number of the check. (Your bank may give you checks that are already numbered.)
2. Write in the correct date. Never write in a future date.
3. Write in the correct name of the person or organization you're giving the check to. Fill in the remaining space with a line—that protects you and the other person from anyone else changing the check.

If you want to collect cash from your bank, write "Cash" or your name on this line. But don't write a check to "Cash" until you are at the teller's window. Otherwise, anyone can cash the check if you lose it.

4. Write in the exact amount of the check in numbers. Start as close as possible to the dollar sign, so that no numbers can be added.

5. Write out the amount of the check in words. (For an amount in the hundreds, write "One hundred twenty-five and 00/100." For an amount less than one dollar, write "Only 57 cents" and cross out the word "dollars" at the end of the line.) Draw a line from the end of the amount to the word "dollars."

6. If you wish, you can use this line to record what the check was for.

7. Sign your name in the same way that you signed the card that the bank gave you when you opened the account.

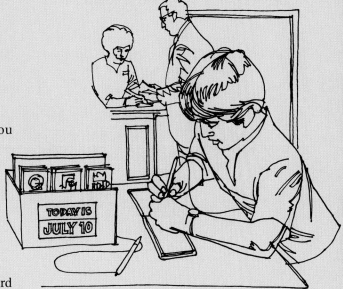

Now that you've written the check, record it in your check register and subtract the amount from your balance, as Randy did.

Check Number	Date	Payee		Deposit		Check		Balance	
								127	17
122	11/14	To Sportslife Magazine						13	95
		For Subscription				13	95	113	22
	11/15	To Deposit						50	00
		For		50	00			163	22
123	11/25	To Dandy Duds						27	98
		For 2 pair pants				27	98	135	24
124	12/1	To Super Sound						17	92
		For 2 records				17	92	117	32
		To							
		For							
		To							
		For							

Borrowing Basics

Credit can be a convenient way to buy costly goods or to spread out the cost of a product. But if misused, credit means too much debt—and that can bring on financial troubles. Here's how to avoid the credit crunch.

Don't use credit to buy extras that you don't need. Ask yourself whether you'd buy the item if you had to use cash.

Compare the cost of buying the product with cash and on credit. It will cost less if you wait and save money for it.

Compare credit cost—can you get a better deal somewhere else?

Hold down the cost of credit by making a larger down payment. The more you pay at the beginning, the less you'll have to borrow.

Pay back credit card charges when you receive the first bill. Then there will be no finance charge.

Read all credit agreements carefully to be sure you understand what the terms are. Ask questions if you need to.

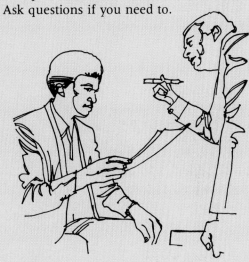

Don't borrow to make too many big purchases at once. Spread your buying time.

Don't give in to pressure. Take your time and consider the purchase carefully.

Looking at Labels

Federal laws require certain information on product labels. Here are examples of what you should look for:

FOOD

1. list of ingredients in decreasing order by weight (this information is required by law)
2. a list of the amounts of nutrients in each serving (not found on all food packages)
3. a list of the percentage of the U.S. RDA that each serving supplies (not found on all food packages)
4. name and address of the manufacturer, packer, or distributor
5. Universal Product Code is found on almost all grocery products. Checkout equipment can read the parallel black lines of various widths and ring up the sale automatically.

FLAKIES WHEAT CEREAL

INGREDIENTS whole wheat, sugar, salt, malt syrup, calcium carbonate, trisodium phosphate, sodium ascorbate, niacinamide (a B vitamin), iron (a mineral), vitamin A palmitate, pyridoxine hydrochloride (vitamin B_6), thiamine mononitrate (vitamin B_1), riboflavin (vitamin B_2).

NUTRITION INFORMATION PER SERVING

	1 oz. serving	1 serving with milk
calories	110	190
protein (g)	3	7
carbohydrate (g)	23	29
fat (g)	1	5
sodium (mg)	370	430
(1305 mg per 100 of cereal)		

0 70177 05060

PERCENTAGE OF U.S. RECOMMENDED DAILY ALLOWANCES (U.S. RDA)

protein	4	niacin	25	vitamin B_{12}	25
vitamin A	25	calcium	*	phosphorus	8
vitamin C	25	iron	25	magnesium	8
thiamine	25	vitamin D	10	zinc	4
riboflavin	25	vitamin B_6	25	copper	6

* contains less than 2 percent of the U.S. RDA of this nutrient

General Cereals, 16 Industrial Drive West, Colesville, PA 18015

CLOTHING

1. a list of the fibers from which the garment is made
2. instructions for washing

50% Wool
50% Cotton

35% Cotton
25% Polyester
20% Rayon
20% Acrylic

DRY CLEAN ONLY

Wash warm, tumble dry

COSMETICS

1. a list of ingredients in decreasing order by amount, including artificial colors (except secret ingredients)
2. name and address of the manufacturer, packer, or distributor

LIP SMOOTH
CONTAINS: 44% Petrolatums, 1.5% Padimate O, 1% Lanolin, 1% Isopropyl Myristate, 0.5% Cetyl Alcohol.

Lip Smooth, Inc., 2123 Wayne Way, Cuyahoga Falls, OH 44223

OVER-THE-COUNTER DRUGS

1. a list of active ingredients (with a note on any that may cause allergies)

2. dosage instructions

3. warnings on usage

4. warnings on combining with other drugs

5. expiration date and product control number

6. name and address of the manufacturer, packer, or distributor

END SNEEZE

Each tablet contains: Phenylephrine HCl 5 mg., Chlorpheniramine Maleate 2 mg., Aspirin 325 mg., and Caffeine 16.2 mg to counteract possible drowsiness from the antihistamine. Do not take this product if you are allergic to aspirin.

Adult dosage: 2 tablets every 4 hours, not to exceed 12 tablets in 24 hours. Children 6–12: 1 tablet every 4 hours, not to exceed 6 tablets in 24 hours.

CAUTION: Do not give to children under 6. Avoid alcoholic beverages and driving a motor vehicle or operating heavy machinery while taking this product. If symptoms do not improve within 7 days or are accompanied by high fever, consult physician before continuing use.

Drug interation precaution: Do not take this product if you are presently taking a prescription antihypertensive or antidepressant drug except under the advice and supervision of a physician.

EXP AUG 88   10005

Wilson Brothers
Box 1999
Orrville, ALA 36701

Unit Three Review

Unit Summary

Chapters 24 and 25.

Your life calls for you to make many decisions. You can develop your management skills to make good decisions. With effective use of your resources—your possessions, money, time, and talents—you can reach your short- and long-term goals.

Chapters 26–28.

Two of your most important resources are time and money. By planning schedules and budgets, you can get the most out of those resources. You should also make those plans flexible so you can adapt to changes. And you have to be sure to follow your plans. You can stretch your money further by saving or borrowing. By learning about the kinds of saving plans and credit available, you can choose the best type for you.

Chapters 29 and 30.

As a consumer, you can make your resources go further and be more satisfied with your purchases once you understand the marketplace. This means understanding advertising and the seller's point of view. You must know how to shop for price and quality. Planning your purchases before making them helps. With planning, you're prepared to get the quality you need for the price you're willing to pay.

Chapters 31 and 32.

Sometimes purchases go wrong. A skillful consumer knows how to solve such problems by visiting a store or writing a letter of complaint. But consumers should be honest, fair, considerate, and responsible in their dealings with businesses.

Chapter 33.

If your skills and interests lie in management or consumer-related areas, there are a variety of interesting jobs. These range from bank teller and personnel manager to entrepreneur and home economist. These careers call for such characteristics as the ability to make decisions, plan and organize, and get along with others.

Review Questions

1. List five resources.
2. What are short-term and long-term goals?
3. How does barter work?
4. How does thinking ahead help you plan the time required for a task?
5. How does a checking account work?
6. How does a credit card work? How does the store get the money that it's owed?
7. What is the difference between fixed and flexible expenses?
8. Why is it important to find out interest rates at several banks before opening a savings account?
9. What are the disadvantages of keeping your savings in your home?
10. What are the disadvantages of buying on credit?
11. Suppose that you are planning to buy a cassette player. How can you compare different models without actually trying them out?
12. Name three types of stores.
13. Why do stores have sales?
14. What five standards can you use to judge quality in an item?
15. What is a warranty?
16. List four consumer rights.

17. When you go to a store to return a product, what should you take with you?
18. How does shoplifting affect all consumers?
19. When is it fair to return a product to a store? When is returning a product unfair?
20. Why are management skills useful in almost every job?

Reading Activities

1. Read a credit purchase contract. Write down any terms or conditions of sale that you don't understand, and discuss them in class.
2. Look up reports on a product that interests you in *Consumer Reports* or *Consumer's Research*. Explain which of the product brands listed you would buy and why.
3. Make a scrapbook of magazine ads. Under each, explain the kind of appeal being used.
4. Find a copy of a product warranty. Read it and then summarize it in your own words. Is the language easy to understand?

Writing Activities

1. Evaluate your skills and talents and those of three friends. How could you share your individual resources with one another?
2. Write a paragraph or two describing the time bandits that seem to be robbing you of time. What can you do to use time more effectively?
3. Pick an object in the classroom and write a sales talk that would persuade people to buy it.
4. Write a letter of complaint to a manufacturer about a video game cartridge that didn't work. Give your letter to a classmate, and discuss how you could make the letter even more effective.

Math Activities

1. Keep a three-week record of how you spend your money. What pattern do you see in your spending? What percentage of your income goes toward each category of spending? How might a budget change this pattern?
2. Investigate the interest rates for passbook accounts and Christmas Clubs at a local bank. Assume that you have $50 to deposit. How much would the money earn in interest in each account by the end of one year?
3. Invite someone with a management job to speak to the class on the importance of math in his or her job. You might want to consider someone in one of the following careers: school financial administrator, museum administrator, store owner, day-care center director.

Group Projects

1. With two or three other students, write a shopper's guide to your town. List your favorite stores by type. Explain why you like them, what kind of products they carry, and when special sales are held at them.
2. Attend a session of small claims court with two classmates. Take careful notes and then recreate the court session for the class with each member of your group taking on a role.
3. With a friend, act out returning an unsatisfactory item to a store. One of you should take the part of the customer, and the other that of the store manager.

FOODS AND NUTRITION

F ood is simple—you get hungry, you buy something, and you eat it, right? While eating may be that simple, there's really a lot more to choosing and preparing foods. Here's a quiz to test how much you know about food. Check your responses against the answers that follow.

Questions

1. Which of these factors influence food choices: taste, family, advertising, peer pressure, ethnic or religious group, region?
2. Which of these foods are fruits: apples, blueberries, cucumbers?
3. The best way to lose weight is to skip breakfast. (True or false.)
4. Snacks are bad for you. (True or false.)
5. Fast-food restaurants serve only junk food. (True or false.)

Answers

1. All of these factors influence your food choices. (See chapter 34.)
2. They all are. Fruits are fleshy foods with seeds inside. (See chapter 36.)
3. False. You should eat three balanced meals to stay healthy. It is especially important to eat a good breakfast. (See chapter 37.)
4. False. Healthy snacks are good for you. But some snack foods give you few benefits. (See chapter 38.)
5. False. You can get healthy food at a fast-food restaurant if you choose carefully. (See chapter 49.)

How did you do on this quiz? The chapters following will explain these points and more about how you choose and prepare food.

Chapter 34 Food and You

Food decisions come in as many types as there are ice cream flavors. What should you snack on? Should you have dinner at home or in a restaurant? What kind of exercises should you do? Should you buy one brand of soup or another? There are so many questions that eating seems confusing.

Eating well, however, pays off in many ways. It makes you healthy. It gives you energy to do the things you want to do. And eating tasty food gives you pleasure. What's better than a cold drink when thirsty?

In this unit, you'll learn about the range of choices you make about food. You'll learn about what foods benefit you and how to prepare them. You'll learn how to choose a good diet and why you should exercise. You'll read about how to plan a menu and prepare a meal. But first, let's see why you need to eat—and why you choose to eat what you do.

Why Do You Eat?

It's almost time for bed. But first, you walk into the kitchen and open the refrigerator for something to eat. Why? There is no one, simple reason for eating. Your desire to eat may stem from one of a number of factors, or from a combination of them.

Hunger

The simplest reason for eating is **hunger**—*the physical desire for food.* To survive, all living things need food and water. You can live for only three or four weeks without food, and for only two or three days without water.

The aroma and appearance of certain foods influence your desire to eat. It might be anything from the smell of popcorn to the sight of a colorful fruit salad.

Your body uses the substances in food for energy, for growth, and for other body functions. When supplies of these substances are running low, you begin to feel tired. And when your stomach is empty, it contracts, producing hunger pains that tell you to eat.

Appetite

If you always eat lunch at noon, you may feel like eating at that time even if you had a big breakfast at ten o'clock. You aren't really hungry, but you have an **appetite**—*a psychological need for food.*

Other factors influence your appetite. The smell of fresh-baked bread or the sight of a juicy peach can spark your desire to eat. So can food that is prepared and served in an appealing way.

Emotional Factors

Food helps meet social and emotional needs, too. Mealtimes are important in everyone's life. A meal may be an occasion for people to get together and talk. And special events and holidays are often marked by special meals.

Selecting and preparing good food can be a way of showing love. If you make a cake for a friend's birthday, you are saying "Happy Birthday!" with more than just words.

Your emotions can influence your eating habits. If you are upset or tense, you may lose your appetite. Or you may eat too quickly and get indigestion. Some people snack too much when they are upset, in an effort to take their minds off their troubles. Others eat very little when they are excited.

What Influences Your Choice of Foods?

When you open the refrigerator for your snack, you're faced with many choices. Will you take the apple, the cheese, or the chocolate cake? A glass of milk or a can of soda? Your decision about what to eat and how to prepare it will be affected by various factors.

Your Personal Tastes

You hate mushrooms, but your best friend thinks that no pizza is worth eating without them. Personal tastes have much to do with the foods people choose to eat.

The senses of taste and smell help us distinguish between the flavors of different foods. The **taste buds** are *sensitive areas on your tongue that identify sweet, sour, salty, and bitter tastes.* **Receptors** are *sensors in the passages of your nose.* They can pick out thousands of different aromas. But no two people respond to flavors in exactly the same way. That's why you and your friend differ about mushrooms.

Your Family

Your food choices are probably influenced by your family. Throughout your childhood, your family may have served certain foods at certain times—eggs at breakfast, for example, or dessert after dinner. These things become part of your eating habits.

Family members may also have passed their personal preferences on to you. And they may have urged you to select certain foods in place of others—vegetables and fruits, for instance, instead of cookies and pretzels.

Your family's way of life also plays a large part in determining what and how you eat. Does your family eat a weekend meal with relatives? What meals do all family members eat together?

Advertising

Magazines, newspapers, television, radio—everywhere you turn, you'll find advertisements for food. Food advertising makes us aware of products and special sales. But it can also influence our choices in some hidden ways that don't always make sense. An ad for soft drinks shows a group of young people at the beach, laughing and having fun as they drink the soda. The ad seems to say that if you drink the soda, you'll have fun. But can the product really make you have fun?

Peer Pressure

As you learned in an earlier chapter, **peer pressure** is *the influence that your friends and others of your age have on you.* Your friends can influence your choice of foods. If they often gather at the pizza parlor or the ice cream shop, these foods are bound to be part of your diet. At times you'll have snacks and meals at a friend's home. The foods there may be quite different from the ones you're used to eating at home.

Ethnic and Religious Groups

Ethnic Background. An **ethnic group** is *made up of people who share a common cultural background.* Everyone belongs

TABLE 1 **Foods from Around the United States**

Region	Typical dishes
New England	lobster, clam chowder, steamed clams, baked beans, maple syrup, boiled dinner
Mid Atlantic	clams, oysters, crabs, duck, scrapple, chicken pot pie
South	smoked ham, fried chicken, grits, corn bread, pecan pie, crayfish, collard greens, black-eyed peas, key lime pie, red snapper
Midwest	corn on the cob, steaks, pancakes, pies, cheese, freshwater fish
Southwest	chili, tacos, rice and beans, barbecued beef, hominy, pickled okra
Mountain States	trout, bass, wild game
Northwest	salmon, oysters, pea soup, berries, fruits, game meats
California	fruits and vegetables, ocean fish
Hawaii	pit-roasted pork or chicken, macadamia nuts

to some ethnic group. Each group has its own food **traditions**, or *customs that have lasted a long time.*

Your eating habits may be affected by these customs. For example, if your family is Italian, you may enjoy spaghetti with a spicy tomato sauce. Foods flavored with hot chili peppers are traditional in many Mexican homes. A family with a Middle Eastern background may serve many lamb dishes. Families of Chinese descent eat rice and crispy stir-fried vegetables.

Because so many immigrants have brought their ethnic traditions to this country, we all have an opportunity to try the special foods of many groups.

Religious Background. Religion may also influence your food choices. Special foods may be eaten on religious holidays.

Egg dishes are eaten at Easter, and matzoth are served during Passover.

Other foods are not eaten at certain times. For example, Roman Catholics do not eat meat on Fridays during Lent.

Many religions have dietary rules. For example, some Jewish people follow strict dietary laws that do not allow them to eat pork or shellfish. Islam has similar laws, and Muslims fast—or keep from eating—at certain times of the year. Strict Buddhists eat no meat, except for fish.

Region

Where you live can also affect your food choices. In coastal areas, seafood is plentiful. In the western plains, grain foods and beef are more likely to be found. In the

F E A T U R E

Exploring Your Eating Patterns

- Jill has a soft-cooked egg, a slice of whole-wheat toast, and a glass of orange juice for breakfast. She takes a container of yogurt and a piece of fruit to school for lunch. After school, she feels hungry. Sometimes she has more fruit and sometimes she eats cookies or potato chips. She eats with her family at dinner, and enjoys a single helping of what is cooked for the family.
- Ron never has time for breakfast. He eats a hot lunch in the cafeteria. After school, he often stops by the ice cream shop with his friends. But he's hungry again by dinnertime, and he often snacks on potato chips or candy after dinner.

How do your eating patterns compare with these two teens? To find out, you'll have to do some careful thinking about your own habits.

For one week, keep a daily log of what, where, when, and with whom you eat. Write down everything—not only what you have at meals, but also what you eat for snacks. Also write down how much of each item you eat. Part of a page might look something like this:

Time	Place	With	Food	Amount
7:15 A.M.	home		oatmeal with milk and sugar	large bowl
			orange juice	8 oz.
12:00	school	Susan	peanut butter sandwich on whole-wheat bread	1
			banana	1
			milk	8 oz.

Use the margin to note any unusual circumstances—a family celebration, an argument at the table, a phone call that interrupted a meal, the fact that you were especially happy or depressed on that day.

Your log will help you see your own individual eating patterns. As you learn more about nutrition, you can check your log to see if what you're eating is healthful. And you'll be able to see how your life-style and other factors affect your eating habits.

Logs may be kept longer than one week. You might like to keep a monthly log. Generally speaking, in a monthly log a pattern will emerge that will be more accurate than the one found on a week's record.

In order for your body to perform in its peak condition, you need to give it fuel. Start each morning with a nutritious breakfast to insure energy throughout the morning.

southern United States, growing seasons are long, and fresh fruits and vegetables are available all year.

Regional differences are less important today than they once were. High-speed transportation and refrigeration have made most foods available everywhere. But specialties like New England clam chowder or Texas barbecue or Louisiana crayfish remain popular in the regions where they were first made.

How Do You Choose What's Best To Eat?

With so many foods to choose from —and so many factors affecting your choices—you might wonder if all eating habits are equally healthful. The answer is no.

Two factors of healthy eating habits are deeply related. They are *good eating habits* and *good nutrition*.

Good Eating Habits

To start with, eating regular meals is important. If you skip breakfast and try to make up for it at lunch, your body will suffer. You won't have much energy during the morning. And your body won't use the food you eat at lunch effectively if you have to digest a large amount all at one time. It is best to eat at least three well-spaced meals a day.

Second, what you eat—as well as when you eat—can help you feel well most of the time. Or it can keep you from doing any task as well as you might. Food is one of the most important factors in making a person healthy, lively, and attractive.

Good Nutrition

To stay healthy, you must nourish your body with the right foods. Good nutrition will give you energy and help you to grow.

As you will see in the next chapter, nutrition is not a difficult subject to learn. Once you know the basic facts, you'll be able to choose the best foods for a healthful diet.

Words to Remember

appetite: a psychological need for food

ethnic group: people who share a common cultural background

hunger: the physical desire for food

peer pressure: the influence that your friends and others of your age have on you

receptors: sensors in your nasal passages

taste buds: sensitive areas on your tongue that identify sweet, sour, salty, and bitter tastes

traditions: customs that have lasted a long time

Questions

1. Why does your body need food?
2. What factors affect your appetite?
3. How do emotions influence your desire for food?
4. List the factors that affect eating habits. Which factors have the strongest influence on your eating patterns?
5. Why should you become aware of your personal eating habits?

Chapter **35** Eating and Nutrition

Objectives

After reading this chapter, you will be able to:

☐ *identify the six classes of nutrients needed by the human body,*

☐ *explain what each nutrient does for your body,*

☐ *find the specific nutrient content of different foods from a table of food values.*

We all know people with very busy schedules. How do such people keep going? The answer is energy. Your body uses energy continually—not only when you exercise, but even when you read and think and sleep. The energy you need comes from the food you eat. Food provides **nutrients**, or *nourishing substances. The study of how the body breaks down and uses these nutrients* is called **nutrition**. Nutrients help in building muscles and other body tissues, in providing energy, and in maintaining good health. They also contribute to shiny hair, clear skin, and healthy teeth.

Nutritionists are *the scientists who study the effects of food on the body.* They divide nutrients into six types: proteins, carbohydrates, fats, vitamins, minerals, and water.

Proteins: The Tissue Builders

Proteins form the basis of all the body's cells. There are more proteins in the body than any other nutrient except water. Proteins even form the major part of hair, nails, and skin. **Protein** is *the nutrient necessary for building and repairing body tissues.* Anyone who is growing needs a great deal of it.

Amino acids are *the building blocks of protein.* The human body needs twenty-two of these amino acids to build tissue. It can make fourteen of them. The other eight must come from food. These eight are called the *essential amino acids.*

Foods that contain all eight essential acids are said to have *complete proteins.* Most such foods are animal products—meat, fish, milk, eggs. Vegetables, fruits, and grains have *incomplete proteins.* They contain many amino acids, but they don't contain all of the essential eight. You can get the essential eight by combining two incomplete proteins, such as beans and rice or nuts and whole grains.

Carbohydrate: Ready Energy

Carbohydrate is *the nutrient that provides ready energy.* If you do not have enough carbohydrate, your body will begin to use stored fat and protein for energy. Carbohydrate is found in many foods, but the best sources are grains, fruits, and vegetables. There are three types of carbohydrates: starches, sugars, and fiber.

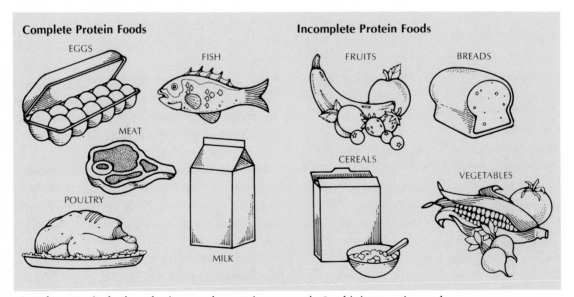

Complete Protein Foods

EGGS

FISH

MEAT

POULTRY

MILK

Incomplete Protein Foods

FRUITS

BREADS

CEREALS

VEGETABLES

Complete protein foods each give you the protein you need. Combining two incomplete proteins, such as beans and rice, can result in a high-quality form of protein.

FEATURE

What Is a Calorie?

When you look at a list of nutrients, you may be surprised to find one term missing—*calorie*. But if a calorie isn't a nutrient, what is it?

A **calorie** is *an amount of energy*. When you ride a bicycle, you use energy, which can be measured in calories. You might use about 250 calories in a half-hour bicycle ride.

You use energy all the time, even when you're asleep. But you use more energy when you're active. This energy comes first from carbohydrates that you've eaten. If more is needed, energy comes from fat that is stored in your body. If your carbohydrate and fat reserves are low, the energy may come from the protein in your muscles—something that you should avoid.

Protein, carbohydrate, and fat can all be described by the amount of calories, or energy, they produce. There are four calories in every gram of protein and in every gram of carbohydrate. There are nine calories in every gram of fat.

If the foods you eat produce more energy than you need, the extra amount is turned into fat, which holds the calories in reserve. This is why people count calories to keep from gaining weight.

But it is essential to consider nutrients as well as calories in your diet. If all the calories you eat are carbohydrate calories, you will have no proteins for body growth. You may not gain weight, but you won't stay healthy. With a little thought, you can both keep your intake of calories down *and* eat a healthy diet.

Starches

Rice, pastas, grains, and grain products such as bread are examples of foods high in starch. Starches are broken down by the body to form a simple sugar called *glucose*. This sugar is then used for energy. Most starchy foods are **complex carbohydrates**—that is, they *supply both energy and other nutrients at the same time.*

Sugars

As it does with starches, your body breaks down the more complex sugars, found in fruits and milk, to form glucose.

Some foods, such as cakes, candy, cookies, and soft drinks, are high in sugar. But these are not the best sources of high energy because they have few other nutrients. And too much sugar can lead to weight gain and dental problems. Fruit and milk are examples of foods that are high in sugar but also contain other nutrients.

Fiber

Fiber, or *roughage,* is *threadlike cells that pass through the body but supply no energy or nutrients.* It comes from the parts of the food that the body doesn't digest.

Fiber plays an important part in digestion by helping to move food through the digestive system. Fruits, vegetables, and whole-grain cereals and breads are all excellent sources of fiber. So are peels and seeds.

Fats: The Misunderstood Nutrients

A certain amount of **fat** is necessary for good health. Fat is *a substance that the body uses to store reserve energy.* Fat is also necessary so that the body can store and use certain vitamins. It helps regulate body temperature. And without fat in the diet, skin and hair problems can develop.

Fat is present in most foods, especially meat, butter, salad dressing, nuts, milk, cheese, baked goods, and snack foods. In fact, nearly all foods contain some fat, except for most fruits and vegetables. This means that it's far more common for people to eat too much fat than too little fat.

Too much fat can lead to serious health problems. The extra fat will be stored in fatty tissue and you will become overweight. Too much of the saturated fats— animal fats in milk and meat, and hard fats like butter—can lead to high levels of cholesterol in the blood.

Cholesterol is a white, wax-like substance that plays an important part in transporting fat and providing hormones. However, high cholesterol and being overweight can lead to heart disease, high blood pressure, hardening of the arteries, and other health problems.

Unsaturated fat, which is found in vegetable oils like corn oil and sunflower oil, can be used. They do not cause the problems that saturated fats can cause.

Vitamins: The Miracle Nutrients

Vitamins are *nutrients that help the body stay healthy and function properly.* They work together to help the body use other nutrients. Vitamins are present in the body in very small amounts. They provide no energy. They form no part of the tissues. But without the right amount of each vitamin, serious illnesses can develop.

The Water-Soluble Vitamins

The B vitamins and vitamin C are water-soluble vitamins. That means that they move through the body in water. They are easily absorbed because the body contains a lot of water. But since the water is constantly being lost, these vitamins are easily lost. You need fresh supplies every day.

There are eight B vitamins. They work together to help the body use other nutrients. They are especially important in helping nerve and brain tissue to develop and work well. They also aid in digestion. The most important of the group are thiamine (B_1), riboflavin (B_2), and niacin. B vitamins are found in milk products, meats, and cereals and breads.

Vitamin C helps the body build cells, which makes it important in healing cuts and bruises. It also helps form strong teeth and bones and healthy gums. Vitamin C is found in citrus fruits.

The Fat-Soluble Vitamins

Vitamins A, D, E, and K are fat-soluble. This means that they travel through the bloodstream attached to small bits of fat.

Vitamin A is necessary for good vision, healthy teeth and gums, and strong bones. It is found in yellow and leafy green vegetables. Vitamin D also helps form bones and teeth, and it helps the body use minerals like calcium and phosphorus. The body can make vitamin D if it gets enough sunlight. Vitamin D is also added to the milk you buy. Vitamin E works with vitamin A, and also helps keep red blood cells healthy. Vitamin K helps your blood to clot.

Minerals: The Body Protectors

Small amounts of minerals are found in most foods. **Minerals** are *elements that form part of many tissues and are needed to keep body processes operating smoothly.*

Calcium and Iron

Calcium and iron are two minerals that you must be careful to include in your diet. *Calcium* is the chief mineral of your bones and teeth. Enough calcium must always be present in the blood so that the heart will beat regularly and blood will clot normally. Calcium also keeps nerves and muscles healthy, and it helps normal growth take

Vitamins are vital to health. Vitamins B and C are water-soluble and need to be replenished every day. Vitamins A, D, E, and K are fat-soluble and are stored in the body.

TABLE 1 Recommended Daily Dietary Allowances (RDA)[1]

Sex-age category	Age (years)	Weight (kg)	(lbs)	Height (cm)	(in)	Food energy (cal)	Protein (g)	Cal-cium (mg)	Iron (mg)	Vita-min A (IU)	Thia-mine (mg)	Ribo-flavin (mg)	Nia-cin (mg)	Ascorbic acid (mg)
Males	11–14	45	99	157	62	2,700	45	1,200	18	1,000	1.4	1.6	18	50
	15–18	66	145	176	69	2,800	56	1,200	18	1,000	1.4	1.7	18	60
Females	11–14	46	101	157	62	2,200	46	1,200	18	800	1.1	1.3	15	50
	15–18	55	120	163	64	2,100	46	1,200	18	800	11	1.3	14	60

[1] Adapted from Food and Nutrition Board, National Academy of Sciences: *National Research Council Recommended Daily Dietary Allowances*, revised 1980.

Key: kg—kilograms; lbs—pounds; cm—centimeters; in—inches; cal—calories; g—grams; mg—milligrams; IU—international units.

place. Dairy products are good sources of calcium.

Iron is essential for building red blood cells. When people do not get enough iron, they develop **anemia**. This is *a condition causing a lack of energy and low resistance to infections.* Teenage girls must be especially careful to get enough iron. Liver and spinach are good sources of iron.

Iodine and Other Minerals

Iodine makes the thyroid gland work correctly. A lack of iodine can cause such problems as weight gain, lack of energy, and a swelling of the neck called *goiter.* Iodized salt contains iodine.

Other important minerals, such as *phosphorus* and *potassium,* are widely available in the foods you eat. The average diet will provide enough of these minerals. People who do not eat meat, however, may get too little *zinc.* This mineral is used by the body in making insulin, which helps the body use sugar.

Sodium is one mineral that people may get too much of. Sodium is present in table salt and in most prepared foods, such as chips, pretzels, and cured meats such as bacon. Some sodium is necessary for body functions, but too much can cause the body to retain water and lead to high blood pressure and other health problems.

Water

About 66 to 75 percent of body weight is water. Water is the basic material of blood and is in all the cells. It helps transport nutrients throughout the body, and it carries wastes away. It helps move food through the digestive system. And it helps regulate body temperature.

Your body is constantly losing water, so it is important to take in enough. People should drink about six to eight glasses of water a day.

Try to visualize what you would look like without water in your body. You would be all dried up like a mummy. If your average weight is 145 lbs. (66 kg), you would only weigh some 44 lbs. (20 kg) without water in your body.

What You Need and What You Get

To plan a healthful diet, you must know what your nutritional needs are and how different foods can help you meet those needs. Nutritionists have carefully studied human needs.

Nutritionists have developed tables of *Recommended Dietary Allowances* (RDAs for short). These tables suggest how much of certain nutrients different people should eat each day to stay healthy. See page 272 for RDA information about yourself.

Food Values

How can you know that you're getting the RDAs of the nutrients you need? Nutritionists have also prepared tables of food values, showing how much of the nutrients are provided by portions of different foods. These tables are collected at the back of this book.

It's important to remember that all the nutrients work together. If you get too little vitamin C, for example, your body won't use calcium or iron well. That is why it's necessary to get the right amounts of each nutrient.

Words to Remember

amino acids: the building blocks of protein

anemia: a condition causing a lack of energy and low resistance to infection

calorie: an amount of energy

carbohydrate: the nutrient that provides ready energy

complex carbohydrate: a substance that supplies both energy and other nutrients at the same time

fat: a substance that the body uses to store reserve energy

fiber: threadlike cells that pass through the body but supply no energy or nutrients

minerals: elements that form part of many tissues and are needed to keep body processes operating smoothly

nutrients: nourishing substances

nutrition: the study of how the body breaks down and uses nutrients in food

nutritionists: the scientists who study the effects of food on the body

protein: the nutrient necessary for building and repairing body tissues

vitamins: nutrients that help the body stay healthy and function properly

Questions

1. What are the six types of nutrients? What can each type do for you?
2. What is the difference between complete protein and incomplete protein?
3. How does complex carbohydrate differ from simple sugars?
4. How does your body use fiber?
5. Can a person be overweight and undernourished at the same time? Explain your answer.

Chapter **36** Which Foods
Have Which
Nutrients?

After reading this chapter, you will be able to:

☐ *explain the purpose and principles of dividing food into five groups,*

☐ *outline the general nutritional differences among the five food groups and give examples of food in each group,*

☐ *use the five food groups to evaluate meals, menus, and diets.*

There is a simple way to plan a nutritious diet. You don't have to look up every meal and snack in a food table! Nutritionists have divided foods into **food groups**, *five categories divided according to the nutrients that foods contain.* These groups are:

■ fruits and vegetables.

■ breads and cereals.

■ milk and milk products.

■ meats, fish, eggs, and beans.

■ "extras."

The last group includes foods, like sweets and oils, that are low in nutrients but high in calories. Plan your daily diet to include the right amounts of different foods from the first four groups. And watch your intake of foods in the fifth group.

Fruits and Vegetables

Fruits and vegetables provide large amounts of vitamins and minerals. They also add fiber to the diet. They are very important sources of vitamins A and C.

Some of these foods provide only a little vitamin A and much vitamin C. You probably know that citrus fruits like oranges and grapefruits are especially high in vitamin C. But other good sources of vitamin C are potatoes, broccoli, tomatoes, cabbage, and peppers. Some, such as broccoli, are also excellent sources of other important nutrients.

Types of Fruits and Vegetables

There are many types of vegetables:

- *Flowers*—Broccoli and cauliflower are both flowers of plants. They are rich in vitamins A and C.

A piece of fruit, a tossed salad, or one medium potato is one serving from the fruit and vegetable group. You need four servings daily.

- *Leaves*—Many leaves are eaten, including cabbage, spinach, turnip greens, mustard greens, and kale. These are excellent sources of vitamin A. Other leafy vegetables, like lettuce, chicory, and romaine, have less vitamin A but more vitamin C.
- *Roots*—Carrots, onions, and potatoes are all grown underground. They are high in vitamins A and C.
- *Seeds*—This group includes corn, beans, and nuts. Many of these vegetables are high in protein.
- *Stems*—We eat the stalks of many plants, including asparagus, broccoli, and celery. They are good sources of fiber and other nutrients.

What about all those other vegetables you eat, like squash, cucumbers, tomatoes, and peppers? Actually, those foods are fruits—just like apples and oranges. All fruits have seeds inside the fleshy part.

You can buy fruits and vegetables fresh, canned, frozen, or prepared. Generally, these foods lose some of their vitamin content when they are processed. **Processing** is *changing a food from its raw form before selling it.* But fresh fruits and vegetables may also lose nutrients if they are kept too long or improperly stored or prepared.

Servings per Day

You should eat four servings from the fruits and vegetables group every day. One serving is an average-size piece of fruit, ½ grapefruit, ½ cup fruit juice or fruit piece, one cup of a vegetable, one carrot or celery stalk, one medium potato, or a bowl of tossed salad.

Breads and Cereals

Cereal means more than what you eat at breakfast with milk and fruit. This term refers to any grain. Foods in this group, which includes all kinds of bread, are important for the carbohydrate they contain. Cereal products also contain B vitamins, iron, and important fats. Finally, these foods provide some incomplete proteins.

Types of Breads and Cereals

Important grains include wheat, rice, oats, barley, rye, and buckwheat. Wheat is the main ingredient in most breads, pastries, breakfast cereals, crackers, and spaghetti and macaroni. Rice is a major food for more than half of the world's population.

All of these grains are available as whole grains, as flour, and in prepared foods ranging from soups to breads. Many products made from grains have been **fortified**. This means that *nutrients have been added to them.*

Servings per Day

Four servings a day from the breads and cereals group are recommended. One serving would be a slice of bread; 1 cup of ready-to-eat cereal; ½ cup of cooked cereal, rice, or spaghetti; or one roll or muffin.

One slice of bread, one roll, or ½ cup of cooked rice is one serving from the bread and cereal group. You need four servings daily.

Milk and Milk Products

Milk and milk products, such as cheese, yogurt, buttermilk, and ice cream, are rich in calcium and phosphorus. And milk is an excellent way to get riboflavin, one of the B vitamins. These foods are also good sources of protein and vitamins A and C. Milk may also be fortified with vitamin D. Nutrient amounts vary depending on the form of the food and the way it was processed.

Types of Milk and Milk Products

Milk can be *liquid, evaporated,* or *dried.* These last two have some water removed.

Liquid milk is usually **homogenized**. In this process, *the fat in the milk is blended with the rest of the liquid.* The result is a more even texture. Liquid milk is **pasteurized**. *The milk is first heated and then cooled.* The action kills harmful germs.

Buttermilk, yogurt, and sour cream are called *cultured* milk products. They contain harmless bacteria that produce a tangy taste and a thick texture.

An eight-ounce glass of milk, one ounce of cheese, or one cup of yogurt is one serving from the milk group. You need four servings daily.

Cheese is also a cultured milk product. It is made from milk curd, which is high in protein and other nutrients. Because it is made by removing liquid from milk, most cheese has much less calcium and many more calories than liquid milk has.

Ice cream, ice milk, and frozen yogurt are all popular desserts made from milk products. Ice milk and frozen yogurt are lower in fat and have fewer calories than ice cream. Because all three are sweetened with sugar, they contain many calories.

Servings per Day

Nutritionists say that teenagers need 32 ounces of milk a day. You could get this amount from four 8-ounce servings of milk. Or you could substitute one serving of milk for an ounce of cheese, or 2 cups of cottage cheese, or 1 cup of yogurt.

Meat, Fish, Poultry, Eggs, and Beans

The foods in this group are important sources of protein. Many of them also supply iron and other minerals, B vitamins, and some vitamin A and vitamin E.

Animal Protein

- *Beef,* which comes from cattle, is rich in iron.
- *Lamb,* from young sheep, has nutrients similiar to those of beef.

  Pork, from pigs or hogs, is very high in thiamine.
- *Liver, kidney, heart,* and *sweetbreads* are packed with nutrients. For example, liver contains large amounts of vitamins D, A, and B, as well as iron.
- *Poultry* includes chicken, duck, turkey, and goose. Chicken and turkey have less fat than beef, lamb, and pork.

Three ounces of beef, 2 eggs, or 1-½ cups of cooked beans is one serving from the meat group. You need two servings daily.

- *Fish* is also high in protein and low in fat. And fish is a good source of iodine.
- *Eggs* supply complete protein and some amounts of almost every nutrient except vitamin C.

Vegetable Protein

Some vegetables—nuts, seeds, and legumes—also provide protein. **Legumes** are *peas and beans like soybeans, lentils, kidney beans, and chick peas.* These vegetable foods are rich in iron and the B vitamins. But the protein they contain is incomplete.

They should be eaten with complete proteins like meats, or with foods like cereals that will complete their proteins. Peanuts are also good protein foods. They, too, must be eaten with cereals to make complete proteins.

Servings per Day

Your diet should include two servings from foods in this group each day. A serving is 2 eggs or 3 ounces of beef, lamb, pork, poultry, or fish, or 4 tablespoons of peanut butter or 1½ cups of cooked beans.

FEATURE

Making Substitutions

Eating foods from the five food groups assures you of good nutrition. But what if you can't eat the foods from one group? For example, many people are allergic to milk. **Allergies** are *unpleasant physical reactions to a food or other substance.* And many other people are vegetarians. For religious or personal reasons, they do not eat meat.

When you don't eat the foods from one group, you have to get the nutrients provided by that group from other foods. You may have to consult a table of food values to find out which foods are high in the nutrients your diet lacks.

If you can't drink milk, for instance, you have to be concerned about getting enough calcium and vitamin A. One serving of collard greens will give you almost as much calcium as a glass of milk, and many times as much vitamin A. Other leafy vegetables—like spinach or chard—and broccoli are also high in these nutrients.

You can also get calcium from certain seafoods—scallops, oysters, canned salmon, and sardines. Dates, rhubarb, and blueberries are high-calcium fruits, and almonds and brazil nuts also contain this mineral. By choosing carefully, you can make sure that your diet gives you the nutrients that you need.

Vegetarians must be careful to get enough protein, because the proteins in plants are incomplete. Vegetarians also must be sure to get the B vitamins, iron, and other nutrients that are found in meat.

Extras

The "extras" are high in sugar or fat but lacking in most other nutrients. They include *fats*, such as butter, margarine, and oil, and *sweeters*, such as sugar, honey, and molasses. This category also includes foods such as candy bars, doughnuts, and jelly.

The extras share one important trait—low nutrient density. **Nutrient density** is *the proportion of nutrients to the calories a food contains.* Soft drinks have a low nutrient density because they contain many calories and few nutrients. They are mostly sugar.

Some foods in the extras group do contain nutrients. Butter and margarine are high in vitamin A, for example. And the carbohydrate in a candy bar will provide quick energy. But eating too much of these foods can be harmful.

Servings per Day

Nutritionists do not recommend a number of servings for foods in the extras group. In fact, they advise people to eat as little of these foods as possible. The few nutrients they provide can be obtained easily from other foods.

A Balanced Diet Plan

Once you know what foods are in each group, you can plan a balanced diet.

It's easy to include all of these foods—even if you are on a weight-loss diet.

Because each food group contains many different foods, you can also eat a variety of foods. That way, you can enjoy many different tastes and textures.

Words to Remember

allergies: unpleasant physical reactions to a food or other substance

food groups: five categories divided according to the nutrients that the foods contain

fortified: nutrients have been added to food

homogenization: blending the fat in milk with the rest of the liquid

legumes: peas and beans like soybeans, lentils, kidney beans, and chick peas

nutrient density: the proportion of nutrients to the calories a food contains

pasteurization: heating and then cooling milk to kill germs

processing: changing a food from its raw form before selling it

Questions

1. What are the five food groups?
2. Which important nutrients do fruits and vegetables provide?
3. If you do not eat meat, how can you be sure to get the protein you need?
4. How many servings of food from each food group should you include in your diet each day?
5. Give an example of a food with high nutrient density and one with low nutrient density.

Chapter **37** # Developing Healthy Eating Habits

Objectives

After reading this chapter, you will be able to:

☐ *explain the importance of regular meals,*

☐ *describe the relationship among exercise, diet, and weight,*

☐ *evaluate different ways of solving diet problems.*

"Learning about food groups in class is easy, Ms. Remsen," Jeff said. "The nutrients and recommended servings are all in our books and charts. But what can I really *do* to make sure my diet is healthy?"

"Well," Ms. Remsen said, "It isn't just *what* you eat, but also *how* you eat that counts."

Ms. Remsen explained to Jeff and his classmates that many factors are important in developing good eating habits. Planning meals is one of them. It is better to eat balanced meals throughout the day than to eat everything at one sitting.

Eating properly also includes preparing the food so that it contains as little fat and keeps as many vitamins as possible. Ms. Remsen also stressed the importance of physical exercise.

Good Eating Habits

Eating well involves carefully selecting from the basic food groups. The United States Department of Agriculture and the Department of Health and Human Resources have other guidelines to help you develop good eating habits:

1. Eat a variety of foods.
2. Maintain your ideal weight.
3. Avoid too much saturated fat and cholesterol.
4. Eat foods with enough starch and fiber.
5. Avoid too much sugar.
6. Avoid too much sodium.

These guidelines are for everyone who does not need to follow a special diet for health reasons. A **diet** is a *planned approach to eating designed to accomplish a certain goal.* A proper diet maintains good health and physical fitness.

Special diets have special goals. One goal may be to avoid illness by staying away from foods you are allergic to. Another goal of dieting is weight control.

Eat a Variety of Foods

Some people find a few foods they like and then stick with them. Try to take advantage of the large variety of foods that our food system supplies. You can lunch on sandwich, soup, salad, fruit and cheese, warmed-up leftovers, or many other foods. You can also vary your breakfasts, as one of the Teen Tips at the end of this unit shows.

By varying your diet, you're more likely to get all of the nutrients you need. And you can have more fun doing it!

Maintain Your Ideal Weight

You can maintain your ideal weight by developing good eating habits, choosing nutritious foods, and exercising. If your weight is more than 10 percent over your ideal weight, you should consider a plan for losing weight. See the last sections of this chapter.

Avoid Too Much Saturated Fats and Cholesterol

Animal and dairy products—and some vegetables—contain saturated fats. Eating too much of these fats has been linked to some types of heart problems.

Substitute beans, fish, poultry, or lean meat for high-fat meats. Trim the fat off meats and take the skin off poultry. Use unsaturated cooking oil, like soybean oil, or corn oil, in preparing your food. Broiling or baking instead of frying will also reduce the fat in your cooking.

Eat Foods with Enough Starch and Fiber

Starch, in moderate amounts, is necessary for proper muscle function. Fiber is important to keep your digestive system in good order. Your body needs bulk and fiber in order to digest food and get rid of waste properly. Try to eat raw fruits and vegetables, whole-grain breads, nuts, and seeds.

All these foods are good substitutes for salts and sugars, especially when you're choosing a snack. A ripe piece of fruit, a fresh stalk of celery, or a tasty slice of wheat bread are all nutritious snacks.

Many people have decreased the amount of red meats in their diet. Instead, they use chicken as a low-cost, low-fat alternative.

Avoid Too Much Sugar and Sodium

Almost everyone enjoys the tastes of sugar and salt. Too much of either of them, though, can cause problems. Foods rich in sugar can harm your teeth and cause you to gain too much weight. Too much salt may contribute to high blood pressure.

You can cut sweets, like candy, and salty foods, like chips, from your diet. Stay away from other salty foods, too, like salted nuts, bacon, and pickles.

If you want to snack, choose healthy snacks: popcorn (unsalted and unbuttered), pizza, dry roasted nuts, ice milk, frozen yogurt, whole-grain cakes and cookies, raw vegetables, fruits, and fruit juices. See the Teen Tips at the end of this unit for more ideas.

Use sugar and salt sparingly in cooking, and avoid adding more at the table. You will find that fresh, well-prepared foods really don't need that much seasoning.

Beyond Food Choices

In addition to the foods you choose to eat, how you prepare them and how you eat them is important, too.

Eating slowly, for example, offers three benefits.

- It helps your body digest the food.
- It gives you a chance to enjoy the taste of the food.
- It helps you know when you're full.

When you eat too fast, you often eat more than you really need.

Planning and Eating Meals

Regular mealtimes are important, because the body needs nourishment throughout the day. Eat three balanced meals and—if you snack—snack wisely.

How much you eat during the day is important, too. Be sure to eat a full breakfast—your body needs nourishment after many hours of sleep. Skipping breakfast is the worst way to diet. Having a good lunch is also important for keeping your energy up during the day.

Preparing Food

Nutritious foods—especially vegetables—can be spoiled by overcooking. Boiling vegetables for too long drains the nutrients out of them. Instead, steam them

T E E N   I S S U E

Eating Disorders

Because being overweight is so common, it seems that everyone is on a diet. Watching your food intake is a good idea. There are times, however, when concern with food gets out of hand. The two eating disorders discussed here are especially dangerous for young teenage girls.

Anorexia Nervosa

Anorexia nervosa is *self-induced starvation*. The victims can actually diet themselves to death. It is very hard to stop them once they start on this dangerous course because the disease affects the mind as well as the body.

The disorder seems to be basically psychological, but no one is really sure of the exact cause. Victims are usually young women. They tend to be overly sensitive and want to be perfect in all they do. When they learn that society encourages thinness, they try to become thin.

They refuse food, or they eat but then make themselves vomit afterward. Often, they exercise to the point of exhaustion.

After a while, undernourishment and overexercise cause the body systems to begin to break down. At this point, the patient is hospitalized and fed through tubes. The treatment is continued until she or he is well enough to receive counseling. But many people with anorexia nervosa do not recover from their breakdowns.

Treatment is long and difficult. It concentrates on building up the body with nutrients while helping the mind get over its problem.

Bulimia

Bulimia involves *alternating food binges and purges*. The victims go on binges of eating huge amounts. Then they use laxatives or vomiting to purge the food from their systems.

Again, the victims are usually young women in their teens and early twenties. Bulimia victims seem to share some common traits with victims of anorexia nervosa. They are generally perfectionists who expect a great deal from themselves. They have low self-esteem and depend on the approval of others. If they fail to get this approval, they turn to food.

Typically, they start out on a strict diet. When they have an emotional problem, they go off their diet by binging. Ashamed of this, they try to make up for it by purging themselves of the food. This response to emotional upset is repeated often.

The constant purging causes severe physical problems after a while. The first step in trying to cure bulimia is to stop the purging. Counseling then tries to uncover the basic worries that lead the victim to this behavior.

The cure is long because like anorexia nervosa the disease affects both the mind and the body.

TABLE 1   Average Heights and Weights of Females and Males, Ages 11 – 17[1]

| | FEMALES | | | | MALES | | | |
| | Height | | Weight | | Height | | Weight | |
Age	Inches	Centimeters	Pounds	Kilograms	Inches	Centimeters	Pounds	Kilograms
11	57.00	144.8	81.47	36.95	56.42	143.3	77.84	35.30
12	59.65	151.5	91.57	41.53	58.94	149.7	87.71	39.78
13	61.85	157.1	101.65	46.10	61.61	156.5	99.11	44.95
14	63.15	160.4	110.87	50.28	64.21	163.1	111.95	50.77
15	63.70	161.8	118.36	53.68	66.54	169.0	125.05	56.71
16	63.94	162.4	123.24	55.89	68.31	173.5	136.93	62.10
17	64.21	163.1	125.00	56.69	69.37	176.2	146.21	66.31

[1] Adapted from National Center for Health Statistics: *NCHS Growth Curves for Children; Vital and Health Statistics*, Ser. 11, no. 165 [DHEW publication; (PHS) 78–1650], November, 1977, pp. 37–38.

quickly in a covered pot with a little boiling water. This method will soften them and still leave them tasty and nutritious.

Frying tends to add fat to already fatty foods, like meats. Slow roasting and stewing or broiling are preferable.

Butter, mayonnaise, and salad dressings add calories but few nutrients. Flavor salads with lemon juice, and serve cheese on toast instead of butter.

Ways to Gain or Lose Weight

The amount of food you need is closely related to the amount of exercise you get. When you take in more calories than you use up in exercise and growing, the extra amount is stored as fat. The best method of weight control is to take in only as many calories as you use. This approach will maintain your weight. If you wish to lose weight, you must use up *more* calories than you take in.

The table shows average ideal weights for people at different ages. If you find that you differ by more than 10 percent from the ideal weight for your size and age, you may want to bring your weight back into line for good health and better appearance. There are several ways to do this.

Gaining Weight

It is not a common problem, but sometimes people are underweight. If you are, you may need to change your attitude toward eating. Try to relax at mealtime. Plan your meals around foods that you like. Eat more frequently. Eat larger portions. And choose foods from the first four groups. You can also snack on high-calorie nutritious foods, such as milkshakes, cheese, and whole-grain sandwiches.

You many even want to look at other parts of your life. Are you getting enough sleep? Are you trying to do too much every day? Slow down, and leave yourself enough time for eating and sleeping.

Losing Weight

When you weigh more than is healthy for your age and size, you are **overweight**. The best way to lose weight is to combine exercise with eating fewer calories.

Exercise. Instead of storing calories as fat, you can burn them off by exercising. You'll also help your heart, lungs, and muscles. You'll look better, stand straighter, breathe more deeply, and get rid of bulges.

Dieting. Reduce your calorie intake while following the guidelines for good eating habits. Eat smaller portions and eat more slowly. Don't skip meals, but choose foods carefully by eating foods from the four main food groups, which are dense in nutrients. Cut out sweet and salty snacks high in calories but low in nutrients. Also cut out rich sauces and fats.

Changing Your Habits. Some people use eating as a way to solve emotional problems. You're not hungry, but you're unhappy—and you eat. When you're tempted to overeat for some reason, try getting away from food altogether. Go for a long walk. Jog for half an hour. Exercise often works off frustration and anger. You feel better—and not hungry—when you finish.

TABLE 2 **Calories Burned in Various Activities**

Activity	Calories burned per hour
Basketball	360–660
Bicycling (5 mph)	240
(10 mph)	420
Dancing, fast	240–360
Field hockey	600
Housework, light	240–300
Karate and judo	700
Mowing lawn (hand mower)	450
Reading	125
Running (5 mph)	600
(8 mph)	1020
Swimming, most strokes	360–750
Table tennis	300–420
Walking, leisurely	300
Watching TV	125

Words to Remember

anorexia nervosa: self-induced starvation

bulimia: alternating food binges and purges

diet: a planned approach to eating designed to accomplish a certain goal

overweight: when you weigh more than is healthy for your age and size

Questions

1. List the five guidelines for a healthy diet.
2. Give at least two examples of how food preparation and planning meals help with weight control.
3. What effect does exercise have on weight? How is food intake related to exercise?
4. List two techniques you can use to gain weight. List two techniques you can use to lose weight.

38 Fact, Fad, or Fallacy?

After reading this chapter, you will be able to:

☐ *explain what is meant by a fad,*

☐ *identify certain food fads that are currently affecting American eating habits,*

☐ *evaluate new diets to decide if they are based on fact or fallacy.*

"If it were not for the belly the back would wear gold." (Russian proverb)

"Stop eating when you are enjoying it the most." (German proverb)

"You are what you eat." (Italian proverb)

"Eat all you want and lose weight!" proclaims an advertisement for a new diet book. Another ad praises the latest "all-natural" vitamin. Meanwhile, your friend tells you about an article she read. It claimed that eating a pound of beets a day would prevent illness.

Traditions aren't the only influences on our food choices. A particular food or a combination of foods can become a **fad**—*something that is highly fashionable for a short time.* When many people rush to try the latest wonder diet or miracle health food, a fad has started. But food fads may have little to do with sound nutrition.

Some Recent Food Fads

Following fashions in food or clothing can be expensive. And believing everything you hear about food can be risky. If you ignore the rules of good nutrition and base your diet on the latest fads, you could damage your health. Use your knowledge of nutrition to decide whether claims made about new diets and fads are true.

People follow fads in diets because they believe that the diets will either help them lose weight or make them healthier. But often these diets are based on false ideas about food, and accomplish neither goal.

Weight-Loss Diets

Many popular weight-loss diets tell people to eat large amounts of protein, but almost no carbohydrate. People on these diets seem to lose weight—at first. But most of what is lost is water. This is quickly regained as soon as the dieter goes back to normal eating. If the diet is kept up for a long time, the body starts to break down muscles to get needed glucose, which it would otherwise get from carbohydrate.

Some weight-loss diets have been based on the mistaken idea that certain foods, such as grapefruit or other fruit, help the body burn fat. In fact, fruits do not help the body burn fat. And people on an all-fruit diet can suffer weakness, dizziness, low blood pressure, and intestinal upsets.

Crash diets are *diets that promise quick and easy weight loss.* They are almost always dangerous to your health, and they usually fail. That's because these diets don't help people change their bad eating habits to good ones.

Some people try to lose weight by taking diet pills or candy. These substances reduce their appetite, so they eat less food at a meal. But this method is not good for permanent weight loss because the people are not changing their eating habits. Once they stop taking the pills or candy, they will begin eating too much again.

Health Fads

Other fads claim to prevent or cure certain illnesses or to increase physical well-being. Sometimes these diets are based on fact. For example, heart disease has been linked to high blood levels of cholesterol. Many diets call for small amounts of protein and fat and larger amounts of grains, fruits, and vegetables. The goal—to lower cholesterol—is healthful, but there is no evidence that this diet will completely prevent heart disease.

Macrobiotic diets are high in brown rice and vegetables. Although all these foods are healthy, dieters must be very careful to avoid becoming undernourished.

Some people think that if vitamins are healthful, large amounts of vitamins must be very healthful. These people take expensive pills that contain large doses of one or more vitamins. But the extra vitamins are of no help, because the body uses only what it needs. And too much of some vitamins can be harmful. Large doses of vitamin A and D, for example, can cause discomfort and illness.

A well-planned diet provides all the vitamins you need—in a tastier form than pills. It provides roughage, moisture, and other nutrients that pills alone cannot give you.

Health Foods—Fact or Fad?

So-called **health foods** are very popular in North America today. These are *foods that are thought to provide better nutrition.* But any clean, fresh food that offers valuable nutrients can be a healthful part of your diet.

What Are Health Foods?

Health food stores sell whole grains, flours, seeds, and nuts not always found in regular grocery stores. They also sell breads and crackers made from these items. They often carry a selection of fruit and vegetable juices and dairy products.

Most of the products are labeled **natural**. This label means that they *contain no chemi-* cal additives and have been processed no more than they would in the average kitchen. Some products are labeled **organic**. These are *made with ingredients that were grown without chemical fertilizers or pesticides.*

Certainly, foods such as whole grains and nuts provide valuable nutrients. But health foods may cost more than other foods. People buy them because they contain no additives and have not come in contact with chemical fertilizers or pesticides.

Additives

Food **additives** are *substances that are added to food during processing.* The most common additives are sugar, salt, and corn syrup. But thousands of other substances are added to food. It is hard to put together a

---

Buying products in a health food store does not guarantee that the product is better. Continue to compare nutrients and costs with brands found in your local supermarket.

meal that does not contain some additives. Additives are used for four purposes.

- *To improve a food's nutritional value.* For example, vitamin D is added to milk. Iron and B vitamins are added to bread, cereals, and flour.
- *To help keep food fresh.* Salt and sugar help keep food from spoiling. Vitamins C and E and the chemical BHT (butylated hydroxytoluene) keep food from changing in color or flavor when it is exposed to air.
- *To make food more appealing.* Food colors, flavorings, and sweeteners fall into this group.
- *To prepare or process foods.* These additives control the acidity of food, help baked goods rise, bleach flour, keep table salt from sticking, keep ice cream smooth, and retain moisture in soft foods like candy.

Steaming vegetables so that they retain their nutritional value is a food trend that has gained in popularity.

Making a Decision

Some people are concerned about the additives in food. They feel that some of the chemicals may be harmful. They also worry that chemical fertilizers used to grow foods are not healthy.

In the United States, all additives must be approved by the Food and Drug Administration (FDA), a federal agency. If an additive is found to be harmful, manufacturers are not permitted to use it. Sometimes, if test results are unclear, products containing the additive may carry a warning label.

Other people feel protected by these tests. They argue that without fertilizers it would be impossible to grow enough food. And without additives, they say, it would be hard to keep food fresh enough to reach all

consumers. They also point out that even organically grown foods often contain traces of chemicals that were already in the soil.

Are special health foods worth the extra money? Are chemical additives, pesticides, and fertilizers a risk? As a consumer, you must make your own decisions. Look for the latest news on food in newspapers and magazines you think you can trust. Reliable sources can help you decide.

Healthful Trends

Not all new fashions in foods are questionable. In fact, three recent trends show that people are starting to pay more attention to nutrition in their diets:

TEEN ISSUE

Facts about Tobacco, Alcohol, and Drugs

Smoking

- Smoking is the number one avoidable cause of death in our society.
- Smokers are more likely than non-smokers to suffer lung cancer, coronary heart disease, and other lung diseases.
- Smokers of low tar and low nicotine cigarettes have less risk of developing lung cancer than other smokers. But they still have a greater risk than non-smokers.
- Risk of heart disease decreases when a person quits smoking.
- About 10 percent of boys aged 12 to 18 smoke. About 13 percent of girls aged 12 to 18 smoke.
- Teens are getting the word—the percentage of teens who smoke has been decreasing since 1975.

Drinking

- More than two-thirds of all cases of violence to spouses or children are alcohol-related.
- About half of the people who die on the highways die as a result of drunk driving. Drunk driving is the greatest threat to 15- to 24-year-olds.
- Alcohol can affect the health of the liver and heart.
- Drinking makes it harder to reason clearly, use judgment, move in a co-ordinated way, and speak.
- Heavy drinkers may neglect good nu-trition because they get too many calories from alcohol.
- Beer and wine have less alcohol than hard liquor. But people tend to drink more of them at a time, which adds up. A six-pack of beer contains the same amount of alcohol as one-half pint of whiskey.
- More than 12 million people in this country are alcoholics. As many more might be problem drinkers.
- Social workers have found that young people can become alcoholics in months, though it takes adults years.

Taking drugs

- *Drugs* include over-the-counter and prescription medicines, as well as il-legal substances like marijuana. Alcohol, caffeine, and the nicotine in tobacco are also drugs. If used incorrectly, all of these drugs can cause problems.
- Overdoses of narcotics can kill.
- Drugs sold on the street may have high dosages or contain other chemicals that can cause bad reactions.
- Marijuana can lead to heart and lung problems, loss of short-term memory, and poor coordination.
- PCP affects perception, which can lead to accidents. An overdose can cause convulsions and passing out.
- Teens are catching on to the dangers of drugs. Use of most illegal drugs by teens has decreased since 1978-1979.

1. *People are choosing healthier foods.* In the past, we have relied on red meat for most of our protein. Now people are eating beans, poultry, and fish, which contain less fat. They're also eating more vegetables. Salad bars are also popular now.

2. *People are preparing food with an eye to good nutrition.* They are more likely to broil meats and fish than fry them, and to steam vegetables rather than to boil them or cook them in butter. People are also cutting down on the salt and sugar they add to food.

3. *People are developing healthier habits.* They're snacking more wisely. And they're exercising more—jogging, walking, and playing sports.

Evaluating Trends—Good or Bad?

How can you decide if a new trend or fad in food is healthful or not? Food manufacturers and those who promote a trend often make confusing and conflicting claims. For example, both low-carbohydrate and high-carbohydrate diets are claimed to help weight loss.

A wise consumer thinks carefully before believing such claims or following food fads. The claims made for special foods or diets can be appealing, but they may be questionable. You must evaluate them. By using your knowledge of nutrition, you can protect your health and save money, too.

Words to Remember

additives: substances that are added to food during processing

crash diets: diets that promise quick and easy weight loss

fad: something that is highly fashionable for a short time

health foods: foods that are thought to provide better nutrition

natural: food products that contain no chemical additives and have been processed no more than they would be in the average kitchen

organic: made with ingredients that were grown without chemical fertilizers or pesticides

Questions

1. What is a food fad? List some food fads that have affected your eating habits.
2. Why do crash diets usually fail?
3. If you eat a balanced diet, do you also need vitamin supplements? Explain.
4. Are health foods always worth the extra money? Explain.
5. Are eating trends always harmful? How can you decide if a trend is harmful or not?

Chapter **39 Planning Meals for the Home**

Objectives

After reading this chapter, you will be able to:

- *plan meals based on nutrition, appeal, and resources,*

- *use the newspaper and the cookbook as planning tools,*

- *develop a varied menu plan.*

You and your family can almost always save money by eating your meals at home. And family meals are a great time for the family to talk about the events of the day and just enjoy being together. But cooking at home requires time, skills in the kitchen, and careful planning.

Cooking at home can be easier if it's a team effort. Why not make a game of it? You can get together with other family members and organize a meal. Everyone can make a contribution to shopping or cooking. And everyone can join in eating it.

Planning meals does not take a lot of time if you are organized and have people pitch in. This chapter can help to start you out on a lifetime of enjoyable meal planning.

Aspects of Meal Planning

What's Going On?

The first thing you need to find out when you begin to plan a meal is how many people will be eating. Next, find out what time is best for the most people. Will someone be at work or at practice?

Once you know who will be there, think about **food preferences**, *the foods that people like best.* Will there be any small children or older people who need special foods served at certain times?

Achieving Nutritional Balance

You'll want to prepare a nutritious meal. In choosing from the food groups, keep in mind what else was eaten during the day.

The heart of most meals is a combination of protein and carbohydrate. Some exam-

---

F E A T U R E

Computers in the Kitchen

For many years, writers predicted that in the future computers would become more widely used in the homes. The future seems to be here. More and more people are buying home computers and using them for budgeting and education. And everyone knows that they can be fun for games!

Many of these computers are being used in the kitchen. People are finding that computers make meal planning and achieving nutritional balance easier. Computer users no longer have to check the cupboards to see if they have a can of tuna—the computer can quickly search its memory to see. No one needs to figure out the nutritional content of a meal. Just ask the computer, and you get the answer in seconds.

Computers do their work based on instructions from *programs.* Food programs fall into three groups.

■ *Meal planning.* These programs help the user put together balanced menus that are economical and tasty.

■ *Diet analysis.* With these programs, a user can learn whether his or her eating habits need to be changed. Some of these programs include the number of calories the person burns each day.

■ *Nutritional analysis.* These programs allow the user to check on the nutrients in different foods.

Some computers are found in kitchen appliances. Microwave ovens (see chapter 45) and automatic coffee makers, for example, contain tiny computers. With these devices, a cook can instruct the machine to turn itself off automatically. Some oven computers even tell the cook how long to cook a food and at what temperature. That leaves the cook with more time to play computer games!

ples are meat and potatoes, beans and rice, chicken and noodles, macaroni and cheese, or a tuna noodle casserole.

To round out this basic meal, add fruits and vegetables—as appetizers, salads, side dishes, or desserts. The dairy group could be included as a dessert (yogurt or ice cream) or as a drink (milkshake or plain milk).

Giving Your Meal Appeal

Some meals just naturally look and taste delicious. What makes them so special? They blend food flavors, colors, shapes, textures, and temperatures successfully.

Flavor. The right combination of flavors makes a meal go well. Sweet flavors can be paired with savory ones (applesauce and pork; cranberry sauce and turkey). Strong flavors go best with mild ones (tomato sauce on spaghetti). But avoid serving two strong flavors in the same meal.

Color. Think about what colors you'll include in your meal. You don't want everything to be the same color—aim for variety. If you plan to serve two vegetables, match carrots with string beans or tomatoes with spinach. Brown rice or green spaghetti are good side dishes for a white-fleshed fish. Add a lemon wedge, a slice of orange, or a sprig of parsley to give a dish an appealing color contrast.

Shape. The size and shape of foods can also be varied for an attractive look. Serving

The cookbook can be a valuable tool for the beginning cook. It contains a wealth of delicious recipes and offers menu ideas, cooking hints, and serving suggestions.

meatballs and brussels sprouts together is boring, since both are round. Replace those sprouts with broccoli and you've got a more interesting meal. If you do serve carrots and string beans, cut the carrots into circles, rather than lengthwise. Then you'll have variety in shape as well as color.

Texture. Think about the texture of foods, too. How do they feel in your mouth when you bite into them? It's a good idea to try for three different textures. A slightly chewy chop, a smooth baked potato, and a crisp salad make a good combination. Remember that you can get a different texture from the same food by preparing it differently. Applesauce has a different feel than a fresh apple.

Temperature. Vary the temperature of foods in your meal, too. Combine a cool salad with a hot soup for an interesting contrast. Or serve a cold vegetable soup and end the meal with a hot dessert.

What Are Your Resources?

Try to be realistic when planning meals. Consider five factors.

- *Time*. If you try to make a long, complicated recipe when you're short on time, you'll feel rushed. Keep in mind how much preparation time a food needs, too. Meats that need to sit in sauces to become tender need extra time.
- *Your kitchen and its equipment*. Be sure that you have all the tools and appliances that you'll need.
- *Skill*. Don't take on a project that's more complex than you're ready for.
- *Money*. Plan your meal within the food budget.

- *Food on hand*. You can save money and reduce waste by using food that you already have on hand. Look in your kitchen cabinets as well as refrigerator for items to use.

Planning Tools

Cookbooks

Your best meal-planning aid may well be your family's favorite cookbook. Most cookbooks have a wide variety of **recipes**. These are *detailed instructions for preparing foods*. Some even suggest what foods to serve with a main course.

When you're searching for the right recipe, look first at the list of **ingredients**, *the individual foods needed to make a dish*. Do you have them all, or can you get them at your local store? Be sure to note how many people your recipe serves. Will you need to add to or subtract from your recipe in order to feed your family?

The recipe should also list what equipment is needed. Read through the recipe to see if you understand the steps and techniques. If you don't, you're probably better off choosing another dish. Chapter 46 will tell you more about using recipes.

Newspapers and Magazines

You can also get good recipe ideas from newspapers and magazines. You can clip ones that you like and make a file of your favorite dishes. Newspapers and magazines also can help you shop for food, as the next chapter explains.

Thinking Ahead

One Step at a Time

Making a family meal can seem like an overwhelming chore, but you can make it easier by doing it in small steps. Suppose that you're making a Saturday night birthday dinner. Make up your menu and your grocery list on Thursday night, shop on Friday, bake a cake on Saturday morning, and cook and serve the rest of the meal Saturday evening.

Here is a checklist of items that can make your mealtimes easier and more relaxing:

- What type of meal will it be (breakfast, lunch, dinner)?
- How many people will be served?
- What dishes will be included (appetizer, main course, side dishes, desserts, beverage)?
- Will the meal be nutritious? Appealing? Easy to prepare?
- What items must you shop for?
- What can be done ahead of time?

Keep Your Plan Adaptable

Now that you've completed your meal plan, remember to be flexible. You might want to prepare something you can add to, in case a family member brings a friend home to eat.

While you're shopping, you may see a bargain you want to take advantage of. You may be able to switch chicken for turkey if it's on sale.

Just be sure when you adjust your plan that you still are offering your family nutritional balance.

And remember to stay within your budget.

Words to Remember

food preferences: the foods that people like best

ingredients: the individual foods needed to make a dish

recipe: detailed instructions for preparing a food

Questions

1. What is the first thing to think about when planning a meal?
2. What five qualities of food can you vary to make an appealing meal?
3. What five resources should you consider in meal planning?
4. Name two sources of meal ideas.
5. How can you make preparing a meal easier?

Chapter 40 Shopping
for Food

Objectives

After reading this chapter, you will be able to:

☐ *select the most appropriate store for your food shopping needs,*

☐ *prepare a shopping list for quick and efficient shopping,*

☐ *describe how to get the best food buys.*

Shopping for food is an art in itself. Chefs at luxury restaurants often go to markets early in the morning to supervise the purchase of foods they will prepare. They look for high-quality foods at the best prices. By planning your food shopping, you can do the same.

The items that are bought weekly for the household should be bought at the greatest savings. Such savings can really add up during the year. Items bought only now and again can be purchased at regular prices if they cannot be purchased at sales.

Deciding where to shop is the first step in getting the best food for your money. The restaurant chef usually purchases food at a wholesale market, but there are many other kinds of stores. The smart shopper uses a store that offers good prices and high quality on the items he or she buys most often.

Types of Food Markets

Supermarkets

Supermarkets have two main advantages: lower prices and wider selection. A *supermarket* is a large store that sells many types and brands of food and grocery products. Customers can buy just about anything they want. Many supermarkets have specialty sections like deli counters or bakeries.

Some places also have discount supermarkets, or "no-frills" supermarkets. They sell a small selection of basic items, like canned goods, cleaning supplies, and paper products, at low prices. These stores have fewer services than supermarkets. For instance, at many no-frills supermarkets, customers must bring their own shopping bags.

Take advantage of the convenient, one-stop supermarket that offers lower prices and a wider selection.

Specialty Stores

Some stores sell only meat, only fruits and vegetables, or only cheeses and bread. The prices at specialty stores are usually higher than those at a supermarket. They attract customers by offering high-quality goods. Some also provide special services, such as getting special cuts of meat or selling fresh fruit in large quantities.

Convenience Stores

A *convenience store* is a smaller store that sells basic items at many locations and for longer hours. They may be open 24 hours a day and are usually open every day, including holidays.

Quick checkout is one thing that makes these stores so convenient. In addition, these stores are usually found at many handy locations.

Other Places to Buy Food

At a *farmer's market*, a consumer can buy produce directly from farmers. The food is usually very fresh and the prices can be quite low. At a *roadside stand*, one farmer sells his or her produce.

Many people today are using co-ops (or cooperatives) to save money on their food bills. A **co-op** is *a group of shoppers who get together to buy large amounts of basic food items at discount prices*. The co-op owners save money by buying large quantities of everything. They also save by operating the store. Only members can shop there.

Preparing a Shopping List

Smart shopping requires careful planning. This involves taking three steps: Use a menu plan, take advantage of sales and coupons, prepare a shopping list.

Using a Menu Plan

Your shopping list will include the foods you need to complete the meal you plan to make. As you plan a meal, check your supplies. Note which items you need to buy, along with exact amounts. A shopping list should be based on menus for several days or a week.

Your menus should be flexible. Change them if you discover a better buy or a higher-quality product when you get to the store. Suppose that broccoli is costly or of poor quality, but green beans are a bargain. Simply substitute the beans for broccoli in your meal plan. While making up your shopping list, check newspaper ads.

You will probably purchase some foods—milk, bread, and eggs, for example—every week. These are **staples**, *basic food items that are used regularly.* Flour and sugar are staples too, but they are usually purchased less often on a regular basis.

Clipping Coupons

A **coupon** is *a printed slip of paper that gives a customer a discount on a particular item.* Coupons are found in newspapers, advertising fliers, and on some product packages and containers.

Some supermarkets offer double or even triple value for coupons. That means that the store subtracts two or three times the coupon discount from a product's price.

Coupons can help you save money if you use them wisely. Don't buy something just because you have a coupon for it.

Outdoor markets are popular. They buy fresh fruits and vegetables in bulk. They usually sell their produce at generally lower prices.

Organizing the Shopping List

The shopping list is your key to successful shopping. With a written list, you're sure to get everything you need.

Your list can be organized in two ways:

1. List the same types of foods together.
2. Follow the layout of the store.

Whichever method you choose, you can follow the same smart shopping practices. Choose canned goods first and put them at the bottom of the cart. Select frozen foods and dairy products last, to prevent thawing and spoiling. Select fresh produce at the end of your shopping, too. That way it can sit on top and won't be damaged.

Locating the Best Buys

Shopping means more than just taking the first item you see on the shelf and crossing it off your list. Planning also goes on at the store.

Looking at Labels

Food labels can tell you a lot about the product you're buying. They can help you compare features of different brands of the same product.

Basic Information. Almost every food label, by law, must contain the following information:

■ Name of product.

■ Weight of contents.

■ Name and address of manufacturer, packer, or distributor.

■ Ingredients.

Ingredients are listed in order by weight—the ingredient with the largest weight is listed first. A can of stew that lists beef first, for example, will have more meat than one listing potatoes first.

Standards of Identity. The government has set standards for what some foods should include. If manufacturers follow these standards, they don't have to list ingredients. If other ingredients are included, they must be listed. Standard foods include catsup, mayonnaise, and peanut butter.

Nutritional Labels. By law, foods that have had nutrients added and products that are advertised as being nutritious must have nutritional labels. These labels include:

■ Serving size and number of servings.

■ Calories per serving.

■ Grams of protein, carbohydrate, and fat per serving.

When a product claims that it is nutritious, it must include a nutritional label. This helps you to compare calories and nutrients.

FINE FOOD

INGREDIENTS—ZUCCHINI, WATER, TOMATO PASTE, SUGAR, SALT, DRIED ONIONS, FOOD STARCH MODIFIED, DRIED GREEN PEPPERS, DRIED CELERY, CITRIC ACID, DRIED GARLIC, CALCIUM CHLORIDE, SPICES.

NUTRITION INFORMATION—PER ONE CUP SERVING

SERVINGS PER CONTAINER—APPROX. 2

CALORIES..............60	CARBOHYDRATE 16g	
PROTEIN...............2g	FAT....................0g	

PERCENTAGE OF U.S. RECOMMENDED DAILY ALLOWANCES (U.S. RDA) PER ONE CUP SERVING

PROTEIN.................	2	NIACIN..................	4
VITAMIN A	30	CALCIUM	4
VITAMIN C	15	IRON....................	8
THIAMINE (VIT. B₁)....	6	PHOSPHORUS..........	6
RIBOFLAVIN (VIT. B₂)..	6	MAGNESIUM...........	8

*WT. OF ZUCCHINI (9-¾ OZ.) BEFORE ADDITION OF LIQUID NECESSARY FOR PROCESSING

Net Wt. 16 oz. (1 lb.) 454 g

Cups ....Approx. 2

For good nutrition eat a variety of foods.

FEATURE

All about Brands

A **brand** is *the particular make of a product, as indicated by an official name or trademark.* There are brands of nearly every food product. The brand is found on the product label, and it is probably the first piece of information you notice.

■ *National brands.* These are the products advertised in television and radio commercials and in magazines. They are the "name brands" that are made and sold across the country.

■ *Store brands.* Larger supermarket chains have their own brands, called *store brands* or *house brands.* They are not advertised as much as the national brands are, and their packaging tends to be simpler. As a result, store brands usually cost less than national brands.

■ *Generic brands.* A new trend in food marketing is **generic products.** These are *no-frills products packaged with no brand or store names.* The cans or packages are usually white with black or blue lettering. These products are generally the cheapest in the store.

Which brand is best? The choice is yours. Many consumers feel that national brands offer better quality and are worth the extra money. Others feel that the quality of all three types is the same, but they want the savings of store brands or generic products. Most consumers choose from more than one type.

■ Percentage of U.S. Recommended Daily Allowance (RDA) of protein, vitamins, and minerals per serving.

Look for signs that one product may be less nutritious than another. "Orange juice drink" has less actual juice than "orange juice."

Universal Product Code. Food labels and packages also contain the Universal Product Code (UPC). This is the small block of parallel black lines of various widths. Because the lines for each product are unique, computerized checkout equipment can read them and ring up the sale automatically. This saves time at the counter.

The Teen Tips in Unit 3 show a Universal Product Code.

Open Dating

Dates stamped or printed on food packages can help you to judge how fresh a food product is. There are two major types of dates.

■ The **pull date** is *the last day a product may be sold.* A label may say, "Do not sell after November 17."

■ The **expiration date** is *the last day a product can be used safely.* This kind of label says, "Do not use after July 1986."

Other types of dates include the *pack date,* which states when the product was made or packaged, and the *freshness date,* which tells when the product will taste best or be most nutritious.

Warning Signs

Careful consumers protect themselves by watching food packages for signs of spoilage:

■ bulging cans, which may contain dangerous bacteria,

■ dented cans, which may have broken seams,

■ rusty cans, which may be old,

■ frozen food packages that are soft or wet, and which may be thawing,

■ stained frozen food packages or those with thin sheets of ice, which may have been thawed and refrozen.

Do not purchase these products. Show them to the store manager, who can take them off the shelves so that other people do not buy them.

Using Unit Prices

Comparing prices can be tricky. Sometimes, you might think you need to carry a calculator to the store with you. Almost all supermarkets post unit prices on their shelves. *Unit prices* are costs of items by ounce or by count. They help you compare the prices of different-sized packages of the same item.

For example, if a 12-ounce box of cereal costs 60 cents, its unit price is 5 cents per ounce. That's a better buy than an 8-ounce box that cost 48 cents—its unit price is 6 cents per ounce. You can use this method to compare brands as well as sizes.

Of course, the larger package is only a better buy if you use all of the product while it is still fresh. Otherwise, the waste will mean you saved nothing.

Words to Remember

brand: the particular make of a product, as indicated by an official name or trademark

co-op: a group of shoppers who get together to buy large amounts of basic food items at discount prices

coupon: a printed slip of paper that gives a customer a discount on a particular item

expiration date: the last day a product can be used safely

generic products: no-frills products packaged with no brand or store names

pull date: the last day a product may be sold

staples: basic food items that are used regularly

Questions

1. Describe the three main types of food markets.

2. How can coupons be used wisely?

3. Explain two good ways to organize the items on a shopping list.

4. What four basic points of information are on all food labels?

5. Explain the two major types of open dating.

6. Describe how unit prices can be used to judge the best buy.

Chapter **41 Selecting and Storing Food: I**

Objectives

After reading this chapter, you will be able to:

□ *identify and select foods in the fruits and vegetables group,*

□ *identify and select foods in the breads and cereals group,*

□ *explain how to store these foods.*

Even a quick tour of a supermarket will give you some idea of the many different forms of food products you can choose from.

To make the best choices, you must consider four factors:

1. how you will use the product,
2. the product's nutritional quality,
3. the price,
4. how long you will be storing the food at home.

In this chapter, you'll read about choosing and storing fruits, vegetables, breads, and cereals. In the next chapter, you'll find out how to select foods in the milk group, as well as meat, poultry, fish, eggs, and legumes.

Selecting and Storing Fruits and Vegetables

This first food group probably offers the most variety of all. You can easily name at least 10 different fruits and 10 different vegetables. There's even more variety than you think, because fruits and vegetables come in four basic forms: fresh, frozen, canned, and dried. Juices are available from many fruits and vegetables, too.

Selecting Fruits and Vegetables

Fresh. *Fresh fruits and vegetables,* also called **produce**, are very nutritious. But how nutritious they are depends on when they were picked. The more time that passes between picking and eating, the more nutrients that are lost.

Produce should look fresh and crisp, not wilted. Larger produce is not necessarily better. Smaller carrots or plums may be more tender than larger ones. Produce should have a healthy color, with no bruises, spots, or sticky areas. Fruit that is juicy will be firm but not hard. Soft fruits are overripe.

You also need to consider price. Most produce is **seasonal**, which means that it is *plentiful only at certain times of the year.* For instance, you see fresh corn in summer but usually not in winter. Buying produce in season can save money.

Frozen. Frozen fruits and vegetables can be a good choice if you are not planning to use the items right away or if fresh fruit is not in season. They retain many of their nutrients—almost as many as fresh produce. And they keep their flavor and color better than canned products. Fruits can be frozen without added sugar. Canned fruits are sold in a sugar syrup or in their own juices.

Canned. Fruits and vegetables in cans can be stored longer. Often, they are easier to use than frozen fruits and vegetables. Very little preparation is required—canned foods need only be warmed.

FEATURE

Produce Seasons

Fruit	Season	Vegetable	Season
apples	all year	broccoli	October–May
bananas	all year	carrots	all year
cantaloupe	May–September	cauliflower	September–January
grapefruit	October–June	corn	April–September
grapes	June–September	green beans	May–August
oranges	November–June	lettuce	all year

When selecting produce, check to see that the leaves are not wilted. The head should be firm but not hard and have a fresh appearance.

In fact, canned fruits and vegetables come in many forms, such as diced, sliced, halved, or whole. For example, you can buy canned pineapple in rings, in chunks, diced, or crushed. Which form you choose depends on how you will use the item.

Dried. Many fruits and vegetables are available dried, from raisins and apricots to mushrooms and onions. Dried fruits can be eaten as snacks or used in prepared dishes.

Juices. Apples, oranges, prunes, and carrots are just some of the many fruits and vegetables that are made into juices. Juices can be fresh, canned, frozen, or frozen **concentrates**. These are *juice products from which most of the water has been removed.* Concentrates may be less costly than other forms of juice.

Storing Fruits and Vegetables

Now that you've chosen a fruit or vegetable, you must make sure that it stays healthy and tasty once you get it home. Storing foods properly helps prevent **spoilage**, which *happens when food is too old to eat or contains bacteria or mold.*

Fresh. In general, fresh fruits and vegetables need refrigeration. Some, like berries and cherries, must be kept as dry as possible until they are served. Others, like lettuce and other leafy vegetables, need to be kept in airtight containers to retain their moisture.

A few products, such as bananas, do much better stored at room temperature. If you have a question about a specific product, the produce manager at your local supermarket would be a good person to ask about products.

Most fresh produce should be used within a day or two of buying it. Apples, though, can stay fresh for three or four weeks. And oranges and other citrus fruits can keep for five weeks in a plastic bag in the refrigerator.

Potatoes and onions can also be kept a long time—two or three months—in a cool, dry, dark place.

Frozen. Frozen products keep well for several months if the temperature in the freezer or freezing compartment is no higher than 0° F (−18° C). If the freezer or freezing compartment is not this cold, frozen fruits and vegetables should be stored for only a few days.

Canned. Canned fruits and vegetables keep for long periods of time if they are stored in a cool, dry place. Storage at no more than 65° F (18° C) is recommended.

Dried. Dried and freeze-dried products do well on the cupboard shelf, tightly wrapped. In very humid weather, however, dried fruit should be refrigerated.

Juices. Juices should be stored according to the package directions.

Selecting and Storing Breads and Cereals

Selecting Bread and Cereal Products

Breads. You can buy bread that has been commercially made or freshly baked. You can also buy bread mixes or the ingredients to make bread yourself. There are many kinds of bread: white, whole wheat, rye, pumpernickel, and corn are some examples. There are also rolls, muffins, biscuits, and other forms of bread products.

You can also buy some frozen bread products. Waffles, bread dough, and rolls come in this form.

Most bread is made from white flour, which is *refined*. This means that the bran and the germ have been removed to give the flour a finer texture and make it keep better. But in taking out the bran and germ, refining also removes much of the bread's nutritional value. When the nutrients, like iron and B vitamins, are put back into the flour, the bread is called *enriched*.

Whole-wheat bread uses the whole grain, including the bran and germ. It is not necessary to enrich whole-grain products.

Bread comes in two types: quick bread and yeast bread. Both rise, or puff up, because chemicals in the dough release gases. What makes the two types different are the chemicals involved.

Quick breads use *baking soda or baking powder to rise*. These chemicals work fast, so that the bread is ready for baking right

Besides high calorie treats, bakeries provide a daily fare of breads and rolls. Some offer an assortment of ethnic desserts and pastries, as well as diet bread.

Quick Breads

Griddle Bake

Hotcakes

Oven Bake

Blueberry muffins

Yeast Breads

English Muffins

Whole wheat bread

How well you prepare a bread depends on the way you heat it, and what you use to make it rise. On the right, we have yeast bread, on the left quick bread.

away. That's why they're called quick breads. Examples are muffins, biscuits, and pancakes.

Yeast breads *rise through the action of yeast,* a tiny plant. When mixed with warm water, the yeast becomes active. Added to dough, it feeds on the starch and releases gas. Bakers knead bread dough to spread the yeast throughout the dough. Refined wheat flour rises more than other flours. For that reason, whole-wheat, rye, and pumpernickel breads have a coarser texture than white bread.

Cereals. Cereals, usually eaten at breakfast, are made from wheat, oats, corn, rice, and barley. Some are ready to eat—such as wheat flakes or corn puffs—and can be served with milk and fruit. Others are prepared hot by being cooked in water. Some cooked cereals are instant—you only have to add boiling water.

To find out if you are getting the most nutrients for your money, check the labels on all cereal products. Make sure that the cereal you choose contains enriched or whole-grain flour.

Also check the labels on products that claim to have a high percentage of added nutrients. If these nutrients are in addition to the usual enrichment of cereal products, they may be unnecessary. A well-balanced diet will supply those nutrients. Also check to see if the product has added sugar. Many ready-to-eat cereals contain large amounts of sugar.

When buying dry cereal products, pay attention to the weight listed on the label rather than to the size of the package. One cereal may seem much more expensive than another one of the same price because it comes in a much smaller box. But the cereal in the larger box may be of the "puffed" variety, and the added air takes up much more space. The two boxes may weigh exactly the same.

Rice. Most rice has its brown covering, or hull, removed. But most of the vitamin B_1 is in that hull. Like enriched bread, enriched or *converted* rice has some of the vitamins put back in. You can also buy brown rice, which still has the nutritious hull.

Some rice products are packaged with sauces. Some rice is instant, meaning that it can be cooked quickly. This type has fewer nutrients.

Pasta. Macaroni, spaghetti, and noodles are also in the breads and cereals group. These products are all called *pasta*, which comes from the Italian word for dough. Some are made from whole-wheat or enriched white flour, but most are made from a special wheat called semolina. Some pasta products have spinach or tomatoes added to the dough.

Pasta comes in all sizes and shapes, from thin strands of spaghetti to little shells and pieces that look like wagon wheels. They all usually taste the same, but the difference in texture or appearance may be important in your recipe.

Storing Breads and Cereals

Bread tastes best when it's fresh, but it can also keep for some time. Wrap breads tightly and store them in a breadbox. In hot weather, store them in the refrigerator. Proper storage also will slow down the growth of mold in the bread.

Refrigerator rolls should be kept in the refrigerator. Bread can also be frozen for a few months.

Dry cereals keep well on the shelf in tightly closed packages. Or they can be stored in airtight containers.

Rice, pasta, and flours can stay fresh for a long time in airtight containers. Refrigeration is not needed except in hot, humid weather or if insects are a problem in the area.

Words to Remember

concentrate: a juice product from which most of the water has been removed

produce: fresh fruits and vegetables

quick breads: breads that use baking soda or baking powder to rise

seasonal: plentiful only at certain times of the year

spoilage: damage that occurs to food that is too old to eat or that contains bacteria or mold

yeast breads: breads that rise through the action of yeast

Questions

1. What are four forms in which you can buy fruits and vegetables?
2. How long can you store most produce?
3. How long can you store frozen fruits and vegetables?
4. Why is some flour enriched?
5. What are the two types of breads?
6. Where should you store cereals and breads?

Chapter **42** Selecting and Storing Food: II

You have a great range of choice when you're shopping for meat. Do you want a steak, a chop, or a roast? Would you prefer stew meat or hamburger? Do you want meat, such as beef, lamb, or pork, or would you rather have fish or eggs?

Milk products give you a variety of choices, too. You can buy whole milk or milk with less fat. You can choose from hundreds of kinds of cheeses. And there are many delightful flavors of ice cream that you can select.

Once you get these products home, keeping them fresh is important. Dairy products and meat are **perishable**. They *can spoil very easily.* Storing them properly helps you use them safely, enjoy their flavor, and avoid wasting money.

Selecting and Storing Milk Products

Selecting Milk Products

Milk offers its rich supplies of nutrients in many delicious forms. But before milk gets to you in any form, it is pasteurized. It is heated to destroy harmful bacteria.

Liquid Milk Products. The dairy section of the supermarket holds many varieties of milk in liquid form. *Whole milk* contains all the nutrients milk has to offer. Included is 3 to 4 percent fat, often called *butterfat*.

Most whole milk is *homogenized*. This means that the fat has been broken down into small particles and evenly spread throughout the milk. As a result, the fat will not rise to the top.

Skim milk is whole milk from which al-most all the fat has been removed. It has most of the nutrients supplied by whole milk, except for fat. Vitamin A, removed during skimming, is put back in.

Two percent milk has more fat than skim milk, but less than whole milk. Although 2 percent milk is a little higher in calories than skim, many people prefer its flavor and texture.

Whole milk, 2 percent milk, and skim milk are usually fortified with vitamin D. This important nutrient must be present for calcium to work well. Vitamin D occurs naturally in very few foods. Adding it to milk makes it easier for everyone to get enough.

If milk isn't homogenized, the fat in the milk rises to the top of the container. This rich substance is *cream*. An ounce of cream contains 110 calories. An ounce of whole milk has only about 20 calories.

Half-and-half is a mixture of cream and

Cheese is rich in protein and nutrients, but its fat content makes it rich in calories, too. Cheese is available in many varieties and most go well with fruit.

milk. It offers some of the rich taste and texture of cream with less fat and fewer calories.

Evaporated milk is whole milk that has been heated to remove more than half the water content. This product is canned and can be stored for long periods of time. Add the right amount of water and you have a product like fresh whole milk.

Another kind of milk has half the water removed. This product, *sweetened condensed milk,* also has sugar added.

Dried Milk. Milk from which all the moisture has been removed is called *dried milk.* Dried milk is an inexpensive powder that contains all the nutrients found in skim milk. It keeps for a long time. Nonfat dry milk can be used for cooking and, with water added, for drinking.

Cultured Milk Products. The taste and texture of milk and cream can be changed greatly by the addition of certain harmless bacteria. These bacteria are grown in colonies called *cultures.* They turn milk and cream into products that have a tangy taste and thick texture. That is why *buttermilk, yogurt,* and *sour cream* are called *cultured milk products.* Buttermilk is made from skim milk, and sour cream is made from cream. Yogurt can be made from either whole or skim milk.

Cheese. Cheese is made from the milk of cows or goats. The type of cheese depends on what milk it's made from and how it's made. There are more than 400 types of cheeses, with over 2,000 different names.

Almost all cheeses can be put in four groups:

1. *Soft*—These range in flavor from mild types like cottage cheese to the tangy French Brie and Camembert.

2. *Semihard*—These are generally mild cheeses like Muenster and Gouda.

3. *Hard*—These cheeses, like Cheddar, Swiss, and Parmesan, usually have strong flavors.

4. *Processed*—These are mixtures of different cheeses combined with seasonings.

Most cheeses have much less calcium per serving than liquid milk has, and they cannot be used entirely in place of it. Cheese, except for low-fat varieties, is also much higher in calories than milk. Low-salt cheeses are also being made.

Other Milk Products. *Ice cream, ice milk,* and *frozen yogurt* are all popular desserts made from milk products. Ice milk and frozen yogurt contain less fat and fewer calories than ice cream. But all three are sweetened with sugar and so contain more calories than liquid milk or regular yogurt that you buy in the store.

Storing Milk Products

Keep fresh milk in the coldest part of the refrigerator. This will help it retain its nutrients and freshness for as long as possible. Putting the milk container away as soon as you have used what you need is also very important. Warmth and light both harm fresh milk. Warmth allows the growth of harmful bacteria, while light destroys the milk's riboflavin.

Other fresh milk products need the same care. Cultured milk products that have not been opened keep longer than fresh milk. The dates stamped on milk products will help you judge their freshness.

Soft cheeses, like cottage cheese, keep for a few days if tightly covered. Hard cheeses,

Convenience Foods

Two dishes of spaghetti with sauce: one took only 20 minutes to prepare, while the other took more than 3 hours. The difference, of course, is that one was prepared from two packages of convenience foods. That did away with the peeling, slicing, chopping, measuring, mixing, and cooking that went into making the other meal from scratch.

The answer to the question, "Which one would you choose to make?" may seem obvious. But a wise consumer thinks of more than time when deciding how to prepare a dish.

When should convenience foods be bought? Items like prepared hamburger patties or jarred spaghetti sauce usually cost more than making these foods from scratch. But they may save you time and effort in cooking. Sometimes this is worth the extra price.

like Cheddar and Swiss, remain fresh for weeks or even months if they are tightly wrapped.

The freezer, of course, is the place for ice cream, ice milk, and frozen yogurt. If the freezer temperature is above 0° F (−18° C), the product should be used within a few days.

Canned and dried milk keep well on the shelf until they are opened and mixed with water. Then they must be refrigerated.

Selecting and Storing Meat Group Products

Selecting Meat Group Products

Red Meat. Beef, pork, lamb, and veal are available in different cuts, depending on the part of the animal that they come from.

For example, you can buy a rib roast or a rump roast, a loin chop, or a flank steak. **Variety meats** are *animal's internal organs*, like the liver or kidneys.

Both the cut and the type of animal determine the tenderness and flavor of the meat. Basically, younger animals are more tender. And the parts of animals' bodies that were not exercised much are also more tender. Legs, shoulders, and necks are examples. Tender meats, like ribs, usually contain more fat and cost more. Proper cooking can make even a cheap piece of meat tender and flavorful.

You can buy meat fresh, frozen, or canned. Check fresh meat for bone, fat, and color if it's in a see-through package. Meat that looks brown and dry is probably not fresh. Some frozen meats are complete dinners. Read the label to find out how much meat is actually in the package.

Processed Meat. Sausages, hot dogs, cold cuts, and bacon are examples of **pro-**

cessed meats. *They have been changed in some way before they get to the store.* They might have been chopped and reformed, had seasoning added, or have been cured or smoked.

Poultry. Poultry, like meat, comes from different birds and in different cuts. You can buy chicken, turkey, duck, or Cornish hens. They come whole, in sections, or in parts such as legs, wings, and breasts.

There are various types of chickens. Broiler-fryers are young and tender, roasters are older, and stewing chickens are the oldest. Its name shows the best cooking method for each type.

Stores also sell frozen and canned poultry products. Many of these products are prepared meals.

Fish. Saltwater fish, like tuna and flounder, come from the ocean. Many fish, such as trout and salmon, come from freshwater lakes, rivers, and streams. There are also many types of shellfish, such as clams, scallops, and shrimp.

Fresh fish are sold in three ways:

1. *Whole*—just as it comes from the water.

2. *Dressed*—scaled, with head, tail, fins, and insides removed.

3. *Cut*—cut in strips (fillets) or in steaks with all bones removed.

You can buy fresh, frozen, or canned fish. Fresh fish comes packed in ice and has bright red gills, firm skin, and clear eyes. It should not have a strong smell. Frozen fish can be bought plain or batter-dipped. Canned fish, like tuna or salmon, comes packed in water or in oil.

Eggs. Eggs are usually bought fresh in cartons of a dozen. Brown eggs and white eggs have exactly the same quality and taste. Eggs can be small, medium, large, or extra large in size.

There are also dried eggs that keep for a long time. Many stores sell egg substitutes, which contain less fat and cholesterol.

Legumes. The many varieties of legumes include soy, navy, pinto, and lima beans, as well as peas and nuts. They come dried and canned. Most dried legumes must soak in water before being cooked. Canned legumes can be used as they are because they have been soaked in liquid.

The four U.S. grades of beef are Prime, Choice, Good, and Standard. Streaks of marbling within the lean meat are clues to the better cuts, like this piece of Prime beef.

Storing Meat Group Products

Proper storage is the first step in using meat and meat group products wisely.

All fresh meat and fish should be taken out of the store wrapper and wiped with a clean damp cloth. Then it should be wrapped loosely in clean foil or plastic wrap and stored in the coldest part of the refrigerator.

All fresh meat products must be used within a few days of purchase. Ground meat should be cooked within 24 hours. Organ meats keep only for 1 to 2 days. Processed and cooked meats can be kept longer.

Eggs, too, need refrigeration to retain nutrients and flavor. Whole eggs should be stored in a covered container to keep them from absorbing food odors.

Dried peas and beans will stay fresh in the cupboard if they are kept in a tightly sealed container. Canned meats and fish keep well on cool, dry shelves until they are opened.

Frozen meat, poultry, and fish must be kept at 0° F (-18°C) or used within a day or two of purchase. If you plan to freeze meat, poultry, or fish, you should do so at once, after wrapping it in as airtight a manner as possible. Write the date of storage on the package. Thaw in the refrigerator.

Selecting and Storing Foods from the "Extras" Group

Fats include butter (a milk product), margarine, cooking oils, and vegetable shortening. Butter and margarine must be kept refrigerated. Oils and shortening can usually be kept on a shelf.

Sugar comes granulated, brown, or powdered. Other sweeteners include honey, molasses, and syrups. These can be stored at room temperature in tightly closed containers.

Words to Remember

perishable: easily spoiled
processed meats: meats that have been changed in some way before they go to the store
variety meats: animals' internal organs

Questions

1. Name four forms of liquid milk. What are the differences among them?
2. What produces a cultured milk product?
3. What are the four types of cheeses?
4. How should you store milk?
5. How does the type of animal and the cut of meat affect tenderness and flavor?
6. What are the three forms in which you can buy fish?
7. How should you store fresh meat?

Chapter **43** Safety and Sanitation

Objectives

After reading this chapter, you will be able to:

☐ *describe precautions to take against common dangers in the kitchen,*

☐ *explain the benefits of sanitary practices in the kitchen,*

☐ *list steps to make sure that foods will be safe to eat.*

You may think that the rule "Handle with care" applies only to packages. But careful handling of food and tools is very important in the kitchen. It involves both safety and sanitation.

In restaurant kitchens, there are many signs that remind employees about safety and sanitation. Some are:

■ Danger—open flame area.

■ Keep floors clean.

■ Place glasses in racks.

■ Put knives back in knife slots after use.

■ Do not stand near the dining room doors.

Safety means following careful work habits to avoid accidents like burns and cuts, electrical shocks, and falls. **Sanitation** involves *keeping yourself, the kitchen, and the food clean, and storing and cooking food properly.*

Safety in the Kitchen

Safety is important for the person doing the actual cooking. But you should also take care to protect others who may be in the kitchen. Careful work habits can prevent accidents from happening, especially to children.

Sources of Danger

Some kitchen dangers are obvious. Knives and open cans are sharp, and an oven or stove that's on is hot. But there are other dangers, too. Metal pots, pans, and tools can get very hot very quickly. Electric burners hold some heat after they are turned off. The food itself can be so hot that it burns what it touches when spilled. And hot grease can splatter, causing burns or even fires.

When using knives, work on a cutting board and cut down and away from yourself. Wash knives separately in hot, soapy water.

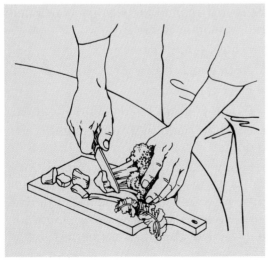

Many electrical appliances can cause shock when they are used near water, have frayed cords, or are used without following instructions. Some kitchens have microwave ovens. If the oven is not used properly, there can be microwave leaks or splattered food. Leaks from gas appliances, like stoves, can also be dangerous.

Finally, cleaning products stored in the kitchen can cause poisoning if swallowed or damage to the eyes if splattered. These products can be very dangerous in a house with children.

Precautions

Here are some safety tips to prevent accidents from happening.

■ Always cut by moving the knife away from you, and always hold a knife by its handle. Use a plastic cutting board.

■ Wash knives separately.

■ Watch out for sharp edges and tops of opened cans.

■ Use a wooden spoon to stir hot foods—metal spoons get too hot.

■ Always use potholders to handle hot pots, pans, and utensils.

■ Keep pot handles turned in over the center of the range—not over other burners—or over a counter so they won't get knocked over.

■ Lift the far side of a pot's lid first, so the steam won't burn you.

■ Keep sleeves and other parts of clothing away from flames and hot burners.

■ Clean all grease from the surfaces of the oven and the stove. Check the vent above the burners, where grease collects.

F E A T U R E

Outdoor Dining

Whether you're barbecuing or back-packing, safety and sanitation are as important outdoors as they are in the kitchen. Here are some safety tips.

Water

- Don't drink from lakes or streams.
- Make sure a supply of water will be available, or bring your own.
- Don't wash dishes in any body of water. Don't put soaps in the water.
- Do not throw garbage into or near the water supply.

Food

- Keep hot foods hot and cold foods cold. Wrap casseroles in layers of newspaper. Use thermoses for hot soups or drinks. Keep cold foods in ice chests, coolers, or insulated bags. Pack them with ice.
- Take special care with foods that spoil quickly, such as milk and egg dishes, and salads with dressings.

- Keep foods wrapped to protect them from bugs and animals.
- Don't eat wild berries or mushrooms. Some are poisonous.
- Throw all garbage in the containers provided, or take it back home with you.

Fire

- Never use a charcoal grill indoors—the fumes are dangerous.
- Never leave a fire, grill, or gas stove unattended.
- Keep a container of water nearby in case a fire flares up.
- Use long matches to light a fire. Never use kerosene or gasoline.
- Rearrange coals with long tongs.
- Use long-handled utensils and mitts to handle food on the grill.
- Be sure that the fire is completely out. Pour water on the coals and scatter them, or scatter them and cover them with dirt.

- Wipe up all spills at once.
- Keep papers away from the stove.
- Smother a grease fire with baking soda or baking powder, or use a fire extinguisher. Never use water.
- Plug in only one electrical appliance in an outlet at a time. Unplug appliances when they aren't in use. Don't yank on cords. Don't drape cords over the counter top.

- Keep electrical appliances away from water. Don't touch them with wet hands.
- Do not use appliances with frayed cords. Do not stick metal objects (like forks) inside appliances.
- For two-plug cords, put the plug into the appliance first, and then into the outlet.
- Insert beaters into a mixer before plugging it in.

■ Never turn on a gas stove if you smell gas. If the burner doesn't light, turn the gas off. Turn all dials to "off" when you're done cooking.

■ Keep dangerous chemicals stored well out of reach. Keep cupboard doors closed. If there are children in the house, lock these doors.

■ When reaching to a high shelf, stand on a stool.

Keeping Germs Away

Protecting the Food

Some dangers in the kitchen are invisible, including bacteria and viruses. These germs are the enemies of good sanitation. They can cause serious illness.

Illness can result from infection. Someone with a cold or flu virus might touch the food or utensils passed on to someone else. That person might become ill.

Another way that germs can cause disease is by **food poisoning**. This happens *when bacteria grow in food until the food actually becomes poisonous. Food containing such poisons* is said to be **contaminated**. The result can be rather mild, like stomach cramps and a slight fever, or it can be very serious.

Salmonella is a bacteria that grows in raw foods like chicken and eggs. Infection from salmonella is very hard to cure. Always wash a cutting board and knife after cutting up chicken.

Another harmful type of bacteria grows in food that's been canned improperly. It causes *botulism*, a very serious illness. If a can bulges, the contents may be infected. Throw such a can away.

You can prevent these illnesses by following good sanitary practices.

Using Good Personal Habits

Keeping yourself clean prevents the spread of infection through the food you prepare and the tools you use. There are six basic rules for personal hygiene.

1. Wash your hands well before working with food and after using the bathroom.
2. Keep your hair out of the food. If your hair is long, tie it back.
3. Use a separate spoon—not your fingers—for tasting food. After you've used the spoon for tasting, wash it.
4. Do not sneeze or cough on food. Use a tissue and turn your head away. (This is the reason for the plastic shields over many restaurant salad bars. These sneeze guards prevent the spread of germs.)
5. Rinse fresh fruits and vegetables to remove dirt and insecticides. Wash tops of cans before opening them.
6. Clean all kitchen equipment. Wash all dishes and tools in hot, soapy water and rinse them in warm water.

Controlling Pests

A **pest** is *an insect or small animal that carries dirt and germs.* Ants, cockroaches, mice, and rats contaminate foods and surfaces with their eggs or with diseases they carry.

Many insecticides and traps are sold to get rid of these creatures. Use a method that is safe as well as effective.

Avoiding the Danger Zone

At *temperatures between 60° and 125° F (15.6° and 51.7° C), bacteria grow and produce poisons rapidly.* This range is called the **danger zone**. Food should not be kept within this temperature range for more than two or three hours.

TABLE 1 Refrigeration Storage

One to two days	Two to three days
ground meat	berries
variety meats	cherries
(liver, etc.)	asparagus
poultry	ham slices
fish	
sweet corn	**Three to five days**
sausage	broccoli
leftover cooked	lima beans
poultry	spinach
	green onions
Three to four days	green peas
leftover cooked	milk and cream
meats and meat	grapes
dishes	peaches
	apricots
Up to one week	fresh meats
cottage cheese	cold cuts
tomatoes	
cauliflower	**Up to two weeks**
celery	butter
eggs in shell	dried beef, sliced
bacon	lemons
whole ham	carrots (tops
lettuce	removed)
	cabbage
Up to one month	
apples	

GERM WARFARE

°C	°F	
121	250	Canning temperatures for low-acid vegetables, meat, and poultry in pressure canner
115.5	240	Canning temperature for fruits, tomatoes, and pickles in water-bath canner
100	212	Cooking temperatures destroy most bacteria. Time required to kill bacteria decreases as temperature is increased
73.9	165	Warming temperatures prevent growth but allow survival of some bacteria
60	140	Some bacterial growth may occur. Many bacteria survive
51.7	125	**Danger Zone.** Temperatures in this zone allow rapid growth of bacteria and production of toxins by some bacteria. (Do not hold foods in this temperature zone for more than two or three hours.)
15.6	60	
4.4	40	Some growth of food-poisoning bacteria may occur.
0	32	Cold temperatures permit slow growth of some bacteria that cause spoilage.*
17.8	0	Freezing temperatures stop growth of bacteria, but may allow bacteria to survive. (Do not store food above 10° F for more than a few weeks.)

*Do not store raw meats for more than five days or poultry, fish or ground meat for more than two days in the refrigerator.

To control growth of bacteria, keep hot foods hot (above 140°F/60°C) and cold foods cold (below 40°F/4.4°C).

U.S. Department of Agriculture, Keeping Food Safe to Eat: A Guide for Homemakers, Home and Garden Bulletin No. 162, Agricultural Research Service, U.S. Government Printing Office.

Using Heat for Safety

High temperatures, such as those reached when boiling food, actually kill bacteria in food. Different foods need to be heated to different temperatures for different lengths of time to accomplish this. For instance, pork must be cooked until its internal temperature is 170° F (75° C). If not, tiny worms in some pork may live to cause a serious disease called *trichinosis*. To be safe, never eat pork that is still pink inside.

Once the food is cooked, keep it hot until it's eaten. Cover and refrigerate leftovers as soon as possible. Don't leave stuffing inside roasted chicken or turkey before storing. The cooked meat insulates the stuffing, which won't cool down quickly. As a result, bacteria will begin to grow.

Using Cold for Safety

Low temperatures slow down the growth of bacteria in food. For this reason, food stays fresh in the refrigerator, but only for a limited time.

Chapters 41 and 42 give information on the best way to store many foods. The table in this chapter lists the storage times for some common foods. Be careful of salads made with dressing such as mayonnaise and various cheeses. Take extra care with foods that spoil more quickly, like milk, eggs, and meat.

Freezing food stops bacteria from growing altogether until the food is thawed out again. During and after thawing, take care to avoid the danger zone.

Words to Remember

contaminated: food containing poisons

danger zone: the temperature range between 60° and 125°F (15.6° and 51.7°C), at which bacteria grow and produce poisons rapidly

food poisoning: when bacteria grow in food until the food actually becomes poisonous

pest: an insect or small animal that carries dirt and germs

sanitation: keeping yourself, the kitchen, and the food clean, and storing and cooking food properly

Questions

1. State one way to prevent each of the four sources of danger in the kitchen.

2. What two ways can bacteria be transmitted in food?

3. List three basic rules for personal hygiene in the kitchen.

4. What is the purpose of washing food before cooking?

5. Why should food be kept at temperatures outside the danger zone?

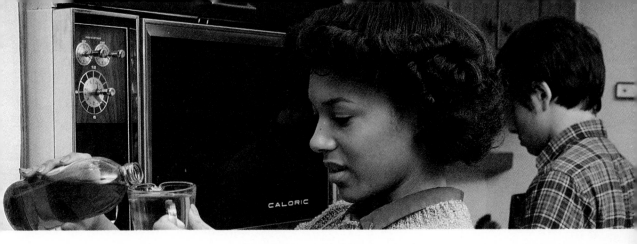

CALORIC

44 Kitchen Utensils

After reading this chapter, you will be able to:

☐ *recognize the most common utensils used in the kitchen,*

☐ *identify which utensil is used for which kitchen task.*

Every worker needs good tools. This is also true of people who work in the kitchen to prepare meals. An important part of kitchen equipment are the **utensils**. These are *simple hand tools, like knives, or containers, like saucepans.* Larger items of kitchen equipment are called **appliances**. You'll read more about them in the next chapter.

Utensils are used for:

■ Measuring

■ Pre-preparation

■ Mixing

■ Cooking and baking

Some of these utensils are very old. The caveman's sharp flint rock is now our modern knife. The wooden spear is now the long kitchen fork. The crude clay pot is now our fancy saucepan or pressure cooker. The ivory hand pick is now our table fork, and the rough wooden grater is now our electric blender.

Measuring Utensils

Measuring Ingredients

Measuring ingredients accurately can make the difference between a good meal and a poor one. Many utensils are available for doing this important task. The basic ones are described here.

Plastic or metal *measuring cups* are used to measure dry ingredients like flour and sugar. They are sold in sets that include cups ranging in size from 1/4 cup to 2 cups. Many are marked with both standard and metric measurements.

For liquids, like milk or water, there are *measuring cups* with pouring spouts. They are graded on the sides in cups, ounces, and sometimes liters. Because they are made of clear plastic or glass, the cook can judge when the correct amount has been poured.

Measuring spoons are used to measure smaller amounts. They, too, come in sets, usually ranging from 1/4 teaspoon to 1 tablespoon.

A few recipes require cooks to weigh ingredients. Small *scales* are available for this.

F E A T U R E

Cooking with Metrics

The metric system of measurement is used in most countries of the world. The United States is gradually converting to this simple system, too.

Metrics are based on the number ten—the decimal system—and all metric units are multiples of ten.

To see how much simpler this is than standard measurements, consider these examples:

Volume 1 liter = 1000 milliliters
                    instead of
        1 quart = 4 cups
        1 pint = 2 cups
        1 cup = 16 tablespoons

Weight 1 kilogram = 1000 grams
                    instead of
        1 pound = 16 ounces

The metric system only seems difficult when we try to convert a measurement from standard to metric or vice versa:

1 liter = 61.025 cubic inches

1 kilogram = 2.2046 pounds

There are tables and formulas that people can use to make these conversions. This may be necessary for some cooking tasks.

Recipes usually give standard measurements, but the more modern method is to use the metric system. There are measuring cups and spoons available in metric units. Cups come in 50, 125, and 250 milliliter sets. Spoons measure 1, 2, 5, 15, and 25 milliliters.

Temperatures are different in standard and metric measurements, too. In metric, temperatures are measured in degrees *Celsius*. In standard measurement, it is measured in degrees *Fahrenheit*.

Measuring Temperature

Some tools measure temperature or time. *Meat thermometers* allow cooks to check roasts to see if they are cooked. *Candy thermometers* do the same job for candies and preserves. Cooks can set *timers* which make a sound that reminds them to check a food that is cooking.

Pre-Preparation Utensils

Few ingredients are simply placed in a pot and allowed to cook. Usually, some things must be done to ready them. These steps are called *pre-preparation*.

Tools for Cutting and Chopping

Two important pre-preparation tasks are cutting and chopping. The tools that help with this work are:

- *Kitchen shears*—for cutting meat, poultry, vegetables, pastries, and dried fruit.
- *Parers*—for peeling away the rind or skin of fruits and vegetables.
- *Knives*—for many uses and in a variety of shapes and sizes. Chef's knives are best for chopping, and paring knives are best for peeling. Bread knives for cutting bread, and carving knives for cutting roasted meats, are used once a food is cooked. Cutting is best done on a *cutting board*, a plastic surface that protects counters or tabletops.
- *Graters*—for shredding or grating vegetables and cheeses. These are tools that have holes with sharp edges.

- *Food mills*—for puréeing foods. Most have disks with different sizes of holes for producing coarser or smoother purées.

Tools for Other Tasks

There are many other pre-preparation tasks besides cutting and chopping. The tools suited to these jobs are:

- *Colanders and strainers*—for draining foods. *Colanders* are bowls with large holes. Legs help them stand in the sink. They are used to drain foods like cooked pasta or potatoes. *Strainers* are fine wire-mesh baskets with handles. They hold a solid food—berries, for example,—and let the water drain off. Strainers come in many sizes. For a small quantity of food, the same work can be done with a slotted spoon.
- *Drainers*—for draining fried foods. They are shaped like flattened spoons with many slots.
- *Funnels*—good for pouring liquids from one container into another.
- *Vegetable brushes*—stiff brushes used for cleaning vegetables.
- *Brushes*—These soft brushes are used to brush water or beaten egg on dough or pastry.
- *Rolling pins*—round tools, made of wood or plastic, used to flatten dough. They can also be used to crush ice.
- *Pastry cloths*—pieces of canvas or plastic that are placed on a counter top and dusted with flour before dough is rolled.
- *Can openers*—used to open cans. They can be either manual or electric. Can openers

PREPARATION UTENSILS

MIXING UTENSILS

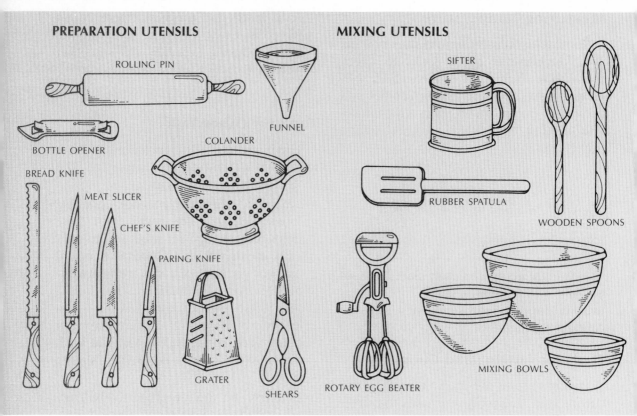

ROLLING PIN

FUNNEL

BOTTLE OPENER

COLANDER

BREAD KNIFE

MEAT SLICER

CHEF'S KNIFE

PARING KNIFE

GRATER

SHEARS

SIFTER

RUBBER SPATULA

WOODEN SPOONS

MIXING BOWLS

ROTARY EGG BEATER

either take the lid completely off or puncture the lid to make a pouring spout.

■ *Bottle and jar openers*—rubber pieces that help you get a good grip for opening twist-off lids.

Mixing Utensils

Many utensils can be used to mix ingredients.

■ *Wooden or plastic spoons*—used to mix ingredients together. These spoons come in many sizes.

■ *Rubber spatulas*—used for scraping or folding. They can clean sticky liquids like honey out of measuring cups or help the cook fold in a new ingredient.

■ *Mixing bowls*—the containers for mixing ingredients. They can be metal, plastic, or pottery. Most are sold in sets that have bowls of various sizes.

■ *Pastry blenders*—half circles of wire held together by a wooden or plastic handle. They are used to blend shortening into flour.

■ *Rotary egg beaters*, also called *hand beaters*, used for mixing batters.

■ *Sifters*—cylinders with a wire mesh base

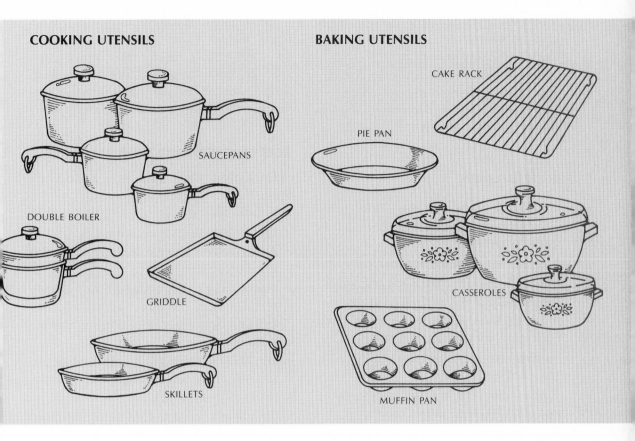

COOKING UTENSILS

SAUCEPANS

DOUBLE BOILER

GRIDDLE

SKILLETS

BAKING UTENSILS

CAKE RACK

PIE PAN

CASSEROLES

MUFFIN PAN

and a metal piece that scrapes it. Flour is placed in the wire base and the metal piece is moved back and forth. The result is a more powdery flour.

Cooking and Baking Utensils

Cooking Utensils

There are many shapes and sizes of pots and pans used for cooking on or in a stove:

- *Saucepans*—for warming, cooking vege-tables, and stewing. They can be large or small, and they have covers. Their sides are higher than their bottoms are wide.

- *Frying pans or skillets*—for frying, saute-ing, and panbroiling. These are low-sided, large-bottomed pans.

- *Griddles*—low, flat pans used for grilling sandwiches and pancakes. A skillet can also be used for this purpose.

- *Broilers*—a pan with a rectangular bot-tom and a wire holding tray. The slots in the tray allow fat to drip down while the food broils.

- *Double boilers*—one saucepan set inside another. The bottom pan is filled with water that boils. The top pan holds the food being cooked. A double boiler is used for making delicate sauces.

■ *Casseroles*—deep-sided cooking containers used for baking dishes like macaroni and cheese. Most are decorated and can also be used for serving.

Baking Utensils

For baking, the following items are used:
■ *Cake pans*—for layer cakes. They can be round or square.
■ *Loaf pans*—for breads or meat loaves.
■ *Baking sheets*—for thin cakes or cookies.
■ *Tube pans*—used for angel food, chiffon, or bundt cakes. They are round and deep, with a hollow tube in the center.
■ *Pie pans*—round pans with sloping sides. They are usually glass.
■ *Muffin pans*—for muffins or cupcakes. Each pan has individual cups.
■ *Cake racks*—wire racks used for holding cake pans or bread while cooling.

Cookware and bakeware are made from many different materials. Some are stainless steel, others are cast iron. Many casseroles are ceramic, glazed for easy cleaning. Some metal pans also have nonstick surfaces to make them easier to clean.

Tools for Working with the Food

Cooks also need some utensils to work with the food as it cooks or bakes:
■ *Wooden, metal, and plastic spoons*—used for stirring soups and stews.
■ *Ladles*—deep-bowled spoons used to dish up soup or stew.
■ *Long-handled forks*—used for turning meat or large pieces of vegetables. They can also help you test cooking food to see if it's done.
■ *Wooden or metal spatulas*—are used to turn foods that are being broiled, pan-fried, or cooked on a griddle.
■ *Tongs*—also used to turn meat or pick up cooked foods like corn on the cob and baked potatoes.

Words to Remember

utensils: simple hand tools, like knives, or containers, like saucepans

Questions

1. What is the difference between utensils used to measure dry ingredients and those used for liquids?
2. Name and describe the uses of four cutting and chopping utensils.
3. For what type of food would you use a rolling pin, a pastry cloth, and a pastry blender? How would you use these tools?
4. How does a double boiler heat foods?
5. What is the difference between a cake pan and a tube pan?

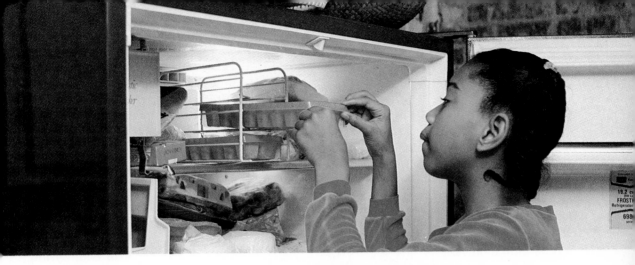

Chapter # 45 Kitchen Appliances

After reading this chapter, you will be able to:

☐ *consider eight factors when choosing appliances,*

☐ *recognize the most common appliances in the kitchen,*

☐ *use appliances to save energy and care for them properly.*

Good equipment is a must for any kitchen worker. In the last chapter, you read about some of the smaller tools that are used in the kitchen. In this chapter, you'll learn about kitchen **appliances**. These are pieces of *equipment that are run mechanically, by electricity, or by gas*.

Some appliances, like electric can openers and mixers, do jobs that you could do by hand. Others, like refrigerators and ovens, do special work.

Some appliances are found in almost every home. Refrigerators, ovens, and ranges are needed to store and cook food. Toasters aren't essential, but they are very common. So are electric coffee makers.

Other appliances are found less frequently. Some families have waffle irons, and may own dishwashers.

327

Buying Appliances

Department stores and kitchen specialty stores are loaded with many different appliances. They sell familiar pieces like ranges, refrigerators, and dishwashers. They also sell smaller pieces like blenders and toaster ovens. And there are special items that are meant for one task—for example, yogurt makers, popcorn poppers, and pasta machines.

Different People, Different Needs

What makes one appliance a necessity and another an extra? It all depends on a family's needs.

One family might have five children and a mother and father who both work outside the home. To cut down on trips to the store, that family would need a good-size refrigerator, and possibly a large freezer as well. A good range would be a necessity. If the family budget allowed, time-saving electric devices would be helpful in preparing large, nutritious meals quickly.

Another family might have only two people, who care little about cooking. They would need very little kitchen equipment.

It isn't only the size of a family that matters. Someone who lives alone might enjoy cooking as a hobby. Such a person might buy special kitchen equipment usually found only in big restaurants.

Deciding on Appliances

In choosing appliances, a family should consider eight factors.

■ *Family size.* As the example above showed, a large family may need appliances that store large amounts of food or save cooking time.

■ *Cooking and eating habits.* A family that cooks very little won't need many appliances. People who have special cooking interests may want appliances that help them—a yogurt maker or ice cream maker, for instance.

■ *Multiple uses.* Some appliances are good buys because they can be used for more than one job. Blenders can chop, grind, blend, and purée. Toaster ovens can toast, bake, and broil. Electric skillets can be used for stir-frying or pan-frying, grilling, or cooking on a griddle.

■ *Time for cooking.* Families that are always on the go may want labor-saving appliances like a self-cleaning oven.

■ *Appliance cost.* A family on a tight budget

Major appliances now come with an energy guide label. This shows how the appliance compares to others in energy consumption.

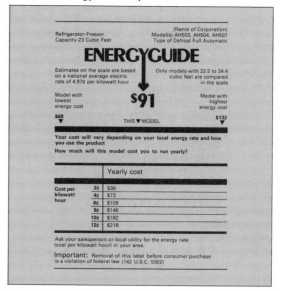

may not think that a self-cleaning oven is worth the extra cost.

- *Safety.* Some appliances have safety features. A blade in a blender may stop turning when the lid is removed, for instance.
- *Warranty.* As in shopping for many goods, consumers should check appliances for their warranty coverage.
- *Energy use.* Appliances cost money to use as well as to buy because they use energy. The federal government requires appliance makers to put special yellow **Energy Guide labels** on all refrigerators, freezers, dishwashers, washing machines, and water heaters. These labels *estimate the cost of running the appliance for one year.* They also compare energy use among models of the same size. You can use these labels to find the model that uses energy most efficiently in your home or neighborhood.

Types of Appliances

Preparation and Mixing Appliances

Many small appliances do the work of hand tools. Some simply do the work faster—an electric can opener is one example.

Also in this group is some complex and costly equipment. Electric mixers and blenders and other small appliances are very helpful to people who enjoy cooking. They can be used on many kinds of foods, and they save time in preparing difficult recipes. Food processors combine the features of other appliances.

Heating Appliances

A variety of equipment is used for heating foods. Some equipment, like kitchen ranges, provides the heat for cooking. Other items, like saucepans and skillets, hold the food as it cooks. Some appliances both heat and hold—for example, electric skillets or electric coffee makers.

Most people need some way to heat food. But a full-size range is not a necessity for everyone. People who seldom cook may do very well with just a hot plate to heat soup or boil water for coffee or tea. An electric skillet could take care of their other cooking needs.

There are other heating appliances besides a full-size range. Many people are

The microwave oven is an efficient, time-saving kitchen appliance that can be programmed to defrost, cook, and simmer.

F E A T U R E

Popular New Appliances

Three new appliances have become popular in recent years. They can add fun and variety—as well as efficiency—to your cooking.

■ *Food processors.* Food processors have very powerful motors and round plastic work bowls. They use different disks or blades to perform various tasks. They can do everything a blender can do, plus more, such as slicing, grating, and shredding. Food processors can also mix dough and purée foods. They cannot completely replace a mixer, however. The processor works so fast that air is not mixed in as much as is necessary for things like cake batter. Many cookbooks give hints on how to use food processors to do various jobs.

■ *Convection ovens.* Convection ovens save time and energy. A high-speed fan circulates the hot air within the oven. This provides uniform heat throughout the oven and speeds up the cooking. Convection ovens can be part of a large oven or separate counter top units. They are good for baking or roasting.

■ *Microwave ovens.* Microwave ovens cook food from the inside out by agitating the molecules in the food. Microwaves can cook food up to 75 percent faster than a regular range can. This saves time and energy and is usually cleaner than regular cooking.

These ovens can heat certain frozen foods and processed foods (like baby food) right in their original containers. They can do everything from boiling water to baking a potato. Microwaves can be separate units or part of a larger one.

Some special techniques and cookware are needed when cooking with microwaves—for instance, metal cannot be used. Many special cookbooks explain how to prepare foods in microwaves.

These three appliances have many benefits. They help the cook save much time and energy. But they can be quite expensive and are considered a luxury by most people. Still, they are very popular these days. Busy cooks or those who cook for many people find them worth the money.

buying microwave ovens. These appliances cook food much more quickly than regular ovens do. Although microwave ovens are expensive, many homemakers feel that the time and energy they save are worth the expense. Some people own both a microwave oven and a range.

Storing and Cooling Appliances

Keeping food fresh before and after it is cooked is an important part of any homemaker's job. A lot of equipment is available for this purpose.

Many foods must be kept cool to stay

fresh. Some products must remain frozen until they are ready to be used. Such items belong in the refrigerator or the home freezer, the largest appliances for storing food in the home.

Refrigerated and frozen foods often must be kept airtight. Aluminum foil, plastic wrap, sealed plastic bags or containers with tight lids can be used for this purpose.

You can also use regular bowls tightly covered with aluminum foil or plastic wrap. You can reuse plastic margarine containers with airtight tops. Or you can buy special airtight boxes for refrigerator and freezer storage.

Using Appliances

Using appliances properly keeps them in good condition. It also helps you prepare your meals while saving money and energy.

Making Substitutions

Camping. Many families enjoy camping and have experience in making do without appliances. Maybe you know how to bake a potato without a stove. Perhaps you can boil water without a pan. You can prepare excellent meals without a lot of equipment.

Grilling. Do you think you need a special sandwich grill to make grilled cheese sandwiches? Try making them in an ordinary frying pan. Or grill them open-faced under the broiler.

Simmering. If a recipe calls for using a double-boiler and you don't have one, try floating a small pan in a larger one partly filled with water. Of course, you must take care that water doesn't spill into the upper pan, but at least you have a double boiler.

While you're still learning, you should seek advice from a person with more experience before substituting equipment. Re-

Be an energy-wise consumer. When baking something in the oven, plan ahead and cook your complete meal, using the oven at the same time. You will save both fuel and money.

member, you don't always have to spend a lot of money. Imagination can be the best equipment of all.

Saving Energy

Appliances run on gas or electrical energy. Using them properly uses less energy—and that helps save money:

- Don't use the oven for small cooking jobs like baking a potato. Use a smaller appliance like a toaster oven or a more efficient one like a microwave oven.
- Don't preheat the oven unless the recipe calls for it.
- Keep oven and refrigerator doors closed.
- Keep appliances clean and in good repair.

Caring for Appliances

Kitchen equipment works best when it is kept clean and when it is used and stored properly. Keeping utensils and appliances clean not only protects your health, it also lengthens the life of the equipment.

Small Appliances. Small appliances such as blenders and toasters require special cleaning. Dirt and grease must be removed to keep them sanitary and working properly. However, putting the electrical unit of such a product in water can ruin the appliance. It is dangerous as well. The manufacturer's instructions will tell exactly how to care for such equipment.

Large Appliances. Large appliances are complicated pieces of machinery and must be treated with care. Never line the broiler of an electric range with aluminum foil. If the foil touches any part of the electrical unit while it is turned on, the entire heating element will burn out. The range will then require major repairs. Worse, anyone nearby could be seriously injured.

To keep a refrigerator working well and to save electricity, prevent a frost buildup in the freezer. Make sure the refrigerator is not too full. To maintain the correct temperature, air must be able to circulate freely. Storing too much food in a refrigerator overworks the motor. An overworked motor may have to be replaced.

Words to Remember

appliance: a piece of kitchen equipment that runs mechanically, by electricity, or by gas
Energy Guide labels: labels that estimate the cost of running appliances for one year

Questions

1. What are four factors that should be considered when choosing appliances?
2. Name an appliance that can be used for preparation or mixing.
3. Give two examples of appliances that can be used for heating.
4. Give an example of an appliance that is used for cooling or storing food.
5. Which is better for warming a loaf of bread: an oven or a toaster oven?

Chapter **46 Following Recipes**

Objectives

After reading this chapter, you will be able to:

☐ *explain the standard parts of a recipe,*

☐ *understand the abbreviations and terms used in recipes,*

☐ *use recipes to schedule and plan for the actual preparation of a meal.*

The recipe is the single most important tool for food preparation. This is true for people who don't cook much, as well as for those who enjoy preparing complicated dishes. Without recipes, all the best equipment and skills would be useless. Recipes tell what foods to purchase and in what amounts. They also give the important details of food preparation.

Here is an informal recipe that a fifth grader made up.

Peanut Butter and Banana Sandwich

■ Get a slice of bread.

■ Spread peanut butter all over it.

■ Cut a banana into thin slices.

■ Put the slices on top of the peanut butter.

Now eat the sandwich with milk. Follow with dessert—the banana slices that you couldn't get on the sandwich.

Choosing a Recipe

Cookbooks

Recipes come from many sources. A cookbook is probably the first place you look when you're planning a meal. Some cookbooks are general. They include recipes for everything from appetizers and snacks to main dishes and desserts. They may even have instructions on cooking methods and equipment. Some cookbooks are specialized. They contain recipes only for desserts, or for vegetarian meals, or for Mexican food.

Other Sources for Recipes

Recipes are also available on individual cards. They can be organized in a file so that you can just pull out the one you need. And recipes can even be found on food packages and cans. These can be clipped out and filed.

Newspapers and magazines also print recipes. And many recipes are simply passed on from one person to another, by word of mouth or on scraps of paper. These are the special inventions of good cooks or the traditional recipes used in a family.

When you are deciding on a recipe, there are three questions to ask yourself.

- Will it taste good?
- Is it complete?
- Will it work for me?

Will It Taste Good?

Sometimes, reading a recipe can cause your mouth to water. You just know how good it will taste. Other times, you see an

There are many cookbooks that you can choose from. Some contain ethnic foods, low-calorie meals, and quick and easy recipes.

ingredient or a combination of ingredients that doesn't really appeal to you.

If a recipe sounds strange, it's probably not a good idea to try that recipe when you're cooking a meal for friends. It's better to test it by yourself first. This is also true when the cooking method is one you've never used before. In fact, you may want to give every new recipe a test run before you serve the dish to guests.

Is It Complete?

Ingredients and Servings. Be sure that a recipe tells you everything you need to know in order to prepare the dish successfully. Obviously, it must list all ingredients.

In addition, the recipe should tell you the number of **portions**, or *servings it will yield*.

You can increase or decrease the amounts of ingredients if you're serving more people or fewer people. Some recipes give nutritional information that will help you plan a balanced meal. For instance, if it is a meat recipe, information may be given about what to serve with the meat course and after it.

Equipment. The recipe should also tell you what equipment is required. Different cooking methods—microwave cooking, for example—may require special cookware or utensils. And it helps if the recipe tells you what to watch out for while cooking—how to mix a batter, for instance.

Temperature and Time. Finally, the recipe must tell you at what temperature and for how long to cook the dish, and how to find out when it's done. For instance, a cake recipe might tell you to bake it at 350° F (176.5° C) for 30 minutes or until a knife gently inserted into the middle comes out clean.

Will It Work For Me?

Before you decide on a recipe, be sure that you can follow it. The ingredients must be on hand or easily available. You must have the equipment needed to prepare the dish. And, of course, you must have the skills required to prepare it. Many dishes are easy to prepare, but certain types of cooking require special talents.

Your decision will depend finally on whether the dish is right for the meal you are cooking. Important factors to consider are how formal the meal is, the time of year, and who your guests are. And, of course, you must decide whether everyone will like the dish.

Reading a Recipe

Because cooking is an art, a science, and a craft, it is written in its own special language. To follow a recipe successfully, you must understand all the cooking terms used.

The list on page 336 contains the major items that you see in recipes.

Abbreviations and Standards

Here are some of the most common abbreviations found in recipes. Most of them refer to units of measurement, either metric or standard. See also the box in chapter 44 for more on the metric system of measurement.

Volume
- l liter
- ml milliliter
- t teaspoon (also tsp)
- T tablespoon (also tbsp)
- c cup
- qt quart
- gal gallon

Weight
- g gram
- kg kilogram
- oz ounce (also used to measure volume)
- lb pound

Length
- mm millimeter
- cm centimeter
- in inch

Temperature
- °C degrees Celsius
- °F degrees Fahrenheit

F E A T U R E

The Language of Recipes

Preparation terms

beat: to mix smoothly, using rapid, regular strokes with a spoon or whisk

blend: to mix two or more ingredients together thoroughly

chill: to refrigerate or let food stand in cold water

chop: to cut into small pieces

cool: to refrigerate or let warm food stand until it is at room temperature

dice: to cut into very small cubes

dredge: to cover food with a light coating of flour or crumbs

grate: to reduce food to very small particles by rubbing it against a rough surface.

grease: to rub a cooking surface with fat to prevent sticking

grind: to reduce to powder by crushing food with a heavy spoon or other utensil

knead: to work a dough with a pressing and folding motion

marinate: to soak food in a sauce for a time to make it tender and flavorful

mash: to reduce to a soft pulpy state by beating or whipping

mince: to cut into very small pieces

mix: to combine two or more foods together

pare: to remove the skin of firm vegetables and fruits

peel: to remove the outer covering, skin, or rind of soft vegetables and fruits

pulverize: to reduce to small particles by crushing, beating, or grinding

purée: to blend food into a smooth, thick paste

sift: to rub flour against a fine sieve to make it more powdery

stir: to mix food in a circular motion

toss: to mix with a lifting motion

whip: to beat a food into a foam, or froth, with a fork or other utensil

Heating terms

bake: to cook by dry heat, usually in an oven (called *roasting* for meat)

baste: to moisten food while it cooks, using its own juices or a sauce

boil: to cook in liquid that is bubbling

braise: to cook slowly in a small amount of liquid in a covered pan

broil: to cook by direct heat, especially in a broiler

deep fry: to cook in hot fat deep enough for the food to float

fry: to cook in hot fat

melt: to heat a solid until it becomes a liquid

poach: to cook in a simmering liquid

preheat: to heat the oven or broiler to the desired temperature before putting the food in to cook

sauté: to cook in a small amount of hot fat

simmer: to cook in liquid just below the boiling point

steam: to cook over boiling water

stew: to cook in liquid at low heat for a long time

toast: to brown food with dry heat

Recipe Formats

Most printed recipes follow a *standard format* that clearly presents the following information:

- name of the dish,
- list of ingredients with exact amounts, in the order in which they will be used,
- time to prepare (not always given),
- oven setting, if any,
- step-by-step directions,
- number of servings.

Here's an example of a recipe:

FRENCH TOAST

2 eggs
1/4 cup milk
1 tablespoon butter or margarine
6 slices white, whole wheat, or raisin bread
applesauce or cut-up fresh fruit

About 10 minutes before serving: Beat eggs slightly with a fork in a shallow bowl or pie plate. Beat in milk. Meanwhile, heat butter or margarine in a large skillet over medium heat. Quickly dip the bread into the egg mixture, coating both sides. Place in the hot skillet and cook until golden brown; turn, and cook on the other side. Top with applesauce or fresh fruit.
Makes 3 servings.

There are three other ways of presenting recipes that you will see in most cookbooks and magazines.

- The *action form* gives directions for a step and then lists the ingredients to use in that step. (See the box on page 338.)
- The *narrative form* puts the ingredients and directions in a paragraph. (See the box on page 338.)
- The *descriptive form* uses three columns and presents ingredients, amounts, and steps. (See the box on page 338.)

Using a Recipe

Using a recipe involves more than just reading and following instructions. You also need to have planning, good timing, and a little creativity to make pleasing dishes.

The cook can increase or decrease the recipe to fit particular needs. Recipes usually indicate the size of the serving and the number of people that can be served with the dish.

Recipe Formats

Action Form

Broiled Tomatoes

Preset oven to broil.

Put in broiler pan:
    4 medium tomatoes, hollowed at top

Mix together:
    1 tsp (5 ml) oregano
    1 cup (240 ml) bread crumbs

½ cup (120 ml) grated cheese

Sprinkle over tomatoes.

Place under the broiler and cook until the crumbs brown.

Yield: 4 servings.

Narrative Form

Hamburger Casserole

For macaroni: Boil 4 quarts of water with ½ tsp (2.5 ml) salt. Add ½ lb (225 g) elbow macaroni and cook until tender but chewy. Drain and return to saucepan.

For hamburger: Meanwhile, sauté 1 chopped onion in 1 tbsp (15 ml) oil. Add 1 lb (450 g) ground beef and brown. Drain fat.

For casserole: Add onion and ground beef to macaroni, stirring to mix well. Salt and pepper to taste. Add ½ cup (120 ml) grated cheese and mix well. Put on low heat to melt cheese.

Yield: 4 servings.

Descriptive Form

Applesauce

Ingredients	Amount	Procedure
Apples, cored and peeled	8	Cut in large chunks; put in pan.
Water	½ cup (120 ml)	Add to pan.
Sugar	2 tbsp (30 ml)	Add to apples and water.
Ground cinnamon	½ tsp (2.5 ml)	Add to mixture.
Ground cloves (optional)	¼ tsp (1.25 ml)	Add to mixture.
		Cover and cook slowly until tender, about 20 minutes. Should be a thick mixture. If chunks remain, mash or purée.

Making a Schedule

Here are the steps for following a recipe:

1. *Get all the ingredients.* Assemble them from your stock in the kitchen or shop for them.

2. *Plan your cooking schedule.* Read the recipe directions carefully and decide how much time you need to prepare the meal or dish. Be sure to allow yourself enough time to get the job done comfortably and safely. If you're in too much of a rush, your meal may not succeed.

3. *Decide exactly what steps you'll take and in what order.* And if you're working with other people, you also have to decide who will do what. Teamwork can make cooking more efficient and more fun.

Getting Ready

Preparation before you start cooking helps you avoid forgetting ingredients or overlooking equipment you need. Take these steps:

1. *Clean up the kitchen.*

2. *Clean work areas so that you'll have plenty of room.*

3. *Lay out all of the equipment and utensils you'll need so they will be handy when you need them.*

4. *Make sure all of the ingredients are on hand.* Some ingredients, like hard-boiled eggs, must be prepared ahead of time. Others—flour, spices, and fruits, for example—can simply be laid out on the table or counter. Still others—milk and mayonnaise, for example—must stay in the refrigerator until they are needed.

Preparing the Food

Now you're ready to prepare the dish. Take your time, follow directions exactly, and complete one step at a time.

Some experienced cooks like to vary recipes. They substitute some ingredients for others, or they use more or less of some ingredients than the recipe calls for.

It's safest, however, to follow a recipe exactly the first couple of times you use it. Once you discover your own tastes and those of your family or guests, you can start to add your own personal touch. This will add variety—and fun—to your cooking and will please your guests.

Words to Remember

portions: the number of servings that a recipe yields

Questions

1. What are three sources of recipes?

2. What three questions should you ask yourself before using a recipe?

3. What does the standard recipe format include?

4. List three things you should do before you start the actual food preparation.

47 Measuring and Mixing

Objectives

After reading this chapter, you will be able to:

□ *measure liquids and solids accurately,*

□ *use pre-preparation equipment safely and correctly.*

You have your recipe chosen and your schedule planned. Now you're ready to go, right? Wrong.

You need to learn many skills to prepare your recipe correctly. You must be able to measure correctly and to pare, peel, slice, dice, chop, mince, beat, and mix. You must know the best way to heat a food. None of these things is difficult, however. With practice, you can learn to do them.

On the following pages, you'll find the practical "how-to's" that will help you to follow that recipe.

In chapter 48, you'll learn about using heat to cook foods in the kitchen.

In chapter 49, you'll learn about how to serve meals at home. You'll study points to keep in mind when you are eating out. You'll also learn about dishes served in other countries.

Measuring

Measuring ingredients accurately can make all the difference in preparing food. Even the best cook cannot judge a cup or a teaspoon by eye alone. It's important to have proper tools for measuring, and to follow standard techniques for using them.

How to Measure Dry Ingredients

Flour, sugar, baking powder, or any other dry ingredient can be measured in measuring cups or spoons.

Flour. Always spoon the required amount gently into the measuring cup. Don't dip the cup into the flour, or shake it once you've filled it. If you do, the flour will pack down and you'll get too much. Level off the flour in the cup with a spatula or a straight-edged knife.

To measure dry ingredients, such as flour or sugar, spoon the required amount into a dry measuring cup and level with a knife.

If your recipe calls for sifted flour, spoon an approximate amount into the sifter. Sift it onto a piece of wax paper. Then pour it into the measuring cup until you have the exact amount you need. Return any unused flour to the container.

White Sugar. Spoon the sugar into the measuring cup and level it off.

Brown Sugar. If the sugar is lumpy, put it in a plastic bag and roll a rolling pin over the bag. Then spoon the sugar into the measuring cup, pressing each spoonful down firmly. Level it off to the desired amount.

Shortening. Spoon the shortening firmly into the measuring cup, packing each spoonful firmly. Level it off, and then scrape it out. A rubber spatula is good both for packing shortening into a cup and for getting it out.

Adapting. Recipes may call for an amount smaller than your smallest measuring tool. Suppose you have only a ¼-teaspoon measure and your recipe calls for ⅛ teaspoon. Fill and level your 1/4 teaspoon. Then, using a spatula or a knife, divide the amount in half and push one-half off the spoon.

How to Measure Liquid Ingredients

Glass or clean plastic measuring cups are used for liquid ingredients. Place the cup on a flat surface. Then pour the amount you need.

Check to be sure that the liquid is at the proper mark by squatting down to look at it at eye level. Don't lift the cup, which will probably tilt it and cause you to misread the amount.

When using thick liquids such as molasses or honey, pour directly from the bottle or the jar into the measuring cup. Dipping a measuring spoon or cup into these liquids will coat the utensil and give you too much. Use a rubber spatula to scrape all the liquid out of the measuring cup.

Special Equivalents

A good cook can save time and trouble by knowing certain **equivalents**, or *different measures that describe equal amounts*. The most common equivalent is for butter or margarine. One stick equals 1/2 cup, or 1/4 pound, or 8 tablespoons.

The following equivalents are also useful to know:

apples	1 lb	3 cups (chopped)
cheese	1 lb	5 cups grated
chocolate	1 oz	1 square
cream	1 cup heavy	2 cups whipped
eggs	4 large	1 cup
flour	1 lb	4 cups
lemon	1 medium	3 to 4 tablespoons juice
milk	1 qt	4 cups
rice	1 cup uncooked	3 to 4 cups cooked

Measuring by Weight

Sometimes people on special diets must have their food weighed exactly. They need a small kitchen scale. Usually, though, it's possible to figure out an equivalent from pounds or ounces to cups or spoons. Some all-purpose cookbooks have tables of weight equivalents.

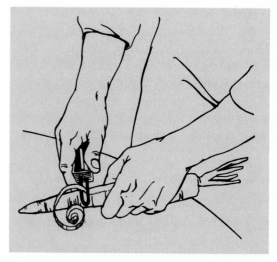

Always pare vegetables, such as carrots or potatoes, away from your body to avoid hurting yourself with the paring tool.

Pre-Preparation Techniques

The following techniques are useful in preparing foods for cooking and in making foods look pretty if they're to be eaten raw. When you do these preparations, be sure to use good sharp tools.

Paring and Peeling

Paring. Removing the skin of firm fruits and vegetables is called *paring*. You might want to pare apples, cucumbers, or potatoes, for instance. A paring knife cuts a rather thick peel.

Paring can also be done with a potato peeler. This cuts a much thinner peel, which leaves more of the vitamins that are concentrated in and just under the skin.

A peeler can also be used to cut vegetables into thin, decorative strips. You can use these thin slices in a salad. They can also **garnish** or *add color to a prepared dish.*

Whether you use a peeler or a knife, always pare fruits and vegetables away from yourself to prevent injury.

Peeling. *Peeling* is removing the skin of soft fruits and vegetables such as peaches, tomatoes, and plums. Though these foods can be eaten with their skins, some recipes call for them to be peeled. Cut into the skin with a paring knife and pull. The skin will come off in pieces. Dipping the fruit or vegetable in boiling water for 30 seconds will make peeling easier.

Peeled fruits and vegetables usually darken in color if not used immediately. This is especially true for apples, bananas, peaches, and avocados. To prevent this, sprinkle the cut surfaces with lemon juice and wrap them in plastic or other airtight covering. Or you can put them in a bowl of water with some lemon juice added.

Slicing, Dicing, Chopping, and Mincing

These techniques are done with a slicing knife, a utility knife, or a chef's knife.

Slicing. To slice meat or a vegetable, steady the food with your opposite hand or with a fork while cutting. Be sure to keep your fingers out of the way.

Dicing. *Dicing* food means cutting it into small cubes. First slice the food in one direction. Then grasp the slices all together and cut them in the other direction. If the cubes are still too large, cut them in half. Diced carrots, beets, or other vegetables can be added to stews or salads.

Chopping and Mincing. To chop food, continue to dice until the food is in smaller pieces. To mince, keep chopping until the food bits are as small as you can make them. Foods used for flavorings—such as onions, garlic, and ginger—should be chopped or minced to give the most flavor to your recipe.

To slice, dice, chop or mince, choose a slicing knife, utility knife, or a chef's knife. Cut down on a cutting board and be careful so that you don't cut your fingers.

FEATURE

Countdown to Mealtime

Cooking a meal is like a countdown —with mealtime as the zero hour. Let's see how Noreen and Jason work together to prepare for the following meal for themselves and two of their best friends:

Beans and franks
Brown bread and margarine
Broccoli
Apples
Milk

They want to spend some time talking with their friends before dinner, so they make it easier on themselves by buying the brown bread and using frozen broccoli.

For the main course, they only need to follow one recipe. It is a simple one to prepare, but very tasty when it is put together carefully:

Beans and Franks

1 pound baked beans, canned
1 pound franks, sliced
¼ teaspoon dry mustard or 1 teaspoon prepared mustard

Preheat oven to 350° F (176.5° C).
Combine all ingredients in a 1½-quart casserole.
Bake uncovered for 20 minutes.

First, they clean up the kitchen. Then, they set the table, read the directions on the package of broccoli, review the recipe, and get out the equipment and utensils they'll need. Then the countdown begins.

The Forty Minute Meal

Zero minus 40 minutes

Jason: Set the oven.
Mix beans, franks, and mustard and put in casserole.
Place casserole in refrigerator.

Noreen: Put margarine on plate, cover, and place in refrigerator.
Wash apples, put in a bowl, and place in refrigerator.
Prepare salted water for broccoli.

Zero minus 20 minutes

Jason: Put casserole in oven.
Set out apples.

Noreen: Start burner for broccoli.
Add broccoli to water when it boils.
Put bread and margarine on table.

Zero minus 1 minute

Jason: Pour milk.

Noreen: Drain broccoli and put on table.

Zero

Jason: Bring casserole to table.

Separating and beating eggs are among the most important kitchen operations. Practice them early in your cooking career to insure getting the technique right.

Separating and Beating Eggs

Separating. **Separating eggs**, or *dividing into whites and yolks*, is tricky, but not difficult. Have two bowls ready. Tap the eggshell lightly, enough to crack it, against the side of one bowl. Holding the crack side up, gently pry apart the two halves. Some of the white will drip into the bowl. Transfer the yolk carefully from one half-shell to the other, allowing the white to drip into the bowl. Continue to do this until all you have left in the shell is the yolk. Drop the yolk into the second bowl.

Beating. You can beat whole eggs or the separated whites or yolks with a fork, a wire whisk, an eggbeater, or an electric mixer. Beating adds air to eggs, increasing their volume. Beaten whites and yolks make foods lighter in texture.

Dredging

Dredging is covering food with a light coating of flour or crumbs. This is also called *breading*. The food should be dry to start. If it's wet, dry it with paper towels. The coating should be thin and should cover the entire surface of the food.

Food such as fish or chicken can be breaded with crumbs, cornmeal, or flour. One efficient method is to put seasoned bread crumbs into a paper bag, add the food, close the bag tightly, and shake. For more elaborate breading, first coat the food with flour, then dip it into beaten egg, and then dip it into seasoned crumbs.

Mixing Dough

Steps in Mixing. To prepare dough, have all the ingredients ready. Read your recipes carefully to be sure that you understand what steps are involved and how much time is needed. In general, dry ingredients are combined in one bowl and wet ingredients in another. Then the two are put together.

Steps in Kneading. Kneading yeast bread dough spreads the yeast throughout the dough. This is the method.

■ After turning your dough out on a floured board or table, flour your hands.

■ Press the ball of dough away from you with the heels of your hands. This will flatten it out.

■ Pull the far end toward you, folding it over. Turn the dough one-quarter turn on the board.

■ Continue to press away and fold over for as long as your recipe directs.

The dough is kneaded enough when you poke it with a finger and the dough springs back.

Steps in Rising. To let a yeast dough rise, rub the dough with butter or oil and put it into a clean bowl. Cover the bowl with plastic wrap or a towel and put it in a warm, dry place.

The recipe should state roughly how long to let the dough rise. You can test its readiness for the next step by poking your finger in it again. This time the dough is ready if the mark your finger left remains.

Words to Remember

equivalents: different measures that describe equal amounts
garnish: add color to a prepared dish
separating eggs: dividing into whites and yolks

Questions

1. How do you measure sifted flour?
2. How do you measure a dry ingredient amount that's one-half of your smallest measuring tool?
3. What three measures are equivalents of one stick of butter?
4. What tools can be used for paring and peeling?
5. Describe a good way to bread food.

Chapter **48 Cooking Food**

Objectives

After reading this chapter, you will be able to:

☐ select the best method for cooking food from the different food groups,

☐ test food for doneness.

Common sense tells you that you don't cook steak in boiling water. But just how *do* you prepare steak? What about vegetables? And why do we cook things—wouldn't it be easier to eat all of our food raw?

It might be easier, perhaps, but definitely not as tasty or as healthy. Heating foods improves their flavor, texture, and appearance. Cooking foods also destroys harmful germs that may be living in them.

Different foods react differently to the same cooking techniques. This is why you broil burgers, but not broccoli. If you roasted eggs in their shells instead of boiling them, you'd get an explosion in the oven.

In this chapter, you'll learn which techniques are best for getting the most flavor and nutrition from different foods. You'll also learn about spices and herbs and which ones flavor certain foods.

Cooking Fruits and Vegetables

Nutrition and flavor are the words to remember when cooking fruits and vegetables. The skin or peel and the part closest to it contain a large amount of the nutrients. Whenever possible, leave on skins and peels. Eating them helps you get the most nutrients from these products.

Using a heavy-bottomed pan lets you cook vegetables at a low, even temperature. This saves energy. So does using the right-sized pan for the amount you are cooking, and the right-sized burner for the pan. If you use pans and burners that are too large for the job, much of the energy heats the air instead of the food.

Boiling and Steaming

Vitamin A, vitamin C, and the B vitamins are easily destroyed by air, heat, and water. When cooking fruits and vegetables, use as little water as possible. Cover the pan, too. This will trap nutrients that might escape in the steam, and will cook the foods more quickly.

Boiling vegetables overcooks them. This causes them to lose most of their vitamins. Better methods are to steam vegetables in a steam basket or simmer them in a small amount of boiling water. After the vegetables are cooked, save the water for use in soups and stews.

Stir-Frying

Stir-frying—cooking quickly in very little fat—is another good method. Test vegetables for doneness by poking them with the point of a knife or a sharp fork. They shouldn't be too hard or too soft, but in between.

Cooking Cereals and Breads

Cooking in Water

Many cereal products, including rice, hot breakfast cereals, and pastas, are cooked in water or some other liquid. Nutrients—especially the B vitamins—escape into the cooking liquid. The key to the preparation of cereal products therefore, is to use as little water as possible. The package will tell you exactly how much water each product needs.

Generally, 3 quarts of water are needed to cook 1/2 pound of pasta. Add the pasta to boiling water slowly to keep the water boiling. This will also keep the pieces of pasta apart. Putting a drop or two of oil in the boiling water helps keep pasta apart, too.

Rinsing rice and pasta products before or after cooking is not a good practice. Water can wash away nutrients.

Cereal products should be cooked until they are just done and no longer. Overcooking destroys texture and nutritive value. Package directions and experience are your best guides to proper cooking times.

Baking

Like any art, baking takes skill and practice. A beginner starts with simple recipes. These recipes may be for quick breads, such as biscuits, pancakes, or banana bread, which do not require kneading and rising time. With a little experience, a baker learns how to handle dough and can move on to more difficult items such as piecrusts and yeast breads.

Breads rise because the starch traps gases that are released by yeast or baking powder.

A quick bread is done when a knife inserted in the center comes out clean. To test a yeast bread for doneness, rap the bottom of the loaf with your knuckles. A hollow sound means that the bread is done.

Cooking Milk Products

Milk

Proteins become tough and stringy at high temperatures, so *low heat* is the rule for cooking milk products. Often, the difference between success and failure is a matter of a few degrees—all the stirring in the world won't save a cream sauce that's been cooked at too high a temperature.

Milk can burn easily. Use heavy pots and pans, which allow milk to heat slowly and evenly. Slow, even heat keeps the milk from burning on the bottom of the pan. Low temperatures prevent the protein from forming a skin over the top of the food and a crust on the side of the pan. (If skins or crusts do develop, you should beat them back into the food. Otherwise, valuable proteins will be lost.) Low temperatures also prevent milk products from boiling over.

Because light quickly destroys riboflavin, its important to cover milk products whenever possible as they cook.

Cheese

Cheese can be sprinkled on top of casseroles or vegetables near the end of the cooking period. Baking or broiling the dish quickly will melt the cheese. Cheese can be melted into a creamy sauce. And, of course, cheese can be served uncooked.

Cheese, like milk, toughens when overcooked. To prevent overcooking, chop, grate or slice the cheese before adding it to the recipe. Low heat and constant stirring also help.

Cooking Foods in the Meat Group

The general principles for cooking foods in this group are based on the reactions of proteins to heat. The more heat, the tougher they become. Medium temperatures are usually the best.

Heating Methods

The different ways to cook meat can be grouped into three categories:

Moist Heat. Moist heat cooking methods use liquid or steam to cook the food. Poaching, simmering, boiling, braising, and stewing all use liquid. Steaming and pressure cooking use steam. These methods are used on a stove top, in the oven, or in a special pressure cooker.

Dry Heat. Many meats can be cooked with dry heat. Baking or roasting in the oven, broiling in a broiler pan or on a barbecue, and grilling in a skillet are all dry heat methods.

F E A T U R E

Nutrients in Food Preparation

Different nutrients react differently to heat.

- *Proteins.* When heated, these nutrients **coagulate.** They *change from a fluid state to a thickened mass.* If cooked at high heat, they toughen.
- *Carbohydrate.* Sugar, a simple carbohydrate, **caramelizes** when heated. It *becomes a liquid and changes color.* Starches, or complex carbohydrate, soften and swell during cooking.
- *Fats.* Animal fats and vegetable oils can survive high heat. However, they break down and taste bitter after they start to smoke. Vegetable oils lose vitamins if they are overheated.
- *Vitamins.* Some vitamins dissolve in water, others in fat. Heat destroys vitamins C, E, and thiamine, an important B vitamin. Exposure to air also causes some vitamin loss.
- *Minerals.* The mineral content of foods is usually stable. It does not change during cooking.

Cooking with Fat. Many foods are cooked on a stove top in fat. Little fat is used for *sautéing* or *stir-frying*. If the food is breaded and there is much fat, the method is called *deep fat frying*. In both methods, the fat should be very hot so that the meat will cook quickly without absorbing the fat.

Beef, Lamb, Pork, Veal

The **cut** of meat is *the part of the animal that the piece of meat comes from.* Cut determines the cooking method.

Tender Cuts. Tender cuts can be cooked with dry heat. Legs of lamb or beef roasts are roasted. Meats should be roasted on a rack in the pan. That way the fat drips down. Another dry heat method—broiling—is good for steaks and chops. Broiling browns meat on the outside and seals in juices and nutrients.

Thinly-Sliced Meats. Thinly sliced meats like minute steaks and ground meats can be pan-fried.

Tougher Cuts. Tougher cuts do best with slow cooking and moist heat, which make them more tender. Pot roasts and short ribs are braised, or cooked in a small amount of liquid. Large chunks of meat and vegetables can be stewed, which uses more water. Browning meats before braising or stewing them helps seal in the meat's juices and produces a more flavorsome dish.

Processed Meats. Processed meats can be cooked many different ways. Hot dogs can be boiled or fried, bacon broiled, and ham baked or pan-fried.

Degrees of Doneness. Beef, lamb, and veal can be cooked to different degrees of doneness, called rare, medium, and well done. Pork should always be well cooked. Do not serve pork if it is still pink inside.

TABLE 1 Flavoring with Herbs and Spices

Herbs	Use with	Spices	Use with
basil	pasta sauces, eggs, tomato dishes, salads	allspice	meat loaf, sweet vegetables, desserts
bay leaf	stews, roasts	caraway seed	noodles, cabbage, bread
dill	pickles, fish, eggs	cayenne pepper	sauces, chicken
mint	lamb, vegetables	chili powder	Mexican food, eggs, stews
oregano	Italian food, tomatoes, pork	cinnamon	desserts, fruits, chicken
parsley	eggs, meats, potatoes	cloves	pumpkin pie, stew, ham
rosemary	lamb, chicken, vegetables	curry	Indian food, meats
sage	stuffing, poultry, pork, soup	ginger	baking, oriental dishes
tarragon	chicken, eggs, vegetables	mustard	meats
thyme	meats, chowders	nutmeg	custards, cakes
		paprika	Hungarian food, eggs
		pepper	most foods except desserts

Meats, vegetables, and fruits can be covered with a liquid and stewed. The tasty cooking liquid adds flavor and nutrients to the dish.

To test roasts for doneness, insert a meat thermometer into the thickest part of the meat. Be sure that it isn't touching the bone. When the correct temperature shows, the meat is cooked. For meats being prepared by other methods, test for doneness by inserting a sharp fork. When the juices are clear and not bloody, the meat is cooked.

Poultry

Chicken, turkey, duck, and Cornish hens can be cooked by using moist or dry heat methods. Frying, roasting, stewing, and broiling are all popular. A bird that is roasted can be stuffed with a stuffing of bread, rice, vegetables, or fruits. Stuff the bird first before putting it in the oven. Test poultry for doneness using the same method as for meat.

Fish

Fish can be prepared in many ways. It is usually broiled, fried, baked, or poached. Shellfish is steamed, boiled, or eaten raw.

Fish cooks quickly. You can tell that it's done when the flesh flakes or separates easily when touched by a fork. Do not overcook fish or it will dry out.

Eggs

Eggs react like other protein foods. When they're undercooked, they will be soft and runny. Overcooked, they will be tough. Eggs can be boiled, poached, fried, scrambled, or baked.

You can also beat eggs and add them to many recipes, such as cakes and custards. The eggs add volume to the other dishes.

Legumes

Dried beans need to be soaked in water overnight or boiled in water quickly to soften. Then they should simmer over low heat for a long time. Lentils and split peas do not need soaking.

Cooking with Fats and Sugar

Fats

Because fats and oils can be kept at high heat, they are used for frying and sautéing. The high heat quickly cooks and seals up the outside of the food. This traps moisture and nutrients inside, without making the food greasy. Deep-fried foods should be drained after cooking by placing them on a paper towel. They should be eaten right away or they will get soggy.

Sugar

Since high heat will caramelize sugar, all foods with sugar must be cooked slowly over low to medium heat. Heavy pans will help prevent overcooking.

Sugar acts as a preservative when cooked with some foods. For that reason, it's often used in canning fruits, preserves, and some vegetables and meats.

Words to Remember

caramelize: become a liquid and change color

coagulate: change from a fluid state to a thickened mass

cut: the part of an animal that a piece of meat comes from

Questions

1. What are the general rules to follow when preparing fruits and vegetables?
2. What is the best method for cooking pasta and rice?
3. How do you test breads for doneness?
4. List the three methods of heating meat.
5. How do you tell when fish is cooked?

49 Serving Meals at Home and Eating Out

Objectives

After reading this chapter, you will be able to:

☐ describe the ways to serve a meal at home,

☐ choose a restaurant meal that is nutritious and tasty,

☐ use good manners when eating at home or dining out.

Suppose you and your family want to eat out. You could choose a fine restaurant for a fancy, leisurely meal. You could go to a diner for a simple, quick one. Or you could get a take-out meal at a fast-food restaurant.

You have similar choices when you serve meals at home. You might serve a formal meal. Or you might prepare a more casual meal, where people serve themselves. Wherever you choose to eat your meal, you'll want to behave in the proper manner.

In this chapter, you'll learn about how to serve meals at home, how to choose a restaurant, and how to act at a meal.

Eating at Home

A Style for Each Occasion

Family Style. Most meals at home are served **family style**. *Food is brought to the table in plates and bowls, which are passed around.* You might fill each person's plate in the kitchen and then bring it to the table. Or one person might serve the main dish, like a roast or a rice-and-bean dish, at the table. Side dishes like rolls or salad can be passed around.

Buffet Style. You may want to serve some meals buffet style. At a **buffet dinner**, *all the food is placed in bowls and platters on a serving table.* Guests serve themselves and go to sit elsewhere. This type of service is good for large parties or family occasions.

Foods at a buffet should be easy to eat

Indoor and outdoor buffets have become very popular in recent years. They are a convenient way to serve food, and the food display heightens the appetite.

with fingers or to cut with a fork. Buffet foods are best if they aren't juicy. Casseroles are often served in buffets.

Buffets can be held anywhere—indoors, outdoors, in the kitchen, the dining room, or the living room. They can be informal, with paper plates, or very formal. The choice depends on the occasion.

Setting the Table

For whatever type of meal you serve, you will have to set the table.

Place Setting. For sitdown meals, you will make individual place settings. A **place setting** is *the arrangement of the tableware each diner will need for the meal.* Each guest should have a plate, a glass, a napkin, and **flatware**—*knives, forks, and spoons.*

A more formal place setting includes more pieces. It might include more flatware, a bread-and-butter plate, and perhaps a salad plate. Sometimes a coffee cup is added.

Buffet Table. Food for a buffet should be set up to make it easy for guests to serve themselves. Put plates at the beginning. As guests walk along the table, they can serve themselves from the bowls and platters. Put serving forks and spoons near the platters. And gravies and sauces should go near the food they are meant for.

Place flatware and napkins at the end of the table. Glasses and beverages are often placed at the end, too.

Special Touches. When you want a meal to be something special, you can add a few decorations. A tablecloth can dress up the table. Be sure it is clean and pressed, and that it hangs evenly around the table. Its color should go well with the rest of the

This place setting is usually found in restaurants where the service is fairly simple. This style of setting also suits most homes.

table settings. You could also use placemats instead of a tablecloth.

You may also want to add a **centerpiece**, *a pleasing decoration placed at the center of the table.* A bowl of fruit or flowers, a set of candles, or a craft object are all examples.

Eating Out

Types of Restaurants

Fast-food chains. You're probably very familiar with the *fast-food chains* in your town, since they're often popular spots for young people. The most well-known fast-food restaurants specialize in hamburgers, tacos, fish, or chicken. Some also offer breakfast. They're usually clean, bright, and inexpensive. You order food at a central area and take it to a table or bring it home. Customers are responsible for cleaning up after their meals.

Family-style restaurants. These places include coffee shops, diners, and specialty restaurants, like those that cook only steak or fish. The term can be applied to any restaurant with a casual atmosphere and good, simple food—meat and potatoes, egg dishes, salads, and hot and cold sandwiches. Usually, these restaurants offer **table service**, in which *waiters and waitresses bring the food to the table.*

Luxury restaurants. Such restaurants offer specially prepared food in elegant surroundings. Luxury restaurants provide

---

F E A T U R E

A Taste of Ethnic Foods

Country	Dishes
Mexico	tacos (crispy filled tortillas with sauce), guacamole (avocado dip), refried beans
Puerto Rico	fried plantain (like banana), viandas (steamed vegetables), beans and rice
Cuba	black bean soup, roast pork, flan (caramel custard)
France	bouillabaisse (fish stew), beef bourguignon (beef stew), crepes (filled pancakes), quiche Lorraine (cheese and egg pie)
Italy	tomato sauce, lasagna (layered pasta, cheese, and meat), veal parmigiana (veal with cheese and tomato sauce)
Germany	sausages, sauerbraten (pot roast), sauerkraut (cabbage), potato pancakes
Greece	spanikopita (spinach and cheese pie), moussaka (eggplant casserole)
Morocco	couscous (steamed bulgur wheat), tagines (vegetable or meat- and-vegetable dishes)
Middle East	stuffed grape leaves, hummus (dip of chick peas), shish kabob (meat and vegetables on skewers), pita bread
India	curry sauces (blend of spices), yogurt, lentil sauce
China	stir-fried meat and vegetables, egg drop soup (chicken with beaten eggs), wontons, (dumplings), tofu (soybean curd)
Japan	steamed fish, sushi (raw fish with spiced rice), tempura (deep-fried vegetables or seafood)

their customers with excellent personal service. They're often chosen by business people who want to entertain clients, or by families who are having celebrations.

Ethnic restaurants. These places specialize in food from other countries. The number of these restaurants has grown recently because of people's increasing curiosity about different food traditions. Ethnic restaurants allow people to sample unusual foods. They can be casual, family style, or elegant.

Selecting Your Meal

The kind of food you order depends on your likes and dislikes. Of course, you'll want to look at the **menu**, *the list of foods that the restaurant offers*. As extra help, some restaurants put pictures of their food on the menu, on the walls, or on table displays.

You can always ask waiters and waitresses any questions you have about the food, such as how it's prepared. You might even ask them for their advice about what to order. Diners with special diet needs can often get special dishes.

Keeping a Nutritional Balance

To keep a good nutritional balance in your food choices, consider what other foods you've already eaten that day. If at lunch you didn't eat a vegetable or fruit, be sure to choose at least one for your dinner.

Fast-food restaurants don't always offer balanced meals. An average meal at a chicken restaurant, for example, is chicken

pieces and potatoes. Only two of the basic food groups—meat and fruits and vegetables—are included. You need to round the meal out with a dairy product and a cereals and breads product.

You can solve this problem by choosing a fast-food restaurant that has a salad bar. Or you can be sure to include fruit juice, milk, yogurt, or vegetables in another meal that day.

Family-style restaurants usually offer foods from all the food groups.

Restaurant Service

When you enter a restaurant for the first time, look around. Is this an informal restaurant where you seat yourself? Sometimes a sign asks you to wait to be seated. If you see such a sign, wait until a host or hostess comes to take you to your seat.

If you wish to get the attention of a serving person to make a request, never shout. Speak in an ordinary voice as he or she passes your table. If the waiter or waitress is across the room, raise your hand and try to catch his or her eye.

After you have received the bill, quickly add it up to be sure that you have the correct total. If there has been a mistake, as occasionally happens, bring the error politely to the server's attention. It will be taken care of quickly.

Tips are *extra money given to waiters and waitresses for good service*. They are customary in all table-service restaurants. Usually, 15 percent of the cost of the food (before taxes) is an acceptable tip. Many customers tip 20 percent of the food's cost in luxury-class restaurants.

Good Manners: Rules or Thoughtfulness?

Whether you eat at home or out, you want the people you're with to feel comfortable and enjoy themselves. Manners are nothing more than showing thoughtfulness for others.

Appearance and Hygiene

Be sure to have washed your hands before you sit down for the meal. Don't comb your hair or put on makeup at the table.

If you spill anything on yourself, go to the washroom and try to clean it off. Don't eat with your elbows resting on the table. Keep your napkin in your lap and use it to clean bits of food off your mouth and hands.

Eating the Meal

If you're a guest, don't begin eating before everyone is served. Usually, you should wait until your host takes a bite. Of course, it you're told to go ahead, it's acceptable to begin eating.

What silverware to use should not be a problem. Smaller forks are for appetizers, salads, and desserts. Larger forks are for the main meal. Large spoons are for soups. Teaspoons are for dessert or coffee or tea. If you're unsure, always use the utensil on the outside first.

If you don't know what a utensil is for, watch the host. Do what he or she does with the unfamiliar piece of flatware.

Conversation

An important part of dining with others—even family—is your mood. Enjoy

People enjoy the service and atmosphere of a restaurant. Good table manners, being courteous, and tipping add to that atmosphere.

the company of the people you're with. Mealtime is for warmth and friendship and fellowship.

Many people have recognized that dinner is the best time of day to get the family together and to discuss the day's events. Family business gets completed quicker at the dinner table.

Finally, when you're a guest at a dinner party, don't leave without thanking the host and hostess—and the parents in the home you're visiting, if they are present. A special word of thanks to the cook is also thoughtful.

Words to Remember

buffet dinner: a meal in which all food is placed in bowls and platters on a serving table

centerpiece: a pleasing decoration placed at the center of the table

family style: a meal in which food is brought to the table in plates and bowls, which are passed around

flatware: knives, forks, and spoons

menu: the list of foods that a restaurant offers

place setting: the arrangement of the tableware each diner will need for a meal

table service: restaurant service in which servers bring the food to the table

tip: extra money given to food servers for good service

Questions

1. What is the difference between a family-style dinner and a buffet?
2. Draw or describe a simple place setting.
3. What are the four types of restaurants?
4. What should you consider when choosing a meal?
5. How should you get a food server's attention?
6. What should you say to the host and hostess when leaving their house after a meal?

Chapter 50 Careers in Food and Nutrition

Chapter

Objectives

After reading this chapter, you will be able to:

□ *identify areas in the job market in which you can use the skills discussed in this unit,*

□ *describe certain jobs in these areas.*

Do you like to measure and combine ingredients to create a tasty bread? Do you enjoy making people feel comfortable and at ease so that they can enjoy their meal? Do you like to plan menus to meet a variety of people's needs? If your answer to any of these questions is yes, a career in foods and nutrition may be for you.

Careers in foods and nutrition are plentiful. Such jobs are among the top ten career slots in the country. These career positions range from farm workers and supermarket checkers to meat cutters and food technologists. They include waiters, dishwashers, restaurant hosts and hostesses, chefs, and food editors and writers for newspapers and magazines. As the country grows, so will the foods and nutrition industries.

Useful Characteristics For Careers in Foods and Nutrition

The careers in this area are quite varied, from dishwasher to chef, from food servers to menu planner. But they all call for similar traits.

Mental Characteristics

■ *Are you interested in knowing about food and food preparation?* The short-order cook must know the correct cooking time for burgers. The dishwasher must know how to make plates and utensils sanitary.

■ *Can you pay close attention to detail?* Bakers must measure carefully, food servers must take orders accurately, and supermarket checkers must ring up the correct prices.

Emotional Characteristics

■ *Can you work well with others?* Few people in foods and nutrition careers work alone. A restaurant staff is a team of order taker, food preparer, busperson, and dishwasher. The ability to cooperate with others is essential.

■ *Do you have a pleasant and friendly personality?* Many people in this field spend much of their time working closely with the public. Making customers feel at ease and happy helps make sure that the customers return.

■ *Are you calm under pressure?* Creating an easy atmosphere can be hard at times. The fast pace of a restaurant kitchen or the late hours of a supermarket can put pressure on the workers.

If you have these characteristics, you may want to look at careers in foods and nutrition. In the next few pages, you can learn about some of those careers. There are many more, of course, but this chapter will give you a sampling of what's available.

Food Processing Careers

Many food careers involve the producing and selling of food products.

Entry-Level Jobs

Farm workers manage food crops. They plant, fertilize, weed, and harvest plant crops. Or they tend and feed livestock. The number of these workers is expected to decrease in the future. In fact, the trend over many years has been for fewer and fewer farm workers to produce more and more food.

Checkers in supermarkets help customers buy food. They total up customers' purchases, take cash or checks, count change, and pack bags. They need to work carefully but quickly—customers prefer not to spend much time in line. Checkers often work part-time.

Jobs That Require Extra Training

Running the supermarket is the *manager*, who sees that the shelves are always stocked with the foods that customers want. Managers must keep track of the store's **inventory**, or *the amount of each* *product in stock.* They also oversee the store's workers and budget. Supermarket managers often have taken college courses. Many simply rise from checker to department head to store manager.

Meat cutters cut and package meat. They may keep track of inventory and even help with buying new supplies. Meat cutters must be extremely careful, for the equipment they use is dangerous. Most cutters learn their jobs through on-the-job apprenticeships. Some are taught in trade schools.

A *quality control inspector* checks the food that is produced in the processing plant. He or she makes sure that the taste, texture, and appearance of the food is up to the company's standards. Some inspectors work for the federal government. Their special concern is safety and cleanliness. Food inspectors are trained on the job.

Jobs That Require Advanced Degrees

Plant researchers study ways to make crops yield more produce. They also try to develop new types of plants that resist disease. These scientists usually have advanced training beyond a college degree. Some work for the government.

Food technologists develop new ways of processing food. They have recently developed a protein-based sweetener, new uses for vegetable protein, and fruit drinks with high nutrition and long shelf life. These scientists study chemistry and biology in college.

Food Service Careers

Besides food processing, the other major group of careers in this field relates to food service. People in these careers work mostly in restaurants and cafeterias.

Entry-level Jobs

The *waiter* or *waitress* is a familiar sight in many restaurants. He or she takes customers' orders and brings them their food. But

A food technologist examines foods to help find more nutritious combinations, safer ways of preserving them, and more interesting ways to present them to the public.

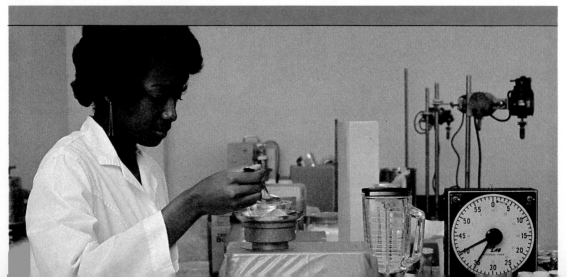

FEATURE

Learning About Job Openings

It's one thing to decide what career you want, but how do you know where the jobs are? Finding a job is hard work, but if you apply yourself, you'll get the kind of job you want.

There is no one way to find a job—in fact, there are many.

- *Applying in person.* For many entry-level jobs, it is best to visit the organization and apply in person. Many large organizations never advertise their job openings. They get enough applicants in this way.

- *Answering help-wanted ads.* This may be the most familiar method. It has the advantage of letting you know exactly what job is open. But ads usually draw many applicants. Your response to the ad must make you stand apart from the others.

- *Using contacts.* **Contacts** are *people you know who know about jobs.* Us-ing contacts can be helpful, since someone who knows you can recommend you to the employer. But you cannot rely on this method alone.

- *Using an employment agency.* Many experienced workers can find a new job through an employment agency. Sometimes, these agencies charge fees that the job seeker must pay. The employer often pays the fee.

- *Entering civil service lists.* People who want to work for the government must enter the civil service system. They need to fill out a form and perhaps take a test.

Whatever method you use to apply for a job, it is important to make a good impression. If you apply in person, dress neatly and speak politely. If you answer a help-wanted ad, write a clear, neat letter that highlights the important points of your résumé.

---

the job goes beyond that. Enjoyment of a meal often begins with how comfortable the waiter or waitress makes customers feel. And many food service workers are asked by customers to recommend dishes. Many of these workers work part-time. Salaries are fairly low but tips add to income.

Dishwashers work in the kitchen. They remove all food and germs from plates and utensils. In smaller restaurants, they might also work at cleaning the kitchen in general or clearing the dining room. These tend to be part-time jobs.

Jobs That Require Extra Training

A restaurant *host* or *hostess* usually learns on the job, although some take courses in food service. These workers supervise the waiters and waitresses. They take reservations, greet customers, and show them to their tables. They may also handle payments by customers who have dined. Many hosts and hostesses begin their careers as waiters and waitresses.

The star of a restaurant, of course, is the *chef* who prepares the food. A smaller res-

The pastry chef in a restaurant works to create delicious desserts and breads.

taurant may have only one or two cooks, but a larger one will employ many cooks. Each one prepares a certain kind of food—pastries, roasts, or soups, for instance. The head chef acts as a manager of all kitchen activities. But he or she also has experience with cooking and may plan the menu. Some chefs even create new dishes. Chefs spend many years learning their profession.

Jobs That Require Advanced Degrees

Editors and writers help the public learn about foods and nutrition. They write articles explaining new ways of using food or describing the latest discoveries in nutrition. These workers write for publishing companies, magazines, newspapers, and food manufacturers. They have college degrees, with training in home economics, English, and journalism.

Dietitians are scientists who use information about nutrition and food preparation to plan meals. They usually work for schools or hospitals. They have a college degree in home economics.

Words to Remember

contacts: people you know who know about jobs

inventory: the amount of each product in stock

Questions

1. What are two mental characteristics required for jobs in foods and nutrition?
2. What are three emotional characteristics required for jobs in foods and nutrition?
3. Describe three food processing jobs, one at each level.
4. Describe three jobs in food service, one at each level.

Tired of cold cereal and milk for breakfast? Trying to avoid snacking on potato chips, but not sure what else you should eat? Want to try making a tasty dish from another country? Here are some ideas to get you started on food choices that offer variety, good taste, and plenty of nutrition.

1. Breakfast in a hurry
2. Snacking for health
3. Supermarket savings
4. A taste from another country

Breakfast in a Hurry

You want to eat breakfast, but you don't think that you have time to prepare eggs and toast or hot cereal. What can you do? Here are a few ideas for breakfast that take just minutes—or less!—to prepare. And each one gives you energy to start the day.

Flavorful Fruit

Add fresh fruit to your cereal. Bananas, berries, and peaches are all delicious.

Pour your favorite fruit juice in a blender and add an egg, milk or yogurt, some ice, and a banana.

Super Sandwiches

Spread peanut butter on whole-wheat bread and sprinkle with sunflower seeds.

Make a cheese sandwich on whole-wheat toast.

Make an open-faced sandwich with leftover meat or sliced hard-boiled egg, top with a slice of cheese, and brown quickly in the broiler.

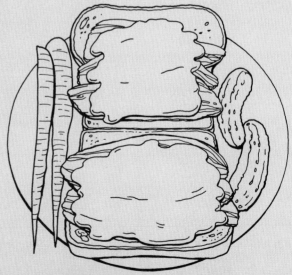

Raid the Refrigerator

Eat that leftover chicken leg.

Quickly warm up a leftover slice of pizza.

Put yogurt in a bowl and top with granola, wheat germ, coconut, or raisins—or all four!

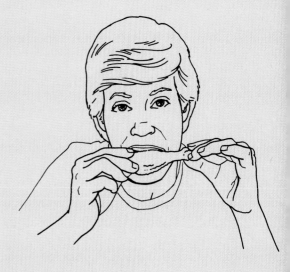

Tasty Treats That Take No Time

Grab a piece of fruit or two.

Munch on a granola bar.

Chew on celery or carrot sticks.

Snacking for Health

You've decided not to eat potato chips, salted nuts, or candy for your snack. But what *can* you eat? Well, there are many nutritious and delicious snack ideas to choose from. Here are some easy ones.

Blender Drinks

1 cup (250 ml) milk
1 teaspoon (5 ml) honey
fresh fruit, peeled (bananas, strawberries, peaches, blueberries, melons, *or* oranges)

Put all ingredients into the jar of a blender and mix at blend speed.

Pour into chilled glasses and serve.

Homemade Trail Mix

3 cups (750 ml) puffed or chex cereal
1 cup (250 ml) unsalted sunflower *or* other seeds
1 cup (250 ml) chopped unsalted nuts
1 cup (250 ml) raisins

Mix all the ingredients, spread on a baking sheet, and bake at 375° F (160°C) for 8 to 10 minutes.

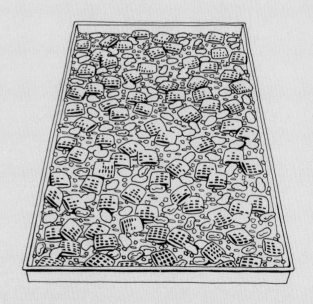

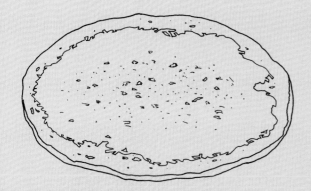

Mini Pizzas

1 English muffin *or* 1 piece pita bread
3 ounces (90 g) cheddar *or* mozzarella *or*
feta cheese, grated
seasoning

Sprinkle cheese on top of bread. Top with
your favorite seasonings (try oregano or
basil with mozzarella or feta).

Broil until cheese melts.

Pocket Sandwiches

½ cup (125 ml) cooked chicken, diced
1 green onion, chopped
¼ cup (62.5 ml) dried raisins
1 tablespoon (15 ml) mayonnaise
1 pita bread

Mix together the first four ingredients.

Slice off the top fifth of the pita bread and
gently open the pocket.

Fill the pocket with the chicken mixture and
serve.

Tuna Spread

1 7-ounce (200-g) can tuna
4 ounces (120 g) cream cheese, softened
¼ teaspoon (1.25 ml) dill

Put the tuna in a bowl.

Add the cream cheese and blend together
using a hand mixer.

Sprinkle the dill into the mixture and mix
thoroughly.

Spoon onto a plate and serve with cucumber
slices, carrot sticks, and crackers.

Supermarket Savings

You can help cut your food bills by shopping wisely. Here are some handy hints for saving dollars:

- Buy large pieces of meat, like whole chickens, and cut them up yourself.

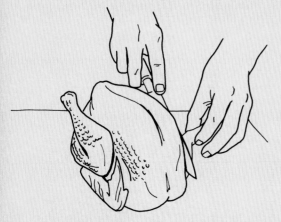

- Buy larger packages of chips, raisins, cookies, or trail mix and separate them into serving size portions at home.

- Buy large sizes of cleaning products, which do not spoil.
- Use coupons for items that you usually buy, and shop at stores that give double or triple coupon value.
- Compare products using unit prices.

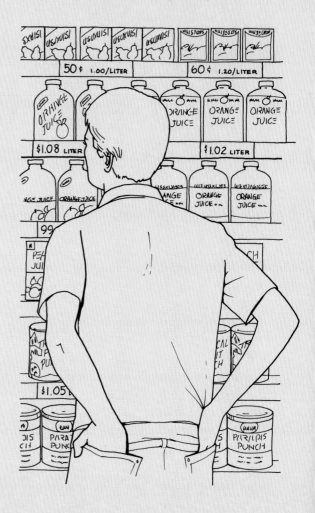

- Avoid displays and impulse buying, especially at the checkout stand—stick to your shopping list.
- Buy cheaper cuts of meat or less expensive protein sources, like poultry, eggs, and beans.
- Buy easy-to-prepare raw foods rather than convenience foods.

- Buy day-old bread for french toast or for stuffing.
- Buy canned goods and paper products in bulk when they're on sale.
- Buy generic products or store brands if you find the quality acceptable.
- Check for bargain produce items. If appearance is not a factor, you can use that vegetable in the evening's meal.

A Taste from Another Country

One way to add variety to your diet is to select a delicious dish from another country. Here are a few ideas you can try.

Marinara Sauce for Spaghetti

A quick-cooking pasta sauce from Italy.
1 clove garlic, chopped
½ cup (125 ml) chopped onion
1 tablespoon (15 ml) olive oil
1 16-ounce (450-g) can whole tomatoes
1 teaspoon (5 ml) basil
salt and pepper to taste

Cook garlic and onion in oil until soft but not brown.

Add tomatoes. Mash with fork while cooking.

Add salt, pepper, and basil, and stir together to blend. Cook about 30 minutes.

Use the sauce as a topping for spaghetti, chicken, or fish, or for homemade pizza.

Beef Tacos

These tasty packets come from Mexico.
8 taco shells
1 cup (250 ml) shredded cooked meat or cooked ground beef
1 cup (250 ml) shredded lettuce
½ cup (125 ml) chopped onion
½ cup (125 ml) chopped tomato
½ cup (125 ml) grated cheddar or Monterey Jack cheese

Spread meat in bottom of taco shell.

Top with lettuce, onion, and tomato.

Add sauce, sprinkle with cheese, and serve.

Sauce
1½ cups (375 ml) canned whole tomatoes
½ cup (125 ml) chopped onion
2 cloves garlic, minced
2-3 tablespoons (30-4 1) chopped green chiles
¼ cup (62.5 ml) water

Combine all ingredients in a bowl and blend well.

Nicoise Salad

This tasty chef's salad comes from southern France.
1 small head lettuce
1 cup (250 ml) cooked green beans
1 can tuna
8 black olives
3-5 green onions, chopped
½ green pepper, cut in thin strips
2 hard-boiled eggs, chopped
4 anchovies (optional)

Tear lettuce into a bowl and add other ingredients. Add dressing and toss.

Dressing
2 tablespoons (30 ml) vinegar
4 tablespoons (60 ml) olive oil
¼ teaspoon (1.25 ml) ground pepper
1 clove garlic, minced

Put ingredients in a jar, and shake to mix well.

Stir-Fried Chicken and Vegetables

This is a delicious and easy Chinese dish.
2 chicken breasts, boned, skinned, and halved, *or* 2 cups (500 ml) cooked chicken meat
2 tablespoons (30 ml) salad oil
1 cup (250 ml) sliced celery
1 medium green pepper, sliced
1 small onion, sliced
1 teaspoon (5 ml) salt
¼ teaspoon (1.25 ml) ginger
1 16-ounce (450-g) can bean sprouts
1 5-ounce (150-g) can water chestnuts
1 cube chicken bouillon
2 teaspoons (10 ml) cornstarch
2 tablespoons (30 ml) soy sauce

Slice chicken into ¼-inch strips.

Heat oil in skillet at high setting. Add celery, green pepper, onion, salt, and ginger. Cook, stirring quickly and frequently, until tender-crisp, about 3 minutes. Remove vegetables.

Stir-fry chicken in oil left in skillet until chicken turns white, about 3 to 5 minutes. (If using cooked chicken, simply warm the meat.)

Return vegetables to skillet. Add bean sprouts, water chestnuts, bouillon, and ½ cup water.

In a cup, blend cornstarch and soy sauce. Stir into skillet, and cook until mixture thickens. Stir constantly.

Serve with rice or noodles.

Unit Four Review

Unit Summary

Chapter 34.

You make many food choices every day. You decide what to eat based on hunger, appetite, emotions, personal preferences, family habits, life-style, advertising, peer pressure, and ethnic, religious, and regional customs.

Chapters 35 and 36.

You should always consider nutrition when making food choices. You need the proper amounts of protein, carbohydrate, fat, vitamins, minerals, and water every day. You can get these nutrients by eating a balanced diet made up of items in the five major food groups: fruits and vegetables; breads and cereals; milk and milk products; meat, fish, poultry, eggs, and beans; and extras.

Chapters 37 and 38.

In general, healthy eating habits involve choosing the best foods, preparing them to get the best nutritional value, and maintaining proper weight. You also need to avoid dangerous or ineffective weight-loss diets or so-called health foods that are not what they seem.

Chapter 39.

You can follow good habits even when eating in the school cafeteria or in a restaurant. At home, however, you really put your knowledge about selecting and preparing good foods to work. In planning meals, you take into account nutrition, your resources, and the flavor, color, shape, texture, and temperature of food.

Chapters 40-42.

Shopping involves deciding on the type of store to visit, making a list, and finding the best buys. You should select the best products available in each food group and store them so they are kept fresh and nutritious.

Chapters 43-45.

In the kitchen, safety and sanitation are major concerns. You should be aware of the dangers and how to avoid them. Learning about kitchen equipment can make cooking easier and more fun.

Chapters 46-49.

When preparing a meal, the recipe is the main tool. It tells you what ingredients are in a dish and how to prepare them. To follow the directions in recipes, you need to know how to measure, mix, and cook foods. Cooking involves using moist heat, dry heat, or fat. Each food is most nutritious—and tasty—if cooked in certain ways. Once the meal is prepared, you can set the table and serve the food in a way that makes mealtime pleasant for your guests.

Chapter 50.

If food selection and preparation appeal to you, you might consider one of the many careers in the food processing or service fields.

Questions

1. Describe three important influences on your food choices.
2. Name the six basic types of nutrients.
3. List the five major food groups.
4. What are some items that you should avoid eating too much of in a healthy diet?
5. Why don't crash diets work?
6. Describe three types of restaurants.
7. Give an example of practicing good manners in a fast-food restaurant.
8. What are three sources of information you can use when planning meals?
9. How can a shopping list be organized?

10. What are unit prices?

11. Why is food storage just as important as food selection?

12. What should you look for when buying fresh fruit?

13. What are the two kinds of safety to be concerned with in the kitchen?

14. Why should you follow sanitary practices in the kitchen?

15. List and describe the uses of three kitchen utensils and three kitchen appliances.

16. What are three things to consider when choosing a recipe?

17. What information should a recipe give?

18. Describe the differences among roasting, frying, boiling, and broiling.

19. How do you measure flour?

20. How do you knead bread?

21. How should you cook vegetables?

22. What is a good cooking method for pork?

23. How can good manners improve a meal?

24. List three careers in foods and nutrition.

Reading Activities

1. Read the five hints for healthy eating habits in Chapter 37. Write a paragraph telling how you follow those rules.

2. Read a recipe from a cookbook you have at home or from a newspaper. Note down any words or procedures that you don't understand. Bring them to class to discuss.

Writing Activities

1. Make a list of everything you ate yesterday. Include the food, the amount, the time, and the place. Write a paragraph about whether you ate a balanced diet yesterday. Explain why or why not.

2. Interview a cook you know. Ask: How do you make up a shopping list? What is your favorite dish to prepare and why? Do you follow recipes closely? If not, what do you do instead? Why do you like to cook? Write two or three paragraphs discussing what you learned.

Math Activities

1. Find a recipe for chocolate chip cookies. First determine the metric equivalents for all measurements given. Then double the recipe, both standard and metric amounts, and rewrite it that way.

2. Take the list you made of everything you ate yesterday (writing activity 1). Determine about how many calories you ate. Make a chart showing that amount as well as the number of calories you burned that day by doing things like walking, running, climbing stairs, or riding a bicycle.

3. Visit a supermarket. Use unit prices to compare the cost of two different brands—or two different sizes of the same brand—of three different products.

Group Projects

1. Have each class member bring in an unusual recipe not found in cookbooks—perhaps a traditional family or ethnic dish—and collect the recipes into a class cookbook.

2. Plan two different table setting arrangements—one for a formal dinner party and one for an outdoor picnic. Have members of the group bring in table items (dishes, flatware, napkins, serving utensils, decorations, etc.). Set two tables and discuss the differences between them.

CLOTHING AND TEXTILES

Choosing, wearing, and caring for clothing involves making many decisions. Sometimes, the choices seem very difficult. You want your clothes to be up-to-date, but you don't have the money to get a new closetful of stylish clothes. How can you adapt what you already own, or buy just enough new items to make your clothes more stylish?

You also make choices depending on how clothes look. Is red a good color for you? Is that print too big or too small to suit your build?

Choices that you make in the store can seem especially difficult. Surrounded by attractive clothes, all looking fresh and new, you're tempted to buy anything. You picture yourself walking into school tomorrow with that sweater on. But is it a good buy? Could you get a similar sweater at another store for less? Is this one well made? Do you really need another green sweater?

Whether you buy your clothes and other items or not, you must decide how to care for them. How you choose to care for your clothes will determine whether they are neat and clean when you want to wear them again.

Finally, what do you do with old clothes? You can leave them in the back of your closet, taking up space and gathering dust. Or you can put them to use again.

In these chapters, you'll read about some of the clothing decisions you make. You'll learn how to make these decisions in the best way for you, to get the most out of your money and your clothes—and to make you look great!

Chapter 51 Clothing and You

Objectives

After reading this chapter, you will be able to:

□ *describe how clothing decisions affect your self-concept,*

□ *explain how clothing choices are based on personal tastes,*

□ *list ways in which you choose clothing for comfort,*

□ *describe how clothing choices are affected by groups.*

At this time in your life, you probably find that your tastes in clothing change easily. One day you want to feel comfortable, and you don't really care what others think of your clothes. Another day, you dress so you can fit in with the crowd. Sometimes, you follow the style of someone you admire.

Experimenting with clothing is part of finding out about yourself. It helps you learn what kinds of clothes make you feel comfortable, with yourself and others.

The choices you make about clothes depend on many things:

■ your self-concept,
■ your personality,
■ your looks,
■ the climate you live in,
■ what you do,
■ the group you belong to,
■ the type of life you lead.

Clothing Choices

Some clothing choices depend on what you plan to do. You probably have certain clothing for school, other outfits for special occasions, and some old favorites for just relaxing. Other choices depend on the weather. Heat, cold, sun, rain, and snow all call for certain kinds of clothing.

Some choices are not so clear-cut. Sometimes, you need to choose between your needs and your wants. You may need a practical jacket that will last for a few years. But you're tempted to buy a jacket in the latest style.

In making these more difficult choices, you have to decide what is important to you. Do you want to dress like your friends, or in your own way? Do you prefer clothes that are easy to care for, or do you not mind hand washing occasionally? Do you like to sew, or would you rather buy clothes ready-made?

Clothes and Your Appearance

Giving First Impressions

When you meet people, your clothes influence how they see you. Clothes serve as a kind of packaging in which you present yourself to the world. Clothing tells other people about your lifestyle, your preferences, and your interests—maybe even how you're feeling on a particular day! Being careful about how you dress will make a good impression on others.

Expressing Your Personality

Your clothes can express your personality. If you wear unusual clothes that set you off from the crowd, you probably like to show your **individuality**, *the ways in which you are different from others.* You think for yourself and enjoy being original.

Sometimes, you want to wear the same type of clothing that your friends wear. You want to feel part of a group. **Conforming**—*being like the people around you*—makes you feel comfortable. You can conform and still be an individual. Though everyone in your group wears T-shirts, the design on yours can reflect what's special about you.

The colors you choose often reflect your inner feelings and preferences, too. A person who wears cool, quiet colors—soft blues and greens—may be showing a calm personality. On the other hand, a bright orange sweater shows your fun-loving, outgoing side.

Clothing reflects your personality, interests and moods.

F E A T U R E

Why Do People Wear Clothes?

We have all seen the pictures of pre-historic people wearing animal skins on their bodies and tiger's teeth necklaces.

Have you ever wondered why they dressed as they did? Have you ever wondered why *you* dress as you do?

Throughout history, people have worn clothes for a variety of reasons. The main ones are for *protection,* for *modesty,* for *identification,* and for *decoration.*

■ **Protection.** The weather is an important reason why people do or do not wear clothes. In northern climates, such as in the Arctic, people wear animal skins and fur for most of the year to survive the snow, ice, and cold. Wearing heavy clothes keeps body heat near the body.

In the south, where the weather is warm, people tend to wear less clothes, so that body heat can escape. People also wear certain clothes for protection when working (firefighters, construction workers, x-ray technicians, etc.) and when playing (football, soccer, baseball, and hockey players, etc.).

■ **Modesty.** Modesty deals with proper dress in a community—when and where to wear a particular garment, and how much that garment covers the body. In many cultures, a man's and woman's body is to be completely covered. In other cultures, people may wear only the slightest garments. Modesty is governed by what a community thinks about the human body and its dignity. Some cultures feel that it is more dignified to cover the body. Other cultures feel that displaying the body is the best way to honor it.

For instance, in the Middle East long robes for both men and women, and veils for women, are considered the correct garments to wear. In the South Sea islands of the Pacific, short skirts for men and women, and no covering for the women's breasts are considered correct and modest.

■ **Identification.** Clothes have always been useful in identifying certain people in a community. The police and soldiers are known by their uniforms. The business suit, the cheerleader outfit, the bride's white gown and veil all identify people—what they do or what they want to be.

In ancient times, royalty was singled out by the amount of purple they used in their robes. The color purple was taken from a liquid found in a certain snail. It was very expensive to produce as a dye. Only kings and high royalty could afford to use it.

■ **Decoration.** People of all cultures have liked to decorate their bodies in various ways. Such decoration helps them to feel better in the eyes of others. It shows that they are unique. It communicates something about their tastes and creativity.

■ People of some cultures paint, tattoo, or scar their bodies. In other communities, the wearing of jewelry and perfume in certain ways is a mark of beauty and acceptance.

Making You Look Better

Clothing can affect your appearance. For example, some designs make your shoulders appear broader or your body seem slimmer. Other designs draw attention to your face.

Colors also affect the way you look. The same style can have surprisingly different effects in different colors.

Learning how color and design change your appearance can help you make your clothing decisions. You'll be able to choose clothes that help you express yourself and look your best. (The next chapter has information on improving your appearance.)

Clothes and Comfort

You also need to choose the right outfit for an occasion so you'll feel comfortable. That means dressing for climate and dressing for activity.

Dressing for Climate

In hot weather, it's best to choose loose-fitting clothes. The loose fit allows air to move over your body, making you feel cooler. Light colors are good, too—they reflect the sun's heat away from your body.

In cold weather, you'll need heavy sweaters, coats, gloves, and boots. Several layers of clothes give extra warmth. You should be sure to wear these extra layers when you are shoveling snow or sledding in the cold.

Wherever you live, you'll probably need a raincoat and other gear for protection from rain.

Climate affects the type of clothing that you wear. In the Arctic, coats, boots, and gloves like these are necessary.

In some places, you'll need clothes for hot summers *and* for cold winters. You may have two completely different sets of clothing.

Dressing for Activity

If you were asked to divide your clothes by type, you'd probably group them according to the activity you used them for. You spend most of your time in school, so most of your clothes are school clothes. Some schools require uniforms. At others, you simply wear what you want.

You would also group together more casual clothes that you use for being with family or relaxing with friends. This group includes your old favorites.

You'd probably separate special clothes for sports, like swimsuits and jogging outfits. These clothes get extra wear because you exercise in them. Clothes for special occasions can go into another group. These would include suits, sports jackets, and dresses. If you have a part-time job, you may need special clothing for it.

Clothes and Groups

At your school, most people might wear jeans to class. But perhaps you and your friends always wear sweaters and skirts, socks and loafers. In your group, you'd feel out of place in jeans.

Belonging to a Group

Being comfortable in a group is important to nearly everyone. When you're dressed like the others in your group, they're more likely to accept you.

School teams and bands have uniforms. Clubs may have special jackets or sweaters. Students wear these special clothes as a way of showing their **identification**. *They can be recognized as belonging to that group.* Wearing a uniform carries a special responsibility. You represent a whole group—the band, team, or school. How you act will influence how other people think of the whole group.

Sometimes, clothes show *special rank within a group*, or **status**. The badges that scouts wear on their uniforms show that they have mastered certain skills.

It's difficult to know how to dress for a new group. You don't want to look out of place, but you don't know what the new group wears. You're most likely to feel at ease if you choose clothes that are moderate and sensible, not too flashy or fancy. If yours is neither the most casual nor the dressiest outfit, you'll probably be comfortable.

Respecting Others' Feelings

Today, comfort is generally the rule in clothes—as long as we don't offend other people. To avoid giving offense, people usually follow the customs of those they are with. Dressing **appropriately**, that is, *in clothes suitable for the occasion*, is important, too. Sometimes, what's appropriate isn't what's most comfortable.

For example, if your parents are taking you out to dinner at a restaurant, you'll probably wear dressier clothes. Jeans aren't really appropriate.

Wearing a uniform carries a special responsibility. People will judge a whole group by your actions. What uniforms do you wear?

Special Occasions

There are also times when dressing appropriately means dressing up. These are special occasions for which you are expected to wear a certain kind of clothing.

- *Parties.* The person who invites you may tell you what to wear. If no one says anything, ask. You can ask the host or hostess, or check on what your friends are wearing.

- *Weddings.* Members of the wedding party often wear **formal clothes**—*tuxedos for the men and long dresses for the women.* What you wear if you're a guest depends on the wedding's time and place.

- *Funerals.* At one time, black was considered the only proper color for funerals. Though this is no longer the rule everywhere, simple designs with dark or neutral colors are usually appropriate.

- *Religious services.* Some groups have strict rules about dress. If you're not sure what to wear to services or within the building, ask a member of the congregation.

- *Stores and restaurants.* Some places have definite rules about appropriate dress. Stores in many areas are forbidden by law to admit customers who are barefoot or without shirts. Restaurants require shirts and shoes. Some insist on ties and jackets.

Clothing Decisions

In the following chapters of this unit, you'll learn how to make important decisions about your clothing:

- You'll find out how to choose fashions and designs that are right for you.
- You'll learn how to plan your wardrobe.
- You'll discover how to decide what to look for when buying clothes, and which stores to shop in.
- You'll discover how you can make your own clothes and choose the materials and patterns that are best for you.
- And last, you'll find out how to care for your clothes so that they'll look and feel better longer.

Words to Remember

appropriate: suitable for the occasion

conform: be like the people around you

formal clothes: dressy clothes, such as a tuxedo or long dress

identification: being recognized as belonging to a group

individuality: the ways in which you are different from others

status: special rank within a group

Questions

1. What factors affect your decisions about what to wear?
2. How does clothing reflect your personality and appearance?
3. What are two kinds of clothing that are worn because of climate?
4. List three needs that clothing fulfills.
5. How are clothing choices influenced by a group?

Chapter 52 Design and Your Appearance

Objectives

After reading this chapter, you will be able to:

☐ *identify the main design elements in clothing,*

☐ *give examples of special effects that can be created using each element,*

☐ *describe how to use all the elements together to achieve a special look.*

Do you think that you're too tall or too short? Too thin or too heavy? That your legs are too long or not long enough? Your shoulders too broad or too narrow?

Few people are completely satisfied with the way they look. This is particularly true when they're young. As you grow to your adult height, your legs and arms suddenly may seem too long. You may become thinner or heavier than you would like to be.

Few of these changes are permanent. Growth will continue to change your build. Watching your diet and exercising will help keep your body in shape. But the results of growth, exercise, and dieting take time. In the meantime, the right choices of clothes can help you look the way you want.

Elements of Clothing Design

If you look carefully at a garment, you can pick out five elements, or properties, of clothing design: *line, proportion, color, texture,* and *print.* All five elements work together to affect the way people look at themselves and others.

Line and You

Shoulder pads change a person's shape by actually adding bulk. High heels actually add height. But a far more common way of making people appear different is by creating an **illusion**. You can use line to make *an image that fools the eye.*

Vertical lines usually have a slimming effect. Because they lead the eye up and down, the distance from side to side seems less. Vertical lines also make you seem taller.

Horizontal lines do just the opposite. They lead the eye from side to side, making the wearer seem shorter and broader. A wide belt makes a tall person seem shorter. A rugby shirt, with its wide horizontal stripes, makes a person look heavier.

Curved lines, such as the curved front of a vest, create a softer effect than either vertical or horizontal lines.

The effect of diagonal lines depends on their length and angle. For example, a short diagonal stripe from the right shoulder to the left hip leads the eye from side to side, creating the illusion of width. A longer diagonal stripe—from the shoulder to the hem of a dress, for example—leads the eye up and down for a slimming look.

Proportion and You

Proportion is *the relationship of one part to another.* Your body has proportions—the length of your upper body, for example, compared to the length of your legs. Clothes also have proportions—for example, in a suit, the length of the jacket in relation to the length of the pants or the skirt.

The parts of an outfit should be in proportion to one another. If you wore large hiking boots with a light chiffon dress, the balance would be all wrong. The boots would overpower the dress.

An outfit should also match the proportions of the person wearing it. Large plaids and big collars look better on tall people than on short people. Tiny prints are better suited to small people than to big people.

By changing the proportions of your clothes, you can change the way you look. For example, a short waist-length jacket can make your legs look longer. A long hip-length jacket could make your legs seem shorter and your upper body look longer.

You can use design elements to disguise physical flaws. Line and proportion can work together to visually change your appearance.

Color and You

Scientists and artists have studied color for many centuries and have arrived at certain basic principles. Understanding some of these principles can help you use color to your advantage.

Understanding Basic Colors

All colors are blends of the three **primary colors**—red, yellow, and blue. The three **secondary colors**—*orange, green, and violet*—are made by mixing an equal amount of two primary colors. Green is a mixture of yellow and blue, orange of yellow and red, and violet of red and blue. All other colors are blends of these six basic colors.

Many different colors are called by the same name. Green, for example, can refer to the color of pine trees or to the color of olives. These two greens are different because they combine the basic colors in different amounts. The pine trees have more blue than yellow. The olives have more yellow than blue. *The name given to each color is* called its **hue**, for example, sky blue, lemon yellow.

There are many variations of a color or hue. There are deep reds that look almost brown and light reds that lean toward pink. Some reds are very bright and others are quite dull. Each color varies from light to dark, and from bright to dull.

The color's lightness or darkness is called its **value**. Darker colors are called *shades*. Burgundy is a shade of red. Forest green is a shade of green. Shades result from adding black to a color—green and black make forest green, for instance.

Lighter colors are called *tints*. They are made by adding white to a color. Pink is a tint of red. Pale green is made by adding white to green.

The brightness or dullness of a color is its

COLOR WHEEL

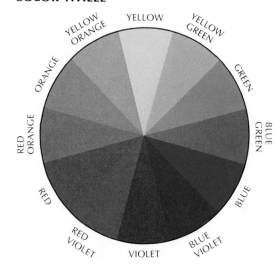

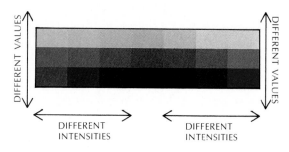

Basic Color Schemes

The color wheel consists of blends of three primary colors—red, yellow, and blue.

intensity. Hot-pink, royal purple, and lemon yellow are thought of as bright colors. Dull colors include some navies, browns, and rusts.

White, black, and gray are called *neutrals*. Gray results from combining white and **1** black. Neutrals are not included in the color **2** wheel.

Color Schemes

In putting together an outfit, you combine or arrange color schemes. Three kinds of color schemes are the most common.

A **monochromatic** color scheme uses *variations of the same color*. If you wore a pale blue sweater and dark blue slacks, your outfit would be monochromatic.

An **analogous** color scheme uses *colors that are closely related*, such as yellow, yellow-orange, and orange. If you topped your blue slacks with a blue-green sweater, your color scheme would be analogous.

Complementary color schemes *combine colors that are direct opposites*, such as red and green. Because orange is the opposite of blue, an orange sweater with blue slacks would create a very complementary color **3** scheme.

Coloring

Your own coloring is probably more complex than you think. Look at your eyes in a mirror. The irises contain flecks of several colors. Brown eyes often have a touch of hazel and blue eyes sometimes seem green.

Hair has many different shades, too. Brown hair may have a touch of red that shows up in a certain light. If you're blond, you may see some brown hairs.

Skin color also has variations. A blue tinge comes from the veins that lie beneath the surface. Redness is caused by the capillaries that bring blood to your skin. The amount of *melanin*, a pigment found in hair and skin, determines whether your skin color is pale or dark.

Study your skin, eyes, and hair coloring to determine what color best suits you. What color of clothing do you recommend that each of these teens wear?

FEATURE

Design Illusions

The best way to learn how to use design elements is to see the different effects that are produced. Look at the pairs of illustrations below. What are the differences in the two garments?

PRINT

LINE

TEXTURE

COLOR

PROPORTION

Prints and You

Prints can be simple stripes or complex arrangements of lines and figures. But whether they are dots, stripes, plaids, or other patterns, prints can have interesting effects on your appearance.

Since prints are combinations of colors, the guidelines for using color apply to prints. A red plaid jacket attracts attention, just as a bright red jacket does. But prints also allow you to wear colors that might not suit you as solids.

The lines of a garment and the print must work well together. A curved seam in a skirt loses its softening effect if the print is a horizontal stripe. Some lines that work well in solid colors get lost in printed fabric.

Prints can make you appear bigger or smaller than your actual size. A shirt with a large, bold print would make you look bigger than one with a small, delicate pattern.

Prints can also emphasize certain features. A border print on a dress calls attention to your legs. A print collar on a solid-color shirt makes people notice your face.

Texture and You

Texture is *the way a material looks and feels.* Satin is smooth and slippery, tweeds are thick and nubby. You can sink your fingers into fur, and you can see through voiles.

Like color, texture can make you look slightly heavier or slimmer. A bulky fabric would make you look heavier than a smoother fabric would. A smooth polyester shirt would make you look slimmer than a heavier velour would.

Your personality, your mood, and the oc-casion may also influence your choices. Some textures are traditionally more casual, like tweeds and corduroys. Others, like velvet and satin, are usually more dressy. But there are no hard rules. For example, tweeds can be used in a long dressy skirt. A sheer fabric can be part of a casual shirt.

The Whole Effect

The line, proportion, and print of clothing—together with color and texture—affect your appearance. Knowing how these elements, or properties, work together can help you find clothes that are best for you.

Design is a complicated matter. However, you learn more about it each time you study a garment. And the best way of finding out if a style suits you is to try it on.

Words to Remember

analogous: closely related colors

complementary: colors that are direct opposites

highlight: emphasize

hue: the name given to each color

illusion: an image that fools the eye

intensity: the brightness or dullness of a color

monochromatic: an outfit using variations of the same color

primary colors: red, yellow, and blue

proportion: the relationship of one part to another

secondary colors: orange, green, and violet

texture: the way a material looks and feels

value: the lightness or darkness of a color

Questions

1. What are the five elements of clothing design?
2. How do horizontal lines and vertical lines affect your appearance?
3. What is proportion? Why should you consider it when you choose a garment?
4. What features of your appearance should you think about when choosing colors?
5. How can you use texture to achieve a different look?

Chapter 53 Clothes and Fashion

Objectives

After reading this chapter, you will be able to:

☐ *explain why fashions change from year to year,*

☐ *describe several ways in which new fashions get started,*

☐ *explain the difference between a fashion and a fad, and what this difference can mean to you.*

A **fashion** is *a style of clothing that is accepted in a society at a given time.* At any one time, certain lines, proportions, colors, textures and prints are favored above others. Fashion sets broad guidelines that help you decide which clothes you want to own at this time in your life.

But fashion is more than just a style of clothing—it has created a whole industry. Hundreds of millions of dollars are spent by this industry on advertising to try to get people to buy clothing. Much of this advertising is aimed at teenagers like you.

It's important not to let fashion tell you exactly what you should wear. What you need and want from your clothes is just as important as what is fashionable. Your tastes, your need to express yourself, your life-style, and your need to feel comfortable should determine what clothes you choose to buy or make.

What Makes Fashions Change

Fashions can change quickly. A style suddenly becomes popular, and everyone seems to be wearing it. Skirt lengths go up or down; pant legs get wider or narrower; sleeves are puffy or smooth. Then, as suddenly as it appeared, that fashion is gone. The same thing happens with accessories. One year neck chains are in. The next year everyone is wearing fancy belts.

Changes in People

Perhaps the main reason why fashions change is that people get bored with their clothes after a while. They want to dress a little differently from the way they dressed two or three years ago.

People also want to say something special about themselves through the clothes they wear. By choosing clothes that are a bit different than those your brothers and sisters wear, you tell the world that you're an individual.

But most people don't like to be completely different. They like to choose clothes that are popular with a certain group—a group that's important to them.

Changes in the World

Many changes have occurred in the way we live. People are much less formal now, and there is more emphasis on comfort. Fashions change to reflect these changes. Clothes have become more suitable for the more active lives we now lead.

Some new fashions result from changes in **technology**—*the methods used to make products.* New fabrics make different designs possible. Once, garments that called for silky materials could only be bought by the rich. Now, such clothes are made in fabrics that are inexpensive to buy and easy to keep clean.

How Do Fashions Start?

The Garment Industry

Clothing fashions are greatly influenced by the **garment industry**. This term refers to *the many different companies involved in producing clothing.* These companies constantly create new designs. Their **designers** are *the people who create new styles.* Designers get their ideas from many sources—history

Some clothing fashions die out as quickly as they begin. Others last for a long time. Think of fashions that have lasted.

and current events; books, movies, and television; travel and the styles of other countries. And they also create new styles of their own.

High fashion—*the expensive clothing created by world-famous designers*—gets wide attention through pictures and ads in fashion magazines. In the past, few people could afford high-fashion clothes, which were completely hand-sewn. And at one time, these very expensive clothes were made mostly in France, which was then the center of the fashion world.

Today, both these things have changed. Many famous designers are now creating clothes that are reasonably priced. These clothes are sold in many stores. As a result, millions of people can now wear designer clothes. And the influence of the Paris fashion market is not as strong as it used to be. Many other fashion centers, including London, Milan, Tokyo, New York, Los Angeles, and Dallas, produce original clothes.

Personalities and the Media

Fashion is influenced by famous people. What celebrities, performers, politicians, and athletes wear is noticed by millions of people. Before you know it, people are wearing the same thing or a copy of it.

Other fashions become popular because they're seen on a popular television show or in a hit movie. People and events in the news also start fashions. New kinds of clothing—a Chinese-style coat, for example, or a Moroccan caftan—may become popular when people who wear them are in the news.

Street Fashions

Street fashions are *started by ordinary people who wear familiar clothing in a new way.* Blue jeans, work overalls, jogging suits, lumber jackets, and cowboy hats and boots all started out as practical clothes. When they began to be used by people for everyday wear, they became street fashions.

These fashions start when a few people try out a new idea. Soon, everyone around them is trying the same thing. Often, no one knows who created the fashion.

Consumer Demand

When there is a need for a different type of clothing, manufacturers start producing it. The new need may come from almost

Designer clothing is no longer a luxury sold to a select few. Today, many people wear affordable designer clothes.

FEATURE

Status Symbols in Clothes

One pair of blue jeans is just like another—or so you might think. But to some people, it's very important to have jeans with a certain designer's label or logo.

Designer labels have become popular in recent years mostly because they are status symbols. They tell the world that the wearer is in style. But designer labels aren't the only status symbols on clothes. Some people buy knitted shirts with a certain symbol, or running shoes that have a certain stripe. Often, these special clothes cost much more than similar items without the logo, symbol, or stripe.

Some designer's names and logos even appear on other items besides clothing, such as luggage, eyeglasses, pens, bedsheets, and chocolates. In most cases, these items aren't made by the same companies that make the clothes.

The designer simply approves the final design and gives the maker permission to use his or her name for a fee.

Famous labels and symbols may mean that clothes are particularly well made or well designed. Some designers did earn their reputations for well-made clothing. But this is not always true. And when a certain designer's clothes become popular, they might be copied in cheaper fabrics or with poorer construction methods. Some companies copy everything, even the label. Of course, this is illegal.

While high-status clothes may cost more, they aren't always the best buy. When you shop for any clothes, think about how they're made, how they look on you, and how long you'll wear them. Designer items that may go out of style or wear out quickly aren't good buys at any time.

anywhere. In recent years, for example, the world's decreasing energy supply changed how people dressed in two ways.

First, it lowered the demand for fibers made from petroleum. In the 1970s, when the price of oil rose sharply, these fibers became more expensive. Natural fibers like cotton and wool became popular again.

Second, the high cost of energy led people to wear more clothing in cold weather. People turned down their heat in winter to save energy. They began wearing sweaters and warmer socks to stay comfortable. The layered look became popular.

Fashions and Fads

What Are Fads?

Some styles are called **classics**—they stay *popular for a long time*. Classics were probably worn by your parents—and even by your grandparents. They may be part of your wardrobe, too. A windbreaker, a blazer, a pullover sweater—these styles have been around for decades.

Other styles are fashionable for short periods and then suddenly lose their appeal.

These *fashions that are very popular but go out of style quickly* are called **fads**. The platform shoe of the 1970s was a fad.

Other styles seem to go through **fashion cycles**—*periods when they are in and out of fashion.* Short skirts, for example, were popular in the 1920s and in the 1960s. They came back in style again in the 1980s.

Building Judgment

It takes experience to be able to tell what kinds of clothes will stay popular. The way to get this experience is to watch fads and fashions over the years and see which ones disappear. In time, this experience will help you make good clothing choices.

A Consumer Strategy

Though some fad items are not expensive, others cost a lot of money. In that case, a fad may be a very poor buy. On the other hand, if you buy only classics, your wardrobe may seem dull.

A good compromise is to buy classics for more expensive clothes, but to get some less costly fad items. T-shirts are examples of inexpensive fad clothes that can keep your wardrobe up-to-date at little cost. You can also follow fads when buying **accessories**. *These are smaller items that are not part of a basic outfit.* Belts, scarves, and jewelry can perk up your clothes for a reasonable amount of money. You can look up-to-date without spending too much.

Words to Remember

accessory: smaller items that are not part of a basic outfit

classic: a style that stays popular for a long time

designer: a person who creates new styles of clothing

fad: a fashion that is very popular but goes out of style quickly

fashion: a style of clothing that is accepted in a society at a given time

fashion cycle: a period when certain styles go in and out of fashion

garment industry: the many businesses involved in producing clothing

high fashion: the expensive clothing created by world-famous designers

street fashion: a fashion started by ordinary people

technology: the methods used to make products

Questions

1. What are two factors that make fashions change?
2. Why would clothing manufacturers encourage fashions to change?
3. Describe two current fashions. Can you tell how these trends started?
4. What is the difference between a fad and a classic?
5. How can knowing about fashion help you make decisions about clothing?

Chapter 54 Fibers and Fabrics

Objectives

After reading this chapter, you will be able to:

- *describe characteristics of natural, synthetic, and blended fibers,*
- *describe characteristics of woven, knitted, and non-woven fabrics,*
- *describe how care is affected by dyes and finishes,*
- *explain the significance of care labels.*

Have you ever bought a piece of clothing that looked great in the store, but turned out to be a big disappointment? Have you spent time on a sewing project only to give it away or throw it out a few weeks later because it shrank after you washed it?

There are many things to know about clothing, aside from what looks good on the hanger. You need to know what kind of fabric it is made of. That can influence how you care for it and how it looks after you've worn it awhile.

Knowing a little bit about fabric can help you:

- get better buys,
- look and feel better in your clothing,
- get more satisfaction from the things you make.

Fibers and Yarns

Fibers are the basic ingredients of all fabrics. They are *the tiny strands that make up yarns.* Fibers can be natural or synthetic.

Most fabrics are made from fibers that have been spun together into yarns. Others, such as felt, are made by shrinking and pressing fibers together until they are tightly tangled in a mat.

TABLE 1 **Characteristics of Common Natural Fibers**

Fiber	Characteristics
Cotton	soft, comfortable, absorbent strong even when wet takes finishes well wrinkles & shrinks unless treated easily laundered
Wool	warm, retains body heat resists wrinkles naturally water repellent can shrink with heat and moisture can be damaged by moths usually drycleaned; sometimes washable
Silk	natural luster soft, flexible, but strong can be damaged by perspiration usually drycleaned; sometimes washable
Linen	cool, absorbent strong, but stiff wrinkles & shrinks unless treated easily laundered

Natural Fibers

Natural fibers are *made from plants or from the hair of animals.*

- *Cotton* is the most common plant fiber. It comes from the seed pod of the cotton plant.
- *Linen* is another fairly common plant fiber. It comes from the stalk of the flax plant.
- *Wool* is made from the hair of sheep. Other animals, like camels, alpacas, goats, and rabbits, provide hair that is also used for wool.
- *Silk* is made by an insect called the silkworm. The fibers come from a cocoon that the worm spins around itself.

Each natural fiber has its own special characteristics. But they all tend to absorb moisture and to allow air to reach your skin, so that you stay comfortable. They keep you warm in winter and cool in summer. However, they usually require special kinds of care.

Synthetic Fibers

Until the end of the last century, all fabrics were made from natural fibers. But today, many fabrics are made from **synthetic** fibers. These are *fibers formed all or in part by chemicals.*

The first entirely synthetic fibers were produced shortly before World War II. These fibers were made of petroleum and other chemicals.

Many synthetic fibers were made to replace or copy natural fibers. Nylon was made to look like silk. Vinyl is a substitute for leather. An advantage of synthetic fibers is that they are easy to care for.

TABLE 2 **Characteristics of Common Synthetic Fibers**

Fiber	Characteristics
Acetate	attractive silk-like look holds shape well may wrinkle and fade usually drycleaned
Acrylic	does not cause allergy lightweight yet warm blends with many other fibers for added bulk resists wrinkles never use a hot iron drycleaned or laundered
Nylon	blends with other fibers for added strength holds shape well doesn't absorb moisture washable, dries quickly
Polyester	resists wrinkles blends with other fibers for wrinkle resistance holds oily stains washable, dries quickly
Rayon	absorbs moisture weak when wet may wrinkle or shrink unless treated usually drycleaned, sometimes washable
Spandex	excellent stretch and recovery combines with other fibers for stretchability washable, avoid chlorine bleach
Triacetate	can be permanently pleated resists wrinkles washable

Yarns

For thousands of years, *fibers have been overlapped and twisted together* to form **yarn**.

Long, straight fibers usually create smooth, silky strands. Short, curly fibers tend to make softer and fluffier strands. The thickness of the yarn also depends on how tightly the fibers are spun.

A **blend** is *a yarn made from two or more different fibers.* The blend can be made of natural fibers (cotton and linen), synthetic fibers (rayon and acetate), or natural and synthetic fibers (cotton and polyester). Blends combine the best characteristics of the fibers from which they are made.

Some of the shirts you buy probably are blends. The label might say "60 percent polyester and 40 percent cotton." This means the shirt will have the good looks and comfort of cotton. But the polyester will make the shirt more wrinkle-free.

Fabrics

Fabric, also called *material*, or *cloth*, is what your clothes are made from. Most fabrics are made by *weaving or knitting yarns or by matting fibers together.*

Woven Fabrics

You may have seen people weave yarn by hand on looms. **Weaving** is *the interlacing of strands of yarn to form fabric.* One set of yarn—called the **warp**—is *lined up in lengthwise rows on a loom.* Another set of yarn—called the **weft**, or **filling**—*is passed over and under these rows in a crosswise direction.*

There are three basic types of weaves.

- *Plain.* Each weft yarn passes over and under each warp yarn.
- *Twill.* Each weft yarn passes over at least two, but not more than four, warp yarns. This action produces a diagonal line in the fabric.
- *Satin.* Each weft yarn passes over four or more warp yarns.

Fabrics are woven on industrial looms that can produce many different weaves. Each type of weave produces a different fabric. The weave determines whether the fabric will be soft or crisp, cool or warm. Woven fabrics hold their shape and are stronger than knits.

TYPES OF FABRIC WEAVES

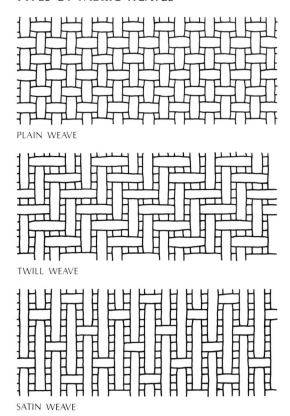

PLAIN WEAVE

TWILL WEAVE

SATIN WEAVE

Plain weave is a simple weave. Twill weave, used for denims, is noted for its strength. Satin weave produces a fabric with shine.

Knit Fabrics

Knitting is another way of turning yarn into fabrics. **Knits** are *fabrics made by looping strands of yarn together row after row, with special needles.* Unlike weaving, knitting can be done with a single strand of yarn, just as people do by hand with knitting needles.

Most knitting is done by machine. Many kinds of clothing, from sport shirts and dresses to T-shirts and stockings, are knitted. Knits are comfortable because they can stretch with movement and return to their original shape. They don't wrinkle easily. Although knits do not fray or ravel, some may run if snagged.

Non-woven Fabrics

Non-woven fabrics usually are made from matted fibers. They all share one special quality—their edges do not fray or ravel when cut. That means they need no special finishing.

Many non-woven fabrics are used on the inside of garments. They may give needed shape to a collar, or firmness to a belt.

Some non-woven fabrics are made so that they will melt when heat is applied to them. These *fusible webs*, as they are called, are used to attach one layer of fabric to another. Fusibles can be used to hold up a hem or to attach decorations and facings to a project.

F E A T U R E

A Fabric Dictionary

Yarns can be woven or knitted into a variety of different fabrics, each with a special look and feel. Here are a few common fabrics.

brocade: a patterned weave that allows for elaborate designs; used for evening dresses and upholstery.

burlap: a coarse, heavy woven fabric made of *jute,* an Asian plant; used for shoes and bags.

calico: a plain weave with a smooth surface and small, colorful prints; used for sportswear.

canvas: a heavy, strong, plain weave; used for sportswear.

chiffon: sheer, light, woven fabric; used for dressy clothes or scarves.

chino: a medium-weight slightly twill fabric; used for pants, uniforms, and some jackets.

corduroy: a weave with rows of cut pile; used for sportswear.

denim: a twill weave with a colored warp and a white weft; used for jeans, and some jackets.

double knit: a knit produced by two sets of needles working two strands of yarn at the same time; used for pants and jackets.

felt: a nonwoven fabric created by matting short fibers with moisture, heat, and pressure; used for facings.

flannel: a weave that is brushed to produce a soft surface; used for shirts and sleepwear.

gabardine: a strong, medium- to heavy-weight twill weave; used for pants.

gingham: a plain weave with a pattern made from dyed yarns; used for curtains and dresses.

jersey: a smooth, lightweight knit used for dresses, shirts, sportswear, and underwear.

lace: a decorative fabric with an open design; used for fancy dresses and trim

oxford cloth: a plain weave with a colored warp and a white weft; used for shirts.

percale: a plain weave with a smooth finish; used for sheets and clothing

satin: a smooth, shiny fabric produced by one of the basic weaves; used for dressy clothes.

seersucker: a woven fabric with a puckered stripe; used for summer suits and sportswear.

taffeta: a crisp, plain weave with a shiny surface that rustles when it moves; used for blouses, dresses, and bows.

terry cloth: a weave or knit with a looped surface that gives a coarse texture; used for towels, bathrobes, and beachwear.

tweed: a weave with colored flecks of yarn on a somewhat hairy surface, usually including at least some wool; used for skirts and suits.

velour: a knit or weave with a thick pile surface; used for sportswear and casualwear.

velvet and velveteen: weaves with a short, close pile; used for jackets and dressy clothes.

Dyes and Finishes

Dyeing is *using a substance to change the natural color of a fiber, yarn, or fabric.* Dyeing can be done at any stage of making fabric. Synthetics can be dyed before the fibers are made, yarns can be dyed, or an entire finished fabric can be soaked in a dye bath. This last method is widely used today. Designs can then be printed on the fabric

Finishes are *substances added to fabric that change the way it looks and feels.*

Some finishes affect how the fabric is used, how it will wear, or what care it requires. Cotton could be preshrunk, for instance. A fabric meant for use in a coat or an all-weather bag could be finished for water resistance. Other finishes provide wrinkle, moth, and fire proofing.

Some other finishes are used to make the fabrics look or feel more appealing. In *napping*, the fabric is brushed to raise the fiber ends. The result is a smooth, soft look. Some finishes make a fabric shinier or crisper.

Care Labels

It's important to know how to care for fabric to keep it looking its best. Laws require fabric and clothing manufacturers to provide labels that tell what the material is made of and how to care for it. These labels should be on clothes you buy. Chapter 62 will describe how to care for fabrics.

Words to Remember

blend: a yarn made from two or more different fibers

dyeing: using a substance to change the color of a fiber, yarn, or fabric

fabric: material made by weaving or knitting yarns or by matting fibers together

fibers: the tiny strands that make up yarns

finishes: substances added to fabric that change the way it looks.

knits: fabrics made by looping strands of yarn together row after row, with special needles

natural fibers: fibers that are made from plants or from the hair of animals

synthetic fiber: fibers formed all or in part by chemicals

warp: yarns lined up in lengthwise rows on a loom

weaves: fabrics formed by interlacing strands of yarn

weft: yarns passed over and under the warp in a crosswise direction; also called *filling*

yarn: the twisted-together fibers that form woven and knitted fabrics

Questions

1. What are fibers? What is the difference between natural and synthetic fibers?
2. What is the advantage of a blend?
3. How is yarn related to fibers?
4. How are fabrics (a) woven, (b) knitted?
5. How is dyeing done?
6. Name three reasons for finishing fabric.
7. Explain the importance of care labels.

Chapter 55 Planning Your Wardrobe

Objectives

After reading this chapter, you will be able to:

□ *take an inventory of your clothes, and see how well they meet your clothing needs,*

□ *use the principle of mixing and matching,*

□ *develop a plan for adding to your wardrobe,*

□ *evaluate different ways of adding to your wardrobe.*

Having suitable clothes for all the different occasions and activities in your life can be expensive. One way to get the most out of your clothes is to plan your **wardrobe—** *the clothes that you own.*

In planning, you have many things to consider. You're growing fast, so you need clothes that allow for growth. Your moods change. Sometimes you want bright colors; other times you want duller ones. You need different clothes for different activities— but you can save by owning clothes that can be used in more than one way.

Finally, you must consider the amount of money you can spend. By looking at the clothes that you have and figuring out what clothes you need, you can use your money wisely. The result will be a more useful wardrobe.

What Are Your Needs?

The way to find what clothes you need is to look at what clothes you have.

What Do You Have?

Go through your closet and drawers and divide your clothes into three groups:

- clothes in good condition that you like to wear.
- clothes that you like but which need to be fixed.
- clothes that you don't wear because you've outgrown them or you don't like them.

It will help if you list the clothes in each group. Remember to include any items in the wash or at the cleaners.

Start by looking at the clothes in the *first group*. What are the characteristics of the clothes you like? Is it the color or texture? Their style or cut? Or do you like how versatile they are—how many different ways you can use them? If you discover why you like some clothes, you'll have a better idea of how to look at your other clothes.

Now take a close look at the garments in the *second group*. By removing a stain or mending a torn knee, you can make these clothes ready to wear again. Is your favorite shirt at the back of your closet because it needs a button? Spend a few minutes to fix it and bring it back into your active wardrobe.

Types of Clothes

A good way to figure out what clothes you need is to divide clothes by what you use them for. There are probably five groups of clothes:

- school clothes,
- casual clothes,
- dressy clothes for special occasions,
- work clothes for a part-time job or for around the house,
- specialty clothes like uniforms or sports outfits.

Look at the list of clothes that you like. Which outfits can you wear for these different types of uses? Remember that many items can be worn in more than one way. A football jersey is a specialty item that can also be combined with a pair of jeans for a casual outfit. The same is true for a leotard—wear it for dance class or combine it with a skirt and blouse for a layered look.

Versatility is your aim. The more uses you get out of your clothes, the more you get for your money. A shirt that can be worn in three different combinations is very handy.

Special Clothes

You have special activities to think about. Do you need special clothing for a favorite sport or for dance lessons? How about parties or religious activities? Outfits for these special events are part of a well-planned wardrobe.

It may help to list your usual activities, and then to write down what clothes you need for them. For instance, you would want a swimsuit for swimming and good winter boots if you shovel snow. Think about future needs, too. Do you have a dressy outfit for your brother's wedding? Could you wear the same clothes you used for the dance in April?

Creative Combining

You'll probably see a few outfits right away—those are the ones you wear often. But if you take a new look at your clothes, you'll find that you have even more possibilities.

Sometimes, different combinations of clothes won't occur to you because you're used to wearing certain pieces together as an outfit—and with nothing else. Mix and match your clothes. That brown sweater will go with your blue pants as well as with the brown ones. If you have a two-piece outfit, try wearing the top with different bottoms and the bottom with different tops. You'll be surprised at how many different outfits you can create this way.

Think of the variety of ways that clothes can be combined. A shirt can be worn by itself, under a sweater, or as a jacket over something else. That's one shirt, and three

entirely different looks! Combine a dressy item, like a silky shirt, with a more casual one, like tweed pants. You'll get more use out of those dressy things you don't wear much, as well as show a very interesting new look.

Experiment with your accessories, too. They can change the style of an outfit. Cowboy boots make dressy slacks look more casual. Adding scarves, belts, ties, and vests changes the look of an outfit. Browse through magazines for more ideas on how to make your clothes go further.

Adding to Your Wardrobe

Now you've looked at your wardrobe to see what you have and what you need. Do you need to make any additions?

MIXING AND MATCHING

A shirt can be worn in several different ways.

What Do You Need?

As you looked at the clothes you own, you probably realized that a few items were missing. Maybe you need a new shirt to go with your suit. Perhaps your old red sweater needs to be replaced. You might have realized that getting a bright red belt could add color to two or three outfits.

You also identified some clothes you need when you thought about special activities. Parties, vacations, sports you plan to play—all these special events may require you to add to your wardrobe.

Changes in seasons may require new clothes, too. Have you outgrown last year's winter boots? Are you too big for your old bathing suit?

Deciding on Additions

Before adding new clothing, you need to answer a few questions:

- What do you really need?
- Will you be able to wear the new item for different occasions?
- Will you be able to wear the new item with other clothes in your current wardrobe?
- Can you create a new look just by adding accessories?

If you're going to be matching new clothes to old clothes to make an outfit, you should think about what colors and textures will match well.

Although there's nothing to stop you from wearing any color with any other one, some combinations look much better than others. And, of course, you have your own likes and dislikes.

So, when planning new additions to your wardrobe, think carefully about what colors the items should be. For example, you probably won't want a black top for your navy pants—that combination isn't too exciting. It would be more interesting to add a color such as light blue or red.

Fabric and texture combinations need to be planned, too. Some textures don't look good together. You may want to try to match a fabric you already have, or to find one that contrasts with it.

When you shop for the new addition, try to take along the article of clothing you plan to wear it with. That way you can be sure

This simple, but well-cut dress can be worn for many different occasions. It will be fashionable for years. Can you tell why?

F E A T U R E

Figuring Cost Per Wearing

The more times you wear a garment, the more value you'll get from the dollars spent on it. One way of finding that value is to compute the **cost per wearing.** This figure is *the total of the purchase price and the cost of cleaning the garment divided by the number of times you wear it.* Let's see if two pieces of clothing that cost that same amount would necessarily be worth the same to you.

Suppose that you buy a very dressy sweater and a pair of slacks. The sweater, which was expensive, had been marked down to $24.99. The slacks cost $25.00.

Throughout the year, you wear the pants 39 times. You wear the sweater only 5 times. The next year you wear the pants another 25 times, until they become too short and a little too tight. The sweater still fits, and you wear it 5 more times that year.

You have the sweater dry-cleaned three times in two years, for a total of $8.25. The pants are washable, so their cleaning cost is only a fraction of the cost of your family's wash—perhaps 50 cents per year.

Figure the cost per wearing for each garment over the two years. First, add the purchase price and the cleaning cost. Then divide by the number of wearings.

Sweater: $24.99 + $8.25 = $33.24
$$\div 10 = \$3.32$$
Slacks: 25.00 + 1.00 = $26.00
$$\div 64 = \$0.41$$

The cost per wearing of the sweater is eight times that of the pants.

---

that your new clothes will go well with what you already have.

Of course, before you make any additions to your wardrobe, you should think again about what you like about some clothes that you already own. Figuring out the colors, textures, and styles that appeal to you will help you choose additions that you'll be happy with.

Making the Additions

You can make additions to your wardrobe in three ways: you can *buy* them, *sew* them, or *recycle* them.

Buying Additions. You can buy ready-to-wear clothes from a store or a catalog. There are a great variety of colors, fabrics, and styles to choose from. By buying the clothes, you are able to have something to wear with little work. Chapter 56 has information on how to shop for clothing.

Sewing Additions. You can choose to make your clothes. Being able to sew frees you to make a garment that's exactly what you want. You have a great range of pattern styles, colors, and fabrics. When you gain experience, you might even design your own clothes!

Sewing has another benefit. It allows you

to make minor changes in store-bought clothes. You can even take advantage of bargains by fixing up secondhand clothes or discounted items. Chapters 58 to 61 introduce you to the basics of sewing.

Recycling. Finally, you can put the clothes that you no longer wear to use. Go back to your wardrobe list. Look at those items you've outgrown or don't like. Could you lengthen the hem to make those pants wearable again? Would a new color make that sweater more appealing? Chapter 63 has more ideas on how to turn old clothes into new.

A Long-Term Plan

Planning your wardrobe gives you the exciting chance to think about how you want to look and make decisions to get that look. It helps you get the most out of your clothes. And it's as simple as these steps:

1. Divide the clothing you have into three groups—those you wear, those you can fix to wear again, and those you can't wear.

2. List all your activities to see what clothes you need.

3. See how many clothes you already have that can meet those needs. Remember that clothes can be versatile, and that you can mix and match and use accessories to make new combinations.

4. Make a wardrobe plan of items you want to add to your wardrobe. Decide whether to add those items by buying, sewing, or recycling.

The results of this planning will be closets and drawers that hold clothes that you like and that you wear. You won't be stuck thinking of what to wear because the only outfit you like is in the wash. You'll have more favorites to choose from!

Words to Remember

cost per wearing: the total of the purchase price of a garment and the cost of cleaning it divided by the number of times you wear it

wardrobe: the clothes that you own

Questions

1. Why should you look at your current wardrobe before deciding what to add to it?

2. What are two ways that you can combine clothes to make new outfits?

3. If you are growing quickly, should you plan to make expensive additions to your wardrobe? Why or why not?

4. What is the advantage of buying ready-to-wear clothing?

5. What are two advantages of being able to sew your own clothing?

56 Shopping for Clothes

Objectives

After reading this chapter, you will be able to:

☐ list the steps needed to prepare for a clothes shopping trip,

☐ identify the different types of stores where clothing can be bought,

☐ describe how to check clothes for quality and ease of care,

☐ explain how to make sure that a garment is a good fit.

Have you ever bought a skirt that you felt you couldn't "live without," only to have it pushed to the back of your closet in a short time? Have you ever bought a sweater at one store—only to see it three days later at another store for less money? Have you ever bought a pair of slacks in "your size" that just didn't fit? And what about the brand new shirt that came apart at the seam and frayed when it was washed?

We can all answer "yes" to at least some of these questions. Buying wearable clothes takes skill. The more you know about clothes:

■ what you want,

■ where to buy,

■ how to find your size,

■ how clothes are made,

the more success you'll have in shopping and finding the right garment for you.

Getting Ready to Shop

First, if you've already made a wardrobe plan (see chapter 55), review it carefully. If you haven't made one yet, do it now. (If you're planning to make the outfit, chapter 57 discusses how to shop for a pattern and fabric.)

Now, write out exactly what you've decided you need. Next to each item, write what you plan to wear it with, possible colors and fabrics, and the size needed. To be even better prepared, bring your measurements.

Wear or bring along the clothes you plan to wear with what you want to buy. If you want to match a color or fabric and can't bring the whole garment along, take samples—the belt, perhaps, or a tiny piece of fabric cut from the inside.

If you plan to wear a particular pair of shoes with your new purchase, wear them or carry them along.

You're almost ready to go, but there are still decisions to be made, both before you leave and while you are shopping. First, you must decide where to shop (see the next section for ideas). Second, you must decide how much you can afford to spend. Don't take more with you than you've budgeted—you may be tempted to buy things that you don't really need.

Department stores feature men's, women's, boys', and girls' departments. Specialty stores often sell one kind of product.

Clothing Stores

Where you buy your clothes will determine the selection you'll find, the prices you'll pay, and the quality you'll select.

■ *Department stores* have several departments offering many styles and sizes for both men and women. They also sell accessories and sewing materials and equipment. They offer a variety of services, such as gift wrapping and free delivery. They may have slightly higher prices than some other stores.

■ *Specialty shops* sell only one type of clothing, such as sportswear, women's clothes, or shoes. A specialty shop may carry labels that the department stores don't stock. Prices may be higher than at a department store. Some of these stores offer extra services, such as making special orders.

Shoplifting: Something for Nothing?

Is shoplifting really a way of getting something for nothing? Hardly.

Everyone pays the costs of shoplifting. Aside from the losses—about $8 billion every year—retailers have to pay the price of more security and of punishing shoplifters who are caught. According to one survey, $406 million was spent on security in a recent year. This includes paying for close-circuit television that watches the selling floors, electronic tags that hang from many items, and salaries for security workers.

These costs are passed on to the customer in the form of higher prices. From 2 to 9 percent of the prices we pay are the result of these expenses.

Shoplifters pay, too. More and more shoplifters are arrested and prosecuted.

Though some sources say that shoplifting has leveled off, the FBI says that the crime is increasing by 20 percent a year. A large number of amateur shoplifters are teens. And an amateur shoplifter has a greater chance of being caught by the new security steps being installed.

What do you think? Is shoplifting a serious crime? Should people be arrested and punished for shoplifting? Why do you think that stores are spending so much on the prevention of shoplifting?

Take an informal survey in your class. What are some of the reasons people shoplift? What are some other ways shoplifters—especially teens—might be stopped?

- *Discount stores* sell clothing and other items at lower prices than department stores do. Discount stores don't always carry the same merchandise as department stores. So don't expect to find the *same* item for less. Of course, a *similar* item may be exactly what you're looking for. Discount stores have fewer services than department stores.
- *Factory outlets* are run by a manufacturer. Their selection includes both high-quality clothing and clothing that is flawed or not perfect. These are labeled *seconds* or *irregulars*. If the flaws aren't serious, the item may be worth buying.
- *Thrift shops* sell second-hand clothing.

Some of the clothing is like new; other styles are from long ago.
- *Mail-order catalogs* are very convenient if you're sure of your size. Often, catalogs explain how to figure your size. You'll have to wait for your order to be delivered, so mail order isn't a good choice for items you need right away. Prices vary. It's a good idea to compare catalog prices with those in nearby stores.

Using the Sales

Sales can be important to anyone buying clothes. But stores hope that you'll buy their regularly priced items at the same time. Remember—no item is worth buying if you won't wear it. Here are traditional kinds of clothing sales:

- An **end-of-season sale** is *held to clear out merchandise to make room for the upcoming season*. Winter coats, sweaters, and ski clothes go on sale in February; bathing suits in July and August.

- Annual sales, such as those on Columbus Day or Washington's Birthday, are aimed to bring in business on a day when more customers can shop.

- Markdowns—or reduced items—are almost always available. These are clothes that, for some reason, didn't sell. The longer an item remains in the store, the more it is marked down.

Know Your Size

Knowing what size you wear first involves knowing which **range**, or *size category*, you fit into. If you shop in the right range, you'll get a better fit. For growing teens, there are several ranges of sizes.

Size Ranges

Female Sizes. Girls can choose from three size ranges. *Girls* clothes may still fit in some styles. The *juniors* range is cut smaller in the waist and larger in the hips and bust than girls. Skirts and pants are usually longer to allow for more height. The *misses* range offers clothes cut slightly larger than those in juniors.

Male Sizes. For boys' clothing, size

ranges are *boys* and *men*. It's possible to grow from the boys range to the men's in just one year, so it's a good idea to keep checking the two ranges for fit.

Special Sizes. Some manufacturers make special sizes in *petite*, *slim*, and *tall* for girls; *slim* and *husky* for boys; and *tall* and *short* for men. And some big department stores have sections showing *preteen*, *teen*, and *college* fashions. You may find more clothes in your size in those departments.

Finding Your Size

Sizes in ready-to-wear clothing are based on the measurements of typical bodies. But no one is typical, so finding the right size can be difficult. Unless you're familiar with a particular label or brand name, never buy clothing without trying it on.

Some blouses and sweaters are sold according to bust size. They're labeled 32 or 34, for example.

Boys' and men's pants are sold by waist and **in-seam measurement**—*the length of the pants leg from the bottom to where the two legs meet*.

If clothing is marked *small*, *medium*, or *large*, give the salesperson your measurements. He or she will tell you which sizes they correspond to.

If you're having trouble choosing between two sizes, it's smart to buy the larger one. Since you're probably still growing, you'll be able to wear the item longer.

You can also allow for growth by looking for skirts and pants with wide hems. You'll be able to let them down later to lengthen the garment. Elasticized waists that leave room for expansion are good ideas, too.

Know Your Garments

Checking the Fabric

Grain. First, check the *grain*. That's the direction the yarns—or strands of fiber—run in the fabric. The lengthwise (vertical) grain should be at right angles to the hem. The crosswise (horizontal) grain should be parallel to the hem. If this isn't the case, the fabric will stretch, lose its shape, or hang poorly. One exception is fabric cut on an angle to allow stretch.

Wrinkling. Take the pinch test. Grab a handful of fabric and hold it tightly for a few seconds. When you let go, does the fabric remain wrinkled? If it smooths out easily, wrinkles will probably smooth out when you're wearing the garment.

Pattern. If the garment is in a plaid or a print, check that the pattern runs in the same direction in all pieces. It should also match at the seams.

Thickness. Hold the garment up to the light. If patches of light come through the cloth unevenly, it will probably wear unevenly. The fabric thickness should be consistent.

Care Information. Look at the labels. Fiber content and care information are required by law. Make sure that the clothes you wear often are made of easy-care fabrics.

Checking the Construction

Seams. First, check the **seams**. They're *the lines of stitching that join the pieces of the garment together*. Make sure that they're straight and smooth with no puckering. The stitches should be secure so the seams won't come apart.

Facings. Next, check the inside of the garment. If the fabric is one that ravels, are the seams finished? Look at the **facings**—*the extra pieces of fabric that finish the edge of a garment*, such as a neckline or armhole. Facings should lie flat and be anchored so that they won't slip out of place.

Hems. Next, look at the **hems**. This is *the bottom edge of fabric turned up and sewn to the wrong side of the garment*. It should have no puckers or wrinkles and no stitches showing on the outside.

You can tell a lot about the quality of construction by checking the seams. Check for straight, smooth seams that won't pull apart.

Fastenings. Check any fastenings that hold the garment openings together. Make sure zippers slide smoothly, buttons are secure, buttonholes are stitched neatly, and snaps or hooks and eyes are firmly sewn.

Trimmings. Last, look at any **trimmings**—*the decorations sewn on a garment*. They should be attached with even, secure stitches so they won't come off.

Checking the Fit

To do this, you have to try the garment on. But don't just stand still. Move around. sit down, reach up, bend. If you can't do any of these things easily, or if the garment sags, gaps, or pulls anywhere, it's probably too large or too small or it just doesn't fit right. Try another size.

Never compromise on fit. A poorly fitting garment will end up, never worn, at the back of your closet.

The Final Decision

Before you buy clothing, you should use the checklist in the table. If you ask those questions and answer them honestly, you'll spend your money wisely.

TABLE 1   **Clothing Buying Checklist**

☐ Does this item fit my clothing plan?
☐ Can I wear it with some of my other clothes?
☐ Is the price within my budget?
☐ What is its cost per wearing?
☐ Could I buy something similar for less?
☐ Could I make this item?
☐ Is it a fad that will go out of style soon?
☐ Does it fit and allow room for growth?
☐ Will this item be on sale soon, so I can save money?

Words to Remember

end-of-season sale: a clothing sale held to clear out merchandise to make room for the up-coming season

facing: an extra piece of fabric that finishes the edge of a garment

hem: the bottom edge of fabric turned up and sewn to the wrong side of a garment

in-seam measurement: the length of the pants leg from the bottom to where the two legs meet

range: category of clothing sizes

seam: a line of stitching that joins the pieces of a garment together

trimmings: the decorations sewn on a garment

Questions

1. What are two things you should do to get ready for a shopping trip?
2. What are some of the advantages of shopping in a department store? What are some of the disadvantages?
3. Give examples of three other stores that sell clothing.
4. What kind of sale might be helpful to you if you were buying clothes for next year?
5. Name two female clothes sizes. Name two male clothes sizes.
6. What are two things to check on fabric?
7. Name two items of construction to check.
8. What are two ways to check for fit?

57 Selecting
Patterns,
Fabrics, and
Notions

Objectives

After reading this chapter, you will be able to:

☐ *determine the correct pattern size to choose,*

☐ *explain how to select a pattern,*

☐ *use the information on the pattern envelope and understand its recommendations,*

☐ *suggest factors that affect your choice of fabric and notions.*

How many times have you found just the shorts you'd been looking for—but they didn't have a pair in your size? Or the duffle bag you wanted costs three times what you could spend?

At times like these, you're glad that you learned to sew! No longer must you hope that you'll find what you want in the color you like and the size you need. You can choose among the hundreds of patterns, fabrics, and colors available. That way, you *know* that you can make the specific item that you want, in the exact size that you need, and in the color that does the most for you and for your wardrobe.

Taking Measurements

The first step in making clothing is getting a pattern. A **pattern** is *a set of written directions and pieces of marked paper that show you how to put a sewing project together.* The pattern tells you how much material you need and shows you how to lay the fabric out and sew the pieces. It also makes fabric suggestions.

To figure out what size pattern is right for you, you first have to measure yourself. Then, using these measurements, take a look at the short descriptions of pattern types that follow. From these, pick your type and your actual size.

Measurements

Here are a few things that you can do to make measuring easier and more accurate.

■ Ask a friend to come over and help you, and write down each measurement.

■ Wear smooth-fitting clothes, a leotard, or underwear when measuring. Do not measure over a bulky sweater or jacket.

■ Wear shoes. That will make your posture close to what it will be when you have on the clothing.

■ Before you start, tie a string closely but not too tightly around your waist. You'll use this for measuring your waist and for other measurements up your back and down to your hips and legs.

■ Stand straight and tall.

■ Always measure around the fullest part of the portion of the body that you're measuring.

■ Be sure that the tape measure is parallel to the floor.

■ Hold the tape measure snugly around your body, but not so tight that it crushes into your skin. That will throw off your measurements.

■ Before writing down any measurement, double-check it. The box shows the measurements that you must take.

Pattern Types and Sizes

Once you've measured yourself, you can identify your body type and your size by comparing your measurements with those on the size chart printed in a pattern book.

Remember that there are different pattern types and different sizes within each type. Female pattern types are misses, misses petite, junior petite, young junior/teen, women, and half size. Male pattern types are boys, teen boys, and men.

A pattern may not match your measurements exactly. The pattern size you choose will be the one within your body type that comes closest to your measurements.

Selecting a Pattern

You've determined your pattern type and your size. Now you can pick a pattern.

Pattern Catalogs and Envelopes

First, go through the **pattern catalogs**. These are *books that show all the projects that can be made from a particular company's patterns.* Each body type has a section in the catalog, so if you're a junior, for instance, you can go to that section to find a pattern.

Special sections of a catalog have ideas for nonclothing projects. These sections are

°F E A T U R E

Measuring Up

Female

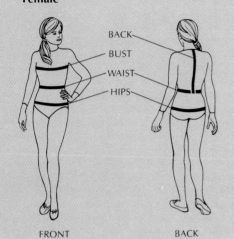

FRONT   BACK

Male

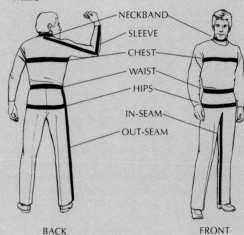

BACK   FRONT

Taking Your Measurements

Depending on the garment you're buying, you will need to take different measurements to determine your size.

In a man's shirt, for example, neck and sleeve measurements are most important. For a woman's dress, the measurements needed to find the right size are bust, waist, and hips.

To find out what size you wear, take your measurements according to the following instructions. Then compare your measurements to those on a size chart. Most clothing stores have size charts available.

How To Measure

Measuring to check your size is not difficult. Remember to stand naturally, and to hold the tape taut, but not tight.

Height   Stand against the wall (barefooted). Have another person make a mark level with the top of your head. Measure from this point to the floor. For pants and skirt measurements, it is best to wear shoes.

Bust or Chest   Measure over the fullest part of the bust or chest, with the tape straight across the back.

Waist   Measure the smallest part of the natural waistline.

Hips   Measure at the fullest part of the hips in a straight line around the body.

Back   Measure from waist to neck.

In-Seam   Place pants that are the correct length on a flat surface. Measure along inner seam from the bottom of one leg to where the two legs meet.

Out-seam   Measure from waist to point where pants bottom breaks slightly on shoe.

Neckband   Measure around the fullest part of the neck for neckband size, adding ½ in or 1 cm for wearing ease.

Sleeve   Bend arm up. Measure from base of neck across center back to elbow, across elbow crook, and up over wrist bone.

FEMALE FIGURE TYPES

YOUNG   JUNIOR   JUNIOR   MISS   MISSES   HALF-   WOMEN'S
JR./TEEN PETITE   PETITE   SIZE

Young Junior/Teen   A size range specially designed for developing pre-teen and teen figures; height is 5′ 1″–5′ 3″ (1.55 – 1.60 m)

Junior Petite   Shorter version of junior; well-proportioned but small; height is 5′–5′ 1″ (1.53 –1.55 m)

Junior   Well-proportioned and trim, but lacks fullness of figure of miss and is shorter-waisted; height is 5′ 4″–5′ 5″ (1.63 –1.65 m)

Miss Petite   Shorter version of miss; height is 5′ 2″–5′ 4″ (1.58 –1.63 m)

Misses   Well proportioned and well-developed figure; height is 5′ 5″–5′ 6″ (1.65 –1.68 m)

Half-Size   A fully developed, smaller figure; height is 5′ 2″–5′ 3″ (1.58 –1.60 m)

Women's   A fully developed, larger figure; height is 5′ 5″–5′ 6″ (1.65 –1.68 m)

After you have taken your measurements, you are ready to determine your pattern type. Match your height and physical build to the type and size that is right for you.

labeled Gifts, Home Decorating, and Crafts. You can find exciting ideas for pillows, totes, and other attractive projects in them.

Front of the Envelope. When you select a pattern, take a good look at the envelope that it comes in. On the front of the envelope, you will find the body type and size that the pattern is made for. You'll also find the price and pattern number.

The front also has a drawing or photograph of how the garment will look when sewn. This often includes a number of views of a garment. A **view** is *a drawing of a different version of the project.* A pants pattern might include views for shorts, bermudas, and full-length pants.

Back of the Envelope. On the back of the envelope is a description of the finished garment. The style and anything that you can't see in the drawing are explained in detail. It also states the number of pattern pieces enclosed and shows a sketch of the back of each view. You'll also find a chart of the body measurements for each size that the pattern is created for.

Other Information. The pattern envelope also says how much material you'll need for each pattern size. It will tell you whether you need more material for napped fabric. It will suggest what kinds of fabrics are best for the pattern you've selected. It will also say if any fabrics are not suitable, such as plaids or diagonal fabrics.

Finally, there's information on sewing supplies needed.

Inside the envelope are the actual pattern pieces and sewing guide sheet.

Choosing for Style

When you buy a pair of pants or a shirt from a store, you can see the piece of clothing all put together. You can also try it on to see how it looks and feels on you. With patterns, you have to rely on the illustrations on the pattern envelope and the descriptions on the back.

You may wonder if the garment will look good on you. One clue might be whether the item is similar to something you have worn in the past. To check, look for a finished garment like it in a store and try it on.

Choosing for Difficulty

Finally, when picking a pattern, take into account how difficult the pattern is. If you're a beginner, you may want to look for patterns marked "easy to sew" or "very easy." Usually, the fewer the pattern pieces, the easier the project.

Remember that details generally are more difficult to sew. Projects with collars, cuffs, fly-front zippers, extra darts, tucks, and topstitching are difficult for beginning students.

Selecting a Fabric

What the Pattern Tells You

Luckily, the pattern envelope tells you what type of fabric will be most suitable for the pattern. A lot depends on the shape of the garment—a soft fabric will be suggested for a soft, gathered shape. Style also matters. For casual clothes, the envelope will probably suggest a more durable, sturdy fabric. Something dressier will be recommended for a special occasion item.

Using Your Own Knowledge

Your Own Experience. Your own feeling about yourself and the clothes you wear will also help you select fabric. What feels comfortable and seems to express your personality? Do you prefer a jacket made of tweed or velveteen? What will the item be used for and where will it be used? Backpacks need sturdy fabric. Placemats need medium-weight, washable fabric.

Seasonal Wear. What time of year do you plan to wear the item? You wouldn't want a heavy wool for summer or a thin cotton material for winter. If you plan to wear the clothing often, you might want to buy a material that wears well.

MALE FIGURE TYPES

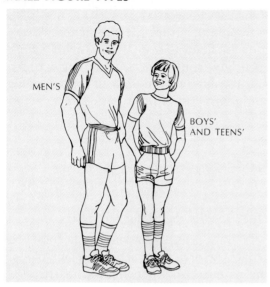

MEN'S

BOYS' AND TEENS'

Boys' and Teens' Size ranges planned for boys and young men who haven't reached adult size; height for boys is 4'–5' (1.23–1.53 m), height for teen boys is 5' 1"–5' 8" (1.55–1.73 m).

Men's Sizes for men planned for an average figure who stands 5' 10" (1.78 m).

Match your height and physical size to the pattern type and size that is right for you.

Fabric Care. Finally, take fabric care into consideration. If you don't want to spend lots of time hand washing and ironing, pick a fabric that is wash and wear with a permanent press finish. If you don't have a lot of money for cleaning bills, avoid a fabric that needs dry cleaning. The salesperson should give you care labels for the fabric you buy.

Sewing Difficulty. Keep in mind the ease or difficulty of working with a fabric. Fabrics with a one-way design or with a nap are harder to work with. So are those that ravel easily. Firmly woven or knitted fabrics are easier to work with.

Looking for Quality

You want what you make to last and to look good. But you need to balance quality with price.

When you've found something that you think you like, unroll the fabric and examine it for flaws. Use the pinch test to see if it wrinkles. If it's a knit, pull it a little to see if it stretches and then recovers its shape.

Find a mirror and drape some of the fabric over your shoulder to see how it looks on you. Consider not only the color and pattern, but also the softness or firmness of the material.

Estimate the total cost of the project by multiplying the cost per yard by the number of yards needed. Add in the cost of the pattern, zippers, buttons, and thread. If that total cost is more than you planned, look for a less expensive fabric. Or shop at another store. You can also compare prices of different projects by figuring the cost per wear.

Deciding How Much Fabric to Buy

Check the chart on the back of the pattern envelope to find out the amount of fabric to buy. Be sure to look at the correct size of the pattern and the view you'll be using. The width of the fabric makes a difference, too.

For certain types of fabric and some patterns, you'll need extra fabric. This is the case with materials that have a nap or pile, like corduroy, velvet, and velveteen. These fabrics are difficult to lay out. When pieces of these fabrics are sewed together, the nap has to face the same way.

You also need extra material for stripes and plaids, which must be matched at the seams. The back of the pattern envelope will tell whether extra fabric is needed.

Selecting Notions

When you're buying fabric and patterns, be sure to buy your notions. **Notions** *are sewing items needed to complete a project.* They include thread, zippers, buttons, other fasteners, seam bindings, tape, interfacings, and trim.

The pattern envelope lists notions that you'll need. Buy all the notions when you buy the pattern and fabric.

Choosing Notion Colors

Notions should look good with your fabric. When buying thread, zippers, binding tapes, and hem tape, pick a color that matches or is slightly darker than the fabric. Buttons can either match the fabric and style of clothing or be used as an attractive accent or contrast. If you're unsure about what style or color to buy, look at some ready-made clothing for ideas.

Choosing Your Thread

The thread you use depends on the fabric you are working with. Cotton-wrapped polyester and 100 percent polyester threads can be used for almost all fabrics. They're especially good for synthetics, knits, and stretch fabrics because they stretch and don't shrink. Use cotton thread for cotton and linen, silk thread for silk and woolens.

Think about the thickness or thinness of the thread, too. You won't want a thick thread for a silky blouse or a thin, delicate thread for a leather jacket.

Words to Remember

catalog: a book that shows all the projects that can be made from a particular company's patterns

notions: sewing items needed to complete a project

pattern: a set of written directions and pieces of marked paper that show how to put a sewing project together

view: a drawing of a different version of the sewing project

Questions

1. What is a pattern?
2. Before you buy a pattern, what things about yourself do you have to know?
3. List four pieces of information found on a pattern envelope.
4. What two factors should you think about when choosing patterns?
5. List three things that you should consider as part of selecting a fabric for a piece of clothing.
6. What are notions? How do you choose the right notions for a particular pattern and fabric?

Chapter 58 Sewing Equipment

Objectives

After reading this chapter, you will be able to:

□ *describe the parts of the sewing machine,*

□ *show how to use a sewing machine,*

□ *identify and describe the purposes of many pieces of sewing equipment.*

People may have begun sewing clothes by using long thorns and strips of leather to attach pieces of animal skin together. The results weren't too good, but they were better than nothing.

We've come a long way since then. Today, even if you sew by hand, you probably use stainless steel needles and polyester thread. But chances are you rarely sew by hand—why should you? With the sewing machine, you can complete your projects faster and more easily.

More than 100 years ago, a Massachusetts machinist named Elias Howe invented a workable sewing machine. His invention revolutionized the making of clothing.

Sewing machines join pieces of fabric together with a lock stitch. This stitch differs from a hand stitch because it requires a thread above the fabric to meet another thread below the fabric.

The Sewing Machine

How It Works

The sewing machine needle pushes the top thread down through the layers of fabric. This thread is caught by a mechanism that winds it around the bottom thread. When the needle comes back up through the fabric, the top thread pulls the bottom thread partway up with it. In a well-adjusted machine, the two threads become locked in the middle of the fabric layers.

The fabric is moved along by a part of the machine called a **feed**. The feed positions the fabric for the next stitch to be made. The process is repeated over and over to create a row of stitching.

The machine is operated by a foot or knee control. A balance wheel can be turned by hand to raise and lower the needle as you begin and end stitching.

Threading the Machine

Each sewing machine model is threaded somewhat differently. Refer to the diagram in your manual for directions. The basic order, though, is the same for all machines. The thread goes from the spool to the upper tension to the take-up lever and down to the needle. The take-up lever should be in its highest position. Thread guides keep the thread from tangling along the way.

You must also insert the **bobbin**, *a spool that holds the bottom thread.* Wind the bobbin on the machine and insert it in the bobbin case according to the directions in your machine's manual.

Adjustments

Sewing machines are made so that you can adjust the type and length of your stitches to suit each sewing job.

There are five main types of stitches.

- The *regular stitch* is a medium-length stitch used for most purposes.
- The *basting stitch* is a long stitch used for holding layers of fabric together temporarily.
- The *reinforcement stitch* is a short, tiny stitch used to strengthen the stitching area at a corner or point.
- The *zigzag stitch* is a sideways stitch used to finish seam allowances, make buttonholes, and sew special seams.
- The *backstitch* is a stitch made in reverse to anchor the thread firmly at the end of a seam.

TYPES OF STITCHES

BASTING ⎯ ⎯ ⎯ ⎯ ⎯ ⎯ ⎯ ⎯

STANDARD ⎯ ⎯ ⎯ ⎯ ⎯ ⎯ ⎯ ⎯

REINFORCEMENT ⎯ ⎯ ⎯ ⎯ ⎯ ⎯ ⎯ ⎯ ⎯

ZIGZAG /\/\/\/\/\/\/\/\/\

Basting   6 stitches per inch (2.5 cm);   long

Standard   10–12 stitches per inch (2.5 cm); medium

Reinforcement   20 stitches per inch (2.5 cm);   short

Different stitches, such as the regular, basting, and zigzag, can be made by adjusting the type and length of the stitch.

F E A T U R E

Basic Parts of the Sewing Machine

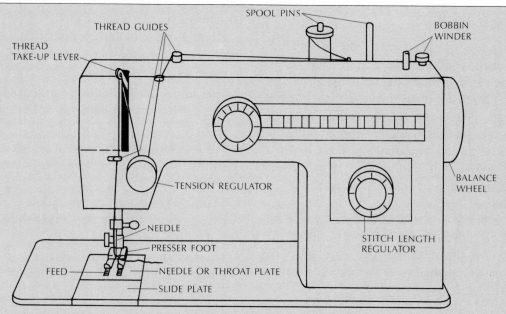

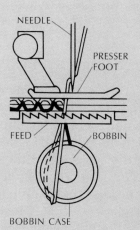

Bobbin Holds the bottom thread, which forms the under half of the stitch.

Bobbin case Holds the bobbin and the tension adjustment for the lower thread.

Feed Rises through the throat plate and moves fabric forward with each stitch.

Presser foot Helps hold fabric in place to keep stitches in a straight line.

Stitch regulator Used to adjust stitch length. On some machines, it also sets the machine to go forward or backward.

Thread guides Hold thread in place.

Needle or throat plate Plate directly under the needle; it has guideline markings to help you keep your stitching straight.

Slide plate A metal plate that covers the bobbin and opens to let you remove the bobbin.

Balance wheel Turns to raise and lower the take-up level and needle.

Bobbin winder Used to wind the bobbin.

Spool pin Holds spool of thread.

Tension regulator Regulates how tightly the thread is pulled as a stitch is formed. (The tension on upper and lower thread must be just right in order to form secure, even stitches.)

Thread take-up lever Keeps thread feeding evenly through the needle.

Needle Feeds the upper thread and forms the upper half of the stitch.

Specialty stitches include the *stretch stitch*, *hemming stitch*, and various *decorative stitches*.

All machines have a dial or lever, called the *stitch regulator*, for setting the stitch length. The higher the number on the regulator, the closer together the stitches. Some machines also have a lever for setting stitch width and for making specialty stitches.

You can also change the tightness of the stitches with the *tension regulator*. This adjusts the tension on the upper thread so that the stitches interlock in a different place. The tension may need adjusting so that one thread does not lay flat against one side of the fabric while the other thread forms large loops on the other side.

Needles

Needles come in different sizes and types for different fabrics. There are two basic types:

- *Sharps*, with a sharp point, are used for woven fabrics.
- *Ball-points*, which have a rounded point, are used for knits.

A bent or damaged needle can cause stitching problems. If a needle seems to be dull, replace it right away.

Accessories

Modern machines have many special features for many kinds of sewing operations. Separate attachments may be needed for some of these operations. To sew zippers, you need a special zipper foot. Other gadgets make hems, gather ruffles, and put on binding.

Caring for the Sewing Machine

The sewing machine needs regular maintenance and careful handling. After each use, the machine should be unplugged, put away in its cabinet or case, and covered.

All machines must be cleaned regularly to keep the moving parts clean of dust and lint. Use a soft sewing machine brush. Be especially sure to keep lint away from the feed area and from the bobbin case. You will find directions for cleaning the machine in the machine's manual.

The machine needs to be oiled occasionally with sewing machine oil. Refer to the manual to see how often to oil the machine and where to place the drops. Carefully wipe away any excess to avoid spotting your fabric.

Other Sewing Gear

Measuring

- *Tape measure*. You'll need one to measure your body measurements. Get one that is 60" long and has inches on one side and centimeters on the other.
- *Yardstick/meter stick*. This is used to measure fabric, check grain lines, mark hems, and draw long lines. The sticks are 36" long, are made of wood, and should have inches on one side and centimeters on the other.
- *Ruler*. A 12" ruler with 1/8" markings can be used to measure and mark lines.
- *Sewing gauge*. This is a 6" ruler with an adjustable sliding marker that's used to measure small areas, like seams or hems.

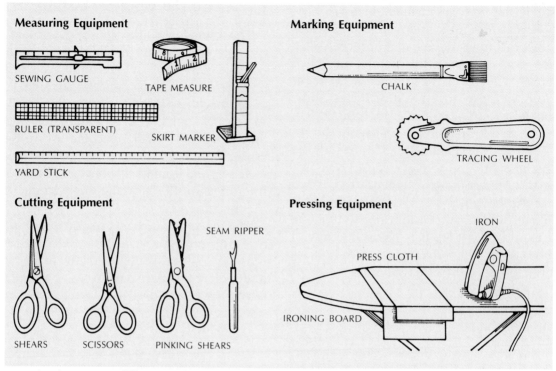

Knowing how to use different sewing equipment will make your work more enjoyable. Use quality equipment. Once you buy it, it will last for years.

- *Skirt marker.* This can be used for marking skirt and dress lengths with pins or chalk.

Cutting

Cutting tools should cut along the whole blade. Buy good tools, which will last a long time. Check your cutting tools regularly to keep them oiled and sharpened.

- *Shears.* These are used to cut out fabric. They have bent handles so that you can lay fabric flat on a surface while cutting. They have 7″ or 8″ blades.
- *Scissors.* Scissors, smaller than shears, are used for trimming and clipping.

- *Pinking shears.* These shears cut fabric in a zigzag. They're used to trim and finish seams and edges on fabrics that don't ravel easily.
- *Seam ripper.* This pen-like object has a small blade for removing stitches.

Marking

Marking tools are used to transfer pattern symbols to fabric.

- *Tracing paper.* This paper comes in several colors. Choose a color that will show up on the fabric without being too dark. Double-faced tracing paper allows you to mark two layers of fabric at one time.

■ *Tracing wheel.* This device is used with tracing paper to transfer pattern markings to fabric. Wheels with saw-toothed edges can be used for most fabrics. Smooth-edged wheels are best for delicate fabrics.

F E A T U R E

How to Machine Stitch

Here are some points to check.

■ Make sure that the machine is plugged in. Turn on the machine light or power switch.

■ Check to see if the needle is inserted correctly and tightened.

■ Fill the bobbin and insert into the bobbin case.

■ Thread the machine correctly, being sure the take-up lever is at the highest position.

■ Adjust the stitch length, width, and tension for your fabric.

■ Sit up straight and don't bend over the machine.

Now you're ready to sew.

■ Raise the needle and take-up lever to the highest position (this prevents the thread from pulling out of the needle when you start stitching).

■ Pull both thread ends back behind the presser foot. (This prevents the thread from tangling as you start to stitch).

■ Place the fabric under the presser foot with the greatest bulk of the fabric to the left of the needle.

■ Line up the seam line directly under the needle. For a regular ⅝" seam, line up the edge of the fabric with the ⅝" guideline marking on the throat plate of the machine.

■ Lower the presser foot.

■ Turn the balance wheel by hand to slowly lower the needle into the fabric.

■ Apply gentle pressure on the machine's foot or knee control, and stitch at a slow and constant speed.

■ Guide the fabric gently—do not pull. Keep your eyes on the edge of the fabric and on the guideline markings, not on the needle.

■ Backstitch to anchor the seam, then stitch to the end of the fabric. Stop when the needle and take-up lever are at the highest position. Or stop and raise the lever by hand, using the balance wheel. Backstitch again.

■ Raise the presser foot.

■ Gently slide the fabric back and to the left. Do not pull it, or you may bend the needle.

■ Clip the ends of the threads.

■ Press the seam.

Sometimes, a problem occurs with stitching. If the needle skips stitches, breaks, or jams, check to see if the machine is properly threaded. Problems are usually the result of incorrect threading of either the upper thread or the bobbin thread. If the threading is correct, check the needle and the tension setting.

■ *Chalk.* Chalk can be used to mark most fabrics, since the markings can easily be brushed off afterwards. Chalk is available as colored squares or pencils.

Small Equipment

■ *Pins.* These are needed to pin the pattern to the fabric and to hold fabric layers together for stitching. They are available with sharp points for most fabrics and with ball-points for knits.

■ *Needles.* Needles for hand sewing come in a variety of sizes and lengths. The smaller the number, the larger the needle. You'll find sizes 7 and 8 good for most purposes.

■ *Thimble.* This metal or plastic item is used to push the needle through fabric. It is worn on your middle finger, which it protects from punctures by the needle.

■ *Pin cushion.* This is better than a box for holding your pins while you sew, since the pins can't spill all over the table or floor. Some have a wrist band so you can wear them while sewing.

Pressing

Fabric should be pressed as you go along—with every seam that you sew.

■ *Iron.* An iron should have a wide temperature range and the ability to steam.

■ *Ironing board.* Your ironing board should be adjustable for comfort. It should have a clean cover and padding.

■ *Press cloth.* Press cloths protect the fabric from the shiny marks caused by an iron's heat. They can be dampened to provide steam.

■ *Tailor's ham.* This firm cushion, shaped like a ham, is used for pressing curved seams and darts.

■ *Sleeve board.* This is two small, narrow ironing boards connected together. It's used for pressing flat areas that won't fit over a normal ironing board.

Words to Remember

bobbin: a spool that holds the bottom thread in a sewing machine

feed: the part of a sewing machine that moves the fabric along

Questions

1. Explain how a sewing machine works.
2. What five stitches does a sewing machine make?
3. What are the two types of sewing machine needles?
4. List three pieces of measuring equipment.
5. What is the difference between shears and scissors?
6. Name two items you can use for marking.

Chapter **59 Layout, Cut, Mark**

Objectives

After reading this chapter, you will be able to:

☐ *adjust a pattern to fit your own figure,*

☐ *prepare the fabric and lay out the pattern pieces,*

☐ *cut out and mark the pieces.*

Keeping your sewing area well organized will help you work efficiently. A cardboard or plastic box or basket can help you keep your materials and equipment together.

Make sure that you have a comfortable place to work. It should include a large, flat surface like a table for measuring and cutting. There should be plenty of light and a comfortable chair. Also useful are a full-length mirror to check your progress and space for your pressing equipment.

There are four steps in the preparation of materials for sewing:

1. preparing your pattern,
2. preparing your fabric, which includes preshrinking and straightening it,
3. laying out and cutting the fabric,
4. marking the fabric.

The result of careful preparation will be a garment that looks good and fits well.

427

Preparing Your Pattern

First, take out your *pattern guide sheet*. This gives you step-by-step information for cutting, marking, and sewing the fabric. One side gives you general instructions, information about pattern symbols, and diagrams for laying out pattern pieces. The other side gives sewing directions. Circle the layout for the pattern size, view, and width.

F E A T U R E

Patterns and Pattern Terms

Adjustment line A double line, where the pattern may be lengthened or shortened.

Buttonholes Marked by lines that show the exact location and length.

Center front and center back Solid lines that show the center of the garment.

Cutting line The heavier outer line, along which you cut.

Darts Consist of two broken lines and corresponding dots.

Dots Used for matching seams and construction details.

Foldline A solid line showing where the fabric is to be folded.

Grainline The heavy solid line with arrows at each end that shows the direction of the grain.

Hemline A solid line indicating the finished edge of the garment.

Notches Diamond-shaped symbols along the cutting line that are used for matching seams.

Placement lines Lines showing the exact location of pockets, zippers, and trims.

Place-on-fold bracket The symbol which shows that the pattern piece is to be placed along a fold of fabric.

Seamline or Stitching line A broken line ⅝" inside the cutting line (unless otherwise noted).

Now, take out the pattern pieces that you'll need. If any pieces are wrinkled, press them with a warm iron to make them smooth and flat.

Write your name on all your pattern pieces, on your pattern envelope, and on your guide sheet.

Next, find your measurements, which you took before you bought the pattern. Compare them with those listed on the pattern envelope to see if you'll need to adjust the pattern.

Checking Pattern Measurements

If your body measurements do not exactly match those listed on the back of the pattern envelope, you may have to make **adjustments**. That means that you'll have to *change the pattern to fit your own size.*

If there's a difference of an inch or more between your measurements and the size measurements on the envelope, you'll probably have to make adjustments. You can check with your instructor to be sure. If a pattern style is loose or full, you may not have to make adjustments.

You can also compare your measurements to those of the pattern by actually measuring the pattern pieces. Measure only from seam to seam—don't include the **seam allowance**. This is *the fabric between the line for cutting and the line for stitching.* Remember that the pattern includes **ease**. This is *extra room that a pattern allows to enable you to wear clothes comfortably.*

Because of the ease, pattern pieces measure slightly larger than the size measurements. The difference might be 3″ to 4″ at the bust, 3/4″ to 1″ at the waist, and 2″ at the hip. Thus, a pattern for 34″ hips would actually measure 36″. Patterns for bathing suits and leotards will have little or no ease. Patterns for stretch fabrics won't have much ease either.

Simple Adjusting

Correcting for length is easy. Some patterns have an adjustment line printed on the pattern where it can be lengthened or shortened.

Shorten by taking a tuck at the adjustment line or at the bottom. If a pattern must be made longer, cut it apart at the adjustment line. Insert a strip of tissue paper in between the two pieces, or add it to the bottom of the pattern. This supplies the extra length you need. Don't forget to adjust all your pieces—both front and back, for instance.

Adjusting for width is a little more complicated. An increase or decrease of 1″ or less can be done at the side seams. Just draw new seam lines parallel to the old, adding tissue paper if necessary. If you have to add or subtract more than 1″, get assistance from your instructor.

Preparing Your Fabric

Preshrinking. To find out if the fabric was preshrunk by the manufacturer, check the label on the bolt when buying the cloth. You could also ask the salesperson.

If the fabric was not preshrunk, you should preshrink it by cleaning it exactly as you'll clean the completed garment. For example, if the fabric is machine washable and dryable, simply wash to preshrink.

FEATURE

Special Fabric Layouts

Some fabrics, such as napped or pile fabrics, plaids, stripes, or border prints, require special layouts. These fabrics demand more time and skill for laying out and for matching designs when stitching than other fabrics do. They are not recommended for beginners. Here are the main things to keep in mind.

- Fabrics with a direction—like napped or pile fabrics, some plaids and stripes, and one-way prints—look right only if the nap or design runs in the same direction over the whole garment.

- When you are matching plaids or stripes, be sure to match seam lines, not cutting lines.

Directional Fabrics

Be sure to place all the pattern pieces facing in the same direction. For napped fabrics, cut with the nap running up for a deeper, richer color. Cut with the nap running down for a lighter, shinier look.

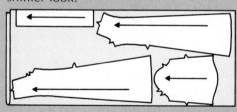

Plaids and Stripes

Place the major vertical line at the center front and center back. Avoid placing a heavy horizontal line at the bust or waist. Match the side seams. Some patterns are marked "not suitable for stripes," because they cannot be matched properly.

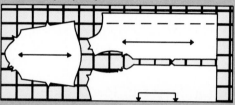

Border Prints

For best results, choose a pattern designed for a border print. Put the print at the hemline.

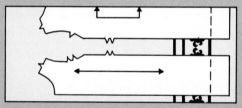

Large Designs

Place pattern pieces carefully on a large design so that circles and flowers are not centered over your stomach or hips.

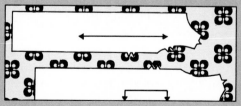

Straightening Ends. Sometimes, fabric gets pulled off grain as it's made. If that happens, you must straighten it before you cut it. The lengthwise and crosswise grains should meet at right angles.

To find out if you're going to have to straighten the fabric, you need to straighten the fabric ends. For a woven fabric, pull a thread across the width of the fabric and cut along this crosswise thread. For a knit, cut along a row of stitches. Then fold the fabric in half lengthwise. If the corners do not match exactly without wrinkling, then the fabric is off grain.

Straightening the Grain. If the fabric is off grain, it needs to be straightened. If it's not straightened before being cut out, it may pull or twist to one side of your body, or the hem may be uneven.

Have someone help you. Open up the fabric and pull the two opposite corners that are too short. Refold the fabric to check that you have pulled enough. If not, repeat.

CUTTING THE FABRIC

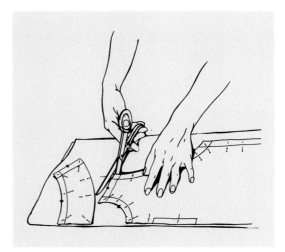

1. Pin along cutting lines and foldline.
2. Use long scissors.
   Cut in steady even slashes.
3. The edge of the pattern should be exactly on the foldline of the fabric.

Double-check the layout directions and the placement of the pattern pieces before cutting.

Laying Out and Cutting

Laying Out

The pattern **layout** is *a diagram in the sewing instructions that shows how to place the pattern pieces on your fabric.* It is planned to waste as little fabric as possible. Special layouts may be given for fabrics with a nap or directional print.

Follow the layout that you circled on the pattern guide sheet. Fold your fabric as shown on the layout, with the right sides together. Smooth the fabric out flat on a surface that is large enough to hold your fabric width. Arrange your pattern pieces on the fabric according to the layout. To avoid mistakes, lay out all the pieces before starting to pin and cut.

First, pin any pattern pieces placed along the fold line. Next, pin the pattern pieces that have grain-line arrows. To make sure that the pieces are exactly on grain, pin only one end of the arrow. Then, measure from each end of the arrow to the **selvage**, *the border of the fabric.* The distances should be equal. If they're not, move the pattern and re-measure. When the distances are equal, pin the other side of the arrow.

Smooth out each pattern piece and pin it diagonally at the corners. Then, place pins about 6" apart at right angles to the edges. Make sure that the pins don't extend into the cutting lines.

Cutting

Before cutting your fabric, double-check. Are all your pieces laid out? Are grain lines accurate?

Use sharp shears to cut accurately and evenly. With your free hand, hold the fabric flat on the table. Cut with long, even strokes, following the pattern's cutting line exactly. Always use **directional cutting**, which is *cutting with the grain of the fabric.* The direction may be shown on the pattern by arrows on the stitching line or by tiny scissors on the cutting line.

Use the points of your shears to cut corners, curves, and notches. Always cut notches *out away* from the cutting line. Cut two or three notches together as one long notch.

Double-check to be sure that you have cut each pattern piece as many times as

MARKING THE FABRIC

Here are the two techniques for transferring markings from pattern to fabric.

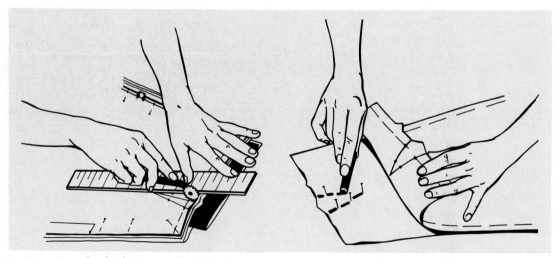

1. A tracing wheel is being used with carbon paper. The paper is folded so that both layers are marked.

2. Pins are pushed through each pattern symbol, then chalk is used to mark both sides of the folded fabric.

The markings on pattern pieces show how to put the garment together. Use carbon paper, tailor's chalk, or "tailor tacks" to transfer the markings from pattern to fabric.

necessary. You may have to remove the pattern piece and lay it out on another area of the fabric to cut it again. If any pattern piece in your layout extends over the folded fabric, cut it out last. Do not remove the pattern from fabric pieces after cutting. They must now be marked.

Marking the Fabric

Printed on your pattern pieces are dots, lines, and other markings. You will have to transfer these markings from the pattern to the wrong side of your fabric. Choose the marking method that seems most suitable for the fabric you're working on.

- *Tracing paper and wheel.* Slide the tracing paper under the pattern so that the color is against the wrong side of the fabric. If you have two layers of fabric to mark, use two pieces of tracing paper, or fold one in half. Roll the tracing wheel once along the line that you want to mark. You can use a ruler to keep the lines straight.

- *Pins and chalk.* Chalk squares or pencils can be used to mark symbols. Push a pin through both pattern and fabric at the symbol to be marked. Then, make a chalk mark on the wrong side of both fabric layers at the pin marking. For a dart (see definition in Chapter 60), start at the edge of the pattern piece and work your way to the point.

- *Thread markings.* You can also use thread to mark fabrics, especially those that cannot be marked by other methods. *Tailor's tacks,* which are several loops of thread, can be used to mark a construction symbol. Long basting stitches can be used to mark the center front or the placement of pockets.

Words to Remember

adjustment: changing a pattern to fit your own size

directional cutting: cutting with the grain of the fabric

ease: extra room that a pattern includes to enable you to wear clothes comfortably

layout: a diagram in the sewing instructions that shows how to place the pattern pieces on the fabric

seam allowance: the fabric between the line for cutting and the line for stitching

selvage: the border of the fabric

Questions

1. What are the four preparation steps before sewing a garment?

2. Why are the measurements of pattern pieces slightly larger than your body measurements?

3. What are the three steps in preparing fabric?

4. What do you follow when laying out the pattern pieces?

5. What is the proper way to cut?

6. What are the three methods of marking?

Chapter 60 Basic Construction

Objectives

After reading this chapter, you will be able to:

☐ *describe the sewing that may be necessary on individual garment pieces,*

☐ *show how to construct the long seams of a garment,*

☐ *explain the technique of attaching fabrics, sleeves, and collars.*

You have marked all your fabric pieces. Spread them out and look at them. You now know how to put the pieces together and where to stitch. You also know where to place buttons and buttonholes, zippers, and pockets. The markings will make your job easier and more accurate.

Now you're ready to assemble—or construct—all the pieces of your project. Soon you'll see it begin to take shape. You'll be using a basic construction technique called **unit construction**—*preparing the separate pieces first, then assembling them in a certain order.*

For example, a shirt has a back, two fronts, and two sleeves. It's easier to construct each unit separately first, pressing each part as you finish it. Once you've sewn all the pieces, you simply put them together.

Preparing the Pieces

Staystitching

Look for all edges that are curved or cut on the bias. Before you do anything else, you'll need to staystitch these.

Staystitching is *a row of stitching on just one layer of fabric that keeps the curved areas from stretching as you handle the fabric.* It is done by machine stitching 1/2" from the cut edge of the fabric in the same direction as the grain.

Shaping Darts

The next step is to stitch your darts. A **dart** is *a triangular fold of fabric stitched to a point.* Darts help shape the fabric to the shape of your body. They're usually located at the waistline, the bustline, and the back of the shoulder. Darts can also be used to shape curved areas in hats and tote bags.

Double-pointed darts taper at both ends. On the outside of your garment, a dart will look like a short seam.

To make a dart, follow these steps:

1. Fold the dart in half, matching markings, and pin.
2. Backstitch at the wide point to secure the threads. Then, stitch from the wide end to the point.
3. Stitch the last two to three stitches at the point right along the fold line so that you don't get a bubble at the point.
4. Tie a small knot at the point so that the threads don't pull loose.
5. Press each dart. Vertical darts should be pressed toward the center of the garment. Horizontal and diagonal darts should be pressed downward.

PINNING AND STITCHING DARTS

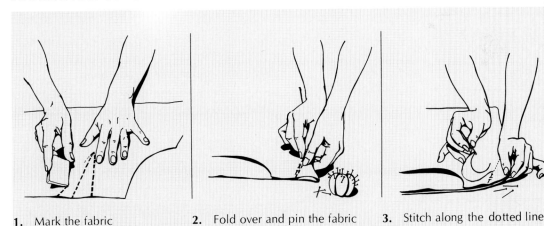

1. Mark the fabric   **2.** Fold over and pin the fabric   **3.** Stitch along the dotted line

Darts, located at the waistline, bustline, and the back of the shoulder, help shape the garment to the body.

Shaping Tucks

Like a dart, a **tuck** is *a small, stitched fold used to give shape.* But a tuck doesn't taper at the end. It makes a small, unpressed pleat in the fabric. Stitch tucks an even distance from the fold. Knot the thread ends as you would for darts, and press the tucks.

Making Gathers

Gathers are *soft folds of fabric that are stitched into a seam.* They can be used at a waistband, cuff, shoulder, or sleeve. Ruffles on pillows or placemats also use gathers. Your pattern will indicate where gathers begin and end.

To gather or ease, make two rows of basting stitches, one along the seam line, the other 1/4" away in the seam allowance. Then, carefully pull up the bobbin thread and slide the fabric along the thread to create the gathers.

Assembling the Pieces

Stitching

Now you're ready to stitch your seams. Adjust your stitch length to 12 stitches per inch for most fabrics; use a longer stitch for heavier fabrics and a shorter stitch for lighter fabrics.

Next, pin the two layers of fabric together with the right sides together; match the notches. Use **directional stitching**, that is, *stitching with the grain of the fabric.* This will keep your seams from stretching as you work on them. Backstitch 1/2" at the beginning and end of each seam to secure the stitching. Most seams are 5/8" wide, unless the pattern has different instructions.

When you've finished stitching one seam, press it before going on to the next one. First, press plain, straight seams flat, just as they were stitched. Then, press the

SOME SEAM FINISHES

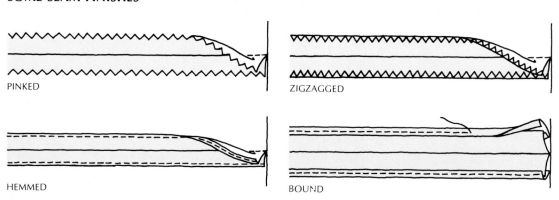

PINKED

ZIGZAGGED

HEMMED

BOUND

The amount of raveling and the type of fabric determines what seam finish to use. Choose from pinked, zigzagged, hemmed, or bound finishes.

seam allowance open, using your finger or the tip of the iron to keep it open completely.

Finishing the Seams

Some fabrics ravel. There are four ways to finish seam allowances to prevent the edges from fraying or raveling. Finished seams also create a neat appearance.

■ *Pinked or stitched-and-pinked*. Trim the edges with pinking shears. For fabrics that ravel easily, stitch 1/4″ from the edge and then pink.

■ *Zigzagged*. Zigzag by machine near each raw edge, using a narrower stitch for lightweight, closely woven fabrics and a wider stitch for heavy, bulky, or loosely woven fabrics.

■ *Hemmed*. This method, also called *clean finishing*, can be used on lightweight and medium-weight fabrics. Turn under the edge of the seam allowance 1/8″ and press, then stitch along the edge of the fold.

■ *Bound*. This method is good for medium- and heavy-weight fabrics. Fold a double-fold bias tape over each raw edge. Place the slightly narrower folded edge of tape on top, and stitch through all the layers.

Adding Facings

Facings are pieces of fabric cut in the same shape as the edges and used to finish a raw edge such as a neckline, armhole, or waistline. They are stitched to the edge and then turned to the inside of the garment. Separate pattern pieces for facings will be included in your pattern envelope. Sometimes, a facing is cut as an extension or as part of the garment. This *extended facing* is then folded to the inside along the fold line. Extended facings are used along the front and back openings of shirts and jackets.

To sew a facing, first construct the facing. Stitch the facing pieces together, then press the seams open. Finish the outer edge of the facing (the unnotched edge), using one of the seam finishes that you read about.

Next, pin the facing to the garment with right sides together. Match the notches and seams, and then stitch. Before you turn the facing under, follow these suggestions to make sure that it will lie flat and smooth:

■ Trim the seam allowance to half its width.

■ If the fabric is thick or if the seams have three or more layers, you'll want to

UNDERSTITCHING FACING

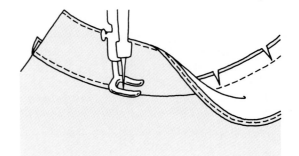

Understitching is a line of straight stitches sewn to prevent the bottom layer of fabric from rolling out. This technique is used for facings, lapels, and similar areas.

Facings on armholes, necklines, and front closings are understitched to lie flat and smooth.

grade or layer, them. *Trim each layer of a seam allowance slightly narrower than the previous one.* Leave at least 1/4" to 1/8" of seam allowance to prevent raveling. Curved seams need to be clipped or notched to let the fabric lie flat. If it curves inward, **clip** the seam allowance by *making small, evenly spaced cuts up to the staystitching line, 1/8"* away from the seam.

FEATURE

No-Problem Pressing

Though an iron is used for both, pressing differs from ironing. Ironing is sliding the iron back and forth, which can stretch the fabric. To **press** a seam or garment, *lift the iron and set it down on the fabric.* This prevents stretching. Steam does the job of pressing. If you're not using a steam iron, you must put a wet press cloth over the fabric. You can buy a cloth specially made for the job or use any lint-free cotton cloth.

After you've steamed one section, lift the iron just above the fabric and move your press cloth elsewhere. Then lower the iron again.

Here are a few good points for no-problem pressing.

- Check the fabric label. It will tell you the fiber content. You can set your iron's temperature control to that setting. If you're not sure of your fabric's fiber content, first test a scrap of fabric with the iron.

- Press the wrong side whenever possible to avoid shine. If you must press on the right side, use a press cloth. Do not use heavy pressure—let the steam do the work.

- Ironing on a towel will keep the pile of raised fabrics such as velvet and corduroy from being crushed. Be sure that the napped surface is against the towel.

- Use a sleeve board for pressing sleeves or pants without creases. If you don't have a board, make one by wrapping a rolling pin or rolled-up magazine in a towel. Insert this roll into your sleeve and press.

- Use a tailor's ham (a round wooden object) for pressing curved seams and darts.

Treat your iron with care. Before using it, read the instructions regarding proper use and storage. Rest the iron on its heel—not face down—when you're working with it. When you're finished, turn the dial setting to off, unplug the cord, and empty the water if it's a steam iron. Don't yank the cord to unplug it, but pull on the plug itself.

Store the iron in a protected place where it won't fall. As with any other electrical applicance, keep it well out of the reach of small children.

Pressing as you go is one of the secrets of successful sewing. With proper pressing, your project has flat seams, well-turned facings, and other neat details. As soon as you're ready to start stitching, set up your iron. You'll need it from start to finish.

TRIMMING, GRADING, CLIPPING, AND NOTCHING FACINGS

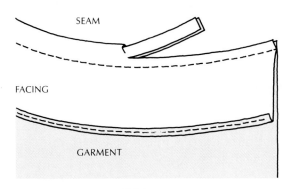

Trimming Cutting off fabric to reduce bulk.

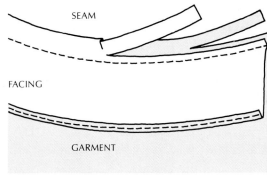

Grading Trimming each layer of a seam allowance slightly narrower than the previous one.

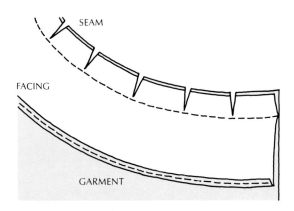

Clipping Making small, evenly spaced cuts in the seam allowance of an inward curve to flatten it.

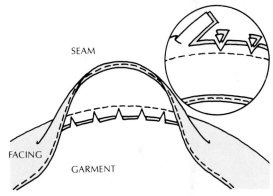

Notching Cutting wedge-shaped sections from the seam allowance of an outward curve to flatten it.

Trimming, grading, clipping, and notching are four frequent steps to take in sewing necklines, armholes, and waistlines.

■ If the seam curves outward, you'll see ripples in the seam allowance. This can be corrected by **notching**, or *cutting wedge-shaped sections so that the fabric lies flat*. When you press the notched seam allow-ance open, it will be smooth and the notched edges will meet.

Now you're ready to turn the facing under. First, press the facing seam flat—the way you stitched it. Then, turn the facing to the inside of the garment and press again.

To hold the facing flat, use one of three methods:

- **Understitch** the facing and seam allowances together. To do this, *open out the facing and machine stitch through the facing and seam allowances.* Do not stitch through the outer layer of fabric.
- *Topstitch* from the right side of the fabric through all the layers.
- *Tack,* or stitch, the facing to seam allowances on the inside.

Pressing

Pressing isn't something you do only when you're all finished making your garment—though you do that, too. Pressing as you go along will guarantee that your seams are flat, darts and tucks are shaped, and facings lie smoothly. As you finish each unit, and before you go on to the next, press it. Check the box in this chapter for tips on no-problem pressing.

Words to Remember

clipping: making small, evenly spaced cuts in the seam allowance of an inward curve to flatten it

dart: a triangular fold of fabric stitched to a point to give shape

directional stitching: stitching with the grain of the fabric

gather: a soft fold of fabric that's stitched into a seam

grade: to trim each layer of a seam allowance slightly narrower than the previous one.

notching: cutting wedge-shaped sections from the seam allowance of an outward curve to flatten it

pressing: lifting the hot iron and setting it down on fabric

staystitching: a row of stitching on just one layer of fabric that keeps the curved areas from stretching as the fabric is handled

tuck: a small, stitched fold used to give shape

unit construction: preparing separate pieces first, then assembling them in a certain order

understitch: to open out the facing and machine stitch through the facing and seam allowances

Questions

1. What does unit construction mean?
2. What are darts, tucks, and gathers used for?
3. What are the four methods of finishing seam allowances?
4. How is a facing applied?
5. When should a project be pressed?

Chapter 61 Adding the Details

Objectives

After reading this chapter, you will be able to:

☐ *identify common fastenings and describe how to attach them,*

☐ *describe how to attach collars and sleeves,*

☐ *apply patch pockets and a simple trim,*

☐ *explain how to make a hem.*

Details can make the difference between an ordinary garment or accessory and one that catches the eye. These finishing details include fasteners, collars, sleeves, pockets, waistbands, casings, hems, and trims. These are the details that people will notice about projects you make. Work carefully to be sure that they look good.

In this chapter, you will learn about:

- *fasteners,* such as buttons, snaps, hooks and eyes, zippers, and hook and loop tapes,
- *special pieces* which many garments call for, including collars, sleeves, pockets, waistbands, castings, hems, and trims.

All these details will spruce up clothes.

Fasteners

Fasteners include buttons and buttonholes, snaps, hooks and eyes, zippers, and hook-and-loop tapes. Buy your fasteners when you buy your pattern and fabric. The quantity and size you'll need are listed on the back of the pattern envelope.

Buttons

There are two kinds of buttons. **Shank buttons** have *a built-in shank, or loop, on the back*. They don't have any holes on the face. Sew them in place with several small stitches through the shank and into the fabric. Use a double strand of thread. Secure the thread with one or two small stitches when you begin and when you finish each button.

Sew-through buttons have *holes in their faces and no shank*. You'll need to make a thread shank to sew them on. This leaves enough room when the button is fastened for the layer of fabric that holds the buttonhole.

To make a thread shank, lay a toothpick or pin on top of the button between the holes. Use double thread and secure the thread with one or two stitches to begin. Sew several stitches over the toothpick or pin and through the fabric. End stitches with the needle and thread under the button. Remove the toothpick or pin and wind the thread several times around the thread under the button. Fasten the thread on the underside of the fabric.

Buttonholes can be made with a zigzag machine or with a special buttonhole attachment. Carefully cut the buttonhole open with the points of your sewing scissors. The pattern has markings showing the location and length of each buttonhole on the pattern.

TYPES OF FASTENERS

SEW-THROUGH BUTTON

SHANK BUTTON

HOOK AND EYE FASTENER

SNAP BUTTON

Select the fastener suitable for the weight and type of fabric. If the right type of fastener is properly attached, the closing of the garment will be smooth.

Snaps

The section of the snap that has the ball should be sewn inside the top flap of the opening. Take several small stitches through one hole, then pass the thread under the snap and sew through the next hole until you've done all four. Rub tailor's chalk on the ball and close the opening. Sew the socket section of the snap over the chalk mark in the same way. Fasten your thread when you begin and when you finish your work.

Hooks and Eyes

Place the hook 1/8″ from the edge of the fabric. Sew several small stitches around each loop or circular hole. Finish with three or four stitches across the end of the hook to make sure it lies flat.

Straight eyes are used for edges that overlap. Chalk the top of the hook and overlap the edges to mark the position of the eye. Attach the eye with small stitches around both loops or circular holes.

Curved eyes are used for edges that meet but don't overlap, such as at the back opening of a blouse. Place the eye so that the curved part sticks out a bit from the edge. Sew in place.

Zippers

Detailed instructions for inserting zippers are given in the pattern guide sheet and in the zipper package. Zippers can be attached in two ways—*centered*, with two rows of stitching, one on each side of the zipper, or *lapped*, with just one row of stitching showing on the outside.

Hook-and-Loop Tapes

Hook-and-loop fasteners consist of two pieces of nylon tape that stick to each other when pressed together. Though they're too bulky for lightweight fabrics, they have many other uses. They're common on parkas, jackets, camping equipment, pillows, and totes. They're even strong enough to hold a decorative quilt on the wall. Attach the tape to fabric by machine stitching around all four sides.

Special Pieces

Many garments call for special pieces, such as collars, sleeves, pockets, and waistbands. They require special sewing techniques.

Collars

You'll find specific instructions for the style of collar to be used on your garment in your pattern guide sheet. However, there are some general guidelines for making collars. The curved edges should be smooth, and the two sides should be evenly matched. Where the collar meets—usually center front—the ends must be the same width and evenly stitched. The undercollar or underside should never show.

To make a collar, first stitch the collar sections together. Interface if necessary. Use short reinforcement stitches for the sharp points. Trim and grade the seam allowances. Understitch the undercollar so that it will lie smooth and flat. Press it carefully. Finally, stitch the collar to the neckline.

F E A T U R E

Hand Sewing

A sewing machine can do just about all the stitching you'll need on a project, but most projects will require some hand sewing. You might be finishing a hem, attaching a fastener, or adding trim by hand. Follow these hints for successful hand sewing.

- Cut the thread on an angle so it will slide through the eye of a needle more easily. Biting or breaking thread frays the end.

- Cut the thread 18" to 24" long—anything longer may tangle or knot.

- Use a single strand of thread except when sewing buttons, snaps, and hooks and eyes.

- Secure stitches when you begin and end by making a few small stitches in one place or by tying a knot.

- Wear a thimble on the middle finger of the hand you sew with to push the needle through the fabric.

- Keep stitches loose to avoid puckering as you sew.

The three most common hand stitches are the backstitch, hemming stitch, and slip stitch. The pictures show how to do them.

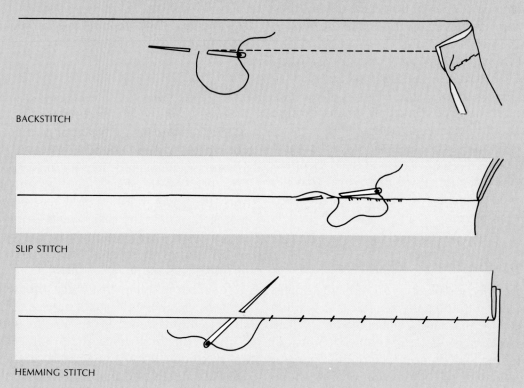

BACKSTITCH

SLIP STITCH

HEMMING STITCH

Sleeves

There are three basic styles of sleeves:

- A *kimono sleeve* is cut in one piece with the top of the garment. It is usually short and loose fitting.
- A *raglan sleeve* has two diagonal seams that run from the neckline to the underarm. It is easy to sew and comfortable to wear.
- A *set-in sleeve* is attached by one seam that goes in a circle over the shoulder and under the arm. The sleeve is gathered or eased across the top between the two notches. Then, the sleeve is pinned to the armhole, the fullness is adjusted evenly, and the armhole seam is stitched.

Pockets

There are many different types of pockets. Two that are particularly easy to sew are in-seam and patch pockets.

In-seam pockets are usually cut along with skirt or pants sections and stitched at the same time as the side seam. Your pattern instructions will tell you how to do this.

A *patch pocket* is sewn to the outside of a garment or project. Finish the top edge of the pocket according to your pattern instructions. Stitch around the pocket 5/8" from the edge. Trim the seam allowance, turn it under along the stitching line, and press. Topstitch the pocket in place, using the edge of the presser foot as a guide for straight stitching. The top corners of the pocket can be reinforced with triangular stitching.

Waistbands

For a firm waistband, use interfacing. To attach the waistband, pin it to the garment, matching notches and seam markings, and follow the pattern instructions. Stitch the seam, and then trim, grade, and clip the seam edges. Press the seam up into the waistband.

Next, stitch the ends of the waistband with the right sides together. Trim, grade,

TYPES OF SLEEVES

KIMONO   RAGLAN   SET-IN

Essentially, there are three basic types of sleeves: the kimono, the raglan, and the set-in. All other types are variations of them.

and clip the corners. Turn the waistband right side out. Stitch the other edge of the waistband in place. Some directions call for topstitching from the right side, while others instruct you to stitch by hand on the inside.

Casings

Casings are used to cover drawstrings or elastic at the waistline of pants, shorts, and skirts, or on one-piece outfits such as dresses and jumpsuits. They're also used at the edge of a sleeve or at a neckline that has a drawstring.

You can create a self-casing by folding back an extension of the fabric at the edge of the garment and stitching it in place. Some casings—for example, those at the waistline of one-piece garments—are made by stitching a strip of bias tape to the inside of the garment.

Leave a 2" opening at the seam to insert the elastic or drawstring. Attach a safety pin to the end of the elastic or drawstring and pull it through the casing. Overlap elastic ends 1" and stitch the casing closed. Or knot the drawstring ends so they won't disappear back into the casing.

Hems

Hems are used at the bottom edge of pant legs, skirts, and curtains, and on shirts, jackets, tablecloths, and beach towels. Sewing hems is the last step in constructing a project.

When marking a hem in a garment, try to get someone to help you. Wear the shoes you'll ordinarily wear with the garment, because heel height makes a difference in measurement. Stand up straight. Have the other person mark the bottom of the hem with pins or chalk, using a yard/meter stick or a special hem marker. Then fold the hem up and pin it. Check the length and evenness in a mirror.

SEWING A HEM

1

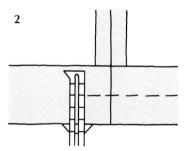

2

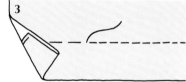

3

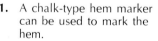

1. A chalk-type hem marker can be used to mark the hem.

2. Make the hem an even width around by marking it with a measuring gauge and chalk.

3. For an interesting finish, you can sew the hem in place with matching or contrasting thread.

The depth of the hem depends upon the style of garment and the type of fabric. Be sure to use one of the seam finishing techniques to prevent raveling.

Next, trim the width of the hem to the desired depth. Pants, sleeves, and shorts usually have hems of 1″ to 2″. On dresses and skirts, the hem should be about 3″ deep. Straight hems can be wider than curved hems. If you are still growing, you may want a wider hem that can be let down in the future.

The hem edge on woven fabrics should be finished to prevent raveling. Use one of the seam finishing techniques, or apply seam tape, bias tape, or lace.

Stitch the hem in place with small, invisible hand stitches. Do not pull the stitches too tight or the hem will pucker. A hem can be topstitched using straight, zigzag, or decorative stitches. Hems can also be fused in place with a fusible web. This method is good for garments that will not be lengthened in the future.

Trims

Trims such as rickrack, braid, ruffles, lace, and appliqués are wonderful for brightening, decorating, and emphasizing the lines of garments, accessories, and household items that you make. Almost all can be bought ready-made and easily attached.

Rickrack is attached with one row of machine stitching down the center. Stitch braid along each long edge. To attach bias binding, place the narrower side on top, folding the wider side underneath. Machine stitch from the right side.

Appliqué is *a cut-out fabric decoration sewn onto another fabric background*. You can buy appliqués or cut them out yourself, but don't use fabric that ravels easily. They can be cut in any shape you choose and sewn on by machine or by hand.

Embroidery can be used to personalize almost anything that you make or buy. You can add your initials or name to a collar, pocket, pillow, or tote. Or use embroidery to create a unique design on a T-shirt or placemat. You can borrow a book from the library to learn how to make the many different embroidery stitches.

Words to Remember

appliqué: a cut-out fabric decoration sewn onto another fabric background

sew-through buttons: buttons that have holes in their faces and no shank

shank buttons: buttons that have a built-in shank, or loop, on the back

topstitching: sewing a decorative stitch on the right side of a garment to emphasize detail

Questions

1. How do you attach a shank button? How do you attach a sew-through button?
2. Which snap section is sewn on first?
3. What kind of an edge is a straight eye best for? A curved eye?
4. What are the three types of sleeves?
5. What are two easy-to-make pockets?
6. Where might casings be used?
7. When are hems sewn?
8. Name two kinds of decorations that can be added to a sewing project.

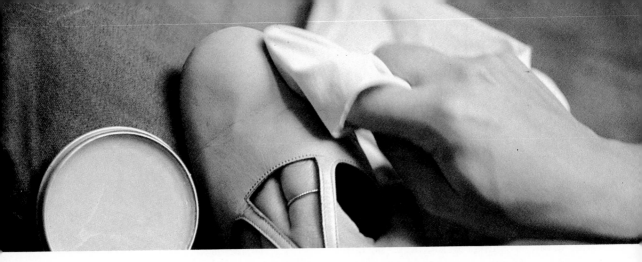

Chapter **62 Clothes Care**

Objectives

After reading this chapter, you will be able to:

☐ *explain how to care for your clothes,*

☐ *describe different ways to clean clothes,*

☐ *describe some simple clothing repairs,*

☐ *outline how to store clothes.*

There are few things more annoying. Just when you're getting ready to go out, you find your favorite outfit dirty or torn. You're so angry, you want to yell at someone—but you know that the someone who should be yelled at is *you*.

Caring for clothes begins when you put them on and ends when you take them off and put them away.

- Put clothes on and take them off carefully.
- Open zippers and buttons fully to prevent breaking them or ripping seams.
- Bathe daily and use deodorant or antiperspirant.
- Protect clothes by using a napkin while eating and by wearing old clothes or an apron when doing messy chores.
- Take care of stains immediately. If you spill something, try to remove it right then. The longer the stain stays, the harder it is to remove.

448

General Care

Daily Care

You can take steps at the end of the day to keep your clothes in condition.

- Before putting clothes away, air them out. Spread them flat on your bed or drape them over a chair.
- Brush off lint and dust. Check each garment to see if it needs repair or has a spot that needs cleaning. A small rip or a loose button takes only a few minutes to fix. But if you ignore it now, the repair may become a major job.
- Set aside any clothes that need to be washed or cleaned.
- Once your clothes have aired, hang them up or fold them. Use curved or wooden hangers for jackets and padded hangers for delicate fabrics. Close zippers and one or two buttons on each piece of clothing.

Occasional Care

Set aside some time every week for making repairs that take longer than the small daily repairs. This is the time to hand wash any items that can't be put in the machine. And if you do all your ironing at this time, you'll save both effort and energy.

You could also do sewing repairs on this fix-it day. Or you could collect all your clothes that need to be fixed in one place—one part of the closet or one dresser drawer. Then, when you have a few minutes to spare, you can make these repairs. You could even repair your clothing while watching television.

Cleaning Clothes

All clothes need to be cleaned, but different garments need different types of cleaning. Jeans with a grass stain will require a more thorough washing than will a shirt that you've only worn once. Though most clothes are washed in water with detergent, some fabrics require drycleaning. And you may have to hand wash more delicate items.

Care Labels

To choose the correct cleaning method, first check the care label. All clothes are required by law to have these care labels. There, the manufacturer tells you what kind of washing, drying, or drycleaning steps to follow. Labels also tell you what not to do, such as "Do no bleach" or "Do not wring or twist."

Increase the life span of your clothes by following a garment's care label cleaning directions.

TABLE 1   **Stain Removal Chart**

Stain	Cleaning Method
Ball-point pen ink	Sponge with rubbing alcohol. Rub any remaining stain with soap or a detergent, then wash.
Blood	Soak in lukewarm water and detergent. If yellow stain remains, apply bleach and rinse well.
Candle wax, chewing gum	Harden by rubbing with an ice cube, then scrape off with a blunt knife or your fingernail.
Chocolate	Rinse in lukewarm water. If brown stain remains, apply bleach.
Cosmetics	Rub detergent into spot and wash.
Grass, flowers, foliage	Work detergent into stain, then rinse. Or, if safe for fabric, sponge stain with alcohol. For use on acetate, dilute alcohol with two parts water.
Grease	Start by using the ice cube method given for candle wax and chewing gum. Then, use lighter fluid to remove the remaining stain.
Nail polish	Do not use polish remover. Sponge with amyl acetate and wash. If necessary, sponge with alcohol mixed with a few drops of ammonia.
Paint, varnish	Rub detergent into stain and wash. If stain is only partially removed, sponge with turpentine.
Perspiration	If garment color has been affected, sponge a fresh stain with ammonia, an old stain with white vinegar. Rinse and launder.
Soft drinks	Sponge with cold water, then wash.

Stains

Sometimes, *dirt has become concentrated in one spot in a garment*. Such a spot is called a **stain**. You may need to give a stain special treatment before adding it to other clothes in a load of laundry. Charts are available that describe how to treat particular stains. Some stains can be removed by spraying them with a prewash spray, letting the spray set, and then washing the clothes normally.

Remember that the longer a stain stays in the fabric, the harder it is to remove. Always try to treat stains either when they occur or soon afterwards.

Sorting Clothes

Before washing the clothes, you must decide which clothes can be washed together. First, separate clothing according to care labels. Put together all clothes that can be machine washed, all those that need hand washing, and all those that need drycleaning. Hand washing is best for delicates, woolens, and silks, as well as for single items that you need to wash but don't have a full load for.

Next, sort out fabrics that might leave lint. Examples are terry cloth and corduroy. And remove heavy items like sheets that might tangle with and tear delicate clothes.

Finally, sort by color. Dye from dark-colored jeans may discolor whites, so they should be washed separately. For these reasons, you need to sort your clothing into piles of items that can be washed together. You might have quite a few piles: sheets, towels, dark colors, light colors, whites, and delicate fabrics.

Washing Clothes

Washing cleans clothes by pushing water between the yarns and fibers. The water

It is important to sort clothes so that you can use the right washing cycles and water temperatures for them.

either dissolves the soil or lifts the particles of dirt away from the fabric. Adding soap or detergent to the water helps remove the soil. The box explains the many types of cleaning products.

You can wash clothes in two ways—by hand washing them or washing them in an automatic machine. Whether the machine is in your home or you use a coin-operated machine, you should follow these steps:

1. Check pockets to make sure that they are empty; close all fasteners.
2. Select water temperature as directed on garments' care labels. To save energy, wash with warm or cold water instead of hot water.
3. Add clothing and detergent to machine. (Read the instructions on the detergent box first—some suggest putting detergent into the machine first, then adding clothing.) Include bleach if you're using it.
4. Use a full load of clothing or reduce the water level setting.
5. Wash clothing. If you're using fabric softener, add it as directed on the package.
6. Remove garments from the washer, and clean the filter.

Drying and Ironing

For best results, check the care labels, and set the correct temperature on the clothes dryer. Synthetics should be dried at a lower temperature than cottons. Be sure to remove your clothes as soon as they've finished drying. Hang them up to prevent wrinkling.

Of course, some clothes can't be put in a dryer. The garment's care label will tell you whether you should hang it on a line or lay it flat on a towel to dry.

Drying on the line can help give your clothes a pleasant, fresh smell. And if you only have a few items to dry, hanging them saves energy. Hanging clothes to dry also avoids shrinkage.

Some fabrics require pressing or ironing to get a smooth finish. Knits and woolens should only be pressed, to avoid stretching. To iron a woven fabric, be sure to iron with the grain line. Check the box in chapter 60 for good tips on pressing.

You can save energy when drying and ironing by following these suggestions.

■ Dry clothes only until dry and remove immediately to avoid wrinkling.

■ Let clothes hang to dry if possible.

■ Iron at the lowest possible temperature setting.

Drycleaning

Many fabrics need to be **drycleaned**, which is *cleaning with chemicals rather than with detergent and water*. After cleaning, the clothes are put on forms that are in the shape of a body and steam is blown through them to remove wrinkles. Special touches, such as creases in trousers, are put in by a steam pressing machine or by hand with a steam iron.

Some fabrics and trimmings are harmed by dry cleaning. Vinyl, for example, can't be drycleaned. If the care label says not to dry-clean, follow the advice. The manager of the drycleaning store will tell you if any trim must be removed before cleaning the garment.

Cleaners may miss spots and stains unless

Some clothes need no ironing. Read the clothing labels to see if you should iron a garment.

you point them out to the counter clerk. And if you know what caused the stain, say so. Otherwise, it may not be identified correctly. The more information *you* provide, the better you will be served.

Some laundromats offer coin-operated dry-cleaning machines. These cost less than professional dry cleaning and remove most soil quite well. However, they don't provide special treatment for spots and stains.

Simple Repairs

No matter how careful you are, sometimes a garment needs to be fixed.

■ *Repairing snags.* Knits often get **snags**, *loops of yarn that are pulled out of the knit*. Use a crochet hook or a snag fixer, which you can buy wherever notions are sold. Grasp the snag with the hook and pull it

TABLE 2   How to Wash Different Loads of Clothes

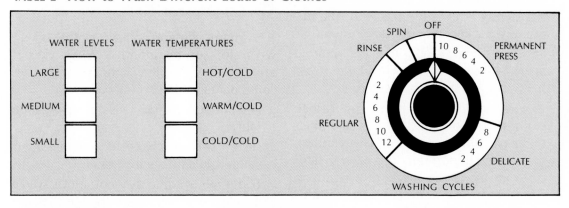

Water Levels
*use **low** for smaller loads, **medium** for average loads, **high** for large loads*

Water Temperatures
***hot, warm, cold.** Use warm and cold temperatures whenever possible for energy conservation*

Washing Cycles
*long cycle, medium cycle, short cycle—wash delicates on **short cycle,** average soiled clothing on **medium cycle,** heavily soiled clothing on **long cycle.***

F E A T U R E

Choosing Laundry Products

Every wash needs a soap or detergent and water. In addition, other products, such as bleaches and presoaks, may be used for special purposes. Always check the care label on a garment. It may warn against the use of one product or another on certain fabrics.

- *Soap.* A cleansing agent made from animal or vegetable fat; used with soft water.
- *Detergent.* A cleansing agent made from chemicals or petroleum; works well in hard or soft water.
- *Presoak.* Helps soak out protein stains like egg, meat juices, and blood.

- *Prewash spray.* Helps remove many types of stains before washing.
- *Water softener.* Softens hard water.
- *Disinfectant.* Destroys bacteria; used if the water is not hot, or if there's an illness in the family.
- *Bleach.* Removes stains and soil; whitens or brightens white items and disinfects.
- *Fabric softener.* Decreases static electricity and makes fabric feel softer.
- *Starch.* Stiffens fabric; used mostly for cotton.

All laundry products include directions. Follow them carefully for best results.

back through to the underside of the fabric. Gently stretch the fabric to smooth out any puckers that the snag caused.

- *Mending seams.* Seams that are coming apart can be stitched by machine or by hand, using a strong backstitch.

- *Patching a hole.* For jeans and casual clothes, iron-on patches are sold that make patching easy. For dressier clothes, matching is important. Cut a piece of fabric from along the inside of a seam or from a seam allowance, and place it under the hole. Turn in the torn edges and stitch around the opening with tiny, hardly visible stitches.

- *Darning a tear.* You can **darn**, or *reweave, straight tears in fabric.* Place the torn edges together. Use an unknotted thread to make small stitches back and forth across the tear. Stitch an extra 1/4″ on either side.

- *Replacing fasteners.* You may have to mend the fabric underneath before replacing a fastener. To attach the new fastener, follow the instructions in chapter 61.

Seasonal Care

In many climates, certain clothes aren't worn for several months. When clothes aren't worn for a long time, they can become damaged in several ways:

- Perspiration and skin oils can weaken the fabric.

- Insects such as silverfish can attack food stains and damage the fibers.

- If the fabric contains wool, moth larvae may eat the fibers, even though they are clean.

- **Mildew**—*a fungus*—may grow on damp fabric, causing stains.

To protect stored clothes:

- Make sure that the clothes are clean, dry, and free of stains.

- Treat woolens with a moth repellent; if possible, seal them in an airtight bag.

- To prevent mildew, make sure that your clothes are completely dry before you put them away, and that they'll remain dry.

- You can also put stored clothes in garment bags or boxes to protect them.

Words to Remember

darn: reweave straight tears in fabric

dryclean: clean with chemicals rather than with detergent and water

mildew: a fungus that damages clothes

snag: a loop of yarn that's pulled out of a knit

stain: dirt that has become concentrated in one spot on a garment

Questions

1. List three things you can do every day to care for your clothes.
2. Why do you need to sort clothes before washing them?
3. What two methods of drying can you choose from?
4. How does drycleaning work?
5. Explain how to protect clothes against moths and mildew.

Chapter 63 Redesigning and Recycling

Objectives

After reading this chapter, you will be able to:

□ *describe ways to get more use out of your favorite garments,*

□ *describe ways to rescue clothes that have fallen out of favor,*

□ *suggest uses for clothes that you can no longer wear.*

When you went through your wardrobe, you found some clothes that you no longer liked or that you couldn't wear. Perhaps a shirt was out of fashion. Or some pants were too short. Whatever the reason, you don't need to throw those clothes away. There are two things that you can do. You can **redesign** the garment—*change it so that it's more in fashion or has an exciting new look.* Or you can **recycle** it—*find a new use for it* in your wardrobe.

Perhaps you have an older garment that fits but doesn't look the way you want it to. Maybe fashions have changed, and last year's shirt no longer looks right. Perhaps the color has faded. You can try a few simple techniques for bringing these clothes back into your wardrobe.

Redesigning a Garment

Lengthening Hems

One problem with those two inches you grew this summer—now your clothes don't fit! You can solve that problem by lengthening the hem.

1. Remove the old hem stitching and press out the crease.

2. Mark the new hemline, turn the new hemline under, and stitch in place. If the original crease does not press out completely, hide it with topstitching or trim.

Does a hem not have enough fabric to lengthen? Then use wide hem facing. Stitch

---

ALTERING HEMS

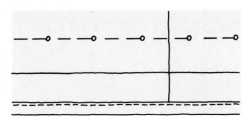

1. After removing the old hem stitching, press out the crease. Then put on the garment so the new hemline can be marked. (It's best to have someone mark the hemline for you, using chalk or pins.)

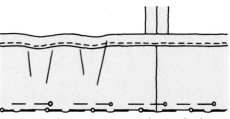

2. Take off the garment and turn the hem under along the chalk or pin line. Use pins to hold the hem in place. Baste the hem ¼ in (6mm) from the folded edge. Try on the garment one more time to make sure the hem is right.

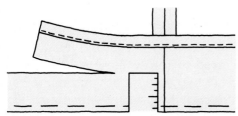

3. If the hem is too deep, measure and mark the desired depth. Cut off the extra fabric evenly. Finish the raw edge with a finish appropriate for the type of fabric and garment.

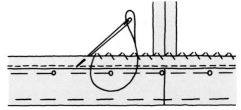

4. Pin the top of the finished hem to the garment, matching seams. Sew the hem to the garment with stitches that just catch the fabric. The stitches should be smooth and invisible on the outside of the garment. Press the completed hem so that it will lie flat.

Fast growing teens will benefit from knowing how to lengthen hems. Use hem facing, a ruffle, or a band of contrasting fabric if there is not enough fabric.

ALTERING SEAMS

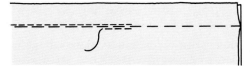

1. Whether you have opened a seam to alter it, or are simply repairing seams, many of the same principles apply. Fix the ends of the old seam that remain, by backstitching about 1 in (24mm) along the old seam line as you start and finish the new stitching.

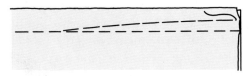

2. Merely restitching a seam is not hard. Pin or baste the two edges together as they were originally, and then stitch along the holes left by the old thread.

To let out a seam, measure how much extra room you want to create, and check that there is enough fabric in the seam allowance. Baste the new seam in a smooth line, *then* remove the old stitching. Check fit by trying on the garment. Then stitch and press open the new seam.

3. To take in a seam, the simplest method is to put on the garment inside out, and pin a new seam line so that the garment fits well. Take the garment off carefully, machine baste along the pinned line, and remove the pins. Press lightly, then check the fit of the garment before final stitching and pressing.

Altering seams allows you to make a garment more comfortable for the wearer. It also gives the garment a longer life in your wardrobe.

---

the hem facing to the bottom of the garment, turn the facing to the inside along the new hemline, press, and sew to the garment. Or you can add a colorful ruffle or band of contrasting fabric.

Altering Seams

To let out a seam, check the seam allowance to be sure that there's enough fabric there. Rip out the old seam as far as necessary. Pin or baste, remove the old seam, and check the fit by trying on the garment. Then finish the new seam.

To take in a seam, put the garment on inside out and pin a new seam line where it feels comfortable. Stitch the new seams, overlapping the original stitching for 1".

Changing the Garment

You can also change clothes to new styles to get more use out of them. Give a shirt or blouse a new look by shortening the sleeves. Turn flare pants into straight legs by taking in the side seams. Turn straight legs into flares by adding a triangle of new material.

There's one other way to restyle—you can turn a garment from one type into another. By removing sleeves from a sweater, you make yourself a vest. Cut off pant legs to make cropped pants or shorts, turn sweatshirts into tops, shorten coats to make jackets. Sewing books—and your own creativity—will give you more ideas.

Creative Measures

You can make old clothes bright and lively by adding decorations. Patches, appliqués, trims, and embroidery can cover holes, hide stains, or simply liven up your clothing. Even if your jeans don't have a hole, decorate them with your initials, or a butterfly, or a sports team emblem.

Use these decorations to make garments that show your individuality. See chapter 61 for directions on how to add them.

Dyeing

Sometimes, the only thing wrong with a garment is its color. You don't like it, or it doesn't go with the rest of your clothes. If so, consider **dyeing** it, or *changing its color*.

You can dye your clothes at home, or you can have them dyed professionally. Professional dyeing costs more, of course, but some garments are worth the extra expense. For successful home dyeing, carefully follow the directions on the dye package.

Home dyeing works best when a light-colored fabric is darkened. Mix the dye with hot water, and then soak the fabric in a sink, a container, or a washing machine. Very dark colors are difficult to obtain since the fabric usually must be simmered in the dye.

Dyes may stain the equipment you use.

For this reason, always get permission to use the sink or container in which you plan to dye your clothes. Never dye clothes in a laundromat.

Tie-dyeing and *batik* are two special dyeing methods that create striking new designs on old garments.

In **tie-dyeing**, *parts of the fabric are tightly wrapped, or tied, so that the dye penetrates unevenly*, producing many different shades of the color. One or several colors may be used in this process.

In **batik** dyeing, *hot wax is poured onto the fabric to coat some areas completely.* When the garment is dyed, the coated areas stay the original color. Only the unwaxed areas take the dye. During the process, the wax cracks, forming thin lines in the final pattern. When dyeing is finished, the wax is removed, leaving a permanent design dyed into the fabric. The same procedure can be repeated several times, using different colors each time.

Recycling a Garment

There are three ways to recycle clothes. You can *pass a garment on* to someone else, *use the fabric in another way,* or *reuse the fiber.*

By recycling clothes in these ways, you're acting responsibly toward the future. Natural fibers need to be grown on land, but with more and more people in the world, that land is needed for food and housing. And synthetic fibers depend on materials that must also be used for other purposes—including energy. When you recycle clothes, there's less demand for fibers, so resources can be used in other ways.

Passing It On

One of the oldest forms of recycling clothing is the hand-me-down. Clothing that you no longer wear can be passed on to a younger sibling, cousin, or niece or nephew. Or you could give it to a friend. Clothing that no longer suits you may be a real find for someone else.

During your teen years, you're likely to be growing fast. This means you may stop wearing garments *long* before they are unwearable. Throwing such clothing out is wasteful. There may be several years' wear left for someone else.

If that someone else can't be found in your family or among your friends, look further. You could earn some money by selling the clothes through a *thrift shop*. This store buys and sells used clothing. Or you could give the clothing to a charity group such as the Salvation Army or CARE.

Clothes that you give away help someone else. They may help a family that has lost everything in a fire or flood. Knowing that your outgrown sweater is keeping someone warm will probably give you a warm feeling, too.

One of the most common methods of recycling in many families is to hand garments down to younger family members after they can no longer be used by older members.

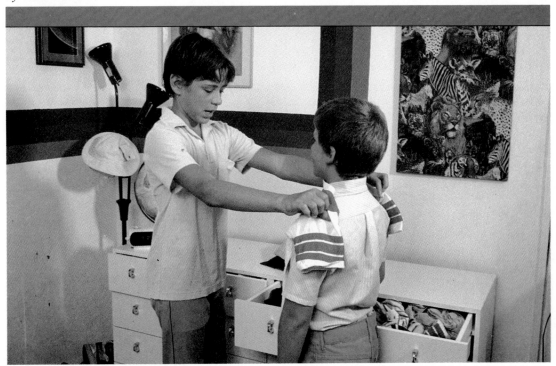

F E A T U R E

The Final Cycle

Garments can be recycled even when they can no longer be used as clothing. The legs of a pair of jeans, for example, can be converted into a sturdy tote bag. And even if only small pieces of the fabric are in good condition, these can be cut out and saved for patchwork. Such pieced fabric can be made into one-of-a-kind vests, shirts, placemats, totes and handbags, or pillows. You could even make an old-fashioned patchwork quilt.

Worn-out garments of soft cotton make good cleaning rags. Be sure to remove all fasteners from the rags before you use them. Otherwise, furniture could get scratched from sharp hooks or button edges. Torn nylon stockings, panty hose, and underwear can be cut up and used to stuff toys and pillows.

Save trim, decorations, and fasteners for use on future projects.

Even if the fabric is totally destroyed, the fibers might still be useful. Fibers can be recycled to make fabrics suitable for use as padding (shoulder pads, for example). Fibers are also used for the rag content in paper. Some cities have organizations that collect old clothes for such recycling. Garments that cannot be used by thrift shops or charities also can be given away for fiber recycling.

There are many reasons for recycling clothes. A lot of them help *you*—they stretch your clothing budget and give you better wear for your money. But when a garment has reached the end of the road for you, don't forget other people. The garment, its fabric, or its fibers may still be useful.

Words to Remember

batik: a dyeing method in which hot wax is poured onto the fabric so that it completely coats some areas, which stay the original color when the wax is removed

recycle: find new uses for old clothes

redesign: change an item so that it's more in fashion or has an exciting new look

tie-dyeing: a dyeing method in which parts of the fabric are tightly wrapped, or tied, so that the dye penetrates unevenly

Questions

1. How do you lengthen a hem?
2. What are the steps for taking in a seam? Letting one out?
3. Where should dyeing be done?
4. Describe tie-dyeing and batik.
5. What are two advantages of recycling clothes?
6. How could you pass clothing you cannot wear on to someone else?

64 Careers in Clothing and Textiles

Objectives

After reading this chapter, you will be able to:

☐ *identify areas in the job market in which you can use the skills discussed in this unit,*

☐ *describe various kinds of jobs in these areas.*

The clothing and textiles industry is among the ten largest industries in the country. It shows every sign of expansion and by the year 2000 will be among the top five industries. Fabrics are needed for all sorts of things, from your pants or skirt to the curtains that hang in your living room.

Careers in clothing and textiles cover a broad range, from clothing design to work in a textile mill to management. Are you interested in fashion? You could apply your knowledge of what people have worn in the past to designing costumes for movies or plays. Someone who likes science could become a textile chemist. If you like crafts, you could become a leather worker.

In this chapter, you'll learn about a few of the fascinating and varied careers in clothing and textiles.

461

Characteristics Useful in Clothing and Textiles Careers

Though there are a variety of jobs in this field, many of them call for similar qualities. If you have these traits, a clothing career may be for you.

Physical Characteristics

To be successful in a clothing career, you first of all need to be able to work hard. The jobs are demanding and put people under a great deal of pressure. Deadlines are always important, and workers often put in long hours.

Mental Characteristics

Are you careful in your work? Do you pay attention to detail? These two traits are very important for a clothing worker, whatever the job. Seams must be sewn to last. Designers need to add that last little touch that makes a garment perfect.

Another important skill is the ability to use shapes. Designers, sewers, and textile workers all get their effects by combining various shapes. If you're good at laying out a pattern in the most economical way, you may have this important skill.

Clothing workers also need a sense of color and design. They combine these elements in their work to create attractive, usable products. Do friends say that your outfits are attractive? If so, your sense of design may be good.

Of course, anyone who works with clothing and textiles must know about fibers. It's also important to be able to organize your work. Clothing jobs often involve following many steps and combining many pieces. To get the job done, you must plan your tasks carefully. If you have the abilities outlined here, you might be just right for one of these careers.

Jobs in Design and Marketing

Many clothing and textile careers have to do with the design and selling of clothes. In one of these jobs, you could combine an interest in fashion with a career in the world of business.

Entry-Level Jobs

Salespeople help customers find what they're looking for and make their purchases. Stores train their sales staffs to answer questions about fabric content, quality, and care of the clothing they sell. Some stores require a high school diploma for their full-time salespeople. The ability to meet and work with the public is also a must. Being a salesperson is often the first step in a career in retail clothing.

Before clothes are offered for sale, someone has to check the incoming orders. This is done by *stock clerks*, who also put price tags on the garments. And they keep track of the merchandise and how the stock is moving. A stock clerk doesn't need any special training. However, being good in math and spelling helps. It's also useful to have a talent for detailed work and to spend time at it.

Jobs That Require Extra Training

Large clothing stores have promotion and publicity departments. In the promotion department, *copywriters* and artists prepare ads. And *display workers* dress windows and set up displays throughout the store. Col-lege writing or journalism courses will help prepare you for a copywriter's job.

Artists and display workers need art training, but these workers may learn many of their skills while on the job.

The *buyer* is one of the most important people in the fashion industry. Buyers con-

---

F E A T U R E

Interviewing for a Job

When someone finds your résumé or application interesting, you may be invited to an **interview.** This *meeting between an employer and a job applicant* is important. It will be the basis for the employer's decision to hire you or not. And it will give you the information you need to decide whether you want to work there.

It's important to make a good impression at a job interview. You're more likely to make that impression if you prepare yourself in advance.

- *Review your résumé.* Refresh your memory about what you've done. If the job requires certain qualifications —such as a license—be sure to bring proof to the interview.
- *Learn about the employer in advance.* Do research in the library or talk to people you know who work or shop there. If your interview shows that you've made this effort, the employer will be impressed by you.
- *Think about some of the questions that you might be asked.* Will you be prepared to work overtime? Can you get along well with others? What do you plan for your future? Thinking about these questions ahead of time will help you give better answers to the interviewer.

- *Come to the interview dressed neatly and appropriately, and be on time.* In fact, try to arrive early. You can spend some time relaxing, looking around the area to learn about the company, and reviewing your résumé.

- *Be ready to ask questions.* It will show that you're interested in the job and that you're thoughtful. And by asking questions, you're sure to learn the information that you feel you need. You could ask what the work involves and what company policies are on training and promotions, for instance.

If you're interested in the job, tell the interviewer as the interview ends. Follow up the interview with a note to the interviewer, thanking him or her for the interview. If you were told that you'd hear from the organization in a certain time and have not, call to find out the status of your application.

nect the designers and garment makers with the stores and shops where clothing is sold. A buyer can work for a large department store, a chain of stores, a mail-order house, or a local specialty store. Large stores have a number of buyers. Each orders only the type of clothing carried in one department. In a small specialty store, the buyer is often the owner of the store.

Buyers must know the tastes and buying habits of their customers. Otherwise, they would not be able to select and buy suitable merchandise. For example, buyers must have a good idea of the colors their customers like. That doesn't mean they can't buy new shades. But they do make sure that they order garments in colors that are popular with their customers.

Jobs That Require a Degree

Large stores often employ *fashion coordinators*. These workers plan fashion shows and develop advertising themes. They often involve community groups, such as school clubs, in their projects. You may have attended or modeled at a fashion show put on by a store.

The fashion coordinator also makes sure that different parts of the store sell clothing and accessories that go well together. They work closely with the buyers. Together they see to it that the different departments in the store are aware of the latest colors and styles. They want to make sure, for example, that a customer who selects a suit in a new fashion color can find matching accessories in other departments.

Garment companies need designers, pattern makers, and sewing machine operators to produce the clothes you wear.

Designers sketch ideas that come from fashion trends, or the sketches may be adaptations of current high-fashion styles.

Fashion coordinators are usually college graduates who majored in home economics or art. In addition, they need to get experience in various positions within a clothing store.

The *designer* is another important person in the fashion industry. Every piece of clothing that a buyer selects—and every piece that you wear—first takes shape in the mind of a designer. Designers choose the fabrics and plan the lines of new garments. They make sketches, and sometimes samples, from which a pattern can be made.

Designers usually get their training in college programs for fashion design and by working with experienced designers. To be successful, designers must keep in close touch with fashion trends.

Store buyers go to clothing manufacturers' head-quarters, like this man's, a few times a year to buy the latest fashions.

Jobs in Clothing Construction and Care

The clothing industry also employs thousands of people who work behind the scenes. These workers are dyeing fabrics or sewing clothes. They are developing new fibers or improving the crop yield of old ones. Or they work in caring for clothes. It's because of this important work that we have such a variety of fabrics, colors, and styles to choose from.

Entry-Level Jobs

The largest number of workers in the garment industry are *sewing machine operators*. These are the people who do the stitching. Machine operators are trained on the job. Beginners start out stitching the easiest seams. Their wages begin with the legal minimum pay, but they can work their way up in responsibility and income. Operators who show ability in working with people become supervisors.

Skilled sewers can work in other businesses also. Drycleaning plants employ *menders* to do repairs and alterations on customers' clothing. Secondhand clothing stores also hire workers with sewing skills for repair work. Many large clothing stores hire *alteration workers* to alter garments, such as suits, to fit customers.

Laundries provide jobs for many different workers. A *machine washer* washes such items as shirts and sheets. He or she must know how to work a huge machine that holds several hundred pounds of laundry. Washers have to choose the right water temperature, suds level, time setting, and amount of agitation for each fabric.

After the laundry is washed, the washer delivers items such as sheets to the *flatwork finishers*. They shake the folds from the sheets. Then, they place the sheets on belts that feed them into ironing machines. Shirts, left damp after the wash, are sent to the *shirt finishers,* who press them.

Jobs That Require Extra Training

Spotters are the real fabric experts. They work mainly for drycleaners. Spotters must know how to choose the right chemicals to remove stubborn spots and stains without damaging the garment. They learn the techniques to use for each type of fabric, chemical, and stain. Because the job involves making a great deal of decisions, it takes six to twelve months to learn. This training can be obtained in a vocational school or on the job.

The *pattern maker* holds the highest paid and most important production job in a garment factory. He or she is a skilled worker who makes a pattern from the designer's original sample. All the patterns of a garment are copies of this first one, so accuracy is very important. Many years of on-the-job experience are needed for this job.

Jobs That Require a Degree

Not all textiles are suitable for making clothing. To find the right kind, research is necessary. *Textile chemists* and *textile engineers* are constantly working on techniques for making yarns and cloths, improving quality, and keeping down production costs. These workers need college degrees and must be skilled in math and science.

Researchers also look for new fibers and finishes. Because of them, we now have wrinkle- and soil-resistant finishes. Even better blends of fibers will probably be developed in the textile laboratories of the future.

Dyers are also highly skilled workers. They work in a textile mill and choose the formulas used for dyeing the textiles. They must know chemistry and understand how the dyes and fibers will react together.

Words to Remember

interview: a meeting between an employer and a job applicant

Questions

1. What physical characteristic is needed for careers in clothing and textiles?
2. Identify three mental characteristics useful for careers in clothing and textiles.
3. Name three jobs in clothing design and marketing—one at each level.
4. Name three jobs in clothing construction and care—one at each level.

You can get the most out of your wardrobe by shopping carefully and by combining garments to make attractive outfits. You can help yourself by making useful projects. Here are some ideas to help you.

1. Should I buy it?

2. Mixing and matching.

3. Sewing safety.

4. Project ideas.

Should I Buy It?

"All right," you say, "I'll try the clothes on in the store before I buy them—but what should I look for?" Here's a checklist.

- Does the neckline lie flat without bulging?

- Are collars and pockets well cut and sewn?

- Is the waistline comfortable?

- Are fasteners attached securely?

- Is the garment too tight, or can you bend, sit, and stretch comfortably?

- Do stripes and plaids match at the seams?

- Are care instructions included?

- Do darts point to the fullest part of your body?

- Does the fitted waistline hug your own waist?

- Are sleeves long enough?

- Is the garment neatly finished at the neck, sleeves, and hems?

■ Are care instructions included?

■ Is the garment neatly finished at the neck, sleeves, and hems?

■ Are fasteners attached securely?

■ Do stripes and plaids match at the seams?

■ Is the waistline comfortable?

■ Are sleeves long enough?

■ Are collars and pockets well cut and sewn?

■ Is the garment too tight, or can you bend, sit, and stretch comfortably?

■ Do the front and back of pants legs hang straight to the floor?

Before making a purchase, answer these questions.
■ Do I need it?
■ Can I wear it for different activities?
■ Will it go with other clothes in my wardrobe?
■ Do I like the color and design?
■ Will it go out of style quickly?
■ Is the price right?

■ Are legs long enough?

Mixing and Matching

How many combinations can you get from these items? Do you see 25 different outfits?

MALE

FEMALE

Sewing Safety

Acting safely is very important in the sewing lab. Below are some steps that you can take to work safely in the lab.

Using the sewing machine

- Use a slow speed when learning how to use the machine.
- Take care to keep your fingers away from the needle.
- Sew carefully over pins.
- Don't lean your face too closely over the needle, in case it breaks.
- Position the cord so that people won't trip over it.
- Disconnect the cord from the outlet before disconnecting it from the machine.
- Close the machine carefully.

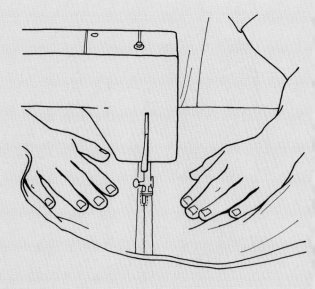

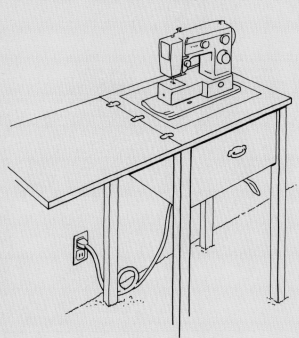

Using sewing tools and equipment

- Keep pins in a pin cushion—never put them in your mouth or clothing.
- Keep shears and scissors closed when not in use.

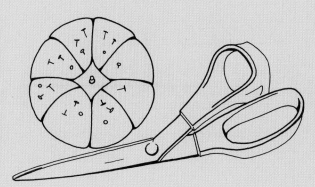

- Pass sharp objects like shears to someone else handle first.
- Store items in a box when you aren't using them.

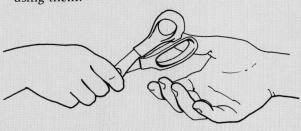

Pressing or ironing

- Don't touch a hot iron.
- Keep your hands away from steam.
- Take care that the iron doesn't get pulled off the ironing board.
- Let the iron cool on a holder in an out-of-the-way place before putting it away.
- Store the iron correctly.

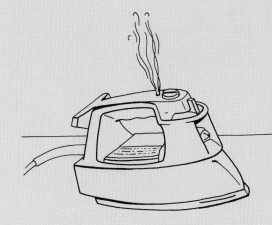

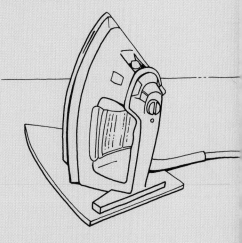

Project Ideas

Looking for a place to store your exercise clothes? Do you want to make your sewing supplies portable? Would you like to dress up your bed? Here are some sewing projects that you can make.

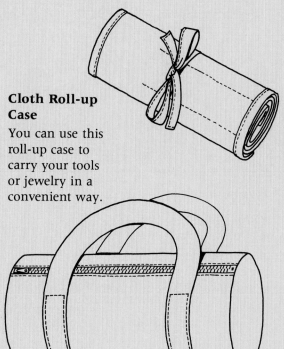

Cloth Roll-up Case

You can use this roll-up case to carry your tools or jewelry in a convenient way.

Wall Organizer

A clever way to store small items by your/the phone, desk, sewing area, or hobby center. Make of all one fabric or mix-and-match.

Zippered Duffle

Use it to carry books, clothes, beach towel or athletic gear. Make of firmly woven medium-weight to heavy-weight fabric. Use colorful webbing for the straps.

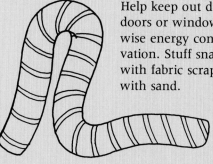

Snake

Help keep out drafts at doors or windows for wise energy conservation. Stuff snake with fabric scraps or fill with sand.

Drawstring Bag

Make it small or large to carry everything from lunch to sleeping bag. Use a slick nylon or heavier-weight cotton fabric. Use nylon cord or a shoelace for the drawstring.

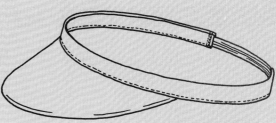

Pillow
A colorful accent for bed or sofa. Use medium weight fabrics that can all be laundered in the same way. Combine different patterns and textures for a one-of-a-kind design.

Sun Visor
Perfect for the beach, pool, biking, tennis or other outdoor activities. Interface brim for long-lasting shape.

T-Shirt
Use a lightweight cotton knit or cotton and polyester knit fabric. Decorate with trims, appliqués, or embroidery!

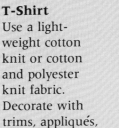

Exercise Roll-Up Mat
Use bright, colorful fabric for this easy-to-store mat. Make one for yourself or for a friend!

Unit Five Review

Unit Summary

Chapters 51-53.

Clothes help you make a good impression and express your individuality at the same time. You wear clothing for comfort, but you also need clothing that fits your life-style.

In choosing clothing, you should take into account the five elements of design: line, proportion, color, texture, and print. You can use these elements to choose clothing that highlights your good points.

Many of our clothing decisions are influenced by fashion—the colors, styles, and combinations that are popular. If you plan carefully, you can keep your wardrobe up-to-date without wasting money on clothing fads that quickly go out of style.

Chapter 54.

Clothes are made of fabrics, which are woven or knit from yarns. These yarns are made from fibers that are natural or synthetic. Each fiber is used to make a fabric with certain characteristics. Sometimes, finishes are added that give fabrics new characteristics.

Chapters 55 and 56.

You can save a lot of money by planning your purchases carefully—analyzing what clothing you have and what you need.

Shopping trips involve planning, too. You need to choose the right store and to check garments for fit and construction.

Chapters 57 and 58.

The materials and tools you use for sewing are very important. A pattern shows what a project will look like, explains how to make it, and lists the materials you'll need to complete it. These materials include fabric and notions, such as buttons, zippers, and trim.

Most sewing is done on a sewing machine, which saves a lot of time. Other tools are used to measure, cut the pattern, and mark the pieces for construction.

Chapters 59-61.

Sewing begins with four steps. You must prepare the pattern, prepare the fabric, lay out and cut the pattern, and transfer the pattern symbols to the fabric. Once these initial steps are completed, you can begin sewing each part of the project and finally put all the pieces together. After the main pieces are joined, you can add details like hems, fasteners, and decorations.

Chapters 62 and 63.

You can get the most out of your wardrobe by caring for your clothes. Wearing and storing clothes properly keeps them fresh. Cleaning them regularly helps, too. You can also redesign and recycle your clothes. Change outgrown or out-of-style garments into new items that fit and look up-to-date. Turn clothes that you no longer wear into useful items like totes or patchwork pieces. Or you can give outgrown clothes to others.

Chapter 64.

The clothing and textile industry employs thousands of workers in a great variety of jobs. People design, sew, sell, and clean clothes. These jobs require certain talents, especially good design sense, and attention to detail.

Questions

1. How does clothing express personality?
2. List three elements of clothing design.
3. What can you do to keep your wardrobe up-to-date without spending money on expensive items that will go out of style?
4. How is a woven fabric and a knit made?
5. What is meant by the phrase *mix and*

match? How does mixing and matching help you expand your wardrobe?

6. List three things you should do to prepare for a shopping trip.

7. What are some questions that you should ask yourself before buying a new garment or accessory?

8. What are sizes based on? How would you go about deciding what your size is?

9. List three pieces of information given on a pattern envelope.

10. Describe how a sewing machine works.

11. Why is it important to lay out a pattern carefully?

12. Why might you have to make adjustments to a pattern?

13. What does *unit construction* mean?

14. List three ways to shape a garment.

15. Name three kinds of fasteners.

16. What is the difference between ironing and pressing?

17. List three things you can do every day to help your clothes last.

18. What are three ways to clean clothes?

19. How might you redesign a shirt that you don't wear because it's no longer in style?

20. What other ways of recycling garments are there besides passing them on to another person?

21. List three jobs in clothing and textiles.

Reading Activities

1. Read the list of fabrics and their characteristics in the box in chapter 54. What fabrics would be good for work clothes? What fabrics would be good for dressy outfits?

2. Read the steps toward good clothing care discussed in chapter 62. Write a paragraph explaining how you could change your habits and take better care of your clothes.

Writing Activities

1. Find a picture of a model in a fashion magazine. Write a description of the garment that the model is wearing, explaining how it uses the elements of design.

2. Write a skit about a teenager who wants to wear jeans to a fancy restaurant against his or her parents' wishes.

3. Describe how to choose a pattern.

Math Activities

1. Find a ready-to-wear garment in a store and write down the price. Go to a sewing supplies store and find a pattern for a similar garment. Figure out the cost of making that garment, including the price of the pattern, fabric, and notions. Compare this cost to the price of the ready-to-wear garment.

2. Suppose a shirt costs $11.99. You think you would wear it 10 times a year for two years. It is washable. Calculate the cost per wearing.

Group Projects

1. Bring to class a favorite garment that is no longer in style. Ask classmates for suggestions on how to redesign it so that you can get more wear out of it.

2. With your classmates and teacher, visit a garment factory. If possible, talk with people who do different jobs and find out about their work. Ask if you can see the different stages a fabric goes through in becoming a garment.

HOUSING AND LIVING SPACE

We all need a roof over our heads. Housing protects us from the cold and from bad weather. It gives us a place we can call our own and a place to put the things we own.

Housing also requires us to make decisions. Some of these decisions involve where you want your housing to be and how big you want it to be. Making these decisions also means deciding how much you want to pay for housing.

Most families share space and also try to give each person some personal space. You can make some decisions about what you want to do with your space. How will you arrange your furniture? Should your desk or your bed be near the window? Where will you store your guitar when you're not practicing? If you find that your clothes are stuffed in the closet, you'll need to find a new way to store them.

You also want your space to be attractive. What can you do to lighten up that dull wall by your dresser? How can you get more color into your room?

Sometimes, you share space. You might share a bedroom with a sibling. You certainly share the living room, dining room, kitchen, and bathroom with other family members. You'll make many joint decisions about how to use that common space.

In this unit, you'll learn about some of these housing decisions. You'll find out what housing involves and what factors to consider in making your decisions.

You'll find out how to use and maintain your space, make your space attractive, live with others, make sure your space is safe, and use resources.

Chapter 65 Living Space and You

Objectives

After reading this chapter, you will be able to:

- □ *explain why living space is important to you,*

- □ *describe how living space meets psychological needs,*

- □ *list the physical needs that housing meets,*

- □ *explain how location, budget, and life-style affect housing decisions.*

Have you ever marked out your space on a beach by putting down your towel, sunglasses, and radio? You said to all the world, "This is my place. Please do not disturb it." And you filled up that space with things that were important to you. Thus, you had a home base at the beach—a place where you belonged.

Everyone needs a place to belong. Remember the movie *The Wizard of Oz*? Dorothy, the main character, dreams that she has marvelous adventures in the strange land of Oz.

Dorothy went to many strange places and did many adventurous things. She met some wonderful people who became her friends.

But, when Dorothy awakened in her own bedroom in Kansas, she said, "Oh, Auntie Em, there's no place like home!"

Meeting Psychological Needs

Like Dorothy, most people find home a warm and comforting place. It doesn't matter if home is small or large, simple or fancy. *Anywhere that people live* is **home**. And home gives us a feeling of belonging.

Privacy

The need for *a place of one's own*—**personal space**—is basic to all of us. Even if it's small or partly shared—for example, your personal space at home—it's a place you feel is your own. You have the privilege of asking people in when you want to, and of keeping them out, too.

This privilege gives you **privacy**—*the ability to be alone now and then*. Everyone needs to get away from it all at times, even if it's only for a couple of hours. You can use that space to clear your mind and make decisions.

Individuality

Your living space affects your self-concept. Personal space says "me."

You express yourself in your own space. That's what you do by displaying your track trophies. Showing your interests, school-books, hobby materials, and record collections tells people that this is your space. Chapter 67 will give you some ideas on how to make your room look the way you want it to.

Later, when you set up your own home, some of these personal possessions will help make a strange place seem familiar. An empty room quickly becomes yours when you put up your favorite poster or arrange a few of your mementos.

Principles and Goals

How you live reflects your principles. Someone who values neatness will organize his space. A person who believes in conserving resources will take steps to save energy. Some people want space for noisy activities, while others prefer a room where they can enjoy quiet activities.

Meeting Physical Needs

Living space does more than let you be by yourself. A home also meets physical needs.

■ *Space for possessions.* Books, records, clothes, pots and pans, furniture, family pictures—people have hundreds of objects. And they need a place to put them. Simply dropping objects in piles on the floor might mean damaging some of them. With no organization, you might never be able to find that report you need for school.

■ *Space for activities.* People live in their spaces, and living means doing many activities. You need space for cooking, bathing, entertaining, working on hobbies, exercising, talking—for anything you do. Many of these areas are used by more than one person. Chapter 68 has more information on how to share these common spaces.

■ *Comfort.* One important job of a home is to protect people from the weather—wind, rain or snow, extreme heat or cold.

It provides shelter. A warm living room comforts you when you come home on a cold day. Part of keeping a home comfortable is caring for it to keep it clean. Just as the whole family shares the space, each person should help clean it. Chapter 69 tells you more about caring for space.

■ *Safety.* In addition to giving shelter, a home protects you and your possessions from crime. But home safety also means accident prevention. A home with an unsteady stairway or no fire escape is not safe. Chapter 70 explains how to make a home safe.

■ *Energy.* We use energy to heat and cool us, cook our meals, and give us light and hot water. We need to use this energy carefully. The cost of energy is rising, so being careful about using it pays off. In chapter 71, you'll read about controlling how much energy you use.

Basic Choices

Everyone looking for a place to live must first ask:

■ *Where* will I live?

■ *What kind* of place will I live in?

■ *How much* can I afford?

Until some decisions are made about these three questions, you can't begin to make an intelligent choice.

Where?

Where your home will be situated is the first decision to make. People have many reasons for choosing a **location**, but two are very important. One is the availability of the kind of work they want. The second is the *availability of the goods and services they want*, that is, the **facilities** the community offers.

We all need a familiar, private place. Personal space is a place to listen to music, to read a book, or just to be alone and to think and dream.

Location. People usually try to live near where they work. Some people—for instance, members of the Armed Forces—move from place to place as their jobs demand. People often leave one community to find work in another. Work, then, is a major factor in choosing where you will live. This is something you should keep in mind when thinking about a career.

Even so, a person might do the same kind of work in a number of different places. How do people choose among them?

Facilities. Basically, people are attracted to a place that offers them the facilities and the life-style they desire.

For instance, if they like theater, shopping, crowds, and excitement, they will choose a city or large suburban area. If they like quiet and the outdoors, they will choose a rural setting.

People also keep in mind such characteristics of a community as the police and fire departments, transportation system, the schools, and recreation facilities.

What Kind?

Homes come in many sizes, shapes, and styles. Here are a few examples.

- *Single-family house*. This building provides the living space for one family. It is not attached to any other building—it stands on its own.
- *Townhouse*. This is one of many single-family units attached on the sides. In the city, these may be called *row houses*. Each family lives in a different unit.
- *Duplex or triplex*. This is a building divided into living spaces for two or three families. The spaces can be side by side or one on top of the other.

All housing choices provide shelter. What advantages do the single-family house, above, and the row houses, below, offer to the people living in them?

■ *Apartment building.* This building contains many separate living units. The living spaces may range in size from one-room apartments to three-bedroom units. If the building is very tall, it is called a *high-rise.* If the people who live in each unit have a patio or bit of lawn, the units are called *garden apartments.*

■ *Mobile home.* This is a factory-made house that is moved to the living site by truck. In the past, mobile homes were smallish and could be moved easily from place to place. Today they are larger and less easy to transport.

Renting or Buying. People get housing by renting or buying. *A renter pays a monthly fee,* called **rent**, *to the person who owns the living space.* An owner actually buys the housing, usually by taking out a long-term loan to pay for it. Owning a home has some financial benefits, but many people prefer renting.

You can rent or buy almost any type of housing. Most single-family houses are bought, but some can be rented. Most apartments are rented, but some can be bought. *Apartment units that are bought* are called **condominiums**.

F E A T U R E

Where Do I Go?

Joel will begin a training program after graduation. He'll also be working part time. He's excited about his new job and the money he'll be making. He feels independent and ready to live on his own. Still, the cost of an apartment is high.

After thinking about his situation, Joel realized that he had three choices.

■ He could live at home during the training period and save his money. When he started earning more money by working full time, he could move into a place of his own.

■ He could move into a small place now and hold down his other expenses until his job became full time.

■ He could move into an apartment with a friend. While he wouldn't have as much privacy, he would still have the satisfaction of setting up his own space.

If you were Joel, what would you do?

Andrea is going away to college. She'll be in another town, so she has to find a place to live. But she isn't sure what kind of place to look for. Andrea can choose from two possibilities.

■ She could live with three other girls in a dormitory room. Her roommates would be people she didn't know at first. But getting to know them would help her make friends at a new place.

■ She could rent a studio apartment near the school. She would have more privacy for studying, but she would have to make more effort to meet people.

If you were Andrea, what would you do?

How Much?

Where you live and the kind of housing you choose is affected by one more decision: how much you can afford. Housing prices vary in different areas. Choosing a location, then, is partly a matter of setting a price limit.

Deciding on a size means looking at your budget, too. Usually, the larger the housing, the higher the cost.

Trade-offs. When choosing housing, many people face trade-offs. They are willing to spend a little more money for a better location, or walk a few blocks more to the bus stop for a little less rent. How you make these decisions will depend on what is most important to you.

Decisions About Housing

These basic choices are among the many decisions that you will be making in the future. Will you buy or rent? Should you take a small apartment and live alone, or share an apartment with roommates? The box describes a couple of these choices.

Even now you make many decisions about your living space, even if you share a room with a brother or sister. Where will you put your albums? How can you store your clothes? Can you redecorate with materials you have on hand, or must you buy supplies?

As you've seen, housing decisions include how a space is kept. How will you use the rooms shared by the family? Will you leave your schoolbooks on the kitchen table when you're done studying? If someone else does that, will you say something? Will you help clean or make your home safe?

As you read the next chapter, you'll find information that will help you make these decisions and many others.

You are not renting or buying housing right now. But, it is wise to know about such things ahead of time. Then you will be better able to make choices when the time comes.

Words to Remember

condominiums: apartment units that are bought
facilities: the goods and services available in a community
home: anywhere that people live
location: where a home is situated
personal space: a place of one's own
privacy: the ability to be alone now and then
rent: a monthly fee paid to the person who owns the living space

Questions

1. List three ways that your living space is an expression of you.
2. What are three ways in which a home can meet your psychological needs?
3. What physical needs does housing fulfill?
4. What are the three basic decisions to make when you are considering a place to live?

66 Organizing
Space

Objectives

After reading this chapter, you will be able to:

☐ *use floor plans to improve traffic patterns in a living space,*

☐ *describe ways to organize a work area,*

☐ *give examples of ways to organize and store different possessions.*

Think of all the things you do in your room—you study, dress, sleep, read, listen to music, perhaps even eat. You use your room for private talks with a friend and for a chance to get away from family noise. Your room may hold your clothes, schoolbooks, records, and almost everything else.

Living space, then, provides people with a place to enjoy themselves, perform many activities, and store their things.

There are as many ways to organize living space as there are people. We all have our own ideas about what we want our rooms to look like.

Some people like rooms with hardly any furniture or small objects. Other people prefer plenty of furniture and keepsakes.

In this chapter, you will be given guidelines on how to get the best use out of the space you have, while you prepare it according to your own tastes.

Organizing Your Furniture

Do you always have to move your desk to be able to play your stereo? Rearranging your furniture could make listening to music easier for you.

Making a Floor Plan

A good way to organize your space is to make a floor plan. You can change your furniture around on paper to see how it fits. That saves you the time and effort of actually moving the furniture!

To make a floor plan, you first need to measure your room. Then draw the room to scale on a piece of graph paper. A **scale drawing** is one in which *the relative sizes of objects are the same as the relative sizes in your actual room.*

Follow these steps:

- Allow a certain number of graph paper squares to equal each foot of space in your room. For example, if the scale you choose allows two squares per foot, a room measuring 8 by 12 feet would be drawn as a rectangle 16 squares wide and 24 squares long.

- Show features such as doors and windows on the plan.

- Add your furniture, allowing the correct number of squares per foot for each piece.

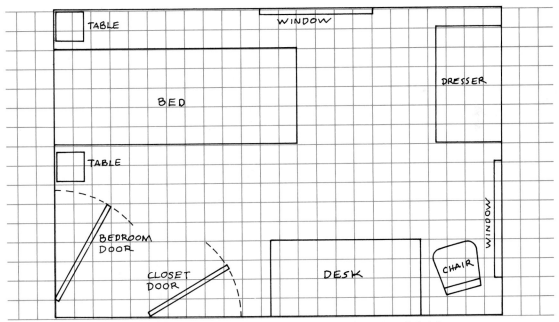

A floor plan is a sketch of a room and its furniture drawn to scale. It is a helpful tool because you can plan space needs before actually moving the furniture.

By using a floor plan, you can see how furnishings will look in a particular **layout**, or *arrangement of furniture.* Try several different layouts until you find one you like. This can save you the trouble of moving furnishings around, deciding they don't look good, and then moving them back again. If you are buying furniture, a floor plan can help you make sure that your choices are the right sizes and shapes.

Considering Traffic Patterns

Think about **traffic patterns**, or *how people move through the space.* Can you move freely from one area of your space to another without tripping over things? If you have to squeeze past a chest every time you walk into the room, try to find another place for the chest.

You should also think about how an arrangement will look. Depending on how furnishings are placed, a room can look cramped or spacious, cluttered or neat.

Creating Different Areas

One way to organize space is to group together furnishings and other items you use for certain activities. You can make many different areas for gathering your belongings:

- *A study area* might include a desk, chair, bookcase, and desk lamp. In your desk drawer would be paper, pens, and pencils.
- *A science area* might include a microscope, magnifying glass, collections of rocks or butterflies, and reference books.
- *The music center* would contain all your records, a stereo, and a cozy chair.

- *A fitness area* could include an exercise mat, jump rope, weights, clothes for working out, and radio.
- *A game area* might include your playing cards, games, puzzles, and a table and chairs.

A Place to Be Active

People also use living spaces for the activities they enjoy. Whether you sew, build models, read, or program a computer, you want room to pursue your hobby.

Of course, many activities need to be done outside the bedroom. Woodworking or staining furniture is best done in a garage or basement. And if you share sewing supplies with your brother or sister, they may be stored in a special place. But you can work on many hobbies and other interests in your own room.

You can *use the same area for more than one activity.* **Multiple use** of space is efficient. A desk can serve for doing homework, working with a computer, or building models. Your bed can double as a place for playing cards, reading, or listening to music. If you push the bed to the wall and add pillows, you've got a couch for reading by day and a bed for sleeping at night.

A Place to Store Things

Living space is important for storing your possessions, the things you own. Putting things safely away protects them from damage, but keeps them handy when they are wanted.

Solving Storage Problems

Storage problems differ from one person to another. But they can all be solved by following a few steps.

Define the Problem. Decide what your storage problem is. You might want someplace to put your athletic equipment. Your sister may want a place for her records. Your friend may want to get out-of-season clothes out of her closet.

Think about How You Use the Possessions. Before deciding how to store things, ask yourself four questions:

■ *How often is the item used?* Something used frequently should be easier to get out than something you rarely need.

■ *Do other family members use it?* If so, you'll need to take their use into account when choosing a storage place. You might even be able to store the item in a different room.

■ *Does it look good on display?* Many objects can be stored and used as decoration at the same time. The next chapter offers some ideas.

■ *Does it require other tools or supplies?* You probably want to keep all your stamp collecting gear together.

What Are the Options? You can store things in many different ways. Your closet, dresser, and desk are the obvious places for clothes and school supplies. But you may be

Set aside a part of your room as a study area. Invest in a comfortable chair, a bookcase, and adequate lighting.

Display your possessions on a shelving unit on the wall. This will protect your valuables and add a personal touch to your bedroom.

F E A T U R E

Organizing Your Room

In the old days of radio comedies, one character was well known for his overstuffed closet. Each week, he would open the closet door to find some tool or other item. As soon as the door opened, the sound effects began— almost a minute of noise told the listeners that this fellow needed help. He needed to organize his closet. Here are a few ideas he could have used to have solved his problem:

- *Crates* can be used to store books, records, clothes, or games. Some plastic models come in bright colors. They can even be used for attractive storage outside the closet.

- *Dishpans or baskets* can be used for clothes that can be folded. You can buy sets that stack.

- *Shoe bags* of cloth, canvas, or plastic are made to fit on the back of a closet door. They can hold not only shoes but also other items.

- *Cardboard boxes* are useful for your out-of-season clothes. Store those clothes on a high shelf, out of the way of your everyday reach. Covered with fabric or wallpaper, these boxes needn't stay hidden in the closet.

- *Double clothes poles* allow you to hang twice as many clothes in the same space. Just position one clothes pole high in the closet and put another halfway down.

- *Towel racks* on the back of the door can hold regularly used items like jackets or running clothes.

- *Empty tissue boxes,* with the top opening enlarged, are a handy place for small items.

- *Gift boxes,* once the gifts are gone, are still useful. Use them to separate types of clothing in your drawer.

Even your walls can be more organized.

- *Pegboard* along one wall makes an easy place to attach hooks for storing everything from hats to tennis rackets.

- *Corkboard* is handy for posters, notes to yourself, and mementos.

able to get more use out of these areas than you think, as the box explains.

Your room has other places to store things, too:

- *Under your bed* there may be space just waiting to be used. Cut off the upper sections of cardboard boxes so they'll fit under the bed. Use these boxes to store sweaters, old magazines, games, or anything else.

- *Bookcases* can hold things besides books. If your bookcase holds books you seldom use, pack them up. Use the shelf space for frequently used items instead.

- *Wall shelves* are good for storing all sorts of things besides books.

Suppose you do a lot of needlework. You could put your yarn, fabrics, and trimmings in baskets on a shelf.

If painting is your hobby, you might keep your art supplies on a shelf in colorfully painted boxes.

Shelf storage space can be attractive as well as useful. Make shelves from boards of wood or pressboard supported by concrete blocks or stacked bricks. Or mount the boards on the wall with brackets. You might want to paint them, stain them, or cover them with adhesive-backed paper.

■ *Walls* can be used for storage in other ways. Put up hooks or pegs and use them to hang jewelry, tote bags, jackets, belts, hats, and sporting goods. Baskets of all types can be hung from the wall and used to hold anything.

Weigh the Alternatives. In choosing between one storage method and another, consider your resources.

Do you have the money to buy the storage units you need? Do you have the skills to make a room organizer out of wood?

If you feel that you don't have much money, you can solve your problem in many other ways. Shop for bargains at garage sales or flea markets. Refinish an old storage unit in the basement. Cardboard boxes for under-the-bed storage are free. Baskets to hang on walls are very cheap. Don't underestimate what you can do. Use your imagination to think up other ways to solve your problem.

Evaluating the Results

An important part of problem solving is evaluating the solution. Did your new use of shelves solve the problem of where to put your records? Are your shoes easier to find in their baskets?

By problem solving and using your creativity, you can make your room more comfortable and your possessions easier to use.

Words to Remember

layout: arrangement of such things as furniture

multiple use: using the same area for more than one activity

scale drawing: a drawing in which the relative sizes of objects are the same as the relative sizes in the actual space

traffic patterns: how people usually move through a space

Questions

1. What are the benefits of organizing your space?
2. How do you make a floor plan? How do you use one?
3. What activities do you enjoy that you could create specific areas for in your room?
4. When solving storage problems, what four questions must you ask?

Chapter 67 Getting the Look You Want

Objectives

After reading this chapter, you will be able to:

☐ describe the elements of design and how to work with them,

☐ list the principles of design and give examples of each,

☐ name various objects that can be used as accessories,

☐ explain how different accessories can be used to give flair to a room.

Maria was discouraged. She was sick of her room and embarassed to take friends there when they came to visit. The pink ruffled curtains seemed childish, and so did her pink and white dresser. Although her toy box was now filled with sewing supplies, it still looked like a toy box. There was no room for her to sew, and her one new possession, a nice desk, didn't fit with anything else in the room.

You may have feelings like this about your own room or the room you share. But it doesn't take a lot of money to give your room a new look. What it does take is a knowledge of the elements and principles of design, and creative use of **accessories**. These *small objects can add visual appeal to a room.*

The Elements of Design

To make your personal space more attractive, you will work with the basic *elements*, or *tools*, of design: color, texture, space, shape, and line.

Color

Interior designers give a lot of thought to the colors they use in a room. Why? Color is powerful and has an immediate effect on your mood. Warm colors, such as red, yellow, and orange, are cheerful and exciting. Cool colors—blues, greens, and purples—are more soothing.

Of course, you can use colors in combination. Choose one color for the walls and accent it with accessories that are other colors.

If you feel that a whole room in red would be too much, use that powerful color for a bedspread or drapes. Neutral colors, like pastels, tans, or white, on the walls and carpet can be easily combined with other colors.

You may need to work around colors already in your room. Perhaps you can paint the walls, but you can't change the floor color. Even so, many colors work well together, so you'll have quite a few to choose from. Look at the color wheel in chapter 52 to see what colors can be combined.

Texture

Another important element of design is **texture**, or *how the surfaces of objects feel*. Are they silky or fuzzy? Rough or polished?

For a formal look, designers use the smooth surfaces of chrome, glass, and polished wood. A more informal look is achieved with rough textures—perhaps a nubby bedspread, handmade plant holders, and a rough board bookcase.

You can also combine textures. A plastic laminated desk contrasts nicely with a shaggy rug.

Space

The size of your room or the room you share is set, but you can make it appear larger or smaller with the right use of space.

Arranging your furniture around the wall will give the feel of more space. Using the same light color for almost everything in the room will unify the space and make it seem larger. Bright, light colors will make it look larger, too.

Taking as much as possible off the floor will also help. Use hanging shelves and sturdy hooks for everything from your book bag to your bicycle.

If the space seems too big, move the furniture toward the center of the room to make it seem more cozy. Darker, richer colors will also make it feel smaller. Or you could divide the room into two living areas, one for sleeping and one for activities.

Shape

The shapes of objects in a room can have a strong effect on a room's atmosphere. A matching set of furniture usually repeats certain forms—the arms of chairs and a sofa may all be curved or straight. Repetition sets a tone for the room.

Many curved shapes in a room give a soft effect. If most of the furniture is angular, the effect will be harder. And if many different forms are mixed together, the effect will be informal—or even confusing. Designers need to think carefully about how different shapes look together in any room that they are laying out for their clients.

Line

Every room has many lines. There is a line at the top of the door, for example, and a line around the base of a lamp. But the atmosphere of a room is most affected by the boldest lines—the ones that stand out for one reason or another.

A room may have tall windows. You could use floor-to-ceiling drapes for the windows and paper the walls with vertically striped wallpaper. Add a tall bookcase and perhaps some full-length portraits or posters. Then the vertical lines will be the boldest element in the room.

Some people feel good in such an "upright" room. Others prefer more horizontal lines, which give a more restful effect. They could use a low bed, a long dresser, and shelves to repeat this line.

Still other people like the motion and excitement created by diagonal lines on walls and furniture.

The Principles of Design

All the elements of design that you have just read about must work together. By using the *principles*, or *guidelines* of design—unity, contrast, emphasis, balance, proportion, and rhythm—you can achieve this goal.

Unity and Contrast

Unity. Imagine a room with square chairs, curved chairs, tall chairs, and short chairs of many styles and colors. It might be hard to relax in such a room. Designers usually advise clients to choose one color scheme, and perhaps one general style of furniture. This helps create a feeling of **unity**. That means that *all objects in a room look like they belong together.*

Unity doesn't mean that a room must have only one color. You can accent a major color like tan walls with pillows and drapes in reds and oranges.

Contrast. A room can be more interesting if it has something that stands out. This can be created by the use of **contrast**—*the difference in color and shape between objects.* A brightly patterned wing chair, for example, stands out when solid colors are used elsewhere in the room.

Emphasis and Balance

Emphasis. An object that stands out receives **emphasis**, or *more attention than other objects in the room.* This effect is stronger if the boldest lines in the room lead the eye toward the center of interest.

You can give greater emphasis to the accessories you display if you don't show too many different things. Too many objects make a room look cluttered.

Balance. Another effect designers work to achieve is balance. **Balance** means that *objects are arranged in an even, pleasing way.* Lack of balance can be disturbing. Suppose all the furniture or bright colors were on one side of the room. Such a room would look unbalanced.

Proportion and Rhythm

Proportion. *A pleasing size relationship among objects* is called **proportion**. A big oak desk that used to be in your mother's office is out of proportion to the wire ice cream parlor chair you use to sit at the desk. It might be best to find a larger and more comfortable chair.

Rhythm. *The regular repeat of line or shape* is called **rhythm**. Rhythm in design is similar to rhythm in music. Striped fabric or pictures hung at regular intervals create rhythm that can be pleasing in a room.

Accessories: The Personal Touch

When planning rooms, designers often speak of major furnishings and accessories.

In a bedroom, the major furnishings might be a bed, a dresser, and a desk. They are fairly expensive items and not often replaced.

Accessories, on the other hand, are small accents. They do a great deal to improve the look of a room, they are fairly inexpensive, and they are easily changed.

Posters, for example, don't cost very much money and can reflect your interest in music or foreign countries. And when your interest changes, you can get a new poster.

What Is an Accessory?

Accessories add interest to a room, such as a splash of color. They can accent or highlight an area, especially if chosen with the room's color scheme in mind.

Some accessories are strictly for decoration. A painting, for example, adds beauty

Give your room a personal touch, with accessories that reflect your hobbies and interests. You might like to display things that you bought or made yourself.

Same Room, Different Looks

Accessories and color can make a great difference in the way a room looks. Look at these two rooms. Each one has the same basic colors and furniture. But by using a different color for accent and different accessories, each teen has created a unique look.

to a room. Other accessories have a double purpose. Besides improving the appearance of a room, they are useful. A calendar that features art prints not only looks attractive, but also tells what day it is.

Accessories and You

Your accessories say a lot about you. By looking at them, a stranger might be able to begin to get an idea of the kind of person you are.

A wicker sewing basket, for example, might show that you like to do needlework. Posters of dirt bikes suggest that you like that sport. By hanging your drawings or displaying your sports trophies, you are saying something special about yourself.

Accessories also please your senses. They help satisfy your sense of beauty. Your plants may give you the pleasant feeling of being in a garden. Even on the darkest day, a bright quilt may make you feel cheerful.

And accessories can bring back memories of places you've been and people you've known. By looking at a collection of seashells, you can walk along the beach in your imagination.

Words to Remember

accessory: any small object that can add visual appeal to a room and make a statement about you

balance: when objects are arranged in an even, pleasing way

contrast: the difference in color and shape between objects

emphasis: an object receiving more attention than other objects in the room

proportion: a pleasing size relationship among objects

rhythm: the regular repeat of line or shape

texture: how the surfaces of objects feel

unity: a feeling that all objects in a room look like they belong together

Questions

1. What are the five elements of design? How can you use them to change the look of a room?
2. What are the six principles of design?
3. Give five examples of objects that can be used as accessories.
4. How could you use an accessory to brighten up a dark dresser top? How could you use an accessory to make a long, blank wall interesting?

Chapter **68** Sharing Space

Objectives

After reading this chapter, you will be able to:

☐ *explain the meaning and importance of shared space,*

☐ *describe how to compromise so that space can be shared with few disagreements,*

☐ *list specific ways in which sharing rooms and homes can be made easier.*

All of us live, work, eat, and play in spaces with other people. So, in addition to having personal space, we also share space with others. Public buildings, streets, theaters, and restaurants are all shared spaces.

Shared space means *any space that is used by more than one person.* Limited space makes sharing necessary. In the home, bedrooms might be shared. Smaller spaces, such as closets and drawers, also might be used by several people.

Shared space also means space that people use together. All family members may use the same room for reading, working, or watching television. This shared space gives family members a place to meet, talk, play, and simply enjoy one another.

Shared space calls for thoughtfulness on the part of the sharers. This chapter will give you some points on helping to make shared space pleasant for all.

Consideration for Others

When you think about the needs of others, you show **consideration** for them. Your family is made up of individuals, each with different needs, tastes, interests, and friends. To live peacefully with them, you must take their different feelings and needs into account. You may sometimes have to adjust your plans to avoid offending some other family member.

Respecting Personal Space

It's important for family members to respect each other's personal space. This means letting other people have their privacy. It means not going into their rooms without first knocking on the door and asking permission. And it means leaving their things alone and not going into their closets or dressers.

Except in special cases—putting the laundry away, for example—make it a rule never to enter anyone else's space without asking permission first.

Respecting Shared Space

Scheduling. You should also be fair and considerate in using shared space. This means that you can't always watch the television show that you want to see. Others must sometimes have their choices, too.

Consideration. Being considerate also means respecting other people's interests by not playing the radio or television too loudly. Also, try to practice musical instruments where they won't bother other people. If you're within their hearing, you're sharing their space.

Neatness. Respecting shared space also means keeping it neat. Leaving the living room, kitchen, bathroom, or workbench neat after you've used it shows consideration. Rinse out the bathtub after a bath. Hang up your towel neatly. Clean up in the kitchen after making a snack. Cleaning up after others is no fun.

Your family will appreciate your thoughtfulness. Other members will probably show consideration for you. That way, the whole family will find sharing space easier and more pleasant.

Keeping shared space clean is important. Messiness can lead to accidents. Dirt and uncleanliness can cause serious illness.

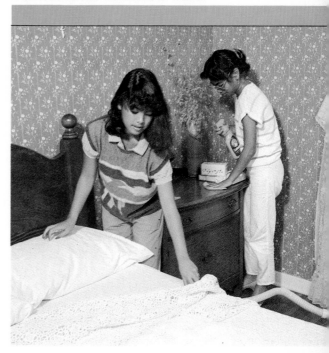

F E A T U R E

Sharing Community Space

You also share space with your neighbors and the other people in your town or city. You share the place where you live. It's important to show consideration for those who share your community as well. What can you do?

1. *Keep public spaces clean.* Trash bins are everywhere. Simply use them.

2. *Keep public spaces in good repair.* People who carve their initials in trees or spray paint their names on walls are damaging property. Breaking windows and streetlights may make some teenagers feel powerful, but vandalism is a childish—and criminal—act.

3. *Allow others to enjoy public spaces.*

A park or museum is meant for all the people. And there's usually enough space for everybody. Don't monopolize the diving board at the community pool, or talk loudly at the library. Talk and sit quietly on buses and trains. Show consideration for others so that they can enjoy using public spaces.

4. *Use public spaces yourself.* Most important, use the public spaces. If all the people ignore them, they go to waste—and the government may decide to close them. By going to the park or the aquarium, you show that you're glad that they're available. And you have fun, too!

Sharing a Room

Sharing small spaces, like a room, takes a lot of consideration and compromise. Each of the people sharing a room must have his or her own personal space and times for privacy.

Together and Alone

Sharing a room has its pros and cons. Often you'll be glad to be able to talk things over with your brother or sister. On the other hand, sometimes you just need to be alone. You and the other person must work together to provide the privacy you both need.

Scheduling. For instance, you might set up times when the room is to be used by only one of you. Suppose you have an important test tomorrow that you must spend a few hours studying hard for. You might ask your sister if you can have the room to yourself for that time. Of course, you'll then do the same for her when she needs the room for something important.

Consideration. Even if you both use the room at the same time, you can show consideration. When you see that the other person is busy, try not to bother him or her. Conversation is nice, but not when one of you is concentrating on something else.

Neatness. Another thing you can do is put your things away after you finish using them. Don't leave your books and papers spread out over the shared worktable when you finish studying. That way your brother won't have to clean them up before starting his work. He'll feel better about letting you have the space again when you need it.

Dividing a Room

It is possible to divide even a small room so that each person gets some private space. The simplest way is to move the furniture to create separate areas for each of you. Try putting beds along opposite walls and desks as far apart as possible. That way you won't distract each other as much.

Bookcases.   There are several ways to divide the room physically. You can set up bookcases back to back down the center of the room. This way each person has storage space for his or her things and also a way of marking off his or her private space. Open shelves would do the same job.

Blinds and Screens.   Another good way to divide up a room is to use roll-up blinds that can be purchased at hardware stores. The blinds are attached to the ceiling and run along the center of the room.

Sharing a room has its pros and cons. It can be fun to talk things over with brothers or sisters, but it can also be hard to have privacy and get work done.

When you or your sister needs privacy, just roll down the blinds. When you're both in the mood for company, you can roll them up and be together. You can also use a folding screen. When you don't want to divide the room, you can fold the screen up and put it in a corner.

Plants. If the room is sunny, you can get the same effect by hanging pots of plants from the ceiling at different heights along the center of the room. This gives a nice, airy effect to the room and still marks off different spaces.

Multi-Levels. If your room is small, you can create more space—and more privacy—by living on two levels. You may be able to set up two loft beds. These beds are set up near the ceiling on solid wooden posts. You climb up to them by ladder, as with bunk beds. The space under the beds can then be used for desks for each person. If you prefer, you can put just one bed on a platform.

Being Together

By sharing space, people share experiences. Each family member may be doing something different in the same room and still enjoy being with the others.

- To use a shared space fairly, you must discuss with your family members your—and their—needs. You can't read that mystery novel you like at the same time that your brother vacuums the room. Your mother can't use the phone if you don't hang up.

- Disagreements about space can be solved in many ways. Some may be settled by talking things over, or by taking turns to use the space.

Consideration and the ability to share are skills you'll always need. You'll always be part of some group—in a family, at work, or at school. If you learn these skills now, you'll find them easy the rest of your life.

Words to Remember

consideration: thinking about the needs of others

shared space: any space that is used by more than one person

Questions

1. Give examples of spaces that might be shared in a family.

2. Tell what consideration is and give an example of how to show consideration for another family member.

3. Describe three ways you can divide a room that you share.

4. How will learning to share space help you now and in the future?

Many of us have been amused by the two men in the television show "The Odd Couple." In this show, one man is very neat, the other is very messy. Together, they represent the extremes of the different ways people take care of their living space.

Being messy may seem funny on television, but in real life it is not so pleasant. Clothes on the floor, dirty dishes on the table, and books and papers all over the place do not make a room inviting. Instead, they may make you want to leave.

Caring for space means keeping it neat and clean. Possessions should be stored where they belong. And floors, walls, and furniture should be kept clean. Cleaning up is not the world's most enjoyable activity. Then why do it? There are three good reasons. Each has to do with you and your well-being. The three reasons affect your pocketbook, your time, and your feelings.

Objectives

After reading this chapter, you will be able to:

☐ *explain the value of home maintenance procedures,*

☐ *describe a routine for keeping your space clean,*

☐ *explain how to clean various areas in your family's space.*

503

Why Care for Space?

Care Avoids Waste

Caring for your things makes them last longer and keeps them in good condition. Then you won't have to spend money replacing them.

Leaving your records scattered around your room may be convenient. But when one of them gets stepped on and scratched, it doesn't seem like such a good idea.

Care Makes Your Life Easier

It is easier to live in a tidy space than in a cluttered one. Whether you want to find a pen, a book, or a baseball mitt, it's easier to find if it's where it's supposed to be.

Care Makes You Feel Better

A cluttered room reflects the way you feel about yourself. It's hard not to be depressed when you are surrounded by disorder. A neat room, on the other hand, makes most people feel better—more in control of things.

Even people who say they don't mind clutter would prefer a neat room, especially if it were cleaned by someone else!

Caring for Your Own Space

Even though your room may be your own space, it's part of your family's home. How you keep up your room is not just a

Where is this teen's sweater? In a corner? On the chair? Under the bed? What would people find if they looked under your bed?

matter of your own personal taste. It has an effect on the overall condition of your home.

Home furnishings and home repair are very expensive. If you don't bother to clean up spills on your floor—nail polish, airplane glue, fruit juice—what is the cost of repairing the damage? If you make large holes in the wall when putting up a poster, who ends up paying to repair the damaged wall? What you do in your own space clearly affects other members of your family.

By caring for your own space and keeping it neat, you are helping the whole family. Money spent on fixing damage that your carelessness caused is money taken away from something else—possibly from something that can benefit you and the whole family.

Getting Started

The first step in keeping your living space neat is to find a storage location for all your possessions. Perhaps your basketball has been in the corner for six months because you just don't know where to put it. You can't find your red sweater because you have no drawer just for sweaters. Follow the suggestions in chapter 66 for creating storage space, and *get organized*.

Policing the Area

Once you have established places for the different things in your room, you must see that they all get there.

Putting things away as soon as you finish using them is a big help. Also, get into a set routine for cleaning and straightening your room.

Time is often short in the morning, especially on school days, so you may want to take a quick 10 minutes and fix up your room when you get home from school. Some jobs—like making your bed—should be done in the morning.

Change your sheets, dust, and vacuum on a regular basis. Check often to make sure that everything is in its place.

Caring for Shared Space

Maintenance of a home—that is, *keeping it in good working order*—is a job for everyone. Your family spends a major part of its resources on your home. It's important to help maintain it, which means taking responsibility for the shared spaces in it.

Assignment of chores. Maintaining a home is done differently in each family. Sometimes, the chores of maintaining the shared spaces are the responsibility of one person. Sometimes, each family member takes a particular job. For instance, one person vacuums, and another dusts.

In any case, you should understand that, as a family member, you have a stake in keeping your home in good condition.

For example, if you see that your mother or older brother is very busy on a particular day, volunteer to clean up the living room, even if it's not your job to do so. Likewise, if you see your father or sister working hard to clean out the garage or shovel snow off the walk, you can offer to give them a hand.

Rotating Schedules. Sometimes, a cleaning job is passed around from one family member to another. You might be responsible for cleaning the bathroom one week. The next week your brother or sister would have the job. This kind of system is called rotating chores.

No matter how the chores are divided up, it's important that they be done and that each person take a part.

Prevention

One of the important areas of maintenance in a home is the **preventive** one. This means *making sure that accidents and damage do not occur.* You can do your part by keeping all the shared spaces in the home neat and safe for anyone who wants to use them.

Leaving your shoes on the floor in the middle of your room may not affect anyone but you. If you leave them on the living room floor, though, a member of your family or a friend may trip on them. In the next chapter, you'll learn more about safety in the home.

What to Do

Cleaning house isn't difficult; you probably know many of the procedures already. There are certain steps for cleaning each area. If you use commercial cleaning products, follow the easy directions on their containers. Misuse of a product can ruin what you're cleaning or be dangerous.

Bathroom. Use a sponge or cloth and scouring powder or liquid to clean the sink basin and bathtub. Then rinse them carefully. You'll need a toilet brush and toilet cleaner to clean and sanitize inside and outside the toilet. For this kind of cleaning, you may want to wear rubber gloves.

You can transform a messy closet into a neat, organized storage space. All you need are some boards, one or two poles, nails, a saw, a hammer, and a measuring tape.

T E E N   I S S U E

Mountains of Trash

We throw away enough garbage every day to fill the New Orleans Superdome from floor to ceiling—twice. That's eight pounds of trash every day for every man, woman, and child. For many years, our trash has been hauled off in trucks to be burned or buried. Our attitude has been, "Out of sight, out of mind."

But today, the problem of where to put all the trash is a very serious one. Burning garbage causes air pollution, and finding places to bury it has become more difficult.

Recycling solid waste, or trash, may provide an answer to this problem.

In the 1960s, when people first became aware of the problem of waste disposal, they formed neighborhood recycling centers.

Many families took part in the effort. They bundled their newspapers, sorted their bottles, and collected aluminum cans.

Then they took these items to the recycling center so that the materials could be reused.

But the problem is still there. Even if every family recycled everything it used, trash would still be around.

That's because only 30 percent of a community's garbage comes from household waste. The rest comes from offices and industries.

If recycling isn't enough, what can you do?

■ *Improve recycling at the community or county level.*

If a recycling center does not exist in your town, find out why. Did one fail from lack of interest? Maybe a good publicity campaign could bring it back.

Sometimes, there is a problem about what to do with the collected materials. Look in the yellow pages of the telephone book under recycling, salvage, or used goods.

Is there a company that will buy the paper, bottles, and cans?

■ *Call or write the public works department and the solid waste commission.*

These are the government groups that collect and handle trash. Ask if anything can be done to encourage recycling in business and industry.

Businesses could collect their own materials for recycling. You could form school groups to help them recycle waste. Schools and offices could buy paper products made from recycled paper.

■ *Visit the dump or landfill and talk to the people who run it.*

Ask if they separate burnable wood from other trash. If they do, people could pick this wood up for their own use.

Find out what's going on in your community. Don't let anything go to waste.

Floors. How you clean a floor depends on the type of floor it is. Vacuum carpeted floors. Use a broom or dust mop on smooth floors. A wet mop and bucket is best for floors that aren't carpeted. Varnished wood floors may need an occasional waxing with a product made specifically for wood floors. Vinyl floors may benefit from a coating of acrylic floor finish, which both shines and protects. Some newer floor coverings have a permanent shine.

Walls. Check the walls for dirt and fingerprint marks. A sponge dampened with a cleaning solution will wipe fingerprints off doors, moldings, switches, drawers, and cabinets. Keep in mind that some paint and wallpaper can be washed, but others cannot.

Windows. To clean windows, you can use a cloth or paper towel with window cleaner. For a cheaper cleaning product, mix four cups warm water, four teaspoons baking soda, and one-quarter teaspoon liquid bleach. Dry the window immediately using a very dry, lint-free cloth or paper towel.

Furniture. Wooden furniture needs an occasional dusting. A dust cloth or duster will do the job. Some people use dusting sprays. For wooden furniture, you may also wish to add wax.

Upholstered furniture may need to be vacuumed. Use a special tool to pick up dirt and hairs that collect in cracks. You may want to turn cushions upside down occasionally to let the fabric wear evenly on both sides.

When to Do It

Some cleaning jobs need to be done more frequently than others. Cleaning your room and wiping out the sink and bathtub or shower after using them are routine chores. The kitchen counter needs to be cleaned after every meal. Chapter 43 has more information on keeping the kitchen clean.

Clean the floors and dust on a regular basis. Waxing floors and washing the windows can be done monthly or even less frequently.

Words to Remember

maintenance: keeping living space and belongings in good working order

preventive: making sure that accidents and damage do not occur

Questions

1. Give three good reasons for caring for your own personal space. How can regular care save money?

2. Give examples of two things you can do to keep your room neat.

3. Describe some chores that should be done daily, weekly, and monthly in a home.

4. What are the advantages of having each person in a home always responsible for the same tasks? What are the disadvantages?

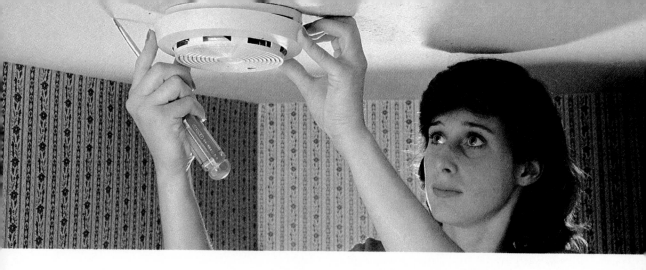

70 Safety in the Home

After reading this chapter, you will be able to:

□ *describe the most common dangers in the home,*

□ *suggest ways to guard against such dangers.*

When you used to play hide-and-seek, you probably yelled "home free" or "safe home." We like to think of "home" this way, but the truth is a little bit different.

In the United States, nearly 25 million home injuries occur every year. Of course, in many homes there are no accidents at all. But unexpected falls, fires, drownings, and poisonings claim lives all the time.

People have accidents in the most familiar parts of their homes. A skid on the rug you walked on a thousand times, a fall over a piece of furniture that has been in the same place for ten years are two common sources of home accidents.

To keep people in your home off the accident list, you must expect the unexpected. Be aware of the dangers, stay on guard, and plan for prevention. Follow the home safety rules described in this chapter. Then you really will be "safe home."

Assessing the Dangers

Before you can take steps to avoid accidents, you have to know what the dangers are. Here are the most common house safety problems.

- *Falls and bumps.* Falling is the most common cause of fatal home accidents. It's also the greatest problem for older people. But anyone, of any age, can fall anywhere—over anything. You can take a tumble down the stairs, skid across highly polished floors, or trip over clutter.

- *Fires and electrical problems.* Fire is the second biggest killer in the home. And burns put thousands of people in the hospital each year. A carelessly tossed, lighted match can become a bonfire. Grease can start an oven fire. Electrical shock accounts for many accidental home deaths, too.

- *Poisonings.* Little children, who can't read labels, are the most likely victims of poisoning. They're very curious and not likely to know about poisonous substances.

- *Cuts.* Cuts may not be as serious as some other injuries, but they are avoidable. Knives or scissors left around are dangerous to children. So are the blades of lawn mowers.

One of the most dangerous areas of the home is under the kitchen sink. Keep harmful detergents and drain cleaners away from children's reach.

Preventing Accidents

Your house contains some danger areas, but many accidents don't *have* to happen. By being careful and safe, you can prevent most serious injuries from occurring.

Preventing Falls

Falls can happen anywhere, but they're most likely to occur in three areas: on floors and stairways and in the bathroom.

Floors. People are more likely to fall on messy or slippery floors. Neatness is one way to prevent these falls. You may be able to find your way in your room in the dark, but others may not. Your mother could trip over your skates. Carefully putting things away will prevent these accidents.

Some people slip on freshly cleaned kitchen or bathroom floors. Simply putting up a sign—CAUTION: WET FLOOR—will tell others that you've cleaned the kitchen. They'll know to walk carefully.

Six other steps will help you make floors safe.

- Wipe up spills immediately, so people won't slip.
- Keep rooms well lit, so people can see objects.
- Anchor down throw rugs with carpet tape or velcro, so they won't skid.
- Arrange furniture so it will not be in people's way.
- Shorten long electrical cords or speaker wires, or secure them with electrical tape to keep them out of walkways.
- Use stepladders to reach high shelves.

Stairs. Lighting is very important on stairways. Stairways should also be kept clear of clutter—they are for walking, not storage. A throw rug at the top of the stairs could slip and send someone to the bottom. A sturdy handrail is a good way to prevent accidents.

Bathroom. Some falls happen in the bathtub and shower. Nonskid mats or strips that stick to the bottom help prevent these falls. Handrails can be put on the wall near the tub or toilet. These are especially helpful to people who have trouble sitting down or standing steadily.

Preventing Electrical Problems

Electrical accidents generally have two causes—problems with outlets and using appliances incorrectly. Here are steps you can take to prevent electrical problems.

Outlets. Pull furniture away from the wall and inspect each cord. Pay special attention to plugs—unplug and plug them in again. Watch for sparks. If you see any, pull the plug out slowly and don't use it again until it's fixed.

Check extension cords and outlets. Avoid putting too much electrical equipment on the same outlet. Connect that extra lamp to some other outlet.

Appliances. Clear all dust away from an appliance's motor after unplugging it. Check all appliances for safe wiring—cords should be well covered with insulation and there should be no fraying.

Never use electrical appliances when you're wet or have wet hands. Unplug appliances and put them away when they're not in use.

Learn how to detect electrical hazards. Check electrical cords for cuts and frayed ends. Be sure that outlets are not overloaded with too many plugs.

F E A T U R E

Organizing a Home Fire Drill

We've all been trained in school to line up and file out if a fire occurs. Some places of business also have fire drills.

But what about a plan for your home? Which exit is best from your room?

Perhaps your family has never thought about this. Yet proper planning for a fire emergency can—and does—save lives. Here's how:

1. *Have a planning meeting that every-one in the family must attend.* Discuss the following safety measures:

   ■ *Escape routes.* What's the best way to get from each room in the house to the outdoors?

   What should you do if the exit is blocked? Where should a chain ladder be kept and how do you attach it?

   ■ *Buddy system.* If there are small children in the home, who can get to them fastest?

   Would it be easier if each family member were responsible for one

other family member?

   ■ *Signals.* Is there some signal—a whistle or a horn—you can use in case of fire?

2. *Get another family member to help you try out each escape route.* Time the route and make adjustments if necessary. Then draw all the routes out. Review the plans with the whole family.

3. *Plan a test with your family.* One person needs to sound the fire signal. Can it be heard in the attic? In the kitchen? In the bathroom with the shower running?

After your planning is done, let a few days pass and stage a fire drill. Wait for a time when everyone is home, preferably in different areas of the house. Then sound the alarm.

This first drill should be followed by another meeting. Discuss any difficulties that came up. Have another drill one week later, and see how it goes.

Preventing Fire

No home can be made entirely **fire-proof**—*completely protected from the danger of fire.* But many steps can be taken to reduce the chance of fire occurring.

Fire Prevention. Checking electrical outlets and appliances is a good first step. But more can be done. Don't store anything near the heater or in the same closet as the furnace. Don't pile papers, wood, or oily rags in a corner—especially near a heat or electrical source.

Keep the kitchen clean to prevent grease fires from occurring. Check the pilot light on a gas stove to be sure that it is working properly. You may want to keep a fire extinguisher in the kitchen, since that's where many fires start.

Use matches safely. Always be sure that a burned match is cold and wet before throwing it in the trash. Cigarettes should be completely put out. And smokers should never smoke in bed. Finally, use fireplaces and wood stoves carefully.

Fire Safety. Sometimes, despite all precautions, a fire occurs. Your family is more likely to survive a fire if it has **smoke alarms**. These are *battery-operated devices that make a loud sound when they sense smoke.* There should be one on each level of your house, and one near the sleeping area. Check the battery regularly to see that the device is working.

A major part of fire safety is knowing how to leave the house if a fire occurs. See the box for some guidelines.

Preventing Poisoning

Closets, medicine chests, cabinets, laundry areas, basements, and garages all hold many poisonous substances. Ammonia, bleach, cleansing powders, cosmetics, detergents, fertilizers, furniture polish, gasoline, kerosene, paint thinner, weed killers—all these are poisons.

Even medicines like aspirin and prescription drugs can be poisonous if too much is swallowed at one time.

Check heating appliances regularly. Usually a representative from the gas company will come to your home to light pilot lights and check gas appliances.

Most poisonings occur in the kitchen, bathroom, and bedroom. And many involve young children, whose curiosity leads them to explore things that they don't know are dangerous.

Preventing poisoning involves these steps.

- Lock up all cabinets, closets, or other storage areas that contain poisons.
- Keep dangerous substances high and out of children's reach.
- Teach children not to swallow these products.
- Purchase medicines that come in child-proof containers.
- Never move medicine to another container that lacks a warning label.

Preventing Cuts

The kitchen, workrooms, and the outdoors are the danger areas for cuts. Proper storage and use of knives and other sharp cooking utensils are the best ways to prevent cuts from occurring. Always store knives with the handle toward the person opening the drawer and the sharp edge away.

Workrooms contain dangerous objects like saws. These tools should be stored out of children's reach, and their blades should be safely covered.

Care must be taken when operating outdoor tools and machinery. Anyone using these machines should keep away from their moving parts. Always wear shoes with closed toes when running a lawn mower.

Words to Remember

fireproof: completely protected from the danger of fire

smoke alarm: a battery-operated device that makes a loud sound when it senses smoke

Questions

1. What are the four main types of accidents that can occur in the home?
2. List three ways that you can prevent falls.
3. List two ways to prevent electrical problems.
4. What device might help you survive in the event of a fire?
5. List five common household substances that are poisonous.
6. What can you do to prevent cuts from occurring?

Chapter **71 Energy Conservation in the Home**

Objectives

After reading this chapter, you will be able to:

□ *explain the importance of conserving resources,*

□ *list the steps that you can take to conserve energy,*

□ *describe old and new ways of decreasing energy use.*

Do you turn the lights off when you leave the room? Do you take quick showers? When you're chilly, do you put on a sweater instead of turning up the heat? Has your family put in insulation, or a wood stove?

You've probably heard your parents and others talk about the rising costs of electricity, gas, and oil. **Conservation** steps like the actions described above help save money. They also *help protect our natural resources from waste, loss, or harm.*

■ Is turning off lights enough to save energy?

■ Can you do more?

This chapter will describe many steps you can take to conserve resources.

What Is Energy?

Types of Energy

Energy is *the capacity for work*. Oil and gas are called energy sources because they provide power to do work. We use energy for two important purposes—to make electricity and to produce heat.

Electricity is supplied by a local utility company. Most utilities produce it by burning fuels—oil, coal, or natural gas. Some use **hydroelectric power**, which is *generated by the force of falling water*. Some use nuclear reactors to make electricity.

Home-heating energy sources vary. Your home might be heated by electricity. Your heating system might burn oil or use natural gas. These are the three main sources of heat. Some homes have wood-burning stoves. Others have coal-burning stoves. And some homes use heat from the sun.

Uses of Energy

If you've ever had a power blackout, you know how helpless you feel without electricity. Almost everything we do requires electrical energy of some kind. The table lists many uses of electricity in your house. How many more can you think of?

Steps to Save Energy

What can you do to conserve energy? First, think about how you use it. Of the average home's energy bill, 41 percent of the cost is for heating and 15 percent is for heating water. Cooling totals 7 percent. The other 38 percent goes for all the appliances, machines, and lights that are run by electricity. Of course, your family's actual energy use may be different. Climate, the size and age of your home, and the size of your family all affect energy use.

Heating and Cooling

Conserving Energy. Heating and cooling together amount to almost half of the average family's energy bill. These are two good areas for cutting back on your use of energy. Here are some ideas.

- In the winter, set your thermostat to 68° when family members are home during the day and 60° when no one is home and at night. Set it low when you're away from home during the day, too. If you

To conserve resources, change some of your habits. When you feel a chill, put on a sweater instead of running up the thermostat.

TABLE 1   Uses of Electricity in the Home

Cleaning appliances	Heating & cooling	Entertainment	Lighting	Food preparation	Personal care
Dishwasher	Air conditioner	Computer	Ceiling fixture	Blender	Electric curlers
Dryer	Fan	Radio	Lamps	Skillet	
Vacuum	Heater	Stereo		Mixer	Electric razor
Washer	Water heater	Television		Oven	Electric toothbrush
		Video game		Refrigerator	Hair dryer
				Stove	
				Toaster	

reduce your home temperature by 6 degrees, you can save up to 15 percent of your fuel bills.

■ If possible, put thermostats in more than one room. Then you can control temperature better.

■ If you use an air conditioner in the summer, raise its temperature setting 6 degrees. This will cut your cooling costs, perhaps by as much as 47 percent.

■ Use fans instead of air conditioners. They are less costly to run.

■ Use drapes to help you control the temperature. On cold days, open them when the sun is shining in, but close them at other times. In summer, closing drapes and shades keeps the house cooler.

■ Close the fireplace damper when you're not making a fire.

Insulation. *Different materials can be put inside walls or ceilings to keep cold out and heat in.* These materials are forms of **insulation**. In some houses, good insulation can lower heating bills by 30 to 35 percent.

Insulation is measured by its *R value*. This stands for its resistance to heat flow. The higher the R value, the better the insulation. Colder climates need higher R values than warmer climates do. Because heat rises, ceiling insulation should have a higher R value than that of wall insulation.

Preventing Drafts. Much heat is lost because warm air escapes through cracks in the walls or around windows and doors. You can prevent this problem by using double-glass or triple-glass windows, and by adding caulking or **weatherstripping** around doors and windows. These *fiber, plastic, or metal strips prevent air leaks*.

Lighting and Appliances

You can save electricity in two ways: *by using it carefully* and *by buying efficient appliances*.

Using Electricity. You can save electricity by following these steps.

■ Save hot water by taking shorter showers. Install water-saving shower heads.

■ Keep the refrigerator defrosted so it works more efficiently.

■ Don't leave the refrigerator door open.

T E E N I S S U E

Five Ways to Save Water

Water is one of our most precious resources, but many people use it carelessly. Saving water isn't difficult. It's a matter of developing good habits. Here are five suggestions that will help you save water every day:

1. *Turn your faucets off completely after use.* Fix dripping faucets and leaks immediately. Did you know that a faucet that leaks one drop of water per second sends 192 gallons of clean water down your drain per month?

2. *Take a short shower instead of a bath, or use a low level of bath water.* A typical tub bath uses 10 to 15 gallons of water, while a 5-minute shower uses only 8 to 12 gallons. Keep your daily showers short.

3. *When you wash your dishes by hand, stopper the sink or use a dishpan for washing.* Washing dishes under continually running water wastes about 30 gallons per meal! If you use an automatic dishwasher, use it (fully loaded) instead of washing dishes by hand. A dishwasher with two meals' worth of dishes will use 11 to 16 gallons of water.

4. *Use the washing machine only when full.* Also, use the special water-saver settings.

5. *Never run your faucet continually when you're shaving, brushing your teeth, or working at the sink.* If the faucet is left on during a 5 minute shave, 6 gallons of water are wasted. Turning faucets on and off as needed is largely a matter of awareness and habit.

■ If you have a dishwasher, wash only full loads. Open the door once the dishes are clean. Let them dry in the air.

■ Wash clothes on warm or cold water settings.

■ Do not overdry clothes in a dryer.

■ Dry clothes by hanging them up, rather than by using a dryer.

■ Shut off electric lights and appliances such as the radio when not needed.

■ Replace high-wattage bulbs with low-wattage ones if light isn't needed for reading or close work.

■ Use fluorescent bulbs, which take less energy than incandescent bulbs.

Buying Appliances. Large appliances are very important purchases. They are expensive to buy, and many use a great deal of energy every day. For this reason, the federal government requires that *Energy Guide* labels appear on many of these appliances. Chapter 45 tells about these labels.

You can also check appliances for energy-saving features. Frost-free refrigerators use more energy than those that require defrosting. If you let the frost build up in the refrigerators that need defrosting, though, the opposite is true. Dishwashers should have controls to skip the drying cycle.

Gas

Three important pieces of home equipment can run on natural or propane gas—the heating system, the water heater, and the range. Follow the gas tips for conserving energy mentioned earlier.

Another way to save gas is to buy equipment with an electronic ignition. Standard gas equipment has a **pilot**. This *thin stream of gas is burned constantly and used to light a larger flame.* By lighting the flame electronically, newer models no longer need the pilot.

Old Energy Savers

Our need to save energy has caused us to begin using older low-cost heating methods. Wood-burning stoves are popular again for heating one room. They are very efficient.

Careful placement and landscaping of a new house can reduce the amount of energy it needs. Houses that are built against hills and surrounded by trees are warmer in the winter and cooler in the summer. If windows face south, they collect more heat.

A New Energy Saver

The sun, our oldest energy source, is being put to new use. Solar energy systems collect and store the sun's power. Some are already being used in many homes as space and water heaters, although a backup heating system is usually needed.

Solar energy is nonpolluting and will be available for billions of years. But scientists must develop more efficient and less expensive ways to collect sunlight before solar power becomes widely used.

Words to Remember

conservation: protecting natural resources from waste, loss, or harm

energy: the capacity for work

hydroelectric power: power generated by the force of falling water

insulation: materials put inside walls or ceilings to keep cold out and heat in

pilot: a thin stream of gas that is burned constantly and used to light a larger flame on gas equipment

weatherstripping: fiber, plastic, or metal strips placed around doors and windows to prevent air leaks.

Questions

1. Why do we need to conserve energy?
2. What sources of power can a utility company use to produce electricity?
3. List two steps your family can take to cut down on home-heating costs.
4. How can you compare different types of insulation?
5. List three things you can do to conserve electricity.
6. What can you do to save gas?

Chapter 72 Careers in Housing

Objectives

After reading this chapter, you will be able to:

□ *identify areas in the job market in which you can use the skills discussed in this unit,*

□ *outline the nature of certain jobs in these areas.*

Housing is one of the basic needs that must be met by all people. Everybody needs some kind of shelter. These homes must be planned and built. They must be furnished, decorated, maintained, and sold.

The largest segment of careers in housing is in construction, the building of homes. These homes may be single-family dwellings or three or four family units.

In the home building industry, people are needed to become masons, plumbers, plasterers, electricians, painters, and paperhangers. Carpenters are by far the largest single group in the industry.

Many people who start in the home building industry move into commercial construction of stores, office buildings, warehouses, restaurants, apartment buildings, and factories.

Characteristics Useful in Housing Careers

Mental Characteristics

- Can you see a finished product by looking at a plan? Housing workers must be able to **visualize**, or *see in their minds*, how a completed project might look. Carpenters must be able to see a table so they can know how to build it. Interior designers need to picture how a certain carpeting will match the furniture.

- Do you like fixing up your room by selecting new colors or rearranging your furniture? Do you have fun picking out new posters for your room or matching frames to photographs for the living room? Your interest in arranging colors and shapes may mean that a housing career is for you.

- Are you interested in learning about the materials used in housing? Plumbers must know about pipes, and carpet salespeople about carpets. Home-security experts must understand locks and alarms. Often, this knowledge is learned on the job, or in a technical school that prepares people for the career.

Emotional Characteristics

- Can you communicate with people easily and work well with them? Kitchen designers and furniture salespeople sometimes work very closely with their customers. They must be able to learn what the customer wants and make him or her feel comfortable. That makes the work satisfying and easier to do. It can also lead customers to recommend the workers to friends.

- Do you pay attention to detail? Housing workers must be thorough and complete. A cabinetmaker must make the tops of cabinet doors line up perfectly. A building inspector must check carefully for safety hazards. If you are patient and thorough in your work, you have this characteristic.

Jobs in Design, Construction, and Sales

Entry-Level Jobs

Landscape gardeners work outdoors most of the time. They mow lawns, prune

The home maintenance industry is among the largest in the country. People are needed to repair anything from can openers to refrigerators.

bushes, and trim trees. Gardeners may work alone or in crews. Some have their own businesses, working at many different homes during the week. Others work for institutions—businesses, colleges, or the government. They care for larger areas.

Construction workers build the homes themselves. This field includes carpenters, electricians, masons, painters, plumbers, and roofers. These workers are usually good at working with their hands and have learned special skills for their trade. Many begin their work as **apprentices**—*helpers*

Architects design houses or other buildings. They draw scale drawings of the inside and the outside of the building. Their work requires precision.

who are trained on the job by senior workers. Construction workers receive good pay, but may be without work when there is little new building.

Jobs That Require Extra Training

When people want help in improving the look of their homes, they might call on an *interior designer.* This professional can redesign one room or a whole house. Depending on the client's budget and wishes, a designer might construct new walls or suggest new color patterns and furniture.

Designers take special courses after high school to get their training. Many designers receive college degrees. They work for furniture stores, architects, or on their own.

A *real estate salesperson* helps people buy and sell homes. Buyers go to a realtor's office and explain what size house they want, what location they want, and how much they can pay. Then the salesperson tries to find a house that matches their needs.

A real estate career requires special training in housing financing and sales.

Jobs That Require an Advanced Degree

Architects actually design buildings and homes. They may design houses for one family or huge apartments for hundreds. They may create a whole new house or redesign the interior of an older one.

Architects must know about the materials used for building and about people's living patterns. They must have some math ability. They must also be able to visualize a completed project while it's still on the drawing board.

FEATURE

On the Job

It's your first day on the job—and you don't know what to do. Everything is unfamiliar and everybody is a stranger. What can you do to be less nervous?

1. *Find out everything you can ahead of time.* When you're hired, ask where you should report, at what time, to whom, and whether you should bring any equipment or supplies. By asking ahead of time, you'll feel more confident when you arrive.

2. *Be yourself with other people.* You'll find it much easier to overcome your nerves if you just act naturally. Don't brag or boast about what you can do—let your work show your skills.

3. *Ask questions when you're unsure about anything.* This is probably the most important rule. Don't sit at your work station wondering what to do. Ask your boss or an experienced co-worker. Don't worry that the question seems dumb. The only dumb questions are the ones that aren't asked when the person thinks of them.

4. *If your employer has an information or policy booklet, find some time to read it.* You may not be able to read it on the job, but you probably can during lunch or in the evening. But be sure to read it. The booklet most likely contains important information about hours, sick days, and work procedures.

5. *Work slowly and carefully.* Start out by trying to understand exactly what you must do and how to do it. Don't try to hurry things through to show people how efficient you are.

6. *Give yourself time to learn your way around.* Few offices are so small that you can learn where everything is in one day. Give yourself a chance.

7. *Be patient in learning other people's names.* One of the most difficult things about a new job is learning the names of many new people. You probably won't be able to do it on the first day—perhaps not even in the first week. Give yourself some time.

City planners work for local governments to guide the growth of an area. First they predict the future population of the area. Then they guess at the people's needs for housing, schools, shopping, recreation, transportation—all the things that make a place livable. Then planners suggest ways to meet these future needs so that the city can grow in pace with the population.

Jobs in Home Maintenance and Use

Entry-Level Jobs

Every one of us can be called a *homemaker*—a person who cares for the home. Homemakers don't just care for a home, they also manage and decorate it. Full-time homemakers usually do much of a family's meal preparation, too.

Many people like to maintain or improve their homes themselves. They need knowledgeable *sales clerks* to advise them on what materials to buy and how to use tools and materials correctly and safely. These sales clerks work at hardware or home improvement stores.

Jobs That Require Extra Training

Large apartment buildings have *superintendents*. Their job is to keep all the housing units in good repair. They must fix leaks, check furnaces, repair broken windows, and do other such jobs. Often, these workers live in one of the units in the building. They may need to be available for emergencies at all hours.

Suppose the cloth on a favorite rocking chair is too worn out to be used anymore. Must the chair be thrown out? Not necessarily. An *upholsterer* can take off the old fabric and put a new covering on the chair, making it as good as new. These workers help people redecorate. And they save older furniture from the junk pile by restuffing and recovering it.

Jobs That Require an Advanced Degree

Home economists can work in the field of housing, just as they can in the areas of food or clothing. Some work in the extension service, an educational program run by the Department of Agriculture and county governments. Others work for businesses.

In all these jobs, home economists offer suggestions and ideas on how to get the most out of housing. They may run workshops for people, write articles, or give speeches. Whatever the method, their goal is to provide information.

Many utility companies have *home service advisers*. These workers visit people in their homes, or they write booklets explaining how to conserve resources.

Words to Remember

apprentice: a helper who is trained on the job by a senior worker

visualize: to see something in one's mind

Questions

1. List two mental characteristics that are important for careers in housing.
2. What two emotional characteristics are important for careers in housing?
3. Identify three careers in the home design, construction, and sales area—one at each job level.
4. Name three careers in the home maintenance and use area—one at each job level.

Your living space is very important. It can be a shelter from noise or a place to have fun. Making it comfortable and enjoyable isn't hard, and the effort pays off with happiness. Here are some ideas for getting the most out of your living space:

1. Solving the decorating blues.

2. Cleaning your room in 15 minutes a day.

3. Using tools around the house.

4. Safety first.

5. Conserving resources.

Solving the Decorating Blues

Have you ever wondered what you could do with your room? Are you tired of feeling that it's too small? Do you want to make it more light? Do you want to put prints up, but you're not sure how to arrange them? Here are some hints that will help you get rid of those decorator blues.

Making your space look bigger

- Move your bed from the center of the room to stand against the wall. This creates more open space.
- Use smaller pieces of furniture.
- Use light colors for floors and walls.
- Put mirrors on one or two walls to create the look of more space.
- Don't buy bedspreads or curtains that have busy designs.

Using lighting effectively

- Place two shaded lamps on low tables to make your room look larger.
- Use tinted bulbs to change or accent a color effect.
- Put bright fixtures on the ceiling to draw the eye upward in rooms with a horizontal design.
- Use spotlights to focus attention on interesting objects.

Decorating your desk

Making these attractive covers is simple. Just get enough fabric to cover each item and glue it on. You could also use contact paper.

Arranging prints

A print or poster need not stand alone. You can create an attractive look by combining more than one. Here are some possible arrangements.

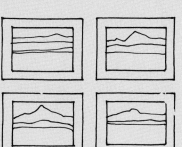

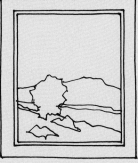

Cleaning Your Room in 15 Minutes a Day

"Clean your room!" your parents say. You'd like to keep your room neater, but it seems like too much work. Actually, keeping your room clean is pretty simple. You need to spend only a few minutes every day to reach your goal. Here's how to plan it.

Every day

Some tasks are easily done every day. These should take you only five minutes or so.

- Make the bed.
- Put your clothes away properly. Put your shoes in the closet.
- Put your school things away neatly when you get home from school or are done studying.
- Put records, equipment, and hobbies away where they belong when you're done with them.

Weekly

Other jobs need be done only once a week. If you decide to do one task each day, it won't take you longer than 10 minutes. There are many different ways you can split up the work. Here is a sample plan:

Monday: Straighten out your desk or study area. File papers away. Stack books and organize magazines. Empty the wastebasket.

Tuesday: Straighten out drawers and closets. Be sure that everything is in the proper place.

Wednesday: Change the sheets on your bed.

Thursday: Dust the furniture.

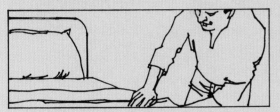

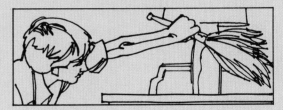

Friday: Vacuum or sweep the floor.

Saturday: Wipe off dust on the walls, around light fixtures, and on window sills.

Sunday: Take a day off to admire your clean room!

Using Tools Around the House

Tools can help you do many jobs, but you have to know how to use them the right way.

Hanging a picture

Suppose you want to hang a framed print. You can use a hammer to put the nail in the wall. Be sure to hold the hammer near the end of the handle. To start, hold the nail in place and tap gently. Be sure to hit the nail squarely.

What if you want to remove a nail? The claw end of the hammer will do the work. But once you've got the nail partly removed, put a block of wood or piece of cloth beneath the head of the hammer. Then its pressure won't damage the surface.

Putting up curtain rods

Most curtain rods are fixed to the wall by screws. You can start a screw hole by hammering a nail into the wall.

There are two types of screwdrivers—the Phillips (bottom) and the straight (top). The slots on the screw will show you which screwdriver to use.

To put in a screw, be sure to fit the screwdriver in the slot squarely. Push against the head of the screw as you turn it.

To hang your curtain rod, insert the topmost screw part way on both sides to hold the rod in place. Add the other screws, tightened part way. Then tighten all the screws.

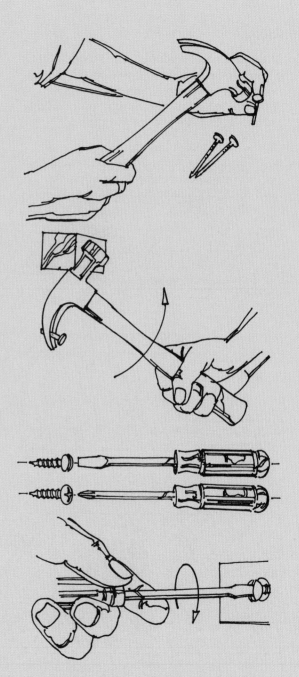

Taking a door off its hinges

You're getting a new desk in your room! But when you bring it home, you find that it's one inch too wide to get through the doorway. What can you do? You should be able to get that desk in by taking the door off its hinges.

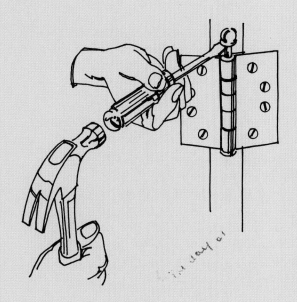

You'll need a hammer and a screwdriver or wedge. Hold the screwdriver or wedge firmly with the point just underneath the ball top of the hinge bolt. A few blows with the hammer should loosen the bolt.

Do the bottom bolt first, then the top one. If the hinges have been painted, you may need to clean dried paint from around the bolt. Once the desk is in your room, put the door back in place and hammer the bolts down.

Taking off a bicycle wheel

You need an adjustable wrench to loosen the bolts that hold the wheel in place. The best way to use a wrench is to put tape or a piece of cloth around the nut you're loosening. Then you're sure not to scratch the nut. Adjust the wrench opening to fit around the nut, then tighten it until the fit is snug. Turn counterclockwise.

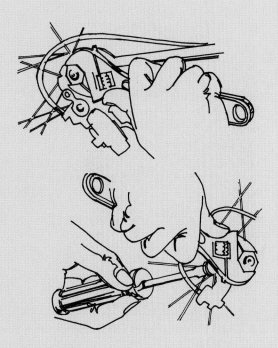

If the nut is around a screw, you may need to use a screwdriver to hold it in place.

If the nut is hard to loosen, apply a few drops of oil. Let the oil soak for a few hours.

Safety First

An important part of living in your home is making it safe. With a few simple steps, you can improve your home's security and protect it—and your family—from the danger of fire.

For security

- Lock doors and windows when leaving, even for a short trip.
- Lock downstairs doors and windows at night.
- Record the serial numbers of all appliances and put the list in a safe place.
- Don't leave cash or valuables lying around.

For fire prevention

- Install smoke alarms—one for each sleeping area and one for each living level.
- Keep electric cords in the open—not under rugs or paper.
- Don't pile up papers, cartons, or oil-soaked rags.
- Have a fire extinguisher handy.
- Keep space heaters away from traffic patterns; be sure that oil heaters are well ventilated.
- Persuade family members not to smoke in bed.

Conserving Resources

Doing your part to conserve resources is easy. It just requires you to think ahead of time. And that forethought has an extra payoff—it can save you money! Here are some things you can do.

Save electricity—and compare usage

Electric companies across the country print useful information on your family's monthly electric bill. Charts show how much power you used this month compared to last month. They may also compare this month's use to the same month last year. You can check these charts to see that your conservation steps are working.

Recycle what you can

Set up separate bins for collecting newspaper, aluminum, and glass. Then take the material to your local recycling center.

Using the car

Our cars eat up millions of gallons of gas. By using them wisely, we can cut down on the number of gallons that are wasted.

ALUMINUM CANS ONLY

- Avoid unnecessary trips by planning to run more than one errand at the same time.
- Car pool to school so that cars aren't used to transport just one person.
- Don't take the car for short trips—use a bicycle or walk. (Then you'll also get some exercise!)
- Keep the car well maintained so it runs efficiently.

Consumer tips

- Buy detergents that are *biodegradable*. These products will not harm the water.
- Buy fabrics and clothes that can be washed and dried at low temperatures.
- Comparison shop for appliances before buying.
- Buy products that are made of recycled materials, or that can be recycled.

Unit Six Review

Unit Summary

Chapter 65.

Your living space is a reflection of you. It says something about your personality, your interests, and how much you care about your surroundings. When people choose housing, they consider cost, physical layout, and location. People can rent housing or buy it.

Chapters 66 and 67.

You can affect your own personal space by the way you organize and decorate it. By changing the layout of your room or creating more storage space, you can make the space more livable. By applying the elements and principles of design, you can create the look you want. Accessories give a room personality and color. They help you express yourself. And changing accessories is less expensive than changing furniture.

Chapter 68.

It is important to be considerate of family members in the spaces you share with them. If you share your room with a brother or sister, you need to be particularly thoughtful. To create private space in a shared bedroom, you can divide the room with dividers or bookcases, or create different levels.

Chapters 69 and 70.

Your living space should be well cared for and safe. Some cleaning tasks need to be done daily or weekly. Others can be done every month or when seasons change. Most home accidents involve falls, fires, electrical hazards, poisoning, or cuts. By being careful, you can prevent accidents from happening.

Chapter 71.

Your family can take steps to conserve energy. You can lower electric, fuel, and water bills. Your conservation measures will also help save our valuable natural resources.

Chapter 72.

There are many jobs in the housing field, ranging from landscape gardener to solar heating researcher. If the material covered in this unit interests you, you may want to consider a career in this field.

Questions

1. How might a person's space reveal his or her personality?

2. What community facilities are important to keep in mind when you choose the location of your home?

3. What is a layout?

4. Why is it important to consider traffic patterns when planning the layout of your room?

5. List four different ideas for increasing the amount of storage area you have in your personal space.

6. What effects do colors have on people's moods?

7. Which materials have textures that give an elegant effect? Which materials have textures that give a more casual look?

8. Explain the importance of unity and contrast in design.

9. What are two benefits of decorating with accessories?

10. Why is it important to learn to share space with others?

11. Give an example of a way to create private space when you share a room.

12. Describe three advantages of keeping your living area clean.

13. List three home-cleaning jobs that should

be done on a daily basis. List three that should be done weekly.

14. What is the most common cause of fatal home accidents? What can be done to prevent these accidents?

15. What steps can you take to check for electrical hazards in your home?

16. Why are smoke alarms important? Where should they be placed?

17. Which natural resources are used for home heating?

18. What steps can your family take to cut its electric bill?

19. Describe what it means to be able to visualize things. Name three careers for which this ability is needed.

20. Why is it important for workers in housing careers to pay attention to detail? Name three careers for which this skill is important.

Reading Activities

1. Look through several issues of craft or decorating magazines. Read and report on any articles describing decorating projects that would make sense in a teenager's room.

2. Research and report on how people share space in Japan, on an Israeli kibbutz, or in the collective villages in China.

3. Read one chapter in a popular book of household hints. Make a list for the class of the 5 or 10 suggestions that seem most useful to you.

Writing Activities

1. Look through decorating magazines for pictures of people's homes. Find one that clearly shows the interests of the people who live there. Cut out the picture. On a separate piece of paper, write a one-page description of the person or family who might live in that house.

2. Visit a discount store. Make a list of things sold there that could be used for storage.

3. Write a letter to your family explaining how you feel about privacy.

4. Interview someone of your grandparents' generation about his or her chores as a teenager. How do they compare with yours? Write a report on your findings.

Math Activities

1. Design a storage unit for your room and make a scale drawing of it.

2. Find out what your family's average monthly heating and electric bill is. Figure out what the bill would be if you cut your energy use by 25 percent and by 33 percent. Multiply the amounts by 12 to figure what your yearly savings would be.

Group Projects

1. Invite an architect to speak to the class about decisions he or she makes in organizing space. If a visit cannot be arranged, ask if a student can interview the architect and report to the class.

2. Make a scrapbook on careers in housing. Each student should research three jobs and write a one-page summary of each. Use a sign-up list so that students are sure to pick different jobs. The summary should describe the training and the mental and emotional characteristics needed for the job. It should also describe the work itself.

APPENDIX

TABLE OF FOOD VALUES

	Amount	Calories	Carbohydrates (g)	Fat (g)	Protein (g)	Calcium (mg)	Iron (mg)	Vitamin A (IU)	Thiamin (mg)	Riboflavin (mg)	Niacin (mg)	Vitamin C (mg)
MILK GROUP												
Cheese, American, process	1 oz/28 g	105	Tr	9	6	174	.1	340	.01	.10	Tr	0
Cheese, Cheddar	1 oz/28 g	115	Tr	9	7	204	.2	300	.01	.11	Tr	0
Cheese, cottage, creamed	½ c/120 ml	117	.1	5	14	67.5	.15	185	.025	.185	.135	Tr
Cheese, cottage, dry	½ c/120 ml	62.5	.5	Tr	12.5	23	.15	20	.02	.10	.1	0
Cheese, cream	1 oz/28 g	100	.2	10	2	23	.3	400	Tr	.06	Tr	0
Chocolate milk	1 c/240 ml	210	26	8	8	280	.6	300	.09	.41	.3	2
Cream, heavy	1 T/15 ml	80	.1	6	Tr	10	Tr	220	Tr	.02	Tr	Tr
Cream, light	1 T/15 ml	30	1	3	Tr	14	Tr	110	Tr	.02	Tr	Tr
Cream, sour	1 T/15 ml	25	1	3	Tr	14	Tr	90	Tr	.02	Tr	Tr
Ice cream 16% fat	½ c/120 ml	175	16	12	2	75.5	.05	445	.02	.14	.5	5
Milk	1 c/240 ml	150	11	8	8	291	.1	310	.09	.4	.2	2
Milk, low fat 2%	1 c/240 ml	121	12	5	8	297	.1	500	.1	.4	.2	2
Milk, skim	1 c/240 ml	85	12	Tr	8	302	.1	500	.09	.34	.2	2
Yogurt, fruit	1 c/240 ml	230	42	3	10	343	.2	120	.08	.4	.2	21
Yogurt, plain, skim milk	1 c/240 ml	125	17	Tr	13	452	.2	20	.11	.53	.3	2
Yogurt, plain, whole milk	1 c/240 ml	140	11	7	8	274	.1	280	.07	.32	.2	1
MEAT, POULTRY, EGGS, FISH, AND LEGUMES GROUP												
Beef, lean (roasted)	3 oz/85 g	165	0	7	25	11	3.2	10	.06	.19	4.5	—
Beef, hamburger, 21% fat	3 oz/85 g	235	0	17	20	9	2.6	30	.07	.17	4.4	—
Chicken (broiled)	3 oz/85 g	240	0	7	42	16	3.0	160	.09	.34	15.5	—
Chicken (fried)	3 oz/85 g	160	1	5	26	9	1.3	70	.04	.17	11.6	—
Eggs (hard cooked)	1	80	1	6	6	28	1	260	.04	.13	Tr	0
Fish, bluefish (baked)	3½ oz/100 g	135	0	4	22	25	0.6	40	.09	.08	31.6	—
Ham, boiled	1 oz/28 g	65	0	5	5	3	.8	0	.12	.04	.7	—
Kidney beans (red beans)	1 c/240 ml	230	42	1	15	74	4.6	10	.13	.10	1.5	—
Lamb shoulder (roasted)	3 oz/85 g	285	0	18	23	9	1.0	—	.11	.2	4.0	—

Food	Measure											
Lentils	1 c/240 ml	210	39	Tr	16	50	4.2	40	.14	.12	1.2	0
Peanut butter	2 T/30 ml	190	6	16	8	20	.6	0	.04	.04	4.8	0
Peas, dried, split	1 c/240 ml	230	42	1	16	22	3.4	80	.3	.18	1.8	—
Pork (roast)	3 oz/85 g	310	0	20	26	9	2.6	0	.46	.21	4.1	—
Sardines	3 oz/85 g	175	0	9	20	372	2.5	190	.02	.17	4.6	—
Tuna, canned in oil	3 oz/85 g	170	0	7	24	7	1.6	70	.04	.1	10.1	—
Turkey, dark meat (roasted)	3 oz/85 g	175	0	7	26	—	2.0	—	.03	.2	3.6	—
Veal cutlet	3 oz/85 g	185	0	9	23	9	2.7	—	.06	.21	4.6	—

FRUITS AND VEGETABLES GROUP

Food	Measure											
Apple	1 (2¾"/63 mm)	80	20	1	Tr	10	.4	120	.04	.03	.1	6
Apricots	3 med	55	14	Tr	1	18	.5	2,890	.03	.04	.6	11
Banana	1 med	100	26	Tr	2	10	.8	230	.06	.07	.8	12
Beans, green	1 c/240 ml	30	7	Tr	2	63	.8	680	.07	.11	.6	15
Bean sprouts	1 c/240 ml	35	7	Tr	4	20	1.4	20	.14	.14	.8	20
Blueberries	1 c/240 ml	90	22	1	1	22	1.5	150	.04	.09	.7	20
Broccoli	1 c/240 ml	40	7	Tr	5	136	1.2	3,880	.14	.31	1.2	140
Cabbage, shredded	1 c/240 ml	15	4	Tr	1	34	.03	90	.04	.04	.2	33
Cabbage, red, shredded, raw	1 c/240 ml	20	5	Tr	1	29	.6	30	.06	.04	.3	43
Cantaloupe	½ melon	80	20	Tr	2	38	1.1	9,240	.11	.08	1.6	90
Carrots	1	30	7	Tr	1	27	.5	7,930	.04	.04	.4	6
Celery, raw	3 stalks	15	6	Tr	Tr	48	.3	330	.03	.03	.3	12
Corn, sweet kernels	1 c/240 ml	130	31	1	5	5	.3	580	.15	.10	2.5	8
Cranberry sauce	½ c/120 ml	202.5	52	Tr	.5	8.5	.3	30	.015	.015	.5	3
Dates	10	220	58	Tr	2	47	2.4	40	.07	.08	1.8	0
Grapefruit juice[a]	¼ c/60 ml	25	6	Tr	.25	6	.05	5	.01	.01	.1	24
Grapes, seedless	10	81	9	Tr	Tr	6	.2	50	.03	.02	.2	2
Lettuce, iceberg	¼ head	17.5	2.6	Tr	.8	18	.45	297	.05	.05	.3	5
Mustard greens	1 c/240 ml	30	6	1	3	193	2.5	8,120	.11	.20	.8	67
Onions, boiled	½ c/120 ml	30	7	Tr	1.5	25	.4	Tr	.03	.03	.2	7.5
Orange	1 (3"/76 mm)	65	16	Tr	1	54	.5	260	.13	.05	.5	66

Note: Although ice cream is a good source of calcium, it also contains many calories, and may lead to weight problems.
Key: Tr—Nutrient present in trace amounts.   [a] Made from concentrate.

TABLE OF FOOD VALUES (cont.)

FRUIT AND VEGETABLES GROUP	Amount	Calories	Carbohydrates (g)	Fat (g)	Protein (g)	Calcium (mg)	Iron (mg)	Vitamin A (IU)	Thiamin (mg)	Riboflavin (mg)	Niacin (mg)	Vitamin C (mg)
Orange juice[a]	¼ c/60 ml	30	7.25	Tr	.5	6.25	.1	135	.05	.001	.22	30
Peaches, peeled	1 (2½"/63 mm)	40	10	Tr	1	9	.5	1,330	.02	.05	1.0	7
Pear, Bartlett	1 (2½"/63 mm)	100	25	1	1	13	.5	30	.03	.07	.2	7
Peas, green, frozen	1 c/240 ml	110	19	Tr	.8	30	2.3	960	.43	.14	2.7	21
Pepper, green sweet, raw	1 med	15	4	Tr	1	7	.5	310	.06	.06	.4	94
Pineapple, cubed	1 c/240 ml	80	21	Tr	1	26	.5	110	.14	.05	.3	26
Potato, baked	1 med	145	33	Tr	4	14	1.1	Tr	.15	.07	2.7	31
Potatoes, French fried	10 pieces	155	18	7	2	9	.7	Tr	.07	.04	1.8	12
Prunes, dried	4 med	110	29	Tr	1	22	1.7	690	.04	.07	.7	1
Raisins (snack package)	½ oz/14 g	40	11	Tr	Tr	9	.5	Tr	.02	.01	.1	Tr
Spinach	1 c/240 ml	40	6	1	5	167	4	14,580	.13	.25	.9	50
Tomatoes, canned	1 c/240 ml	50	10	Tr	2	14	1.2	2,170	.12	.07	1.7	41
Tomato, raw	1 med	25	6	Tr	1	16	.6	1,110	.07	.05	.9	28
Tomato juice	6 oz/170 g	35	8	Tr	2	13	1.6	1,460	.09	.05	1.5	29
BREAD AND CEREALS GROUP												
Bread, white enriched	1 slice	70	13	1	2	21	.6	Tr	.08	.06	.8	Tr
Bread, whole wheat	1 slice	65	14	1	3	24	.8	0	.07	.03	.8	Tr
Bread, pumpernickel (⅔% rye)	1 slice	80	17	Tr	3	27	.8	0	.09	.07	.6	0
Corn flakes, fortified (25% RDA)	1 c/240 ml	'95	21	Tr	2	V	V	V	V	V	V	13
Crackers, saltines	4	50	8	1	1	2	.5	0	.05	.05	.4	0
Egg noodles, enriched	1 c/240 ml	200	37	2	7	16	1.4	110	.22	.13	1.9	0

Food	Measure											
Pasta, enriched, (macaroni cooked, etc.)	1 c/240 ml	190	39	1	7	14	1.4	0	.23	.13	1.8	0
Rice, instant, enriched	1 c/240 ml	180	40	Tr	4	5	1.3	0	.21	V	1.7	0
Rice, enriched	1 c/240 ml	185	41	Tr	4	33	1.4	0	.19	.02	2.1	0
Rice, puffed, whole grain	1 c/240 ml	60	13	Tr	1	3	.3	0	.07	.01	.7	0
Wheat, farina, quick	1 c/240 ml	105	22	Tr	3	147	V	0	.12	.07	1	0
Wheat flakes, fortified, 25% U.S. RDA	¾ c/180 ml	105	24	Tr	3	12	4.8	1,320	.40	.45	5.3	16
Wheat, puffed, whole grain	1 c/240 ml	55	12	Tr	2	4	.6	0	.08	.03	1.2	0
Wheat, shredded, whole grain	1 large biscuit	90	20	1	2	11	.9	0	.06	.03	1.1	0
Wheat, whole grain cereal	1 c/240 ml	110	23	1	4	17	1.2	0	.15	.05	1.5	0
OTHER												
Bacon, fried crisp	2 slices	85	Tr	8	4	2	.5	0	.08	.05	.8	—
Butter	1 T/14 g	100	Tr	12	Tr	3	Tr	430	Tr	Tr	Tr	0
Doughnuts, glazed	1	205	22	11	3	16	.6	25	.1	.1	.8	0
Honey	1 T/21 g	65	17	0	Tr	1	.1	0	Tr	.01	.1	Tr
Margarine, regular	1 T/15 g	100	Tr	12	3	3	Tr	470	Tr	Tr	Tr	0
Mayonnaise	1 T/15 ml	100	Tr	11	3	3	.1	40	Tr	.01	Tr	—
Nuts, peanuts, salted	1 c/240 ml	840	27	72	37	107	3	—	.46	.19	24.8	0
Nuts, walnuts	1 c/240 ml	785	19	74	26	Tr	7.5	380	.28	.14	.9	—
Oil, corn	1 T/15 ml	120	0	14	0	0	0	—	0	0	0	0
Pizza, cheese	1 slice	145	22	4	6	86	1.1	230	.16	.18	1.6	4
Popcorn, plain	1 c/240 ml	25	5	Tr	1	1	.2	—	—	.01	.1	0
Salad dressing, Italian	1 T/15 ml	85	1	9	Tr	2	Tr	Tr	Tr	Tr	Tr	—
Salad dressing, Italian low calorie	1 T/15 ml	10	Tr	1	Tr	Tr	Tr	Tr	Tr	Tr	Tr	—
Seeds, sunflower	½ c/120 g	405	14.5	34.5	17.5	87	5.15	35	1.42	.17	3.9	—
Sugar	1 T/12 g	45	12	0	0	0	Tr	0	0	0	0	0

Note: All fruits and vegetables fresh unless noted. Vegetables fresh cooked unless noted.
Key: [a] Made from concentrate. Tr—Nutrient present in trace amounts. V—Varies by brand; consult label.

GLOSSARY

Note: Numbers in parentheses indicate the chapter where the term appears.

accessory: smaller items that are not part of a basic outfit (53); *also,* any small object that can add visual appeal to a room and make a statement about you (67)

additives: substances that are added to food during processing (38)

adjustment: changing a pattern to fit your own size (59)

adolescence: the time of growth from child to adult (2)

adopted child: a child who is permanently taken into a new family through a legal agreement (8)

age span: the number of years between children (8)

aides: workers who assist higher-level workers with their jobs (16)

allergies: Unpleasant physical reactions to a food or other substance (36)

alternative: a way of solving a problem (5)

amino acids: the building blocks of protein (35)

analogous colors: closely related colors (52)

anemia: a condition causing a lack of energy and low resistance to infection (35)

anorexia nervosa: self-induced starvation (37)

annual percentage rate (APR): the percentage cost of credit on a yearly basis (28)

antidotes: remedies to counteract the effects of poisons (21)

appetite: a psychological need for food (34)

appliance: a piece of kitchen equipment that runs mechanically, by electricity, or by gas (45)

appliqué: a cut-out fabric decoration sewn onto a fabric background (61)

apprentice: a helper who is trained on the job by a senior worker (72)

appropriate: suitable for the occasion (51)

backstitch: a stitch made in reverse to anchor the thread firmly at the end of a seam (58)

bake: to cook by dry heat, usually in an oven (called *roasting* for meat) (46)

balance: when objects are arranged in an even, pleasing way (67)

barter: the direct exchange of one resource for another (25)

baste: to moisten food while it cooks, using its own juices or a sauce (46)

batik: a dyeing method in which hot wax is poured onto the fabric so that it completely coats some areas, which stay the original color when the wax is removed (63)

beat: to mix smoothly, using rapid, regular strokes with a spoon, whisk, beater, or mixer (46)

blend: to mix two or more ingredients together thoroughly (46); also, yarn made from two or more different fibers (54)

blended family: a new family, created by the marriage of two people who were married before and have children (7)

bobbin: a spool that holds the bottom thread in a sewing machine (58)

boil: to cook in liquid that is bubbling (46)

brainstorming: a "free-for-all" approach to problem solving that gets you to think of all possible solutions to a problem (9)

braise: to cook slowly in a small amount of liquid in a covered pan (46)

brand: the particular make of a product, as indicated by an official name or trademark (40)

brocade: a patterned weave that allows for elaborate designs; used for evening dresses and upholstery (54)

broil: to cook by direct heat, especially in a broiler (46)

budget: a plan for spending your money (27)

buffet dinner: a meal in which all food is placed in bowls and platters on a serving table (49)

bulimia: alternating food binges and purges (37)

burlap: a coarse, heavy fabric made of *jute,* an Asian plant, used for shoes and bags (54)

calico: a plain weave cloth with a smooth surface and small, colorful prints; used for sportswear (54)

calorie: an amount of energy (35)

canvas: a heavy, strong, plain weave; used for sportswear (54)

carbohydrate: the nutrient that provides ready energy (35)

caregiver: someone who takes care of children (17)

caring: the emotional bond that one person feels for another (11)

carmelize: become a liquid and change color (48)

catalog: a book that shows all the projects that can be made from a particular company's patterns (57)

centerpiece: a pleasing decoration placed at the center of the table (49)

characteristic: a special feature of a person being described (1)

chiffon: sheer, light, woven fabric, used for dressy clothes or scarves (54)

child abuse: harm, injury, or sexual molestation of a child, usually by a parent or guardian (20)

childproof: to make an area safe for children (20)

chill: to refrigerate or let food stand in cold water (46)

chino: a medium-weight twilled fabric; used for pants and uniforms (54)

chop: to cut into small pieces (46)

classic: a style that stays popular for a long time (53)

clergy: religious workers (16)

client: the person who is given advice and information (16)

clipping: making small, evenly spaced cuts in the seam allowance of an inward curve to flatten it (60)

coagulate: change from a fluid state to a thickened mass (48)

commitment: wanting to make a love relationship work (15)

communicating: sending messages from one person to another (3)

comparison shopping: comparing features and prices of different brands of the same item before you buy (30)

complementary colors: colors that are direct opposites (52)

complex carbohydrate: a nutrient that supplies energy and other nutrients at the same time (35)

compound: to figure interest due and add it to the principal (28)

compromise: a way of solving a problem in which each person gives up something in order to find a solution that satisfies everyone (9)

concentrate: a juice product from which most water has been removed (41)

condominiums: apartment units that are bought (65)

conflict: a problem that arises in a relationship (6)

conform: be like the people around you (51)

conservation: protecting natural resources from waste, loss, or harm (71)

consideration: thinking about the needs of others (68)

consumer: a user of goods and services (29)

contacts: people you know who know about jobs (50)

contaminated: food containing poisons (43)

contingency: an unforeseen event (26)

contrast: the difference in color and shape between objects (67)

convenience store: a store that is open long hours and offers quick service at high prices (29)

cool: to refrigerate or let warm food stand until it is at room temperature (46)

co-op: a group of shoppers who get together to buy large amounts of basic food items at discount prices (40)

corduroy: a weave with an extra warp or weft that produces a nap; used for sportswear (54)

cost per wearing: the total of the purchase price of a garment and the cost of cleaning it, divided by the number of times you wear it (55)

coupon: a printed slip of paper that gives a customer a discount on an item (40)

crash diets: diets that promise quick and easy weight loss (38)

creativity: the ability to use your imagination to do things in new ways (23)

credit: the extension of permission to borrow money (27)

crush: an intense, but usually passing, love-like feeling (14)

cut: the part of an animal that a piece of meat comes from (48)

danger zone: the temperature range between 60° and 125° F (15.6° and 51.7° C), at which bacteria grow and produce poisons rapidly (43)

darn: reweave straight tears in fabric (62)

dart: a triangular fold of fabric stitched to a point to give shape (60)

deadline: the date by which a task must be completed (26)

decision: the choice you make between different possibilities (5)

deep fry: to cook in hot fat deep enough for the food to float (46)

default: backing into a decision by not deciding (5)

denim: a twill weave with a colored warp and a white weft; used for jeans (54)

department store: a store offering a wide variety of items in several different price ranges under one roof (29)

designer: a person who creates new styles of clothing (53)

developmental task: an ability mastered at a given stage, such as crawling in the first year, or walking in the second (18)

dice: to cut into very small cubes (46)

diet: a planned approach to eating designed to accomplish a certain goal (37)

directional cutting: cutting with the grain of the fabric (59)

directional stitching: stitching with the grain of the fabric (60)

discount store: a store that sells nationally advertised brands at reduced prices (29)

distract: to lead children away from something they shouldn't do by interesting them in another activity (20)

double knit: a knit produced by two sets of needles working two strands of yarn at the same time; used for pants and jackets (54)

down payment: a first, partial payment on something you buy (28)

dredge: to cover food with a light coating of flour or crumbs (46)

dryclean: clean with chemicals rather than with detergent and water (62)

dyeing: using a substance to change the color of a fiber, yarn, or fabric (54)

ease: extra room that a pattern includes to enable you to wear clothes comfortably (59)

electronic funds transfer (EFT): banking and paying bills automatically with the use of computers (27)

emotional appeal: the suggestion that an advertised product will make you feel better about yourself (29)

emotional maturity: being secure enough in your own self-image to be able to meet the emotional demands and responsibilities you face (22)

empathy: a helper's ability to understand what the client is experiencing (16)

emphasis: an object receiving more attention than other objects in the room (67)

end-of-season sale: a clothing sale held to clear out merchandise to make room for the upcoming season (56)

energy: the capacity for work (71)

Energy Guide labels: labels that estimate the cost of running appliances for one year (45)

entrepreneur: someone who opens a new business to provide a product or service that he or she thinks people will want to buy (33)

entry-level job: a job in which little or no experience is needed (16)

environment: the culture you're raised in (2)

equivalents: different measures that describe equal amounts (47)

ethnic group: people who share a common cultural background (34)

expectation: what you want from a relationship (6)

expenses: the things that you spend your money on (27)

expiration date: the last day a product can be used safely (40)

extended family: a family that includes not only parents and children, but also grandparents, and possibly uncles, aunts, and cousins as well (7)

fabric: material made by weaving or knitting yarns or by matting fibers together (54)

facilities: the goods and services available in a community (65)

facings: extra pieces of fabric that finish the edge of a garment (56)

factory outlet: a store in which a manufacturer sells extra merchandise directly to consumers (29)

fad: something that is highly fashionable for a short time (38)

family: a group that provides major support and care for its members (7)

family life cycle: the stages a family goes through from the time the parents marry until after the last child leaves home (10)

family style: a meal in which food is brought to the table in plates and bowls, which are passed around (49)

fashion: a style of clothing that is accepted in a society at a given time (53)

fashion cycle: a period when certain styles go in and out of fashion (53)

fat: a substance that the body uses to store reserve energy (35)

feed: the part of a sewing machine that moves the fabric along (58)

felt: a bonded fabric created by applying moisture, heat, and pressure to short fibers; used for facings (54)

fiber: threadlike cells that

pass through the body but supply no energy or nutrients (35)

fibers: the tiny strands that make up yarns (54)

finance charge: the money that you pay to the lender for allowing you to use credit (28)

financial stability: the ability to meet all your expected everyday living costs (22)

fine-motor skills: the control over smaller muscles, such as in the hands (18)

fireproof: completely protected from the danger of fire (70)

first aid: what can be done right away to help the victim of an accident (21)

first impression: the image people have of someone they've just met (3)

fixed expenses: important set expenses that you need to pay—costs that you are committed to (27)

fixed goal: a goal that can only be met at a certain time (4)

flannel: a weave that is brushed to produce a soft surface; used for shirts and sleepwear (54)

flatware: knives, forks, and spoons (49)

flexible expenses: expenses that don't stay the same, which you can make new decisions about in each budget (27)

flexible goal: a goal that can be reached at many different times (4)

food groups: five categories divided according to the nutrients that the foods contain (36)

food poisoning: when bacteria grow in food until the food actually becomes poisonous (43)

food preferences: the foods that people like best (39)

formal clothes: very dressy,

such as a tuxedo or long dress (51)

fortified: nutrients have been added to food (36)

foster child: a child who is taken into a family temporarily (8)

fry: to cook in hot fat (46)

gabardine: a strong, medium- to heavy-weight twill weave; used for pants (54)

garment industry: the many businesses involved in producing clothing (53)

garnish: add color to a prepared dish (47)

gather: a soft fold of fabric that's stitched into a seam (60)

generic products: no frills products packaged with no brand or store names (40)

gingham: a plain weave with a pattern made from dyed yarns; used for curtains and dresses (54)

goal: the steps you take to satisfy your needs and wants or to follow your principles (4)

goods: merchandise that can be bought (30)

grade: to trim each layer of a seam allowance slightly narrower than the previous one.

grease: to rub a cooking surface with fat to prevent sticking (46)

grooming: making yourself look neat, clean, and trim (3)

gross-motor skills: the control over large muscles, such as those in the legs (18)

guidance: telling children what behavior is acceptable and what is not (17)

health foods: foods that are thought to provide better nutrition (38)

hem: the bottom edge of fabric turned up and sewn to the wrong side of a garment (56)

heredity: the genes you inherit from your parents (2)

high fashion: the expensive

clothing created by world famous designers (53)

highlight: emphasize (52)

home: anywhere that people live (65)

homogenization: blending the fat in milk with the rest of the liquid (36)

hormones: chemicals that cause you to grow and mature (2)

hue: the name given to each color (52)

human resources: personal qualities that each of us possesses (25)

hunger: the physical desire for food (35)

hydroelectric power: power generated by the force of falling water (71)

identification: being recognized as belonging to a group (51)

illusion: an image that fools the eye (52)

impulse: doing what you feel like doing at the moment (5)

impulse buying: buying something without having intended to (29)

income: the money you take in and have available to spend (27)

independent: living on your own and setting up your own household (15)

individuality: the ways in which you are different from others (51)

ingredients: the individual foods needed to make a dish (39)

in-seam measurement: the length of the pants leg from the bottom to where the two legs meet (56)

insulation: materials put inside walls or ceilings to keep cold out and heat in (71)

intensity: the brightness or dullness of a color (52)

interest: a fee paid for the use of money (28)

interest rate: the percentage

of the principal that will be paid as interest (28)

interests: the things you enjoy doing (16)

interview: a meeting between an employer and a job applicant (64)

inventory: the amount of each product in stock (50)

jealousy: feeling hurt and resentful when a boyfriend or girlfriend spends time with someone else (14)

knead: to work a dough with a pressing and folding motion (46)

knits: fabrics made by looping strands of yarn together row after row, with special needles (54)

lace: a decorated fabric with an open design; used for trim (54)

layout: a diagram in the sewing instructions that shows how to place the pattern pieces on the fabric (59); also, the arrangement of such things as furniture (66)

legumes: peas and beans like soybeans, lentils, kidney beans, and chick peas (36)

location: where a home is situated (65)

long-term goal: something that you plan to accomplish farther in the future (4)

loyalty: the quality of being faithful to others, especially when they need it (11)

maintenance: keeping living space and belongings in good working order (69)

managing: planning to make the best use of time, money, abilities, and other resources (24)

manners: the way you behave toward other people (3)

marinate: to soak food in a sauce for a time to make it tender or flavorful (46)

mass media: television, magazines, movies, and newspapers—the means of communication (12)

material: a possession that you use to make other things (25)

melt: to heat a solid until it becomes a liquid (46)

menu: the list of foods that a restaurant offers (49)

mildew: a fungus that damages clothes (62)

mince: to cut into very small pieces (46)

minerals: elements that form part of many tissues and are needed to keep body processes operating smoothly (35)

money: something that has an agreed-upon trading value (27)

monochromatic outfit: one using variations of the same color (52)

multiple use: using the same area for more than one activity (66)

muslin: a plain weave from light to heavy weight; heavier muslins are used for interfacings (54)

natural fibers: fibers that are made from plants or from the hair of animals (54)

natural food products: ones that contain no chemical additives and have been processed no more than they would be in the average kitchen (38)

needs: things that are essential (4)

notching: cutting wedge-shaped sections from the seam allowance of an outward curve to flatten it (60)

notions: sewing items needed to complete a project (57)

nuclear family: parents and children sharing a household(7)

nutrient density: the proportion of nutrients to the calories a food contains (36)

nutrients: nourishing substances (35)

nutrition: the study of how the body breaks down and uses nutrients in food (35)

nutritionists: the scientists who study the effects of food on the body (35)

objective: being able to listen without becoming emotionally involved (16)

organic: made with ingredients that were grown without chemical fertilizers or pesticides (38)

overweight: when you weigh more than is healthy for your age and size (37)

oxford cloth: a plain weave with a colored warp and a white weft; used for shirts(54)

parallel play: playing alongside each other, rather than together (18)

pare: to remove the skin of firm vegetables and fruits (46)

parenting: meeting children's physical, mental, and social needs (17)

passive activities: activities that are watched or listened to, but not taken part in (19)

pasteurization: heating and then cooling milk to kill germs (36)

pattern: a set of written directions and pieces of marked paper that show how to put a sewing project together (57)

pediatrics: the study of children's health (23)

peel: to remove the outer covering, skin, or rind of soft vegetables and fruits (46)

peer pressure: the influence your friends and others of your age exert on you (6)

percale: a plain weave with a smooth finish; used for sheets (54)

perishable: easily spoiled(42)

personal space: a place of one's own (65)

pest: an insect or small animal that carries dirt and germs (43)

pilot: a thin stream of gas that is burned constantly and used to light flame on gas equipment (71)

place setting: the arrangement of the tableware each diner will need for a meal (49)

poach: to cook in a simmering liquid (46)

portions: the number of servings that a recipe yields (46)

preheat: to heat the oven or broiler to the desired temperature before putting the food in to cook (46)

prejudice: an opinion or feeling that is not based on fact (12)

pressing: lifting the hot iron and setting it down on fabric(60)

preventive: making sure that accidents and damage do not occur (69)

primary colors: red, yellow, and blue (52)

principal: the amount of money you have in a bank account (28)

principles: your beliefs about what is right and what is wrong and your guidelines for living with yourself and with others (4)

priority: the goal that is most important to you (4)

privacy: the ability to be alone now and then (65)

processed meats: meats that have been changed in some way before they go to the store (42)

processing: changing a food from its raw form before selling it (36)

procrastination: the tendency to put things off, to delay (26)

produce: fresh fruits and vegetables (41)

proportion: a pleasing size relationship among objects (67)

protein: the nutrient necessary for building and repairing body tissues (35)

pull date: the last day a product may be sold (40)

purée: to blend food into a smooth, thick paste (46)

quick breads: breads that use baking soda or baking powder to rise (41)

range: category of clothing sizes (56)

receptors: sensors in your nasal passages (35)

recipe: detailed instructions for preparing a food (39)

recycle: find new uses for old clothes (63)

redesign: to change an item so that it is more in fashion or has an exciting new look (63)

references: the names of people who can tell an employer more about you (33)

reflex: an automatic, involuntary response (18)

relationship: a special bond formed with another person (6)

reliability: the quality of being someone others count on (11)

rent: a monthly fee paid to the person who owns the living space (65)

resources: the things you use to help you meet your goals (24)

résumé: a paper that states what career you are looking for and summarizes your background (33)

return policy: a store's rules for allowing a customer to return an item in exchange for another item, or perhaps for cash (32)

rhythm: the regular repeat of line or shape (67)

role: a part you play when you interact with others (6)

role-playing: pretending to be someone else (19)

sanitation: keeping yourself, the kitchen, and the food clean, and storing and cooking food properly (43)

satin: a smooth, finished fabric produced by one of the basic weaves; used for dressy clothes (54)

sauté: to cook in a small amount of hot fat (46)

savings account: an account that holds your savings (28)

savings bond: a certificate that represents money that you lend to the government (28)

scale drawing: a drawing in which the relative sizes of objects are the same as the relative sizes in the actual space (66)

seam: a line of stitching that joins the pieces of a garment together (56)

seam allowance: the fabric between the line for cutting and the line for stitching (59)

seasonal: plentiful only at certain times of the year (41)

secondary colors: orange, green, and violet (52)

seersucker: a woven fabric with a puckered look produced by alternating tight warp rows with loose ones; used for suits (54)

self-awareness: the sense of who you are and what you're like (2)

self-concept: the picture that you have of yourself (1)

selvage: the border of the fabric (59)

separating eggs: dividing into whites and yolks (47)

services: the work performed by one person for another (30)

sew-through buttons: buttons that have holes in their faces and no shank (61)

shank buttons: buttons that have a built-in shank, or loop, on the back (61)

shared space: any space that is used by more than one person (68)

shoplifting: stealing goods from stores (32)

short-term goal: something that you can accomplish right away (4)

sibling: a brother or sister (8)

sift: to rub flour against a fine sieve to make it more powdery (46)

simmer: to cook in liquid just below the boiling point (46)

single-parent family: a family headed by only one parent (7)

skills: the things you can do well (16)

small claims court: a court in which consumers and businesses present their complaints informally, and a judge decides the case (31)

smoke alarm: a battery-operated device that makes a loud sound when it senses smoke (70)

snag: a loop of yarn that's pulled out of a knit (62)

special children: children who develop physically or mentally at a different rate than the average child (8)

specialty store: a store that sells only a certain type of merchandise (29)

spoilage: damage that occurs to food that is too old to eat or that contains bacteria or mold (41)

stage: a period when a child is able to perform new tasks (18)

stain: dirt that has become concentrated in one spot on a garment (62)

staples: basic food items that are used regularly (40)

status: special rank within a group (51)

staystitching: a row of stitching on just one layer of fabric that keeps the curved areas from stretching as the fabric is handled (60)

steam: to cook over boiling water (46)

stereotype: a fixed mental picture of what someone or something is like (12)

stew: to cook in liquid at low heat for a long time (46)

stir: to mix food in a circular motion (46)

street fashion: a fashion started by ordinary people (53)

stress: physical or emotional strain or tension that can be caused by changes in our lives (10)

substituting: using one resource in place of another (25)

synthetic fibers: fibers formed all or in part by chemicals (54)

table service: restaurant service in which servers bring the food to the table (49)

taffeta: a plain weave with a shiny surface that rustles when it moves; used for evening dresses (54)

taste buds: sensitive areas on your tongue that identify sweet, sour, salty, and bitter tastes (35)

technology: the methods used to make products (53)

terry cloth: a weave or knit with extra yarn left in loops for a coarse texture; used for towels or bathrobes (54)

testimonial: an ad in which a public figure is shown to use a product to promote sales (29)

texture: the way a material looks and feels (52)

thrift shop: a store that buys and sells used clothing (63)

tie-dyeing: a dyeing method in which parts of the fabric are tightly wrapped, or tied, so that the dye penetrates unevenly (63)

tip: extra money given to food servers for good service (49)

toast: to brown food with dry heat (46)

tolerance: the ability to accept people as they are (11)

tool: a possession that helps you use your other resources more efficiently (25)

topstitching: sewing a decorative stitch on the right side of a garment to emphasize detail (61)

toss: to mix with a lifting motion (46)

trade-off: giving up something in exchange for something else that you want more (24)

trade or professional association: a group of workers that educates the public about the work they perform (23)

traditions: customs that have been followed for a long time (34)

traffic patterns: how people usually move through a space (66)

traumatic changes: ones that cause severe emotional shock which may take some time to heal (10)

trimming: the decorations sewn on a garment (56)

tuck: a small, stitched fold used to give shape (60)

tweed: a weave with colored flecks of yarn on a somewhat hairy surface, usually including at least some wool; used for skirts and suits (54)

understitch: to open out the facing and machine stitch through the facing and seam allowance (60)

unit construction: preparation of separate pieces first, then assembling them in a certain order (60)

unit prices: the prices of items by ounce or by count (30)

unity: a feeling that all objects in a room look like they belong together (67)

utensils: simple hand tools, like knives, or containers, like saucepans (44)

value: the lightness or darkness of a color (52)

vandalism: marring or destroying someone else's property (32)

variety meats: animals' internal organs (42)

velour: a knit or weave with extra yarn that creates a loop, which is clipped; used for sweaters (54)

velvet and velveteen: weaves with a short, closely woven pile; used for evening clothes (54)

view: a drawing of a different version of the sewing project (57)

visualize: to see something in one's mind (72)

vitamins: nutrients that help the body stay healthy and function properly (35)

wants: things you desire to make life more enjoyable (4)

wardrobe: the clothes that you own (55)

warp: yarns lined up in lengthwise rows on a loom (54)

warranty: a written statement from a manufacturer or retailer, promising to repair or replace a defective product, or to refund your money (30)

weatherstripping: fiber, plastic, or metal strips placed around doors and windows to prevent air leaks (71)

weaves: fabrics formed by interlacing strands of yarn (54)

weft: yarns passed over and under the warp in a crosswise direction; also called *filling* (54)

worker theft: on-the-job dishonesty (32)

yarn: the twisted-together fibers that form woven and knitted fabrics (54)

yeast breads: breads that rise through the action of yeast (41)

INDEX